The Well-Tempered Announcer

ROBERT A. FRADKIN

A Pronunciation Guide to Classical Music

INDIANA UNIVERSITY PRESS BLOOMINGTON & INDIANAPOLIS

The paper used in this publication meets the minimum requirements of American National Standard for Information Sciences—Permanence of Paper for Printed Library Materials, ANSI Z39.48-1984.

Manufactured in the United States of America

Library of Congress Cataloging-in-Publication Data

Fradkin, Robert A., 1951—
The well-tempered announcer : a pronunciation guide to classical music / Robert A. Fradkin.
p. cm.
Includes bibliographical references.
ISBN 0-253-21064-X (pbk. : alk. paper)
1. Music—Terminology—Pronunciation. 2. Names, Personal—Pronunciation. I. Title.
ML109.F73 1996
780'.14—dc20
95-360

1 2 3 4 5 01 00 99 98 97 96 MN

PRELUDE

A Tribute to WFOS-FM

WFOS-FM is a high school radio station in Chesapeake, Virginia. It has been sponsored by that city's public school system since 1955 and is run entirely by high school students under the leadership of two adults, manager Dennis McCurdy and engineer David Desler. The station is unusual in that over half its programming is classical music. Every summer about fifty students sign up for a two-week course to learn how to run a radio station, concentrating on engineering, advertising, and legal issues. The graduates then take over the announcing duties. Most of them do not have a background in classical music or in the languages involved in announcing it. In 1985, Mr. McCurdy and others had assembled an in-house, typewritten pronunciation guide to help the announcer-trainees manage the names and terms associated with classical music. That guide contained a few hundred names with "user-friendly" phonetic approximations in terms of whole English words, for example, "Berlioz = *barely owes.*"

The present book began in 1991 as a community outreach to those teenagers. I discovered the station on moving to Norfolk, Virginia in 1990, soon realized that the announcers were high school students, and was impressed that they had chosen to immerse themselves in that foreign classical atmosphere while providing a valuable service to the community. I called Mr. McCurdy and offered to assist the students in using those phonetic spellings more effectively and in making educated guesses at names not in the existing list. He invited me to conduct a pronunciation workshop as part of the summer courses of 1992-94. This was a natural and useful way for me, a professor of languages and linguistics and an amateur musician and classical music enthusiast, to combine my profession with my lifelong hobby.

After the first session in 1992, WFOS senior announcer, Aimee Shaffer, updated the list from the station library, and I supplied phonetic spellings and what were intended to be a few brief comments on systematic correspondences between letter and sound in several languages. One comment lead to another, and before long, the project had escalated into a full-fledged manual for training current and future announcers in the fundamentals of reading names in a wide assortment of languages with reasonable certainty.

I want to thank the WFOS high school trainees for their eagerness to try the unfamiliar. Special thanks go to Messrs. McCurdy and Desler for their devotion to the station and their enthusiasm for this pronunciation project from the beginning.

Other Acknowledgments

First of all I thank the top-flight classical announcers of WHRO, the Norfolk National Public Radio affiliate (Dwight Davis, Raymond Jones, Hope Mihalap, Arthur Zanville), who were very generous with their time, expertise, and encouragement.

In summer 1994, I introduced myself to the two radio stations I had grown up listening to near Boston, commercial WCRB and public WGBH, and asked for advice on how this non-announcer could make the book maximally useful to the announcing profession. They were all very enthusiastic and helpful. Robert J. Lurtsema (WGBH), as I then learned, was a member of the board of the Association of Music Personnel in Public Radio. He called Jonathan Palevsky (WBJC, Baltimore), that organization's president, who invited me to give a pronunciation workshop at the 1995 AMPPR national conference. My thanks go to Robert J., Jonathan, and to Diane Finlayson (WGMS, Washington) for their initial consultations and resulting friendship.

I have also profited from delightful conversations with other announcers I met at that 1995 AMPPR conference and elsewhere, among whom are David Srebnik and Kati Kershaw (KEDT, Corpus Christi), George Walker (WFIU, Bloomington), Taylor Lewis (WSCI, Charleston), Ted Weiner (WDAV, Davidson), John Fischer (KSUI, Iowa City), Susan Prince (WMNR, Kent), Laurence Vittes (Naxos and Marco Polo labels), Bill Boggs (WRIU, Kingston and Harvard University Press), Rex Levang and Bob Christiansen (Minnesota Public Radio). Naturally, I take full responsibility for any errors in the text, factual, phonetic, or typographical.

Three people from my high school and college days, with whom I long ago lost touch, contributed significantly to waking me up to classical music. They may not know that and may never see this book, but thanks anyway to Jon Kates, Nikhil Bhattacharya, Shirit Bitter.

I also thank my wonderful wife, Goedele Gulikers, for her feedback, patience, and for notes on her native language, Flemish/Dutch.

Finally, for his constant encouragement, inspiration, wisdom, and unflagging optimism in all matters professional and personal, I thank my father, Irving.

OVERTURE

Why This Guide?

The purpose of this guide is to provide the systematic linguistic tools that classical radio announcers need for reading the names of composers, conductors, performers, titles of compositions, music terms, and place names in a wide assortment of European and East Asian languages. Professional and amateur musicians can also benefit from this book, as well as musicologists, audiophiles and CD collectors (not to mention employees in record stores), anyone involved in the arts or their management, and newscasters. Classical announcers, of course, face the most names in the course of a day's work, and their pronunciation of names reaches the widest audience. This book will serve seasoned professionals as a reference guide and novices as a training guide. (High school principals and college deans could also use it to prepare for reading off names on graduation day.) By applying a few basic notions of sound and spelling, a classical announcer will be able to determine:

1. what language a name is in
2. how that language uses its letters to represent its sounds, and
3. (perhaps most important for the practical business of announcing) which sounds of normal English speech come closest to representing the original.

This is not a dictionary of music and musicians. It is a book about language and the connections between alphabet letter and speech sound. The primary goal of this project is to inform and train, but the secondary goal is to break through the traditional snobbery surrounding classical music and to dissolve the mystery and "foreignness" of reading names in other languages. This is one of the reasons for the deliberately (in places) informal style of this book. Music and other languages are fun, after all. The hope is that working through this book will remove at least one barrier to people who may feel alienated from or intimidated by classical music and the languages associated with it.

Each of the languages discussed here uses its letters to represent its sounds in reasonably systematic ways—even English and French, believe it or not. Therefore, the practical goal of this book is to have the user learn how to read most names straight off the printed page without the intermediary step of an English-based phonetic spelling. The native spelling can, in most cases, serve as its *own* transcription. Announcers do not need to learn to speak all these languages; they just need to let the native spelling speak to them. They can accomplish this end by acquainting themselves with the principles explained in the Interludes and in Movement 4. Many people are content simply to sound out each name individually from the phonetic spellings in Movement 2 or just learn each one by heart without appealing to larger general principles of sound/letter correspondence. For them, the explanations may seem like the proverbial "I asked him what time it was and he told me how to build a clock." Others will enjoy seeing the names as specific examples of larger language phenomena.

The Old "Native vs. Anglicized" Controversy

This perennial topic was discussed at the 1995 conference of the Association of Music Personnel in Public Radio. The present author gave a workshop there on pronunciation for the airwaves and took an informal survey of attitudes in the profession. Many of the one hundred announcers in attendance expressed a preference for a "softly anglicized" pronunciation, while some believed in pronouncing each name "correctly" in its native accent. Still others felt no obligation to change their English speech habits at all, just as they did not for non-English names that are already widely accepted as English: Paris = [pa-rihs], ≠ [pah-ree]; Mexico = [mehk-sih-koh], ≠ [meh-khee-koh], etc.

This book supports the "reasonable accuracy" view of pronunciation proposed by Percy Scholes in his 1938 *Oxford Companion to Music*, pp. 1186-1189, as noted in Bibliography II. People have a right, in principle, to be called any way they choose, and in most European countries the spelling of a name corresponds more or less to its sound. If Louis XIV came to the U.S. we can expect that he would want to be called [loo-ee], and he should expect to hear something *reasonably* close to that, such as [loo-ee] but not [loo-ihs]. English-speaking announcers can set as a goal a pronunciation of a name accurate enough that its owner would recognize it if he or she heard it announced on the air. This does not require the exact phonetic detail of native speech or of singers' diction. Ideally, that pronunciation should not call attention to itself by breaking the rules of English speech, but those rules can be bent quite a bit and still be considered English. Any way that an announcer is comfortable accomplishing that goal is the right way for that person.

Most of the announcers at the AMPPR meeting agreed that it sounds odd (even pretentious) to engage in video-lingual gymnastics, that is, to pronounce (or try to pronounce or think they are pronouncing) each name in its native original in the middle of an otherwise English sentence. Names should flow together with normal English speech just as European announcers splice names in other languages smoothly into their own native speech. Announcers who know another language well sometimes favor that language while they anglicize others. Let consistency be the guide. So many recordings nowadays are multinational that it becomes unwieldy for most people (though a delight for some) to announce a concerto of the Frenchman Camille Saint-Saëns performed by the Hungarian Jenő Jandó playing with the Orquesta Nacional de España conducted by the Russian Yevgeny Svetlanov recorded by Deutsche Welle in Bydgoszcz, Poland.

No one expects announcers to speak the approximately thirty languages surveyed here, and they can do their job perfectly well without having a lovely "foreign" accent. Some announcers report that audiences find a too-correct accent off-putting. And there is the question of consistency: some people hold the more familiar western European languages to a more rigid standard than they do the languages of the less well-trodden territory east of Vienna—and none of them would attempt, or even think it appropriate, to reproduce the rising and falling tones of Chinese. This guide proposes a comfortable English compromise for all the languages involved. An announcer can achieve a respectable degree of accuracy by having an idea of the original sound and the least obtrusive way of accommodating that sound to an English mouth. In short, they need to know how much *to* say and *not* to say.

To that end, this guide offers for many names a range—not a hierarchy—of pronunciations in, admittedly, impressionistic terms from "full-native" to "half-native" to "half-English" to "full-English." The author tries to suggest—but not to dictate—which variant(s) work(s) best on the air and which frequently heard variants are better left inside the announcing booth. The aim is to give announcers some basic principles of language, sound, and graphic representation so that they can make an informed choice.

Caveat Dictor

This author has learned from three decades of listening to classical radio stations on both U.S. coasts and several points in between that there is a large range of acceptability, but there *are* limits. A radio audience will not blink if Toscanini (full-Italian: ["toss"-kah-nee-nee]) comes out as half-English [tahs-kuh-nee-nee] or ["tusk-a-knee"-nee]. If, however, the person at the microphone tries, in the interest of correctness or faithfulness to the original, to reestablish Borodin as full-Russian [buh-rah-deen] instead of the now-accepted full-English ["bore-a-dean"], listeners might fail to recognize him altogether or, ironically, might think the announcer is putting on pseudo-foreign airs. It goes without saying that a station's switchboard will light up with irate phone calls if the first syllable of Wagner sounds like what a dog does with its tail or if Mozart comes out like portraits painted by one's mother—and Heaven forbid if Verdi rhymes with "birdie"! Audiences assume announcers are supposed to know better—and now announcers have a self-teaching reference guide designed specifically for their needs.

Many musicians and announcers feel that their job is to play music. They may not be interested in the sound of the composer's name or they may feel uneasy uttering non-English sounds. They can take comfort from the idea that the sounds of normal English speech are perfectly adequate to the task. The challenge is learning to *see* these sounds in print. No announcer—or listener—should never feel low-brow for substituting English [k] for German [kh] in "Bach" or [yoo] for French [ü] in "Debussy," but they should also know how far not to go: [deh-byoo-see] is a reasonable accommodation, but [duh-byoo-see] is not justified, and [duh-"bus"-ee] is just wrong, the result of imposing English values on the French letters. On the other hand, some announcers and listeners *are* interested in language and the language-related terminology that helps them mention on the air or in conversation with colleagues and fellow listeners what the differences are between the "native" sound and the compromise version. (The Interludes give a few linguistic insights into the characteristics of English and other languages that contribute to anglicizing. The conventional names for "that little whatchamathingy" over the "c" in "Janáček" and the "little doo-hickie" under the "c" in French "François" are also given in several places.) A classical announcer should also have a reasonable idea of how to cope with European and Asian names in the news, such as the Polish president Lech Wałęsa or the Bosnian Serb leader Radovan Karadžić. (This book cannot deliver on names of South Asia, the Middle East, Africa, Native America, or other places that may be in the news but that have different musical traditions from Western diatonic classical music.)

Reading about the *sound* of language on the mute pages of a book can be an elusive endeavor for those unaccustomed to it. It is like learning ballet from a manual without being able to see a teacher or a performance. The way that a reader interprets verbal descriptions of body movements depends on the way s/he moves in general. Pronouncing Danish or Korean purely from the phonetic hints given here may give a reasonable impression, appealing in its own rights, but it would probably not be "correct" to a specialist. Many readers and listeners may disagree with some of the phonetic spellings offered here, but they need a way of expressing their objection other than "This is the way I heard X-announcer say it."

Letters often do as poor a job of representing the sounds and flow of speech as words do of describing the grace of a dancer so that another person can imitate it. Letters, for example, do not take into consideration the crucial elements of word stress (which syllable gets the emphasis) and sentence rhythm (which words to skip over quickly, tuck under the breath, stop on, draw out, and group together in a single breath). A European announcer who did not know English might have no trouble getting out the name of Gershwin, but a longer quotation like "The rain in Spain stays mainly in the plain," which is made up mainly of monosyllabic words, might pose some difficulty. There is no visual clue on the page to tell a reader to skip lightly over some of them ("the," "in," even "stays") and to articulate others ("rain," "Spain") more precisely or with more gusto. (See Interlude 4 for more details.) The present book always indicates word stress and tries to suggest phrase stress but stops short of hints on reading long titles or extended quotations of opera lyrics.

Structure of the Book

The guide is divided into four "movements."

Movement 1 gives the transcription techniques used in the book, discussion of the sound symbols, and explanations of the symbols ✍ 𝄞 ♪ (for people) and ◆ (for ensembles, titles of pieces, music terms and place names).

Movement 2 is the Alphabetical List of personal names, terms, and titles. Each name bears a language designation to suggest the reading techniques you need to have in mind in order to pronounce it with reasonable confidence. The phonetic spellings are provided to remove the guesswork, suggest acceptable variants or compromise pronunciations, and offer commentary on the reasons a name sounds the way it does or appears on paper as it does.

Movement 3 rearranges the list by language. This provides self-guided training in recognizing what a typical French or Hungarian spelling looks like and usually sounds like.

Then follow several short *Interludes* on general notions of language, especially of the properties of English sound and spelling that contribute to what is usually called "anglicizing."

Movement 4 goes into detail on the letters each language uses to represent its sounds, as far as an English mouth is concerned. The languages are grouped mostly by genetic families (Romance, Germanic, Slavic and Baltic, Finno-Ugric) or close cultural connection (Japanese, Korean, Chinese) with references to similarities and differences within and across families.

The *Coda* sections provide several charts reviewing sound and letter across languages: the diacritic signs, the languages that have them, and the affect these marks have on the sound value of the letter; those languages in which a single letter has different sounds under different circumstances; the letters and letter combinations that most often confuse readers.

The *Finale* is an annotated bibliography of music reference books that do and do not provide phonetic help with commentary on each. The bibliography is divided into three sections: works that have no phonetics (to save the user the trouble of seeking them out for that purpose), works that do have phonetics, and works that are either not on music or that are for singers, that is, where the phonetic explanations are far more explicit than an announcer needs for broadcasting.

Suggestions for Using the Book

Phonetic spellings can look strange at first, and reading them takes practice. Here are some hints in the same spirit as those suggested over half a century ago by Percy Sholes in the *Oxford Companion to Music*, p. 1130:

- Use your station's program guide ahead of time to pull the records and CDs you will be playing on any given day or a few days ahead.
- Practice pronouncing the names you will need so that there are no surprises at the microphone. (Piece the syllables together and then work on making them smooth.)
- Keep this book in the broadcasting booth and flip through it as the music plays. (This is not the kind of book that one might sit down and read from cover to cover. Some of the information is repeated in several places in the hope that you will find it when and where you need it.) Compare it with any of the items mentioned in the bibliography to get a well-rounded idea of symbol and sound.

- Compare notes with fellow announcers. Drill each other so that your station can establish its own consistencies (not to mention policies for handling listeners who call in to remark on an announcer's performance and suggest the "correct" pronunciation).
- Get familiar with some of the languages. Even a semester of one or more of them at your local college would help. If a whole course does not fit into your schedule, seek out the college or high school teachers of these languages for a series of organized consultations. (Explain that you want to achieve a comfortable compromise pronunciation and acquire a minimal vocabulary that will help you decipher titles or terms. Note that a native speaker of the language who is not a teacher of that language may be of less help to you than you think.)
- If you have not already had a course in phonetics or in general linguistics, try one. It will help clarify much of the material in this book. (Such a course is not guaranteed to be designed for this specific purpose, but you can consult with the linguistics professor on how best to use this book. Keep in mind that not all linguistic theoreticians are good speakers of other languages.)
- Above all, ENJOY YOURSELF with music and languages.

Limitations

This book is *not* a complete listing of the names of every musician, title of every piece, song, mass, cantata, opera (and character in the cast and aria), or orchestra of the past four hundred years. It is a *selected* list based on *some* of the catalogues of *some* recording companies. Not all languages are equally represented or treated in equal depth. This is not meant to exclude or diminish any nation's musicians or musical production. If a name you need to pronounce is not in the list, do not despair: take a good guess. As for the accuracy or completeness of the explanations, anyone who knows these languages will quibble with some statements. For example, Polish has two kinds of [ch] (spelled <cz> and <ć>), and German <ch> can represent either [kh] or something close to [sh]. No attempt is made to call attention to or represent these subtleties. Plain English [ch] and [k(h)] will suffice on the air. Linguists will recognize references to topics in phonological or morphological theory, but there is no attempt at linguistic analysis. This is a book *by* a linguist for a readership assumed to be *non*-linguists.

MOVEMENT 1

TRANSCRIPTION AND OTHER BASICS

Transcription Conventions

<Letter> vs. [Sound]

The main concern of this book is representing the sounds of language. The familiar twenty-six letters of our Roman alphabet have to do double duty: to serve as both "themselves" (visual units on the English printed page) and "sound symbols" capable of representing the sounds of any of the more than twenty languages discussed here. In the phonetic transcriptions* in the lists in Movements 2 and 3, the following visual clues are intended to let you know when the letter is serving as the letter and when it is the sound symbol. Let us use 'x' to represent any letter.

[x] SQUARE BRACKETS indicate the pure speech *sound*, regardless of how any given language spells it. The name Dvorak is [dvor-zhahk] with a [zh] sound, that seems to have no letter—unless the record company has kept in the wedge mark (called haček = [hah-chehk], discussed below) over the <ř> in Dvořák.

<x> ANGLE BRACKETS give the pure visual *letter*, regardless of the sound it represents in any given language. The <c> of Cécile (Chaminade) is [s], while the <c> of Cecilia (Bartoli) is [ch]. (The separate sections on French and Italian in Movement 4 explain more.) In English, <s> can signal [s] in "No excuse" (noun), [z] in "Excuse me" (verb), [sh] in "pressure," [zh] in "pleasure," and even [no sound] in "island." In Movement 4, dashes show the position of the

---

* This book uses the term *transcription* rather than *transliteration* because it underscores the *sound* of language irrespective of the ways that language spells those sounds. For example, the Russian name for Brahms is a transliteration because it spells silent German <h> with its closest letter, though it has the sound [kh]. A transcription would represent just the vowel [ah].

letter within a word: <x-> is "x as the first letter." <-x-> is "x in the middle of a word, especially a consonant between vowels," and <-x> is "x as the last letter." For example, in English <s-> = [s]; <-s-> and <-s> = [s] or [z]. (Compare to German, where <s->, <-s-> = [z], while <-s> = [s]. In French and Dutch <u> = [ü], while in the rest of Europe <u> = [oo].

"xxx" QUOTATION MARKS surround a whole English word together with its associated sound, irrespective of its spelling. This technique is sometimes effective than an awkward transcription. The sound of Pergolesi can be transcribed phonetically as [pehr-goh-lay-zee] or audio-visually as the whole words ["pear-go-lazy"]; Claudio = [klow-dee-oh] or ["cloudy"-oh]; Rakhmaninov = [rahkh-mahn-"enough"] (whether you pronounce this English word [ee-nuhf] or [uh-nuhf]). Sometimes you really have to say these aloud to get the point and then still use your imagination a little. Not all names lend themselves to this kind of audio-visual play. Sometimes such a representation works for only part of a syllable, as in Rakhmaninov = [rahkh-mah-nee-n"off"]. It may be a little shocking to the eye to see quotation marks in the middle of word or syllable, but it makes the point.[*]

= Read this EQUAL SIGN as "as in..." or "sounds just like, almost like, like part of, rhymes with..." You will have to use some intuition to know how close the clue actually comes. Speakers with different regional accents may differ. The phonetic clue may cover the entire name, as in Borodin = ["bore-a-dean"] and Beaux Arts = ["bows are"] or only part of the name, as in Strauss = ["house"], where <au> = [ow]. See "How to Read the Lists," below.

≠ The DOES NOT EQUAL SIGN means "does *not* sound like, do *not* read as," meaning that you should resist your natural English inclination. Note these names, marked "sounds like—or almost like—X, but not like Y":

Strauss	= "house"	≠ "sauce"
Bach	= "bock" (beer)	≠ "back"
Hans	= "wants"	≠ "hands"
Saint-Saëns	= "sand fonts"	≠ "saint pains."

In plain English these mean that you should read Strauss to rhyme with "house," not with "sauce" (because German <au> and English <ou> = [ow]) and similarly for the rest. This "≠" sign keeps you from falling into frequent announcing traps, like Verdi = ["bear"-dee], ≠ ["birdie"], where it is clear that

[*] It is no stranger than pairing number and letter symbols, where each has to be read as the syllable that names it. This is the technique in license plates like "IW84U" (= "I wait for you" with [w] + "eight" = "wait") or "DOUN102" (= "Do you intend to?").

only the sound of <er> is at issue and not the value of <v> as [v]. This also keeps you from "overdoing" or "re-foreignizing" Americanized names, such as Mancini = ["man-see-knee"], ≠ [mahn-chee-nee].[*]

The above notations help to capture larger generalities that frequently catch announcers off guard. They serve as shorthand for whole statements like "The letter X has the sound Y in the word Z in language Q." For example, "French <ch> = [sh]" takes less space than the prose, "The letter combination 'ch' in French gives the 'sh' sound, as in 'machine'." Similarly, "Italian <ch> = [k]" means "Italian uses the digraph 'ch' for the single consonant [k]." (See Interlude 3 for the term "digraph.") In English, then, <ch> = [ch] in "chair," [sh] in "machine," and [k] in "ache." The brackets and quotation marks also make obvious when a letter of the alphabet or syllable composed of them is being used to represent a sound in general or the particular sound it has in a particular word. For example, [sugar] in square brackets might be the sound of the name Sue Garr, but "sugar" in quotation marks means the word with the sound [shoo-ger], where the vowel in [shoo] = "shook," ≠ "shoot."

xx-x This vi-sual de-vice u-ses hy-phens to di-vide words into syl-la-bles at the same time that an un-der-line in-di-cates which syl-la-ble re-ceives the stress or ac-cent. This is préferable to úsing a stréss márk óver the vówel in quéstion, since thát márk óften has óther fúnctions or gets lóst in phótocopying. Most dictionaries and other reference books put that stress mark either just before or just after the stressed syllable, and you have to make sure you know which strategy a given book uses. (See Interlude 4 on Stress Management.)

Options and Alternatives

√ CHECK MARK indicates "also OK to pronounce as. . ." as in Tosca = ["toss"-kah], (√ [tahs-kuh]).

👓 → 👂 "The way it looks (👓) is the way it sounds (👂)." This means, "Use your English reading intuition." Transcription of obvious English names serves mainly to keep you on your phonetic toes, but space limits the number of these in the lists. John Williams poses no reading or pronunciation problem, but the transcription [jahn wihl-yuhmz] is a convenient exercise in reading transcription, because you already know the answer. Ultimately, almost all the names in this book, with the help of the language designation, could be marked in this "what you see is what you hear" style.

---

[*] Robert J. Lurtsema (WGBH, Boston), who is interested in language issues, interviewed Mancini on the air, and the maestro said that he enjoyed speaking Italian and took pleasure in the Italian pronunciation of his name, though he did not use it professionally.

Which Phonetic Transcription?

There are several different transcription systems in current use, including dictionary phonetics, International Phonetic Alphabet (IPA), and other variations on English spelling. This book uses a "phrendly phonetic" transcription based largely, but not entirely, on actually occurring English spellings of individual sounds, but the combinations are often not as in English. This makes it similar to the *NBC Handbook* (Bibliography II) and to the whole-word approach of McConkey's *Klee As in Clay* (Bibliography III). Some IPA symbols are given below as an attempt to tie the different systems together and make using other books more efficient.

Note that English "silent letters" are not represented in the phonetic spelling. Compare these three representations of a simple English sentence:

• Standard English spelling	Thumb your nose at fate.
•"Phrendly phonetics"	thuhm yohr nohz at fayt
• IPA	θʌm jɔr nɔ^{w}z æt fɛ^{j}t

The <b> of "thumb," the <u> in "your," and the "silent <e>" in "nose, fate" are not represented because they have no sound. (Phrendly phonetics seems to contain its own silent letters, especially <h>, but just consider it part of the "uh" and "oh" complexes.) This transcription does not use capital letters, either, because their sounds are no different from those of the lower-case letters. This is why Beethoven is [bay-toh-vuhn], not [Bay-toh-vuhn]. Not seeing capitals when you expect them also takes your eye some getting used to. (The mirror image phenomenon occurs in German, where every noun begins with a capital letter, whether it begins a sentence or not.)

Your eye is already used to several different spellings for most English sounds, and the whole point of this book is to get you used to the ways other languages use letters to represent their sounds so that you will eventually free yourself of the need for transcriptions. The main transcription in the "phonetic spelling" column of the lists uses only the underlining convention for the stressed syllable and reserves the square and angle brackets for the commentary in parentheses below the name.

Is the Glass Half-Full or Half-Empty?

The terms "full-Russian, half-French, half-English, full-English" are introduced here to suggest a range of acceptable pronunciations between the original language and normal English. This is, essentially, the author's judgment as a listener and not as a musician or a broadcaster. These gradations are not a scientific measurement but are based on comparative phonetics principles and the realities of the announcer's job behind the microphone. For example, Prokofiev is "full-Russian" [prah-"cough"-yehf] with three syllables and with Russian <o> = [ah] before the stressed syllable. In "half-Russian" (or half-English)—that is, observing only some of the rules of Russian and leaning toward English rules—[pruh-"coffee"-ehf] has four syllables and typical

English [uh] before the stressed syllable. (See Interlude 3 on vowels.) Both variants are good for announcing. Pavarotti is full-Italian [pah-vah-"wrote-tee"] or [pah-vah-wrought-tee], depending on how particular your English mouth is about that Italian vowel, complete with Italian "double-[t]," but this is too fussy for most English-speaking announcers. Half-Italian [pah-vah-"row-tee"] or [pah-vah-"raw-tea"] is preferable with a single [t]. Half-English means (1) making the vowel before the stress into [uh], (2) reading <o> as [ah], rather than Italian [oh], and (3) pronouncing the <t> between vowels as a "flap" instead of full [t]. (See Interlude 2 on consonants.) This gives half-English [pah-vuh-rah-tee] (also [pah-vuh-"rot"-ee]). Any of these is good for announcing. Full-English, then, would mean reading the first <a> = [a], that is, [pa-vuh-"rod"-ee] (where [pa-vuh] = "have a") and "rod" simply underscores the flap character of the [t]. You are, of course, free to choose this pronunciation, and now you will be able to explain to critical listeners or colleagues what you are saying and why.

Sound Symbols

Vowels

SYMBOL	SOUND *with notes on spelling in several languages*
[ah]	as in the exclamation, "Ah!" or the words "taco, Hobbit." The term "broad-a" is often used for this sound. The usual dictionary symbol is double-dotted symbol [ä] as in "father." In American English this is the same sound as so-called "short-o," written with a "breve" as ŏ in Hobbit = [hŏ-bit]. IPA uses just [a], as do all European languages, thus, [fah-ther, hah-biht]. Watch out for the combination <ar>. In English it gives the vowel sounds of both "car" and "care," of "starring" (in an opera) and "staring" (at the stars). For many speakers of American English, in "Barry married Mary" all three words rhyme with "airy," while for others only Mary rhymes with "airy." Be aware that in the other languages in this book <ar> is always [ahr], sometimes written [ar].
[a]	always as in "hat rack," never "hot rock." This is often called "flat-a." (See Interlude 3 for the terms "broad" and "flat.") The word "hat" will appear here phonetically as [hat], and "hot" will be [haht]. Note these pairs: "habit, Hobbit" = [ha-biht], [hah-biht]; "latter, later" = [la-ter], [lay-ter]. IPA uses the composite symbol [æ]—like an "a" and "e" fused at the hip—as in [hæt, hæ-bɪt, læ-ter]. Old English used this letter, called "ash." Dictionaries typically use the short mark, called "breve," as in [hăt, hă-bĭt, lă-ter].

[oh]	as in the exclamation “Oh!” and the words “coat, tote, toe, show.” Most languages have a more “clipped” version of this sound, compared to English’s more drawn-out one. Compare note on [aw] below. This [oh] is often called a “tense” or “close” vowel, while [aw] usually signals a “lax” or “open” vowel. English has both. Many languages have only one of them or a sound in between. IPA uses just [o].
[uh]	as in the hesitation “Uh...” spelled in English “hut, ton, flood, couple,” even twenty.” This is the vowel called “shwa,” more on which in Interlude 3. IPA uses two symbols for this: [ʌ] when it is stressed, as in [hʌt, tʌn, flʌd, kʌpəl]; [ə] when it is unstressed, as in the first syllables in “majority, sterility, civility, police.” In IPA, then, “a suspect” and “I suspect” would be [ə sʌspɛkt] and [aj səspɛkt]. A word with both is “succumb,” given in this book as [suh-kuhm] and in IPA as [səkʌm]. French <e> with no accent mark also has this sound, as does Albanian <ë>.
[eh]	as in “Eh?” and as in “bed, said, bread, any.” You may occasionally see a single [e] for this sound, usually with additional commentary or “whole word” helps. IPA uses a cursive small capital [ɛ]. As in the “Barry-Mary” issue mentioned above, watch out for the spelling <er>. In Europe it is almost always [ehr] or [“air”]. However, English “very” may be [veh-ree] or rhyme with “vary” = [v“air” -ree], depending on where you come from in the U.S.
[ih]	as in “pretty, busy, English, women,” and the usual “sit.” This “ih” is not a normal English spelling, but plain <i> is too uncertain, since it is “long” in “line,” short in “linen,” and either in “live (gig)” and “live (for today),” not to mention [ee] in “chlorine.” It is necessary sometimes to make the sound look *really* different to keep lifelong English reading habits from taking over. IPA uses either a small capital [I] or a “barred-<i>,” as in [prIti, bIzi, wImIn], [prɨti, bɨzi wɨmɨn] or in this book [prih-tee, bih-zee, wih-mihn].

The <h> symbol, then, is quite popular in this book, and it appears as part of a two-symbol unit far more often than as the separate consonant sound [h].

[ee]	as in “sweet, seat, receipt, Pete, machine.” IPA uses plain [i].
[oo]	serves for two sounds: the exclamation “Oo!” and its other spellings (as in “Choose a few shoes, but don’t lose the lute or put glue in the soup”) and the sound of “The woman should put the book here.” Dictionaries often distinguish these with the long sign (macron) [o͞o] for the “shoot” and short sign (breve) [o͝o] for the sound “sugar.” This book will use an accompanying English word. Most of the languages involved here really have only the sound of “shoot” and not of “sugar.” IPA uses plain [u] vs. a small capital [U] or [ʊ]. Thus, “The suitor wooed” vs. “The soot from the wood” in IPA look like [sut, wud] vs. either [sUt, wUd] or [sʊt, wʊd]. French has <ou> = [oo], and Dutch has <oe> = [oo].

[aw]	as in "raw, talk, mall, toss, pause." In most languages this is something between [aw] and [oh]. Some users of this book will no doubt disagree with some of the transcriptions on this point, but to use IPA [ɔ] would not clarify. Compare the note on [oh], above, and try reading a few familiar names to get a sense for the range of sound this symbol covers.
[ow]	as in "brown house," ≠ "low blow" and Strauss = [strows], ≠ "Stroh's" (the beer from Detroit.) IPA renders this, rightly, as a combination of [ah] + a quick [oo], usually symbolized as a superscript [w], namely, [aʷ].
[er]	as in "hurt, dirt, Bert, word, heard" and the unstressed vowel in "major, wager, curtail." This is the sound of "fir, sure" as opposed to [ehr], which is literally [eh] + [r], as in "fair, Cher." German spells this <er> at the ends of words (Biber) or in the middle (Dittersdorf). It is not really English [er], but less distinct, more like [uh]. This sound combination is also the recommended substitute for German, Hungarian, etc., <ö>, on which see below.
[y]	This sign serves for both a vowel and a consonant. When it is the only vowel in a syllable it has the same sound as in the little words "my, by, fly" and "sigh, pie": Heinrich = [hyn-rihkh], Haydn = [hy-duhn], and Bernstein = [bern-styn]. This is the combination of [ah] + a quick [ee]. IPA symbolizes this as [aj] or with a superscript [aʲ]. If any other vowel letter follows this sign in the transcription, then the [y] represents the consonant sound in "yes, yuck," and the hidden [y] sound in "music, pure, cute, unit, beauty" = [myoo-zihk], [pyoor], [kyoot], [yoo-niht], [byoo-tee]. Other transcription systems vacillates between [y] and [j] for the consonant sound. More on this under consonants below.
[ay]	as in "day, weigh, fate, grey, great, café." In most European languages, <e> represents this sound or, more precisely, a sound in between [eh] and [ay]. (See the note on [oh] above.) IPA uses [e] or the combination of [ɛ], mentioned above, plus superscript [j] for [ɛʲ].

FRONT ROUNDED VOWELS. Two vowel sounds that do not occur in English need a special symbol: two dots above, called by the German name "umlaut" = [oom-lowt]. French, Dutch, the Scandinavian languages, Hungarian, and Finnish have these sounds as well. In linguistic terms, they combine the tongue position of [ee] and [eh], namely, where the front of the tongue is in the front of the mouth, with the lip rounding characteristic of [oo] and [oh]. (Hence the term "front rounded." See Interlude 3.) As far as this book is concerned, you always have the option of pronouncing them as indicated here or as the equivalent English sounds [oo] instead of [ü] and [er] instead of [ö].)

[ü]	Round your lips for [oo], then say [ee], as in Debussy (= duh-bü-see). If you get it right it will blend in and not sound pretentious. A respectable substitute is plain [oo] or [yoo] in [duh-byoo-see]. IPA uses either this [ü] symbol or, following Scandinavian spelling, [y], as in [də-by-si]. French and Dutch have plain <u>.
[ö]	Think British for "hurt, word" but without the [r] part. This is so close to regular English [er] that you can easily get by with that, as in Arnold Schoenberg = [shön-behrg] or [shern-behrg]. IPA uses the crossed-through symbol [ø], which is the standard spelling in Norwegian and Danish. French and Dutch have <eu>. German, Swedish, Hungarian, Finnish and Estonian have <ö>.

NASAL VOWELS. French, Polish, and Portuguese have nasal vowels. French uses no special symbol for its nasal vowels, just the letter sequence "vowel + <n> or <m>" without another vowel following, for example, "fin" vs. "fini." IPA transcribes these vowels with an over-squiggle called *tilde*, as in [fãn] vs. [fee-nee] (meaning "end" vs. "finished"). Portuguese looks like French for the vowels [eh], [ee], [oo], for example, "bem, Jobim" good, Jobim), which IPA would give as [bẽ, zhoh-bĩ], though the quality is more as in "bang, bing" than in French). Portuguese uses a tilde for the combination <ão> = [ãhn] + [oh], that is, nasal [ow], which is represented here as [õw]. Polish has an underhook on <ę, ą> for nasalized [ẽhn] and [õhn] (not [ãhn]!). In the symbols given below, both the tilde and the <n, m> techniques are superimposed. The squiggle alerts you to the nasal quality of the indicated vowel, but if you are uncomfortable pronouncing that, you can always choose to pronounce the "vowel + consonant [n]."

[ãhn] = nasal [ah]	as in French: Jean = [zhãhn] (√ [zhahn]). This is the man's name. Compare the woman's name Jeanne = [zhahn], with no nasal vowel.
[õhn] = nasal [oh]	as in French: Chausson = [shoh-sõhn] (√ ["show"-sawn"]).
[ẽhn] = nasal [eh]	as in Polish: Walesa, spelled <Wałęsa> = [vah-wẽhn-sah] or [vah-wehn-sah].
[ãn] = nasal [a]	as in French: Chopin = ["show"-pãn] or ["show-pan"]; printemps = [prãn-tãhn] or [pran-tahn] (meaning "spring"). Strictly speaking, this sound is right in between nasalized [eh] and [a], and other books may give [ẽ], as in [prẽhn-tãhn]. Also good. Note that the word "femme" = [fahm] has no nasal vowel and an unexpected [ah].
[ũhn] = nasal [uh]	as in French "un" (the indefinite article for grammatically masculine nouns). "Prélude à l'après-midi d'un faune" = [pray-lüd ah-lah-preh-mee-dee dũhn-fohn]. (The feminine indefinite article "une" = [ün] with no nasal vowel.)

[ĩn]	= nasal [ee]	as in Portuguese: Jobim = [zho-bĩn] or [zho-"bean"] (with [n], not "beam" with [m]).
[õw]	= nasal [ow]	as in Portuguese: João = [jwõw].

Consonants

The following consonants are used quite consistently all over Europe for the same sounds as in English, so the letter is the same as the sound symbol. You can class them by the part of the mouth involved in their production, more on which in Interlude 2:

<p, b, m, f, v>	=	[p, b, m, f, v]	Lip(s), both or just lower
<t, d, n, r, l>	=	[t, d, n, r, l]	Back of upper teeth
<k>	=	[k]	Back of roof of mouth.

The following sounds require some adjustment of your ear-eye habits:

SYMBOL	SOUND *with notes on spelling in several languages*
[s]	*always* as in "us, sign, cats, caps." In English <s> represents [z] just as often, as in "is, as, design, cads, cans." The [s] of phonetic spelling is *not* the same thing as <s>, the English letter. When you are supposed to say [z] you will see [z] in the transcription. This is not so easy a habit to break, and there are frequent reminders in the lists. See also Interlude 1. Note that French and Portuguese also have the under-hooked <ç>(called c-cedilla) for [s]. Hungarian has the digraph <sz>, and German has the special letter <ß> (called "ehs-tseht").
[g]	*always* "hard g," *never* "soft g." Always as in "Gil gets Gertrude a gift," and not [j] as in "Gerry dropped Ginger's gems in the giblets." English <g> can give either [g] or [j] before the vowel letters <i, e> and always [g] before other vowels. The phonetic syllable [gee] here is always so-called "hard" as in "gear," while the exclamation "Gee!" is so-called "soft" [jee]. (See Interlude 2 for more on the terms "hard" and "soft" consonants.)
[k]	English <c>, <ck>, and <qu> all represent [k], so "back" = [bak], "ache" = [ayk], "quack" = [kwak]. The symbol [c] does not occur in the transcription at all. The English letter <c> has no sound of its own. It is either [s] in "city" = [sih-tee], [k] in "country" = [kuhn-tree], and occasionally [sh]. Generally speaking, northern and eastern European languages use <k> for this sound, while southern European languages use, variously, <c, ch, qu>. Albanian uses <q> for $[k^y]$. See below.

[sh]	as in "shoot, sure, pressure, facial, spatial, nation." Other specialized symbols for this sound include several kinds of "adjusted-s": <š>, called s-wedge (and s-haček in Czech, Lithuanian, etc., and the occasional terms chevron and caret are best left aside), <ś>-acute (Polish), <ş>-cedilla (Romanian, Turkish), IPA "elongated s" [ʃ] (called "esh"). There are also several digraph strategies for this sound: English and Albanian <sh>, Polish <sz>, Dutch <sj>, French <ch>. Note also German <sch>, Portuguese <x>, and Hungarian plain <s>.
[zh]	as in "measure, azure, garage." There is no consistent way to spell this sound in English. The <zh> convention, usually associated with Russian names like Dr. Zhivago and Brezhnev, is adopted here consistently. Other specialized symbols for this sound are <ž> (z-wedge or z-haček, as in Czech, Latvian), <ź> (called z-acute, as in Polish), <ż> (dotted-z as in Polish), and IPA elongated-z <ʒ> (called yogh = [yohkh], which was actually a letter in Middle English). French uses simple <j>. Other digraph strategies are Hungarian <zs>, Dutch <zj>, and Albanian <zh>. In American English, "garage" is [guh-rahj] for some people and [guh-rahzh] for others.
[ch]	as in "church, future" and the normal speech of "What do you want?" = [wuh-chuh-wahnt]. (Compare "What did you want?" below.) Note also <č> (c-wedge or c-haček as in Czech, Slovenian, etc.), <ć> (called c-acute as in Polish, Serbo-Croatian), <ç> (called c-cedilla as in Turkish and Albanian). Digraphs include English and Spanish <ch>, Hungarian <cs>, Polish <cz>. German recognizes this sound as the combination of [t] + [sh] with the complex <tsch>. IPA also combines symbols for [^{t}ʃ].
[j]	*always* as in "judge, jury, educate, gem, Ginger" and the normal speech of "What did you say?" = [wuh-juh-say]. (Educated people don't like to admit they say this, but they really do. See Interlude 2.) The letter <j> in most of Europe is [y]. For [j], Serbo-Croatian has both crossed <d> and haček <dž>. Polish has accented <dź> and dotted <dż>. IPA recognizes the compound nature of this sound as [^{d}ʒ]. Turkish uses plain <c>. Albanian has <xh>.
[ts]	as in cats, but in English it occurs only as a sequence of sounds at the ends of words. Several languages treat it as a single sound that can also begin words. Practice making it as a single unit. German and Italian spell this sound <z>. German also spells <-tz-> and Italian also spells <zz>. Romanian has <ţ> (t-cedilla). Several languages use plain <c>.
[w]	as a separate consonant in "wise" = [wyz], as part of a consonant cluster in English "quick"= [kwihk]; Italian "questo, Guido" = [kwehs-toh, gwee-doh], and as the quick closure of the diphthongs such as [ah + w] = [ow]. Portuguese has two of these in "João" = [jwõw]. Note also Italian <ao> = [ow] as in "Ciao, Paolo" = [chow, pow-loh] and Dutch <ou> = [ow] in "oud hout" = [owt howt] (old wood).

[y]	as a consonant, most of Europe spells it <j>. English speakers have no trouble forming consonant clusters such as "cute" = [kyoot], "butte" = [byoot], "mute" = [myoot], that is, where the following vowel is [oo]. Many languages have clusters with [y] as the second consonant and any of several vowels, such as Italian "chianti" = [kyahn-tee], Russian Liadov = [lyah-duhf]. English speakers tend to pronounce a separate syllable, as in [kee-ahn-tee], [lee-ah-duhf]. Such instances will be noted in the lists.
[kh]	as in the slightly raspy [k]-like sound in German "Bach" and English "yech." The term "guttural" is often used to describe this throaty sound, but the fact is that it is not really throaty at all. Do not gurgle or expectorate too loudly. (See German in Movement 4.) Keep it kinder and gentler for the sake of your station's microphones and your listeners' speaker systems. Announcers who are uncomfortable with this very un-English sound may substitute a plain [k] in German, Dutch, and Russian. In Dutch the letter <g> always represents this sound. Spanish spells this sound <j> and <x>, and a plain [h] is a better substitute, hence the frequent transcription [(k)h] in Spanish names in the lists. IPA uses the symbol [x], which is the letter for this sound in Greek. "Bach" and "Jose" in this book are [bahkh] and [(k)hoh-say], while in IPA, they are [bax] and [xose]. Many books use the German spelling <ch> to transcribe this sound from Russian and other languages, but since Russian has both a [kh] and a [ch] some ambiguity could arise. The relatives of the linguistic, Noam Chomsky = [chahm-skee], in Eastern Europe were—and in Israel are still—[khohm-skee]. Some Russian names, like Heifetz, come into English with <h> for original [kh].
[th]	as in both "That northern weather" and "Thad's quick thinking thwarted Theo." Contrast them in an Elizabethanesque sentence like "Thy thigh is this thick." Accompanying words in the lists give the clue. See also Interlude 1. IPA uses the Old English letter [ð] (called "eth") for this and Greek [θ] (called "theta") for think. The three above examples in IPA look like this: ðæt norðərn wɛðər θædz kwɪk θɪŋkɪŋ θwortəd θio ðaj θaj ɪz ðɪs θɪk.*

* Old English used <ð> for "bathe" and <þ> (called "thorn") for "bath," but by the Middle English period they were both replaced by the combination <th>, even though each is a single sound. Modern Icelandic still uses them in both upper case<Ð, Þ> and lower case <ð, þ>. Albanian contrasts <t, th> as in "tick, thick," and also <d, dh>, as in "dough, though." Welsh has <t, th> and <d, dd>. Note that <Đ> is also the upper case of Serbo-Croatian crossed <đ> = [j]. (You also see <Đ> in Vietnamese, but that takes us a little far afield.)

How to Read the Lists

On Alphabetical Order

Some personal names with a "de," "la," "van," or other separate element (usually a definite article or preposition in the original language) are given twice: once alphabetically under that little word and again under the main part of the last name. For example, Manuel de Falla occurs as both "Falla, Manuel de" and "de Falla, Manuel." Titles of most pieces occur only once with that little word as the first word alphabetically, since that is how pieces are most often introduced from CD liner notes. (Be careful, though: standard musicological books and library catalogues alphabetize by the first *main* word, as in "Sacre du printemps, le." This book does not assume a knowledge of French grammar, and finding the readable title "Le Sacre du printemps" directly in the list is more secure. Note, too, that French capitalizes only the first word of a title, not every main word, as English does. Some pieces, like "La Bohème," are often called just "Bohème" by opera-insiders. If space were not a consideration, titles would also be entered twice.)

The Alphabetical List is given in four columns:

NAME (Last, First), TITLE, ENSEMBLE, or TERM [*Translation of title or term*] (Composer of piece, meaning of term, identification of place)	**TYPE** Picture symbol for person, piece, term	**LANGUAGE** Letter(s) for suggesting letter-sound correspondences.	**PHONETICS** Readable spelling with commentary in smaller type in parentheses.

The NAME/TITLE column gives a person's surname first, then given name. For announcing, of course, you have to reverse them. Read titles and names of ensembles as they appear. Original-language titles are followed first by an English translation in italics enclosed in square brackets. (Some radio stations announce some titles in the original language and others in English. Other stations tend to use predominantly English.) The title translation is followed by the name of the composer in plain type in parentheses. The same symbol ◆ marks both musical terms and geographical places. Terms are followed by either a translation in italics in square brackets or an explanation in parentheses. Places are identified in parentheses.

The TYPE column shows the type of person, group, piece, or term with the following more or less mnemonic signs:

People		Pieces, Places, Terms			
✍	Composer (Writes music.)		Name of ensemble or orchestra (Clear why?)		Title of a ballet or choreographic piece (because legs are so crucial).
𝄞	Conductor (Reads music.)		Title of instrumental piece (Any single instrument or combination.)	◆	Term (musical, musicological) or geographical place
♪	Performer (Makes music.)		Title of vocal piece: song, cantata, motet, opera, etc. (because the face is so crucial)		

In a few cases the "conductor" symbol 𝄞 is used for choreographers (also a kind of conducting) and the performer symbol ♪ includes dancers.

The LANGUAGE letter refers to the letter/soud correspondences of a language, not necessarily to the country of origin of the name. (This is analogous to laying a yellow filter over a red, white, and blue picture to get an orange, yellow, and green one.) See the "What's in a Name?" section.

A	Armenian	G	German	P	Polish
B	Bulgarian	Gk	Greek	Pt	Portuguese
C	Chinese	H	Hungarian	R	Russian
Cz	Czech	Ir	Irish	Rm	Romanian
D	Dutch	I	Italian	S	Spanish
Dn	Danish	J	Japanese	SC	Serbo-Croatian
E	English	K	Korean	Sk	Slovak
Es	Estonian	L	Latin	Sv	Slovenian
F	French	Lt	Lithuanian	Sw	Swedish
Fn	Finnish	Lv	Latvian	W	Welsh
		N	Norwegian		

"Dutch" includes the Flemish-speaking northern half of Belgium. "English" includes The United States, Great Britain, and the whole anglophone world. "French" includes francophone southern Belgium and western Switzerland. (The ending "-phone" forms adjectives meaning "speaking a certain language.") "German" includes Austria and northern (allemanophone) Switzerland. "Portuguese" includes (lusophone) Brazil. "Spanish" includes Spain and hispanophone Latin America. Other languages are mentioned in the phonetics column when need be.

The PHONETICS column gives one or more phonetic spellings with notes on letter/sound issues, variants, and occasional other relevant information.

Here are some whole examples taken from the lists for reading practice:

Name	Type	Lang.	Phonetics (with commentary)
DORATI, ANTAL	𝄞	H/E	"door"-ah-tee, ahn-tahl (Hungarian stresses the first syllable, but even Maestro D. seems to prefer half-English ["door-rot"-ee] with second syllable stress, not full-Hungarian ["door"-ah-tee].)

This indicates that A.D. is a conductor of Hungarian background but who pronounces his name more according to English than to expected Hungarian norms.

MAISKY, MISCHA	♪	R/G	my-skee, mee-shuh (Russian born but German spelling of <ai> for "eye" and <sch> for [sh].)

This contains the information that M.M. is a Russian performer, though his name appears in German spelling. He has been an Israeli citizen for over twenty years, but that is irrelevant to pronouncing his name on the air.

PAGANINI, NICOLÒ	✍	I	pah-gah-nee-nee, nee-koh-loh (√ half-Italian [pah-guh-nee-nee, "nickle-oh"] or half-English [pa-guh-nee-nee]. Stop short of full-English [pa-guh-"ninny"].)

This means that N.P. was an Italian composer. (He is not marked ♪ even though he was also an astounding violin virtuoso since there are no extant recordings of him from the mid-nineteenth century. It is OK to pronounce him somewhat as in English, but don't go all the way.)

HAROLD EN ITALIE [*Harold in Italy*] (Berlioz)	🎸	F/E	ah-ruhld ãhn ee-tah-lee (Full English is the norm.)

An instrumental (in this case, orchestral) piece by Berlioz, which he no doubt called by the French name, but which is always announced on English-speaking radio in English.

IL TROVATORE [*The Troubadors*] (Verdi)	🎭	I	"ill" troh-vah-toh-ray

This Italian opera is always announced in the original. The English translation is purely for reference and explanation to the listening audience.

BAYREUTH (city in Germany)	◆	G	by-royt (Not to be confused with capital of Lebanon: Beirut = [bay-root].)

Place in Germany of musical significance, in this case, the site of famous Wagner festivals.

ALLEGRO [*brisk*]	◆	I	full: ah-lay-"grow" half: ah-leh-groh half-English: "a-leg-row"

Music term meaning "brisk." Three pronunciation options are offered: full-Italian with an [ay] vowel, half-Italian with an [eh] vowel, and half-English with both a stressed [eh] and an unstressed [uh], that is, the English words ["a-leg-row"] sound like [uh-leh-groh].

What's in a Name?

People and Places

The language designations given in the lists are meant only to give you the main hint you need in order to pronounce the name. This could refer to the language of last/first name, main/secondary country of origin/residence, language of pronunciation/association. You cannot tell how to read Richard Wagner, for example, unless he is marked *E* for "think English" = ["rich"-erd "wag"-ner] or *G* for "think German" = [rih-"card" vahg-ner]. (Whether it is ["card, shard" or khard] is another question.) The same holds true for many first names that European languages have in common. The same spelling may sound different or a slight spelling difference may accompany the sound difference.

Same (or almost same) spelling, different sound:

Vincent	=	E:	vihn-sihnt	Marie	=	E:	muh-ree
		F:	vãn-sãhn			F:	mah-ree
Robert	=	E:	rah-bert	Albert	=	E:	al-bert
		F:	roh-behr ("row-bare")			F:	ahl-behr
Peter	=	E:	pee-ter	Joseph	=	E:	joh-sehf
		G:	pay-ter			F:	zhoh-zehf
		D:	Pieter = pee-ter			G:	yoh-zehf
Paul	=	E:	pawl	Ivan	=	E:	y-vihn
		F:	pohl			R:	ee-vahn
		G:	powl			Cz:	ee-vahn

Slight spelling difference and slightly different sound:

E:	Herman	=	her-muhn	E:	Alan	=	a-lihn
G:	Hermann	=	hehr-mahn	F:	Alain	=	ah-lãn
E:	Paul	=	pawl	E:	Albert	=	al-bert
I:	Paolo	=	pow-loh	S,I:	Alberto	=	ahl-"bear-toe"
S:	Pablo	=	pahb-loh				

E: George = jorj

G:	Georg	=	gay-org	S:	Jorje	=	(k)hor-(k)hay
F:	Georges	=	zhorzh	P:	Jerzy	=	yeh-zhee
I:	Giorgio	=	jor-joh	Cz:	Jiří	=	"year"-zhee
H:	György	=	jerj, jörj	R:	Yuri	=	yoo-ree
D:	Joris	=	yor-ees		Georgi	=	gee-ohr-gee

E: Joseph (in addition to above)

P:	Józef	=	yoo-zehf	R:	Iosif,	=	yoh-seef
H:	József	=	yoh-zhehf		Yosif		
					Osip	=	oh-sihp

E: Gregory

G:	Gregor	=	greh-gohr	R:	Grigori(j)	=	gree-"gorey"
F:	Grégoire	=	greh-gwahr	U:	Hryhory	=	hrih-hoh-ree
P:	Grzegorz	=	gzheh-gawsh				

and the ever-popular "John" = [jahn] with its European varieties

F:	Jean	=	zhãhn	G:	Johann	=	yoh-hahn
D:	Jan	=	yahn	I:	Giovanni,	=	joh-vah-nee,
					Gianni	=	jah-nee
Pt:	João	=	zhwõw	Cz:	Ivan	=	ee-vahn
S:	Juan	=	(kh)wahn	R:	Ivan	=	ee-vahn
Gk:	Iannis	=	yah-nees	Ir:	Sean	=	shawn.

Proper names can be particularly capricious about matching letter with sound. They often preserve old spellings, as in Dutch names with <ey> and <uy> for modern <ei> and <ui> or Hungarian names with old <cz> for modern <cs>. Sometimes names show natural phonetic properties that spelling might mask, as in Thomson and Thompson (with inserted <p>, on which see Interlude 2). Other pairs such as Stewart-Stuart, Lewis-Louis, Lawrence-Laurence have no difference in sound. In American society many first names have several spellings, such as Carol(e), Ann(e), Sara(h), Ja(y)ne. Some names are deliberately inventive and individualized, such as Karen-Karin-Karyn-Carin = [ka-rihn], Elle = [eh-lee]. Some men's vs. women's names differ only by spelling such as Bobby-Bobbie. Some European countries restrict children's names to a standardized list of traditional names, often saints' names.

Place names can also have two pronunciations for the same spelling. Thames is [tehmz] if you mean the river in London but [thaymz] for a river in Connecticut and a street in Newport, Rhode Island. Monticello is [mahn-tih-cheh-loh] if you mean Thomas Jefferson's house near Charlottesville, Virginia, but [mahn-tih-seh-loh] is one of the main streets in Norfolk, Virginia—and for that matter, Charles is [charlz], with <ch> = [ch], while Charlotte, Chicago, Michigan all have <ch> = [sh]. The German poet Goethe [gö-tuh] or [ger-tuh] would be quite surprised to hear the Chicago street that bears his name pronounced [goh-thee],* but in Chicago any other pronunciation of the street is incorrect. If King Louis XIV left his palace at Versailles = [vehr-"sigh"] and came to the city in Indiana with the same name he would hardly recognize [ver-"sails"]! Some of these variant pronunciations represent historical or linguistic developments, while others suggest that the locals either did not know the sound of the original foreign name or else felt linguistically independent enough to make it conform to their own letter/sound rules. (See the notes on Don Giovanni/Juan and Don Quixote in Movement 2.) Nonetheless, you cannot tell which one you are dealing with just by looking at the letters on the mute page. If you do know the original language you will fight an uphill battle to "correct the barbarism." Each pronunciation is right in its own context. Thus, Detroit and Des Moines must be English [duh-troyt] and [duh-moyn(z)]. If your travel agent tries to book you to the "correct" French [duh-trwah] and [deh-mwahn] you won't get very far.

The language letters in these lists are not the same as a person's citizenship. Musicians are often a mobile lot and have more than one passport for many personal or political reasons. Many either keep the original pronunciations of their names or adapt them to the local pronunciations of their home base. Immigration clerks at Ellis Island were not trained phoneticians and played a role in spelling and pronunciation changes in this country.

Local attitudes toward "foreign" names also play a role in how people pronounce their names. The town of Berlin, New Hampshire, changed the stress of its name to Berlin during World War I so as not to sound too German. Stanley Kowalski from *A Streetcar Named Desire* is definitely full-English [kuh-"wall"-skee] and not Polish [koh-vahl-skee]. Often the first and last names come from different languages for reasons of mixed parentage, personal preference, or the prevailing fashion of in-groups and out-groups in politics or the world of the arts. In the Austro-Hungarian Empire the standard language was German, often at the expense of local "minority" languages such as Czech and Hungarian, which were suppressed for a long time. This is partly why the Hungarian Liszt (= "list") has a German first name, Franz = [frahnts]. No present-day Hungarian would call him anything but native Ferenc = [feh-rents]. Sir Georg Solti is a Hungarian = ["shoal-tea"] who grew up well after Austria-Hungary, but he goes by the German first name Georg = [gay-org] and not by the native Hungarian György = [jerj]. He has long been a British subject—a knighted one, at that—and for the past quarter century has been the conductor of the Chicago Symphony. Some announcers now call him full-English George = [jorj], though some sources suggest that he, himself, prefers Georg. Such people are marked in the lists with a slash-letter, such as *H/G* or *H/E*, to suggest that one part of the name is read according to one language system and another part according to another.

---

* There is a third variant: the astronomical observatory owned by Indiana University is named after its donor, Goethe Link = ["gay-tea"].

Of Firsts and Lasts

Considering that some announcers and many audiences object to "accent-switching" from name to name in a single sentence, it is interesting that American announcers seem to have developed the habit of switching *within* a name. Sometimes this has to do with how much a household word a musician is. There is a tendency for Italians and Germans to remain Italian and German, even if they are well known, unless a German name like Robert = [raw-bert] (Schumann) has an identical English name [rah-bert]. Most announcers do not translate names, that is, Johann S. Bach is never John, and Antonio Vivaldi is never Anthony. French names seem to be more likely to come through an English filter. In this author's experience of radio listening, Vincent D'Indy is announced as [vihn-sihnt] as often as [vãn-sãhn] even if the same announcer does a flawless [dãn-dee]. Frédéric Chopin is almost always [freh-drihk]. Nonetheless, Pierre Boulez is never Peter. Russians succumb to English more often than not. Any Aleksandr = [ah-lehk-sahndr] is likely to become Alexander = [a-leg-zan-der]. Mikhail Glinka is given in musicological reference works as Michael. Pyotr Ilyich Tchaikovsky has a long tradition of being Peter Ilitch on the English airwaves. (This author recommends half-Russian [pyoh-ter ihl-yihch].) Several Russian Sergei's are better known in the west as French Serge (Koussevitsky all the time and Prokofiev half the time). Whether they, themselves, preferred the foreignism or simply thought they were making it easier on English speakers is hard to say. Jan Sibelius explicitly preferred French Jean. (As for Russian "endearing" names—Yasha for Yakov, Sasha for Aleksandr, Tolya for Anatolii—see the footnote on Heifetz, p. 59.)

Language, Ethnicity, Religion, and Politics

Language designations are not the same as country designations. Some of these languages are spoken in more than one country, and the question of language variety comes to the fore. In this author's opinion, American announcers need never try to pronounce a British name with a British accent. If both an American and a British musician are named Carla Carter, they will both be [kar-luh kar-ter]. No announcer need switch to [kah-luh kah-tuh] for the second unless s/he is British, an eastern New Englander, or a Charlestonian, in which case both will have [ah]. Robert Johnson will be pronounced as American [rah-bert jahn-suhn] and not British [raw-buht jawn-suhn]. (One of the basic differences between standard British and standard American is the value of the <o> letter. Both varieties have so-called "long" <o> = [oh] in "wrote," but the American English "short" <o> = [ah] in "rot" vs. British [aw], more or less.) As for British variants of names, this book *does* recommend following British practice as long as doing so does not go against American phonetics. The only two that come up often enough to discuss are Ralph Vaughn Williams = [rayf], ≠ [ralf] and Lennox Berkeley = [bar-klee], ≠ [ber-klee].) The same consistency applies to other languages spoken in more than one country. If, for example, Western Hemisphere Spanish is more natural for a given announcer he or she should feel free to use it even for names from Spain, and vice versa. Both varieties are equally respectable for announcing.

The early 1990s in Eastern Europe saw tremendous political changes that affect the current names of countries and languages and perhaps the likelihood of encountering more names in the that language in the near future. In the former Czechoslovakia there never was a language or nationality called "Czechoslovakian." The Czechs in the western half spoke Czech, and the Slovaks in the eastern half spoke Slovak. The two languages are closely related, and more or less the same reading techniques apply to both for announcing purposes. The two parts are now the independent Czech Republic and Slovakia. The Hungarians are unrelated ethnically or linguistically to the Czechs and Slovaks, but all three have been close neighbors for centuries and many names show properties of two or all three.

The Soviet Union (1917-1991) was a multi-ethnic entity, but it tended to label all its musicians Soviet, and in America this was often equated with Russian. The Soviet Union ceased to exist on January 1, 1992, and all the fifteen former Soviet republics are now independent states. The burden falls on music announcers and newscasters to get familiar with all those previously little-known languages. Many of the place names that have become known in the West in their Russian guise are now asserting their native pronunciation and spelling.

Russian and Ukrainian are distinct languages, but Russia has dominated the Ukrainian area politically for centuries and russified it extensively. In the nineteenth century the term "Little Russia(n)" referred to Ukrain(ian), but modern Ukrainians find that offensive. When announcing such pieces as Tchaikovsky's "Little Russian" symphony, do yourself the favor of explaining this anachronism to the audience to avoid charges of insensitivity.* Aram Khachaturian is Armenian, although his "Sabre Dance" appears on many recordings of "Russian show pieces." In this book the peoples of the Causcasus (Georgians, Azerbaijanis) and the other Turkic peoples to the east (Uzbeks, Turkmen, etc.) are barely mentioned. On the Baltic coast Lithuanians and Latvians are neighbors and distant cousins. The Estonians to their north are related to the Finns. Of course, ethnic Russians still live in these new states, and the current-day Russian Republic is still multi-ethnic. Many of these problems still need to be ironed out in virtually all cultural material that announcers use.

The former Yugoslavia (also spelled Jugoslavia, literally, "Land of the Southern Slavs") was a federation of republics. The several peoples speak related Slavic languages (west to east: Slovenian, Croatian, Serbian, Macedonian). Croatian and Serbian are virtually the same language with regional differences and are called together Serbo-Croatian. The differences are connected with religion as well. The Serbs are

---

* Some radio stations have taken to renaming it the "Ukrainian symphony," but that is a little like changing Stephen Foster's 19th-century lyrics from "darkie" and "gay" to "'Tis summer; the African Americans are merry." (Incidentally, the English "the" in "the Ukraine" was inserted into the English name in the nineteenth century, but neither Russian nor Ukrainian has ever had definite or indefinite articles. It is now becoming standard in Western sources to delete "the" and call the country "Ukraine.")

Eastern Orthodox Serbs. The Croats are Catholic, and the Bosnians in between them are Moslem. Now that the federation has disintegrated and the Serbs and Croats have started to exaggerate their linguistic differences, it is politically proper to speak of two languages, Serbian and Croatian. (The Serbs write it with Cyrillic letters, and the Croats and Bosnians write it with Latin letters. The term "Bosnian" has not yet come to indicate a separate language.) Nonetheless, this guide will continue to use "Serbo-Croatian" for this language.

This book is not responsible for every musician's personal genealogy, but some people have some notes in the phonetic column. For example, Zubin Mehta is marked *E*, though he is from India with roots that go back to old Persia. Pinchas Zukerman is also marked *E*, though he is Israeli, but you do not need to learn any special tricks for reading Hebrew.

More on Slash Designations

As was mentioned above, two designations are given for people who are associated with one country by ethnic origin—and usually, therefore, for pronunciation purposes—but who made their careers in the other. Frédéric Chopin is marked *F/P*. He is mostly associated with Poland and wrote some typically Polish music, but he made his career in 19th-century Paris. His father was French and "Chopin" is a French spelling. See note in the entry on F.C. in Movement 2. Alan Hovanhess, marked *E/A*, has the opposite situation: American-born, so you read his name as in English. He strongly identifies with his Armenian heritage and writes a lot of music based on Armenian themes. His *A* designation has nothing to do with the way you read him, while Chopin's *F* designation does. Vincent Persichetti, marked *I/E*, is also American-born, but you need some of the techniques of reading Italian to get him out as ["purr"-sih-<u>keh</u>-tee], since if you read it like English he might be ["purr"-sih-<u>cheh</u>-tee]. The first name Vincent is not a really good clue as to the language of origin or residence, since it may be French [vãn-<u>sãhn</u>]. Besides, people whose last names suggest another place are not obliged to have first names from that place, too. Henry Mancini, mentioned at the beginning of this movement, does not have to have a first name Enrico just because his last name is Italian. He would be marked just *E*, not *I* or *E/I*.

MOVEMENT 2

ALPHABETICAL LIST

Review the "Transcription Conventions" and "How to Read the Lists" sections in Movement 1 for the arrangement of the Name-Type-Language-Phonetic columns.

A

A LIFE FOR THE CZAR (Glinka)		R	English [zahr] is the norm. (Glinka's original title was Ivan Susanin = [ee-vahn soo-sah-neen], see below since it is the name of the hero, a peasant who saved the tsar's life. Tsar Nicholas I, himself, decided that *A Life For the Czar* was more fitting. In the Soviet-era *Ivan Susanin* was restored for ideological reasons to downplay the tsar and play up the peasant.)
AACHEN (city in Germany)	◆	G	ah-khehn (German <aa> = [ah].)
AARHUS/ÅRHUS (city in Denmark)	◆	Dn	ohr-hoos (Danish <aa> = <å> = [oh].)
ABBADO, CLAUDIO	𝄞	I	ah-bah-doh, "cloudy"-oh (√ [uh-bah-doh], with <d> = [flap], as in Interlude 2, and he would probably still talk to you if you called him ["claw"-dee-oh].)
ABRAVENEL, MAURICE	𝄞	E	uh-brah-vuh-nehl, maw-rees
ABU HASSAN (Weber)		G/E	ah-boo hah-sahn (≠ [a] as in "cab" or "fasten"!) ("Abu" is not a name by itself but Arabic for "father of." Abu Hassan is a man whose son is named Hassan.)
ACCADEMIA DI SANTA CECILIA, ROME		I	ah-kah-day-mee-ah dee sahn-tah cheh-chee-lyah (√ half-English [ah-kuh-deh-mee-uh] but not full-English [a-kuh…].)
ACCADEMICI DI MILANO		I	ah-kah-day-mee-chee dee mee-lah-noh

ACCARDO, SALVATORE	𝄞 ♪	I	ah-kar-doh, sahl-vah-toh-ray (√ half-English [sal-vuh-tor-ay uh-"card"-oh].)
ADAGIETTO [*somewhat slow*]	◆	I	full: ah-dah-jeh-toh (<t> = [t]) half: ah-dah-jee-eh-toh (<t> = [flap]) half-English: uh-dah-jee-eh-toh (Not full-English [uh-da-jee-eh-toh].)
ADAGIO [*slow*]	◆	I	full: ah-dah-joh half: ah-dah-jee-oh half-English: uh-dah-jee-oh (half-French: ah-dah-zhee-oh) (≠ full-English: uh-da-jee-oh, as in "badge"!)
ADAM, ADOLPHE CHARLES	✍	F	ah-dahm, ah-dolf sharl (√ full-French [ah-dãhn].)
ADDINSELL, RICHARD	✍	E	"add-in-sell," rih-cherd
ADDRIAENSSEN, EMANUEL	✍	D	ah-dree-ahn-sen, eh-mah-noo-ehl
ADELAIDE SYMPHONY ORCHESTRA		E	a-duh-layd
ADÉLAIDE OU LA LANGAGE DES FLEURS [*Adelaide or the Language of the Flowers*] (Ravel)		F	ah-deh-lehd oo-lah-lahn-gahj deh flör
ADRIANA LECOUVREUR (Cilea)		F	ah-dree-ah-nah luh-koov-rör
AEOLIAN A. CHAMBER PLAYERS A. QUARTET OF LONDON		E	ay-oh-lee-uhn
AGON (Stravinsky)		E	ay-gahn
AGRELL, DONNA	♪	E	uh-grel, dah-nuh
AGUADO, DIONYSIO	✍	S	ah-gwah-doh, dee-oh-nee-syoh
AKIYAMA, KAZUYOSHI	𝄞	J	ah-kee-yah-mah, kah-zoo-yoh-shee
ALAIN, MARIE-CLAIRE	♪	F	ah-lãn, mah-ree-klehr
ALBANESE, LICIA	♪	I	ahl-bah-nay-zay, lee-chah (√ [ahl-buh-nay-zay], but ≠ [al-buh-nay-zuh].)
ALBENIZ, ISAAC	✍	S	ahl-bay-neeth, ee-sahk (He was from Spain, so <z> = [th] is more authentic, but if you know Latin American Spanish well, stick with <z> = [s].)
ALBINONI, TOMASO	✍	I	ahl-bee-noh-nee, "toe"-mah-zoh (√ half-English [al-buh-noh-nee].)
ALBION ENSEMBLE		E	"Al"-bee-uhn ahn-sahm-"bull"
ALBRECHTSBERGER, JOHANN GEORG	✍	G	ahl-brekhts-behr-ger, yoh-hahn gay-org (√ [ahl-brecks-"bear"-ger], but ≠ [al-brecks-"burger"].)
ALBUQUERQUE CHAMBER ORCHESTRA		E	"Al"-buh-ker-kee
ALCESTIS (V. Fine)		E	ahl-sehs-tihs

ALCINA (Handel)		I	ahl-chee-nah
ALDWINCKLE, ROBERT	♪	E	awld-"wink"-uhl, rah-bert
ALEKO (Both Tchaikovsky and Rakhmaninov wrote one.)		R	ah-leh-koh (Name of main character in opera. Full-Russian [ah-lyeh-kuh] is unnecessary.)
ALEXANDROV, BORIS	𝄞	R	ah-lehk-sahn-druff, boh-rihs (="Horace, chorus." Full-Russian [bah-rees] is unfamiliar to most audiences.)
ALFVÉN, HUGO	✍	Sw	ahl-fehn, hyoo-goh (The accented <é> is not a stress mark, just a Swedish spelling flourish.)
ALLEGRETTO [*somewhat brisk*]	◆	I	full: ah-leh-greh-toh half: ah-luh-greh-toh (but ≠ a-luh-greh-toh like "alligator")
ALLEGRO [*brisk*]	◆	I	full: ah-lay-"grow" half: ah-leh-groh half-English: "a-leg-row"
ALMEIDA, ANTONIO DE	𝄞	Pt	ahl-may-duh, ahn-toh-nee-oh day
ALPERYN, GRACIELA	♪	P	ahl-peh-rihn, grah-tsyeh-lah
ALSO SPRACH ZARATHUSTRA [*Thus Spake Zarathustra*] (R. Strauss)		G	ahl-zoh shprahkh tsah-rah-too-strah (Use this full-German—so <also> ≠ English [awl-soh]—or full-Engish with [zah-ruh-thoo-struh] and old "spake," not "spoke.")
ALTMEYER, THEO	♪	G	ahlt-my-er, tay-oh
ALVA, LUIGI	♪	I/S	ahl-vah, loo-ee-jee (Italianized name of a Peruvian singer. Full Spanish name: Luis Ernesto Alva Talledo.)
ALWYN, KENNETH	𝄞	E	"all-win" (= awl-wihn)
AMADEUS QUARTET		E	ah-muh-day-uhs
AMAZONAS (Villa Lobos)		Pt	ah-mah-zoh-nuhsh
AMELING, ELLY	♪	D	ah-muh-ling, eh-lee
AMÉRIQUES (Varèse)		F	ah-meh-reek
AMOUR ET SON AMOUR [*Love and His Love*] (Franck)		F	ah-moor ay-sawn-ah-moor
AMSTERDAM LOEKI STARDUST QUARTET		D	loo-kee (Dutch <oe> = [oo].)
ANDA, GÉZA	𝄞 ♪	H/G	ahn-dah,gay-zah (Hungarian name with <z> = [z], not German where <z> = [ts]. He is a Swiss citizen, however.)
ANDANTE [*moderately slow*)]	◆	I	ahn-dahn-tay (≠ full-English "Ann Danty" or "Aunt Auntie"!)

ANDANTINO [*a little faster than Andante*]	◆	I	ahn-dahn-tee-noh (≠ "Ann Dan Tina"!)
ANDERSON, LEROY	✍	E	6ə→ (luh-roy)
ANDRÉ, MAURICE	♪	F	ãhn-dray, moh-rees
ANDREA CHÉNIER (Giordano)		F	ahn-dray-ah shehn-yay
ANDREESCU, HORIA	𝄞	Rm	ahn-dray-ehs-koo, hohr-yah (The two <e>'s are separate.)
ANDRIESSEN, HENDRIK	✍	D	ahn-dree-sen, hen-drihk
ANGELES, VICTORIA DE LOS (See also De Los Angeles, V., below)	♪	S	ahn-kheh-lehs, vihk-toh-ree-ah deh-lohs (√ [duh "loss" an-juh-lihs], like California city.)
ANGELICUM CHAMBER ORCHESTRA		E	"Ann"-jeh-lih-kuhm
ANGERER, PAUL	𝄞	G	ahn-ger-er, powl
ANICHANOV, ANDRÉ	𝄞	R	ahu-neeu-chah-nuhf, ahn-dray
ANIEVAS, AGUSTIN	♪	E/S	ah-nyeh-vahs, ah-goo-steen
ANIMAUX MODÈLES (Poulenc)		F	ah-nee-moh moh-dehl
ANTÁL, MÁTYÁS	𝄞	H	ahn-tahl, mah-tyahsh
ANTHEIL, GEORGE	✍	G/E	an-"tile," jorj (American, so read <an> as in "can," but <th> and <ei> as in German [t] and [y] = "eye.")
ANTIGONAE (Orff)		E	"an"-tih-guh-nee (Original is German, but announce as English "Antigone," as given.)
ANTIQUA MUSICA ORCHESTRA		L	an-tee-kwuh moo-zee-kuh
APOLLO (Stravinsky)		E	uh-pah-loh
APPALACHIAN SPRING (Copland)		E	either [a-puh-lay-"shin"] or ["apple-at-chin"] (Copland seems to have preferred the first.)
APPASSIONATA [Full title is "Piano sonata #23, Appassionata"] (Beethoven)		I	ah-pahs-yoh-nah-tah (General European, as given, or half-English [uh-pahs-yuh-nah-tuh]. Resist full-English versions with "passion" and "at-a" in them.)
ARABELLA (R. Strauss)		G/E	ah-ruh-beh-luh
ARAIZA, FRANCISCO	♪	S	ah-rah-ee-sah, frahn-sees-koh (He is Latin American, hence <z> = [s]. If you know European Spanish better, use it. See Albeniz above.)
ARBEAU'S ORCHÉSOGRAPHIE		F	ar-bohz or-keh-zoh-grah-fee
ARENSKY, ANTON	✍	R	ah-ren-skee, ahn-"tone"
ARGERICH, MARTHA	♪	G/S	ahr-geh-rihkh, mahr-tah (Argentinian, but an apparently German background, that is, <ch> ≠ [ch], as in Spanish.)

Name			Pronunciation
ARIADNE AUF NAXOS [*Ariadne on (the Island of) Naxos*] (R. Strauss)		G	ah-ree-ahd-nay owf nahk-sohs
ARICO, FORTUNATO	♪	I	ah-ree-koh, for-too-nah-toh
ARITA, CHIYOKO & MASAHIRO	♪	J	ah-ree-tah, chee-yoh-koh & mah-sah-hee-roh (Half-Japanese [mah-sah-hee-roh] may be more familiar. In the unstressed [hee] syllable you hear the [h] but skip over the [ee]. See Japanese in Movement 4.)
ARLECCHINO (Busoni)		I	ahr-leh-kee-noh (<ch> = [k].)
ARNAUD, LEO	✍	F	ahr-noh, lay-oh
ARNE, THOMAS	✍	E	ahrn (= "aren't")
ARRAU, CLAUDIO	♪	S	ah-row, klow-dee-oh (= "arouse," ≠ "row," which would be [roh]. Strictly speaking, you should separate the vowels into [rah-oo], but in normal speech it comes out [row], anyway.)
ARRIAGA, JUAN CRISOSTOMO	✍	S	ah-ree-ah-gah, (kh)wahn kree-soh-stoh-moh (√ full-English [kruh-sahs-tuh-moh].)
ARROYO, MARTINA	♪	S/E	ah-roy-oh, mahr-tee-nah
ARS REDIVIVA		L	ars "ready"-vee-vuh (= "farce," ≠ "cars")
ASHKENAZY, VLADIMIR	♪ 𝄞	R	ahsh-keh-nah-zee, vlah-dee-meer (√ half-Russian [ahsh-kuh-nah-zee, vla-duh-meer], since he is so well established in the West. The next-to-last syllable stress [ahsh-kuh-nah-zee] is frequently heard but unnecessary. And do avoid ["ash"-kuh-na-zee] with [a] as in "ash" and "snazzy"!)
ASSAD, SERGIO & ODAIR	♪	Pt	ah-sahd, sehr-zhoo & oh-dah-"ear" (Brazilian brothers, guitar duo.)
ASSAI [*rather*]	◆	I	ah-sy ("a-sigh") (An adverb attached to tempo markings, as in "allegro assai.")
ATTERBERG, KURT	✍	Sw	ah-ter-behr, koort (This final <g> is best left silent. In full-Swedish it produces a different quality of <r> with a hint of a syllable. Some sources say this makes <berg> close to [-berry], but that is overstated.)
AUBER, DANIEL FRANÇOIS	✍	F	oh-"bear," dahn-"yell" frãhn-swah (*Do* pronounce final <r>.)
AUGER, ARLEEN	♪	F/E	oh-zhay, ahr-leen (American singer with French last name. Do not pronounce final <r>.)
AULOS ENSEMBLE		E	"ow"-luhs

AUSTBØ, HÅKON	♪	N	owst-bö, haw-kohn
AX, EMANUEL	♪	E	→
AYO, FELIX	♪	I	"eye"-o, fay-"licks"
AZRUNI, SAHAN	♪	E	ahz-roo-nee, sah-hahn (Actually, Iranian, but in this book English is the catch-all language for such minorities.)

B

BAAREN, KEES VAN	✍	D	bah-ren, "case" vuhn
BABA YAGA (Liadov)		R	bah-buh yah-gah (Name of a witch in Russian folklore immortalized in this symphonic poem and in Mussorgsky's *Pictures at an Exhibition*. She lives in a hut that stands on chicken's legs and constantly spins. She travels in a mortar and pestle, not on a broomstick. Half-Russian is given here. Full-Russian is [yih-gah].)
BACCHUS ET ARIANE (Roussel)		F	bah-küs ay ah-ree-ahn
BACH, ANNA MAGDALENA (NOTEBOOK)	◆	G	bahkh, ah-nah mahg-dah-lay-nah (Collection of short pieces, some instrumental, some vocal.)
BACH, CARL (KARL) PHILIPP EMANUEL	✍	G	bahkh, karl fih-"lip" eh-"man"-yoo-uhl (= "Bock" with a raspy or breathy end, but not too gurgly or ejective. Full-German [eh-mah-noo-ehl] is overkill.)
BACH, JOHANN CHRISTIAN CHRISTOPH FRIEDRICH SEBASTIAN	✍	G	bahkh, yoh-hahn (≠ full-English [yoh-han].) krihs-chuhn (√ full-German [khree-styahn].) krihs-tawf free-drihk suh-"bash"-chuhn (= "sub-bastion." Full-German [zeh-bah-styahn] is unnecessarily over-zealous.)
BACH, WILHELM FRIEDEMANN FRIEDRICH ERNST	✍	G	bahkh, vihl-helm free-duh-mahn free-drihk ehrnst (="air"nst)
BACHIANAS BRASILEIRAS (Villa Lobos)		Pt	bahk-yah-nahsh brah-zeel-"air-ish" (Brazilian pieces inspired by, in the style of, and dedicated to Bach.)

BACHWERKEVERZEIGNIS (= BWV)	◆	G	bahkh vehr-kuh fehr-tsykh-nihs (An apparent monster word, but made of three manageable parts: Bach-Werke-Verzeignis, that is, "Bach's Works Catalogue," one of the cataloguing systems for the more than 1,000 works of J.S. Bach. See also Schmieder.)
BACIU, ION	𝄞	Rm	bah-choo, yohn
BACKHAUS, WILHELM	♪	G	bahk-"house," vil-helm
BACQUIER, GABRIEL	♪	F	bah-kee-ay, gah-bree-ehl (Full-French = [bah-kyay].)
BADEN-BADEN RADIO ORCHESTRA	🪑	G	bah-duhn bah-duhn
BADURA-SKODA, PAUL	♪	G	bah-doo-rah-skoh-dah, "Paul" (√ full-German *powl*)
BALAKIREV, MILY	✍	R	bah-lah-kee-rehf, mee-lee (√ [buh-lah-kuh-rehv]. Slonimsky 1992 specifically cautions against [ba-lah-kee-rehv].)
BALANCHINE, GEORGE	𝄞	E/R/F	ba-luhn-sheen, jorj (The "conductor" symbol is loosely applied here for "choreographer." The name looks French and is normally pronounced as in half-English as given. He was Georgian, born Balanchivadze = [bah-lahn-chee-vah-dzeh].)
BALANESCU QUARTET	🪑	Rm	bah-luh-nehs-koo
BALLADEN DER LIEBE [*Love Ballads*] (Bruch)	🐸	G	bah-lah-duhn dehr lee-buh
BALLI, HEINZ	♪	G	bah-lee, hynts (="pints")
BALLO DELLE INGRATE (Monteverdi)	👤	I	bah-loh deh-lah-een-grah-tay
BALOGH, JÓZSEF	♪	H	bah-lohg, yoh-zhehf
BALTSA, AGNES	♪	Gk	bahl-tsah, ag-nihs (Full-Greek first name is [ahg-nee] but use this English equivalent for announcing.)
BAMBERG PHILHARMONIC	🪑	G	bahm-behrg
BANK, JACQUES	✍	D	bahnk, zhahk
BANOWETZ, JOSEPH	♪	E	👓→🔔
BÄR, ALWIN (BAER)	♪	G	"bare," ahl-vin (<ä> and <ae> are alternate spellings.)
BARBIERI, FEDORA	♪	I	bar-byeh-ree, feh-"door"-ah (3-syllable last name, not 4-syllable "Barbie-airy.")
BARBIROLLI, JOHN	𝄞	E	bar-buh-roh-lee
BARBOTEU, GEORGES	♪	F	bar-boh-tö, zhorzh
BARDON, PIERRE	♪	F	bar-dõhn, pyehr

BARENBOIM, DANIEL	♪ 𝄞	E	"barren"-boym, dahn-yehl (√ "bar"-en-boym, in which case he should really be marked "G/E" or more accurately Yiddish. Full-English "bear"-uhn-boym is also OK, as is English "Daniel." He was born in Argentina and grew up in Israel.)
BARGEL, WOLFGANG	♪	G	bar-guhl, vohlf-gahng
BARLOW, JEREMY	♪	E	"bar-low," jeh-ruh-mee
BARSONY, LÁSZLÓ	♪	H	bahr-shohn^{y}, lah-"slow" (Hungarian <s> = [sh], <sz> = [s].)
BARTO, TZIMON	♪	E	"bar"-toh, tsee-mohn (Stage name of an American pianist.)*
BARTÓK, BÉLA	✍ ♪	H	bar-tohk, bay-lah (√ ["bar-talk"] but not [bar-tahk] or ["bell"-uh]. English puts given name first for Béla Bartók, while a Hungarian-produced CD would list him family name first as Bartók Béla without a comma. Re-reverse him for announcing. Same goes for Franz Liszt vs. Liszt Ferenc.)
BARTOLI, CECILIA	♪	I	"bar"-toh-lee, cheh-chee-lyah
BASTIEN ET BASTIENNE (Mozart)	🎭	G/F	bah-styehn ay bah-styehn (This is one of the few places where you do have to distinguish between "nasal vowel" and "vowel + [n]" since it makes the difference between the masculine and feminine.)
BATIZ, ENRIQUE	𝄞	S	bah-tees, en-ree-kay
BAUMANN, HERMANN	♪	G	bow-mahn, hehr-mahn (= "bow," what a gentleman does, not what you shoot an arrow with.)
BAUMANN, JÖRG	♪	G	bow-mahn, yörg (= yerg)
BAVARIAN RADIO SYMPHONY ORCHESTRA	🪑	G	buh-"very"-uhn
BAX, ARNOLD	✍	E	6ə→ɑ
BAYERN (= BAVARIA)	◆	G	by-"earn" (The German name for this southern part of Germany.)
BAYREUTH (city in Germany)	◆	G	by-royt (Wagner made this place famous.)
BEACH, MRS. H. H. A. (= Amy Marcy Cheney)	✍	E	6ə→ɑ (After marriing Dr. H.H.A. Beach she specified that she wanted to use his name.)

* The name is meant to look European, but from where? No European language has an equivalent of Simon with [ts] instead of [s]. Furthermore, no language begins words with <tz>, except a few Russian words transcribed in French, and Russian Simon is Simyon = [seem-yohn]. German has <tz> = [ts] in the middle or at the end of a word. German and Italian can begin words with <z> = [ts]. Czech and Polish always spell [ts] as <c>. See note on Ravel's Tzigane.)

BEATRICE DI TENDA (Bellini)		I	bay-ah-tree-chay dee-tehn-dah
BÉATRICE ET BÉNÉDICT [*Beatrice and Benedict*] (Berlioz)		F	bay-ah-trees ay-beh-neh-dihkt (A fuller French would be [bay-nay-dihkt], but full-English [bee-trihs and beh-nuh-dihkt] is the norm for announcing.)
BEAUTIFUL GALATEA, THE (von Suppé)		E	ga-luh-tay-uh
BEAUX ARTS TRIO		F	boh-zahr (Carry this French <x> over to the next vowel as [z]. French <eau> = [oh], and the final consonants are silent.)
BEECHAM, THOMAS		E	6ϑ→
BEETHOVEN, LUDWIG VAN		G	bay-toh-vehn, lood-vihg vahn (= ["pudding fun"] ≠ ["budding van"].*)
BELLINI, VINCENZO		I	beh-lee-nee, veen-chehn-dzoh (√ half-English [buh-lee-nee].)
BELSHAZZAR'S FEAST (Walton)		E	"bell"-shuh-zahr (This is an Aramaic name from the Biblical book of Daniel, which begins and ends in Hebrew but switches to Aramaic from Chapters 2 to 8. This German spelling with <zz> represents Aramaic [ts]. Also pronounced ["bell"-shaht-sahr].)
BENVENUTO CELLINI (Berlioz)		I	behn-veh-noo-toh cheh-lee-nee (Half-English will have <t> = [flap], which may come into transcription as [behn-vuh-noo-doh].)
BENYACS, ZOLTÁN	♪	H	ben-yahch, zohl-tahn
BEOGRAD, BELGRAD(E) (capital of Serbia)	◆	SC	bay-oh-grahd (English ["bell-grade"] or [behl-grahd] is also good. The variation comes from the fact that Serbo-Croatian <l> in closed syllable becomes <o>. See Movement 4.)
BERBERIAN, KATHY	♪	E	ber-beh-ree-uhn, ka-thee
BEREZOVSKY, BORIS	♪	R	beh-reh-zohf-skee, boh-rihs (Full-Russian [byeh-ryeh-zohf-skee, bah-rees] is too much.)
BERG, ALBAN		G	behrg, ahl-bahn (= ["bare"g], ≠ [al-buhn "berg"] as in "iceberg.")
BERG, GUNNAR		Dn	behrg, goo-nahr
BERGANZA, TERESA	♪	I	behr-gahn-dzah, teh-ray-zah

* Full-German is [bay-toh-fehn, lood-veek], with <v> = [f], but the suggested half-German is more natural. Do not rhyme with "flood wig van." As for "van" vs. "von," German noble families have <von> with a vowel between "fawn" and "fun," while Dutch names can have <van> = [vuhn] or "fun" whether they are noble or not. LvB's grandfather was from what is now Belgium and kept "van" when he moved to Germany. English reads <o> as [ah], in any case. Our Mr. B. is so well known that [vahn] is fine. Reserve full-English [van] for large motor vehicles.

Name			Pronunciation
BERIO, LUCIANO	✍	I	beh-ree-oh, loo-chah-no
BERKELEY, LENNOX	✍	E	"bar"-klee, leh-nuhks (Most American announcers observe British English <er> = [ahr], as in "clerk, Derby" = [klahrk], [dahr-bee]. See also under Ralph Vaughn Williams for another Britishism.)
BERKES, KÁLMÁN	♪	H	behr-kehsh, kahl-mahn
BERLIOZ, HECTOR	✍	F	behr-lee-ohz, ehk-tor (= ["barely owes"] with final <z>. Full-French [behr-lyohz] is too correct.)
BERMAN, LAZAR	♪	R	behr-muhn, lah-zahr
BERNARD, ANDRÉ	♪	F	behr-nahr, ãhn-dray
BERNSTEIN, LEONARD	𝄞 ✍ ♪	E	"burn"-styn (= "shine", ≠ steen), leh-nerd
BEROFF, MICHEL	♪	F	beh-rawf, mee-"shell" (French Michel is a man's name, and Michelle is a woman's name. They sound the same.)
BERWALD, FRANZ	✍	Sw/G	behr-vahld, frahnts (≠ [ber-"walled"]. Swedish composer, but his name looks and sounds German.)
BESNARD, GUY	♪	F	beh-nahr, gee
BEZNOSIUK, LISA	♪	E	behz-noh-syook. lee-suh (Names in <-iuk> are mostly Ukrainian. Hard to tell how her family pronounces it.)
BEZRODNY, SERGEI	♪	R	byehz-rohd-nee, sehr-gay
BIAŁYSTOK (city in Poland)	◆	P	byah-wih-stohk (√ half-English [byah-lih-"stock"].)
BIBER, HEINRICH VON	✍	G	bee-ber, hyn-rick fuhn
BIEDERMEIER ENSEMBLE WIEN	🪑	G	bee-der-my-er ahn-sahm-buhl veen
BIGGS, E. POWER	♪	E	bihgz, ee "power"
BILGRAM, HEDWIG	♪	E	"bill"-gruhm, "head-wig"
BILSON, MALCOLM	♪	E	"bill"-suhn, mal-kuhm
BINNS, MALCOLM	♪	E	bihnz, mal-kuhm
BIRET, IDIL	♪	H	bee-reht, ee-"dill"
BIRKELAND, ØYSTEIN	♪	N	beer-kuh-lahnd, öy-stayn (oy-stayn)
BISENGALIEV, MARAT	♪	R	bih-sehn-gah-lyehf, mah-raht
BIZET, GEORGES	✍	F	bee-zay, zhorzh
BJOERLING, JUSSI	♪	Sw	byör-ling, yoo-see (= byer-)
BLAVET, MICHEL	✍	F	blah-vay, mee-shehl
BLEGEN, JUDITH	♪	E	blay-gun, joo-dihth (First <e> = [ay], typical of "general European." Second is unstressed as [uh], typical of German.)

Name			Pronunciation
BLITZSTEIN, MARC	✍	E	blihts-styn
BLOCH, ERNEST	✍	G	blohkh, ehr-nest (more like the vowel sound in "talk" than in "block")
BLOMSTEDT, HERBERT	𝄞	E/Sw	bluhm-steht (He is of Swedish background, not German, so <stedt> = [steht], ≠ [shteht].)
BLOOM, MYRON	♪	E	bloom, my-ruhn
BLUM, DAVID	𝄞	E	bluhm (="plum")
BLUME, NORBERT	♪	E	bloom, nor-bert
BOCCHERINI, LUIGI	✍	I	boh-keh-ree-nee, loo-ee-jee (√ [bah-kuh-ree-nee])
BOEHMER, KONRAD	✍	G	bö-mer, kohn-rahd (= [ber-mer], ≠ [kahn-rad].)
BOËLLMANN, LÉON	✍	F/G	boh-ehl-mãhn, lay-õhn (Also run together as [bwehl-mãhn] or simplified to ["bell"-mãhn]. The name is Alsatian, hence the German look and French sound. The <oë> with diaresis keeps the <e> separate and prevents you from reading German <oe> = <ö> = [ö].)
BOGAARD, ED	♪	D	boh-khard, ehd (The Dutch also use English first names.)
BÖHM, KARL	𝄞	G	böm (= [berm], like "perm," but British-like with no "r" sound.)
BOIELDIEU, FRANÇOIS	✍	F	bwahl-dyö, frãhn-swah (√ [-dyer] all in one syllable as in "fir.")
BOITO, ARRIGO	✍	S	bo-ee-"toe," ah-ree-go
BOK, HENRI	♪	F	bohk, ãhn-ree
BOLCOM, WILLIAM	✍ ♪	E	"bowl"-kuhm
BOLERO (Ravel)	🎸	F	buh-"lair"-oh (Bolero is a kind of Spanish dance. This particular one is played so often that the half-English suggested here is better than full-Spanish [boh-leh-roh]. Ravel's piece was choreographed but is almost always performed nowadays as an orchestral piece.)
BOLET, JORGE	♪	S/E	boh-leht, jorj (He is Cuban but says [jorj], not Spanish [hor-hay], and definitely not French [zhorzh boh-lay].)
BOLLING, CLAUDE	✍ ♪	F	"bowling, clawed" (Full-French [klohd] = "load" is too much.)
BOLOGNA (city in Italy)	◆	I	buh-"loan"-yuh (Italian <gn> = [n^y].)

BOLSHOI (BOLSHAIA, BOLSHAYA) BALLET, OPERA, ORCHESTRA, THEATRE		R	bahl-shoy & bahl-"shy"-uh (Also spelled Bolshoy, an adjective meaning "great, grand." Bolshoi is the masculine form and Bolshaia, the feminine. Half-English would be ["bowl"-shoy], which is preferable to full-English ["bowl"-shoy]. It is the name of the hall in Moscow and the opera and ballet troupes associated with it. The Russian nouns [bah-lyeht], [ahr-kehstr], and [tay-ahtr] are grammatically masculine, and "opera" = [oh-pyeh-ruh] is feminine.)
BONELL, CARLOS	♪	S/E	boh-nehl, kar-lohs (√ buh-nehl)
BONFIGLIO, ROBERT	♪	I/E	bohn-fee-lyoh, rah-bert
BONYNGE, RICHARD	𝄞	E	bah-ning, "Richard"
BORGUE, DANIEL	♪	E	borg, da-nyuhl
BORIS GODUNOV (Mussorgsky)		R	bah-rees guh-"dune-off" (This full-Russian is just unfamiliar enough to sound wrong to audiences. The English-speaking world seems to have dubbed it ["bore"-ihs goo-duhn-"off"]. Same issue as Borodin, below.*)
BORODIN, ALEXANDER	✍	R	"bore-a-dean" (He is best known in this full-English form. Audiences may not recognize his as full-Russian [buh-rah-deen].)
BOROWSKA, JOANNA	♪	P	boh-rohf-shak, yoh-ah-nah
BOSKOVSKY, WILLI	𝄞 ♪	G	"boss-cough-ski," vih-lee
BOSMANS, HENRIETTE	✍	D	"boss"-muhns, hehn-ree-eh-tuh
BOSNIA-HERCEGOVINA (HERZEGOVINA) (Part of former Yugoslavia)	◆	SC	"boss"-nee-uh "hair"-tseh-goh-vee-nah (√ [bahz-nee-uh] or [bawz-nee-uh]. Hercegovina is also good, and it is spelled with <c> = [ts] or in German Herzegovina with <z> = [ts].
BOTTESINI, GIOVANNI	✍	I	boh-teh-zee-nee, joh-vah-nee (√ [bah-tuh-zee-nee]; 3-syllable [joh-vah-nee], not 4-syllable [jee-oh-vah-nee].)
BOTVAY, KÁROLY	♪	H	boht-vy, kah-roy (Hungarian <ly> is not a syllable, just the consonant [y].)
BOULANGER, LILI	✍	F	boo-lãhn-zhay, lih-lee
BOULANGER, NADIA	𝄞	F	boo-lahn-zhay, nah-dyah

* The resemblance of this name to the common English surname Goodenough made possible the spoof name "Boris Badenoff," the Russian spy caricature who, with his sidekick Natasha, plotted against "moose and squirrel" in the Rocky and Bullwinkle cartoons of the cold war 1960s.

BOULEZ, PIERRE	𝄞 ✍	F	boo-lehz, pyehr (He does pronounce the <z>.)
BOULT, ADRIAN	𝄞	E	"bolt," ay-dree-uhn
BOUR, ERNEST	𝄞	D	(= "flour" in one syllable)
BOURNE, JEAN-LUC	♪	F	boorn, zhãhn-lük (√ zhahn-Luke with optional nazalization, as in *Picard*, for you Trekkies.)
BOURNEMOUTH (city in England)	◆	E	born-muhth (Home of the Bournemouth Sinfonietta.)
BOURRÉE (a kind of Baroque dance)	◆	F	boo-ray
BOWYER, KEVIN	♪	E	"boy"-yer
BOYD, DOUGLAS	♪	E	boyd, duh-gluhs
BRABEC, EMANUEL	♪	Cz	brah-bets, eh-mah-noo-el
BRAHMS, JOHANNES	✍	G	brahmz, yoh-hah-nehs (Half-German with <s>= [z] is normal. Full-German [brahms] = "comps" minus the [p] and with <s> as [s], though this is too correct for American radio.)
BRANSLE (a kind of Baroque dance)	◆	F	brãhn-luh
BRATISLAVA (captial of Slovakia)	◆	Sk	brah-tih-slah-vah (Czech and Slovak stress first syllable.)
BRATSCHE (viola)	◆	G	brah-chuh
BREAM, JULIAN	♪	E	breem, joo-lee-uhn
BREDA (city in Holland)	◆	D	bray-dah
BREDICEANU, MIHAI	𝄞	Rm	bray-dee-chah-noo, mee-"high"
BREMBECK, CHRISTIAN	𝄞	G	brehm-behk, khrees-tyahn
BRENDEL, ALFRED	♪	G/E	bren-duhl, al-frehd (Full-German [ahl-freht] is unnecessary.)
BRNO (city in the Czech Republic)	◆	Cz	ber-noh (Two syllables: the <r> really does serve as the first vowel.)
BROUWER, LEO	✍	G/S	brow-er (= "tower"), lee-oh (German name, but from Cuba.)
BROWN: IONA, JAMES, TIMOTHY	♪	E	"eye"-oh-nuh, 👓→🔔
BRT (Belgian Radio and Television)	◆	E/D	Read as [bee-ahr-tee]. (The Flemish-Belgian national media: Belgische Radio en Televizie = [behl-khih-suh rah-dee-oh ehn tay-lay-vee-zee].)
BRUCH, MAX	✍	G	brookh, "Max" (= ["brook"] with [kh] at end. √ full-German [mahks].)
BRUCKNER, ANTON	✍	G	"brook"-ner, ahn-"tone" (≠"Ann"-tahn.)
BRUGES = BRUGGE (city in Belgium)	◆	F/D	broozh (Full-French [brüzh], also known by its Flemish name, Brugge = [brü-khuh].)

Name			Pronunciation
BRÜGGEN, FRANS	♪ 𝄞	D/G	brü-guhn, frahns (√ [broo-guhn]. He is Dutch but this German spelling with <ü> for [ü] seems to be the norm. Keep <g>= [g], as in German, since full-Dutch <g> = [kh] in [brü-khuhn] might sound overdone.)
BRUNNER, EDUARD	♪	D	brü-ner, ehd-ward
BRUSON, RENATO	♪	I	broo-zohn, reh-nah-toh
BRUSSEL [D] = BRUSSELS [E] = BRUXELLES [F] (capital of Belgium)	◆	D/E/F	bruh-suhlz (English is the norm. French Bruxelles = [brük-"sell"]. Dutch Brussel = [brü-suhl].)
BRYMER, JACK	♪	E	bry-mer
BRYN-JULSON, PHYLLIS	♪	E	brihn-jool-suhn
BUDAPEST (capital of Hungary)	◆	H	boo-duh-pehst (This half-English is the norm. Full-Hungarian is [boo-dah-pehsht], the union of the two former cities of Buda and Pest. Hungarian <s> = [sh].)
BÜHLER, FRANZ	✍	G	bü-ler, frahnts
BÜLOW, HANS GUIDO VON	♪	G	bü-loh, hahns gee-doh fuhn (German <ow> here is [oh], not "of" or "off." See note below under Flotow.)
BUMBREY, GRACE	♪	E	buhm-bree
BURDICK, JAMES OWEN	♪	E	ber-dihk, jaymz oh-wen
BUSCH, FRITZ	𝄞	G	"bush" (as in what you beat around)
BUSONI, FERRUCIO	✍	I	boo-zoh-nee, feh-roo-choh (Full-Italian first name is 3 syllables; English is 4-syllable [fuh-roo-chee-oh].)
BUXTEHUDE, DIETRICH	✍	G/Dn	"book"-stuh-hoo-duh, dee-trikh (Pronounced like German, but he his family had settled in Denmark long before him. See *Greene's Encyclopedia* for details of his background.)
BUYSE, LEONE	♪	D	"buy"-suh, lay-oh-nuh
BWV (See Bachwerkeverzeignis)	◆	E	Read as [bee-"double-yoo"-vee]. (Not a fancy car, just the abbreviation for Bachwerkeverzeignis.)
BYCHKOV, SEMYON	𝄞 ♪	R	"bitch"-"cough", seem-yohn
BYDGOSZCZ (city in Poland)	◆	P	"bid"-gohshch (Polish <sz> = [sh] and <cz> = [ch].)
BYLSMA, ANNER (BIJLSMA, BŸLSMA)	♪	D	byl-smuh, ah-ner (= "honor) (The <y> or <ÿ> is the alternate spelling for Dutch <ij>. See Movement 4.)
BYRD, WILLIAM	✍	E	"bird"

C

CABALLE, MONTSERRAT	♪	S	kah-by-yay, mohn-seh-raht
CALLAHAN, CHARLES	♪	E	ka-luh-han, chahrlz
CALLAS, MARIA	♪	E/Gk	kah-lahs, mah-ree-ah (American born, Greek father, spent several years in Greece, so [kah-lahs] and not "callus" or "callous" = [ka-lihs].)
CAMERATA Part of several ensembles' names: •C. ACADEMICA DES MOZARTEUMS SALZBURG •BERN, HUNGARICA, KÖLN		L/G	kah-muh-rah-tah •ah-kah-day-mee-kah dehs moh-tsahr-tay-ooms zahlts-boorg •behrn, hoon-gah-rih-kah, köln
CAMPRA, ANDRÉ		F	kahm-prah, ãhn-dray
CANINO, BRUNO	♪	I	kah-nee-noh, broo-noh
CANTABILE [*singingly*]	◆	I	full: kahn-tah-bee-lay half: kahn-tah-buh-lay (≠ "can-tab"-uh-lee)
CANTATA	◆	F	full: kahn-tah-tah (<t, t> = [t, t]) half: kuhn-tah-tuh (<t, t> = [t, flap])
CANTELLI, GUIDO	𝄞	I	kahn-teh-lee, gwee-doh
CANTILENA		S	kahn-tee-lay-nah (Full-Spanish as given or half-Spanish [kahn-tuh-lay-nuh. English "can't-a-lane-a" is easily avoidable.)
CANTUS (Pärt)		L	kahn-toos
CAPELLA CLEMENTINA ISTROPOLITANA		L	kah-peh-lah (√ [kuh-peh-luh]) kleh-men-tee-nah ee-struh-puh-lee-tah-nah
CAPITOLE DE TOULOUSE ORCHESTRA		F	kah-pee-tohl duh too-looz
CÁPOVÁ, SILVIA	♪	Cz	tsah-poh-vah, seel-vee-yah
CAPRICCIO	◆	I	full: kah-pree-choh half: kuh-"preachy"-oh
CARDILLAC (Hindemith)		F	kahr-dee-yahk
CARMINA BURANA (Orff)		L	kahr-mee-nuh boo-rah-nuh (Avoid [byoo-rah-, buh-rah-, ber-ah-], cf. pp. 11, 179.)
CARMIRELLI, PINA	♪	I	kar-mee-reh-lee, pee-nah (√ half-Italian "car"-muh-relly)
CARNAVAL DES ANIMAUX [*Carnival of the Animals*] (Saint-Saëns)		F	kahr-nah-vahl dehz-ah-nee-moh (A symphonic work with a text spoken by a narrator, hence the double picture. Announce it in English.)
CARUSO, ENRICO	♪	I	kah-roo-zoh, ehn-ree-koh (√ kuh-roo-soh)

CASADESUS, GABY & JEAN	♪	F	kah-sah-duh-sü, gah-bee & zhãhn (French <e> with no accent mark often drops out in speech. You may hear [kah-sahd-sü], but four syllables are also good.)
CASADESUS, ROBERT	♪ ✍	F	kah-sah-duh-sü, roh-behr
CASALS, PABLO	♪ 𝄞 ✍	S	kah-sahlz, pah-bloh (Half-Spanish as given or half English [kuh-sahlz], but ≠ full-English [kuh-salz] = "Sal's" or [kuh-sawlz] = "Saul's." Full-Spanish is kah-sahls with final <s> = [s] with the same [s/z] issue as discussed above for "Brahms." He was Catalan, born Pau Carlos Salvador Defilló.)
CASTELNUOVO-TEDESCO, MARIO	✍	I	kah-stehl-nwoh-voh-teh-deh-skoh, mah-ree-oh
CASTOR ET POLLUX (Rameau)		F	kah-"store" ay-poh-lüks
CAVALLERIA RUSTICANA (Mascagni)		I	kah-vah-leh-ree-ah roo-stee-kah-nah (No "rusty cans," please!)
CECCATO, ALDO	𝄞	I	cheh-kah-toh, ahl-doh
CELEBIDACHE, SERGIU	𝄞	Rm	cheh-leh-bih-dah-keh, sehr-joo (≠ full-English [cheh-luh-buh-da-kee, ser-joo].)
CEMBALO [I], CLAVECIN [F] (harpsichord)	◆	I, F	chem-bah-loh, klah-vuh-sãn
CÉPHALE ET PROCRIS OU L'AMOUR CONJUGAL [*Cephalus and Procris or Conjugal Love*] (Grétry)		F	seh-fahl ay-proh-kree oo-lah-moor kõhn-zhü-gahl (seh-fuh-luhs & proh-krihs: two characters from mythology.)
CHABRIER, EMANUEL	✍	F	shah-bree-ay, ee-"man"-yoo-el (French last name, but first name usually as in English.)
CHACONNE (type of musical structure)	◆	F	full: shah-kohn half: shuh-kahn
CHAILLY, RICCARDO	𝄞	F/I	"shy"-yee, rih-"card"-oh
CHALIAPIN, FEODOR	♪	R	shah-lyah-pihn, fyoh-der (French spelling of a Russian name, also Chaliapine. English may come out as "Fyodor Shalyapin" and German as "Fiodor Schaliapin.")
CHAMBRON, JACQUES	♪	F	shahm-brõhn, zhahk (Full-French = [shãhn-brõhn].)
CHAMINADE, CECILE	✍	F	shah-mee-nahd, suh-seal
CHANG, HAE-WON	♪	K	chahng, heh-wohn
CHARPENTIER, MARC-ANTOINE	✍	F	shar-pãhn-tyay, mark ãhn-twahn (3 syllables, not half-English 4-syllable [shar-pahn-tee-ay].)
CHAUSSON, ERNEST	✍	F	"show"-sõhn, ehr-nest

Name			Pronunciation
CHAVEZ, CARLOS	✍	S	<u>chah</u>-vehs, <u>kar</u>-lohs (√ [-vehz], and definitely not French-like [shuh-<u>vehz</u>]. See notes on Casals and Brahms, above.)
CHEDRIN, RODION	✍	R	shcheh-<u>dreen</u>, roh-dee-<u>ohn</u> (French spelling for full-Russian Shchedrin, on whom, see below.)
CHEIFITZ, HAMILTON	♪	E	<u>shay</u>-fits (See note on J. Heifetz, below.)
CHEN, GANG	✍	C	chuhn, gahng
CHEN, PI-HSIEN	♪	C	chuhn, pee-shuhn
CHENEY, AMY MARCY	✍	E	<u>chay</u>-nee (See above: Beach, Mrs. H.H.A.)
CHERKASSKY, SHURA	♪	R	"chair"-<u>kahs</u>-skee, <u>shoo</u>-ruh (Shura and Sasha are Russian nicknames for Aleksandr. See note on Jascha Heifetz.)
CHERRIER, SOPHIE	♪	F	sheh-ree-<u>ay</u>, soh-<u>fee</u>
CHERUBINI, LUIGI	✍	I	keh-roo-<u>bee</u>-nee, loo-<u>ee</u>-jee
CHILINGIRIAN STRING QUARTET		E	"chillin'-<u>gear</u>"-ee-uhn
CHIŞINĂU = KISHINEV, KISHINËV (Captial of Moldova, old Bessarabia)	◆	Rm/R	kee-shee-<u>now</u> (The Russian name has been more common, but the Romanian spelling is coming into style.)
CHISTYAKOV, ANDREI	𝄞	R	chee-styah-"<u>cough</u>," ahn-<u>dray</u>
CHOÉPHORES (Milhaud)		F	koh-ay-"<u>four</u>"
CHOPIN, FRÉDÉRIC (FRANÇOIS) [= Frederyk (Franciszek)]	✍	F/P	"show"-"<u>pãn</u>," freh-duh-<u>reek</u> frãhn-<u>swah</u> (√ half-French with 1st syllable stress ["<u>show</u>"-pãn] or English Frederick ["<u>show</u>-pan"]. Avoid "show pin" or "chopping." *)
CHÖRE FÜR DORIS (Stockhausen)		G	<u>kö</u>-ruh für "Doris"
CHÔROS (Villa Lobos)		Pt	<u>shoh</u>-roosh (a type of Brazilian piece)
CHORZEMPA, DANIEL	♪	E	kor-<u>zem</u>-puh
CHU, WANHUA	✍	C	choo, <u>wahn</u>-hwah
CHUNG, KYUNG WHA	♪	K	chuhng, <u>kyuhng</u>-wah (Korean <u>= [uh], not European [oo].)
CICCOLINI, ALDO	♪	I	"chick"-oh-<u>lee</u>-nee, <u>ahl</u>-do (Neither ["<u>all</u>-dough"] nor [<u>al</u>-doh].)
CIMAROSA, DOMENICO	✍	I	chee-mah-<u>roh</u>-zah, doh-<u>men</u>-ih-koh (√ half-English [chih-muh-<u>roh</u>-zuh, duh-<u>mehn</u>-uh-koh].)

---

* The French last name Chopin is from his father. F.C. made his name in the salons of Paris, but the Poles claim him as their cultural hero. To read <Chopin> in Polish is [<u>khoh</u>-peen], which one never says. To represent the French sound in Polish spelling you need <Szopen>, which you may occasionally encounter, along with his Polish first and middle names [<u>freh</u>-deh-rihk frahn-<u>chee</u>-shehk].)

CIRQUE DE DEUX (Gounod)		F	seerk duh dö
ČIURLIONIS, MIKOLAUS KONSTANTINAS	✍	Lt	choor-lyoh-nees, mee-koh-laws (="louse") kohn-stahn-tee-nahs (Lithuanian is one of the "haček" languages, in which <č> = [ch].)
CIVIL, ALAN	♪	E	sih-vuhl (as in "Keep a ~ tongue.")
CLARINADE (Gould)		E	kla-rih-nahd
CLAVECIN [F], CEMBALO [I] (harpsichord)	◆	F, I	klah-vuh-sãn, chem-bah-loh
CLEMENCIC, RENÉ	♪	G	kleh-mãhn-seech, reh-nay (He is Austrian but may have had roots in Serbo-Croatian speech territory, where it might have looked like "Klemenčić" and would have sounded like [kleh-mehn-cheech].)
CLEMENTI, MUZIO	✍	I	kleh-men-tee, moo-tsee-oh (√ half-English [kluh-mehn-tee], but ≠ full-English [-"many"] with the [t] missing. You are also welcome, but not obliged, to do the first name as 2- syllable Italian: [moo-tsyoh].)
CLIBURN, VAN	♪	E	kly-"burn, van" (≠ Dutch [vuhn])
CLUJ-NAPOCA (city in Romania)	◆	Rm	kloozh-nah-poh-kah
CLUYTENS, ANDRE	𝄞	F	klü-tãhn, ãhn-dray (√ kloo-tahn)
COCHEREAU, PIERRE	♪	F	koh-shuh-roh, pyehr
COE, JANE	♪	E	koh, jayn
COENEN, LOUIS	✍	D	koo-nuhn, loo-ee
COLLARD, JEAN-PHILLIPE	♪	F	koh-lahr, zhãhn fee-leep (≠ "collard." That leafy green vegetable sounds like [kah-lerd].)
COLLEGIUM Part of name of several ensembles:		L	koh-lay-gee-oom (Some people prefer to pronounce such Latin terms in full-English: [kuh-lee-jee-uhm].)
C. AUREUM; C. MUSICUM			aw-ree-oom; moo-zih-koom (If you do say [kuh-lee-jee-uhm], then [myoo-zih-kuhm] is more consistent.)
COLOGNE (= Köln, Germany)	◆	E	kuh-"loan" (German = [kerln])
COMISSIONA, SERGIU	𝄞	Rm	koh-"missy"-oh-nah, sehr-joo
CON BRIO [*brightly*]	◆	I	kohn bree-oh (≠ "con" or kahn)
CON FUOCO [*furiously*]	◆	I	kohn fwoh-koh
CON MOTO [*with motion, quickly*)]	◆	I	kohn-moh-toh
CONCENTUS MUSICUS VIENNA		L/G	kohn tsehn-toos moo-zee-koos

CONCERTGEBOUW (Concert Hall in Amsterdam)	◆	D/E	kohn-sehrt-guh-"bow" (√ [kuhn-sehrt-guh-bow], as in "how," which is Dutch for "concert building." Try full-Dutch [kohn-sehrt-khuh-bow], though your audience may misinterpret your efforts as pseudo-foreign affectation.)
CONCERTO/S, CONCERTI (singular/plural)	◆	I	full: kohn-chehr-toh/tee half: kuhn-"chair-toe/s" (Either Italian plural [-tee] or English plural [-toes"] is fine. Other pairs: F: concert/s = both [kõhn-sehr] S: concierto/s = kohn-syehr-toh/s] G: Konzert/en = [kohn-tsehrt kohn-tsehr- tuhn].)
CONCIERTO DE ARANJUEZ (Rodrigo)	🎸	S	kohn-thyehr-toh day ah-rahn-khwayth (The *Aranjuez Concerto* for guitar is named after a place in Rodrigo's native Spain, so the European Spanish pronunciation is, strictly speaking, more "correct," but Latin American Spanish [kohn-syehr-toh day ah-rahn-khways] = "waste," ≠ "ways" is fine. See p. 18.)
CONDIE, RICHARD P.	𝄞	E	kahn-"dye"
CONLON, JAMES	𝄞	E	kahn-luhn
CONN, MICHAEL	♪	E	kahn, my-kuhl
CONSORTIUM MUSICUM	🪑	L	kuhn-"sore"-tee-uhm moo-zee-koom
CONSTABLE, JON	♪	E	kahn-stuh-buhl, jahn
CONTA, IOSIF	𝄞	Rm	kohn-tah, yoh-seef
CONTES D'HOFFMAN [*Tales of Hoffman*] (Offenbach)	🎭	F	kõhnt "doff"-mahn (The French title to the opera by the German Offenbach based on the stories of the German E.T.A. Hoffman. Announce it in English.)
CONTINUO (as in "basso continuo")	◆	I	kohn-tee-noo-oh (bah-soh…) kuhn-"tin-you"-oh
COPLAND, AARON	✍ 𝄞 ♪	E	"cope"-luhnd, a-ruhn (= "baron")
CORBOZ, MICHEL	𝄞	F	kor-bohz, mee-shehl
CORELLI, ARCANGELO	✍	I	koh-rel-lee, ark-ahn-jeh-loh (This full-Italian with double [ll] is probably too correct for most announcers. Half-Italian [kuh-reh-lee] is normal, but half-English [ar-"can"-juh-loh] is avoidable.)
CORELLI, FRANCO	♪	I	koh-reh-lee, frahn-koh
CORIGLIANO, JOHN	✍	I/E	kor-ree-lyah-noh, jahn
CORRÉ, PHILLIPE	♪	F	"core"-ay, fee-leep

Entry			Pronunciation
CORTOT, ALFRED	♪	F	kor-"toe"
COSÌ FAN TUTTE [*That's What All the Women Do*; literally *Thus Do All the Women/Girls*]] (Mozart)		I	koh-zee fahn too-tay (You often hear ["cozy"-fahn-"tootie"], even though the grave accent on <ì> is a stress mark = [koh-zee]. As for grammar, Italian "tutti" = [too-tee] is a *masculine* plural pronoun, that is, "all men" or "all people." The form "tutte" = [too-tay] is *feminine* plural, that is, "all women.")
COSTA, SEQUEIRA	♪	Pt	kohsh-tuh, seh-kway-ruh
COSTELLO, MARILYN	♪	E	kah-steh-loh, ma-rih-lihn
COUPERIN, FRANÇOIS & LOUIS	✍	F	"cooper"-rãn, frãhn-swah & loo-ee
COWELL, HENRY	✍	E	"cow"-uhl
CRESCENDO [*gradually louder*]	◆	I	full: kreh-shehn-doh half: kruh-shehn-doh (Italian <ce> = [cheh], <sce> = [sheh].)
CRESPIN, REGINE	♪	F	krehs-pãn, reh-zheen
CRIME ET CHÂTIMENT [*Crime and Punishment*] (Honegger)		F	kreem ay shah-tee-mãhn
CSÁRDÁS (CZÁRDÁS) (kind of Hungarian dance)	◆	H	char-dahsh (Both spellings occur.)
CSER, PÉTER	♪	H	chehr, pay-tehr (= "chair")
ČSSR (Czecho-Slovak Socialist Republic)	◆	Cz	Read "Czecho-Slovak" as part of name of an orchestra.
CUATRO SOLES (Chavez)		S	kwah-troh soh-lays
CUI, CÉSAR	✍	F/R	kü-ee, seh-zahr (Read like French, but he was Russian. Full-Russian is [kyüy, tseh-zahr]. Sometimes you hear single-syllable [kwee].)
CURZON, CLIFFORD	♪	E	ker-zuhn, klih-ferd
CZERNY, CARL	♪ ✍	G/Cz	chehr-nee, kahrl (Austrian pianist of Czech background. Czech was his first language. The old spelling <cz> has been replaced in modern Czech by <č> = [ch].)
CZĘSTOCHOWA (city in Poland)	◆	P	chẽhn-stoh-khoh-vah
CZIDRA, LÁSZLÓ	♪	H	tsee-drah, lahs-loh (<cz> is an older spelling. In modern words it is replaced by <cs> = [ts].)

D

Entry			Pronunciation
D'AMORE (oboe d'amore, viola d'amore)	◆	I	dah-"moray" (Baroque varieties of these instruments.)

D'ANGLEBERT, JEAN HENRI		F	dãhn-guhl-behr, zhãhn-ãhn-ree
D'INDY, VINCENT		F	dãn-dee, vãn-sãhn (= ["dandy"] with a Hollywood French accent, stressing the last syllable. First name is often given as English [vihn-sent], but no need.)
DA CAPO CHAMBER PLAYERS		I	dah-kah-poh
DA CHIESA (Sonata da chiesa = Church sonata)	◆	I	full: dah-kyay-zah half: duh-kee-ay-zuh
DALLAPOZZA, ADOLF	♪	I/G	dah-lah-poh-tsah, ah-dohlf
DALTON, MITCH	♪	E	dawl-tuhn
DANÇA DOS MOSQUITOS [*Dance of the Mosquitos*] (Villa Lobos)		Pt	dahn-sah doosh moo-skee-toosh (Sounds just like Spanish <dansa>. Portuguese uses <ç> = [s] before <a>, as in French. Unstressed <o> = [oo] and <s> at end of syllable is [sh].)
DANÇAS AFRICANAS [*African Dances*] (Villa Lobos)		Pt	dahn-suhsh ah-free-kah-nuhsh
DANSES CONCERTANTES [*Concert Dances*] (Stravinsky)		F	dãhns kõhn-sehr-tãhnt (Compare Portuguese <dança>.)
DAPHNIS ET CHLOÉ [*Daphnis and Chloë*] (Ravel)		F/E	daf-nihs and kloh-ee (Announce in English, but full-French is [dahf-nees ay-kloh-ay], just for the record. Note that in French Chloé, <é> with acute = [ay], while in English Chloë, <ë> with diaresis means to pronounce <e> as a separate syllable. For English, this means [ee]. It was originally a ballet, but hardly anyone one stages it nowadays.)
DARGOMYZHSKY, ALEXANDER		R	dahr-guh-mihsh-skee, "Alexander" (Full-Russian is more like [duhr-gah-mwihsh-kee] with a hint of a [w] after the [m]. Some sources transcribe <ï> = [ih], viz., Dargomïzhsky. A French spelling, Dargomijsky, with <j> = [zh] and <i> = [ee] also occurs.)
DAS HERZ [*The Heart*] (Pfitzner)		G	dahs- hehrts
DAS KLAGENDE LIED [*The Plaintive Song*] (Mahler)		G	dahs-klah-guhn-duh leed
DAS LIED VON DER ERDE [*Song of the Earth*] (Mahler)		G	dahs-leed-vohn-dehr-ehr-duh (Full German [dahs leet-fuhn…] is too correct, and full-English [das leed vahn der er-duh] goes too far.)
DAS RHEINGOLD [*The Gold in/of the River Rhine*] (Wagner)		G	dahs-ryn-"gold" (This half-German is fine. Full-German [gohlt] is too much.)
DAS WOHLTEMPERIERTE KLAVIER [*The Well-Tempered Clavier*] (J.S. Bach)		G	dahs-vohl-tehm-puh-reer-tuh klah-veer (This title had to be in this book.)
DAVIDOVICH, BELLA	♪	R	dah-vee-doh-vihch, beh-luh

DAVIDSBÜNDLERTÄNZE [*Dances of the League of David*] (Schumann)	🎸	G	dah-veedz bünd-ler "tents"-uh
DAVIS, COLIN	𝄞	E	kah-lin *or* kuh-lin (≠ ["colon"])
DE FALLA, MANUEL (also Falla, Manuel de)	✍	S	duh-fy-yuh, mahn-"well" (Some sources give [deh-fahl-yah] because he was from Spain. See Movement 4 on Spanish <ll> = [y, l^y]. Both are good.)
DE GAETANI, JAN	♪	I/E	duh-gy-uh-tah-nee, jan
DE GROOT, FRANK	♪	D	duh-khroht, frahnk (Dutch <g> = [kh]; <oo> = [oh].)
DE LA TOMASA, JOSÉ	♪	S	deh-lah-toh-mah-sah, hoh-say (√ full-English [hoh-zay])
DE LARROCHA, ALICIA (also Larrocha, Alicia de)	♪	S	deh-lah-"roach"-ah, ah-lee-thee-ah (She is Spanish, so <ci> = voiceless [thee] in "think." She would also come to claim her dinner reservation if she were paged as [ah-lee-see-ah].)
DE LEEUW, TON	✍	D	duh-lay-ü, tohn (√ [duh lay-oo])
DE LOS ANGELES, VICTORIA	♪	S	deh-lohs-ahn-kheh-lehs, veek-toh-ree-ah (Full-English "Victoria" and the California city are often heard, too.)
DE NEVE, GUIDO	♪	D	duh-nay-vuh, khee-doh (Belgian)
DE PALMA, PIERO	♪	S	deh-pahl-mah, pyay-roh
DE PEYER, GERVASE	♪	E	duh-py-er, jer-vis (He is British, though he looks French.)
DE PRIEST, BRIAN	𝄞	E	duh preest
DE RIJKA, HELENUS	♪	D	duh-ry-kuh, heh-lay-nüs
DE SABATA, VICTOR	𝄞	I	deh sah-bah-tah
DE VRIES, HAN	♪	D	duh-vrees, hahn (Dutch has both Hans and Johan as equivalents of "John." Han is a short form of Johan.)
DE WAART, EDO	𝄞	D	duh-vart, ay-doh (Dutch <w> before a vowel is [v].)
DE ZEEUW, CHANTAL	♪	D	duh-zay-ü, shahn-tahl (Dutch <uw> is [ü] at end of word.)
DEBOST, MICHEL	♪	F	duh-bohs, mee-shel
DEBRECEN (city in Hungary, old spelling Debreczen)	◆	H	deh-breh-tsehn (Full-Hungarian has <e> = [a], but [da-bra-tsan] is for English mouths and ears.)
DEBUSSY, CLAUDE	✍	F	duh-bü-see, "clawed" (√ half-French [duh-byoo-see] or half-English [deh-byoo-see], but [duh-byoo-see] and [duh-"bus"-ee] are out.)

Name			Pronunciation
DEGENNE, PIERRE	♪	F	duh-zhehn, pyehr
DEKKERS, MINY	♪	D	"deck"-ers, "mini"
DEL TREDICI, DAVID	♪ 𝄞	I/E	dehl treh-dih-chee (American of Italian background, hence no insistance on [dehl-tray-dee-chee].)
DELALANDE, MICHEL-RICHARD	✍	F	deh-lah-lahnd, mee-shehl ree-shar
DELDEN, LEX VAN (See also van Delden, Lex)	✍	D	dehl-den lehks vuhn
DELIBES, LEO	✍	F	duh-leeb, lay-oh
DELIUS, FREDERICK	✍	E	dee-lee-"us" (German-born but grew up British.)
DELLO JOIO, NORMAN	✍ 𝄞	E	deh-luh-joy-oh
DELOS CHAMBER ORCHESTRA		E	deh-lohs
DEMENGA, THOMAS	♪	G	duh-men-guh, toh-mahs
DEPLUS, GUY	♪	F	duh-plü, gee
DER FERNE KLANG [*The Distant Sound*] (Schreker)		G	fehr-nuh klahng
DER FLIEGENDE HOLLÄNDER [*The Flying Dutchman*] (Wagner)		G	dehr flee-gehn-duh hoh-lehn-der (If you go for German, keep it consistent. Some people get the first two words out in full-German but switch to full-English for "Hollander" = hahl-lihn-der.)
DER FREISCHÜTZ [*The Free Shooter*] (Weber)		G	dehr-fry-shüts (√ shoots)
DER HÄUSLICHE KRIEG (Schubert)		G	dehr-hoys-lih-khuh kreeg
DER JASAGER [*The Yes Man*] (Weill)		G	dehr-yah-zah-ger
DER MOND [*The Moon*] (Orff)		G	dehr-mohnt
DER RING DES NIEBELUNGEN [*The Ring of the Niebelung*] (Wagner)		G	dehr-ring dehs-nee-beh-loong-uhn (Also called simply "Wagner's Ring Cycle" or just "The Ring." A Niebelung is a kind of dwarf, in this case, Albericht, who starts the 20-hour ball rolling in "Das Rheingold" by stealing some magic gold to make a magic ring. The comedian Anna Russell does a wonderful "analysis" of the cycle on a record from the late 1950s.)
DER ROSENKAVALIER [*The Rose Cavalier*] (R. Strauss)		G	dehr-roh-zehn-kah-vah-leer
DER SCHAUSPIELDIREKTOR [*The Impresario*] (Mozart)		G	dehr-show-shpeel-dee-rehk-tohr (The Transcription Police caught you with your guard down. Your eye assumed <show> = [shoh], but it is [show] = ["shower"]. One of those painfully long, but easily disassembled German words: schau = "view," spiel = "play, act," so schauspiel is "theater." The "direktor" part is self-explanatory.)

Name			Pronunciation
DER WILDSCHÜTZ [*The Poacher* or *The Voice of Nature*] (Lortzing)	🎭	G	dehr-vihld-shüts (√ [-shoots])
DERVAUX, PIERRE	𝄵	F	dehr-voh, pyehr
DES KNABEN WUNDERHORN [*The Youth's Magic Horn*] (Mahler)	🎭	G	dehs-knah-bihn voon-der-horn (<oo> = "wooden." The grammar of the phrase is inverted compared to normal German speech "Das Wunderhorn des Knaben" = "the horn of the young man.")
DES PREZ, JOSQUIN	✍	F	deh "pray," zhohs-kãn
DEUTSCHE WELLE	◆	G	doy-chuh veh-luh (Literally "German Waves," the national broadcasting service. German <eu> = [oy] and the final <e>'s are not silent. Many a novice has fallen into the trap of saying something like "douche well.")
DEVIENNE, FRANÇOIS	✍	F	duh-vyehn, frãhn-swah
DEVREESE, FRÉDÉRIC	✍ 𝄵	D/F	duh-vrayz, freh-deh-reek
DI BONAVENTURA, ANTHONY	♪	I/E	dee-boh-nah-ven-too-ruh, an-thuh-nee (√ [duh-bah-nuh—], but ≠ [—ven-cher-uh].)
DI STEFANO, GIUSEPPE	♪	I	dee-steh-fah-noh, joo-zep-pay
DIABLE À QUATRE (Adam)	💃	F	dyah-bluh ah-kah-truh (Full-French words are one syllable each: dyahbl, kahtr.)
DIAGHILEV, SERGEI (also Dyagilev, Diaghileff)	𝄵	R/F	dyah-gih-lehf, sehr-gay (Take 𝄵 here as choreographer, specifically of the Ballets Russes. Half-Russian = [dee-ah-guh-lehv]. The <gh> spelling is to preserve <g> = [g]. Often with the French first name Serge = [sherzh].)
DIALOGUES DES CARMÉLITES [*Dialogues of the Carmelites*] (Poulenc)	🎭	F/E	Announce in English. Poulenc actually specified that it should always be performed in the language of the audience.
DIANE ET ACTÉON (Rameau)	🎭	F	dee-ahn ay ahk-tay-õhn
DICHTER, MISCHA	♪	G/E	dihkh-ter, mee-shuh (German spelling, but he was born in Shanghai of Polish-Jewish parents and grew up in U.S.)
DICHTERLIEBE [*Poet's Love*] (Schumann)	🎭	G	dihkh-tuh-lee-buh
DIDO AND AENEAS (Purcell)	🎭	E	"die-dough" and "a-knee-us" (Some people say a more European ["a-"neigh-us"]. English is fine here, especially since [dy-doh] is never classicized to [dee-doh.)
DIE ENTFÜHRUNG AUS DEM SERAIL [*Abduction from the Seraglio*] (Mozart)	🎭	G	dee ehnt-fü-roong ows dehm seh-ry ("Seraglio" = [suh-rahl-yoh], the Turkish harem.)

Entry			Pronunciation
DIE FLEDERMAUS [*The Bat*] (J. Strauss)		G	dee-flay-der mows (The German title is the norm, not English.)
DIE FRAU OHNE SCHATTEN [*The Woman Without a Shadow*] (R. Strauss)		G	frow oh-nuh shah-tuhn (= "cotton")
DIE GEZEICHNETEN [*The Stigmatized*] (Schreker)		G	guh-tsykh-nuh-tuhn
DIE GLÜCKLICHE HAND [*The Lucky Hand*] (Schoenberg)		G	glük-lih-khuh hahnd (√ -hahnt)
DIE MEISTERSINGER (VON NÜRNBERG) [*The Master Singers (of Nürnberg)*] (Wagner)		G	dee-my-ster-"zinger" (fuhn nürn-behrg)
DIE SCHÖNE MÜLLERIN [*The Beautiful Miller Girl* or *Miller's Daughter*] (Schubert)		G	dee-shö-nuh mü-luh-rihn (German is more frequent here than English.)
DIE SCHÖPFUNG [*The Creation*] (Haydn)		G	dee-shöp-foong (English is the norm.)
DIE SEEJUNGFRAU [*The Mermaid*] (Zemlinsky)		G	dee-zay-yoong-frow
DIE SIEBEN TODSÜNDEN DER KLEINBÜRGER [*The Seven Deadly Sins of the Petit Bourgeois*] (Weill)		G	zee-buhn toht-zün-den dehr-klyn-bür-guh
DIE WALKÜRE [*The Valkyries*] (Wagner)		G	dee-vahl-kü-ruh (= the [val-kuh-reez])
DIE WINTERREISE [*The Winter Journey*] (Schubert)		G	vihn-tuh-ry-zuh (Think "winterizer" with a German accent.)
DILETSKY, NIKOLAI		R/U	dih-leht-skee, nih-koh-ly (A Russian spelling for this Ukrainian composer and theorist of the 16th century. The Ukrainian-Polish spelling is "Dylecki, Mikołaj" [mee-koh-"why"]. The German spelling "Dilezki" also occurs.)
DIM LUSTRE (R. Strauss)		G	deem-loo-struh
DIMINUENDO [*gradually softer*]	◆	I	duh-mihn-yoo-end-oh
DITTERSDORF, KARL DITTERS VON		G	diht-ters-dorf, karl, diht-ers "fun"
DMITRY DONSKOY (Rubinstein)		R	dmee-tree dahn-skoy (Name of medieval Russian military hero. The ending <skoy> is always stressed and <sky> is not.)
DOHNANYI, CHRISTOPH VON		H/G	dohkh-nah-nyee, kree-stawf "fun"
DOHNANYI, ERNST VON		H/G	dohkh-nah-nyee, ehrnst "fun" (You also hear dohkh-nah-nyee, but stick to Hungarian first-syllable stress.)
DOLCE [*sweetly*]	◆	I	dohl-chay

Name			Pronunciation
DOLEZAL, VLADIMIR	♪	Cz	doh-leh-zahl, vlah-dee-meer (Czech stresses first syllable, so not Russian [vlah-dee-meer] or Bulgarian [vlah-dee-meer].)
DOMARKAS, JUOZAS	𝄞	Lt	doh-mahr-kahs, yoo-oh-zahs
DOMINGO, PLACIDO	♪	S	doh-meen-goh, plah-see-doh (He's from Spain and lived in Mexico. No doubt he answers to both [plah-see-doh] and [plah-thee-doh], but there is no justification for Italian [plah-chee-doh] or the stress on other than the first syllable.)
DON	◆	I	dohn (This is the honorific title "Don," meaning "sir," and not the English nickname for "Donald." Several opera characters bear this title. Half-English [dahn-] is also fine.)
DON CARLO(S) (Verdi)	🎭	I(S)	dohn-kahr-loh(s) (√ half-English [dahn-…]. Announce in Italian or Spanish. This is, after all, an opera about a Spaniard written in French by an Italian.)
DON GIOVANNI [*Don Juan*] (Mozart)	🎭	I	dohn-joh-vah-nee (This Italian version of the name Don Juan is used only for the opera. The literary character is otherwise known by full-Spanish [dohn khwahn] or half-English [dahn wahn]. The British, following Lord Byron's poem, read full-English [dahn-joo-uhn]. No one, though, tries to translate this as "Sir John." See Don Quichotte-Quixote below.)
DON PASQUALE (Donizetti)	🎭	I	dohn-pah-skwah-lay (√ half-English [dahn puh-skwah-lee])
DON QUICHOTTE [*Don Quixote*] (Massenet)	🎭	F	dõhn kee-"shut" (This is the French version of the familiar Spanish [dohn kee-khoh-tay], half-English [dahn kee-hoh-tee]. You could transcribe it "donkey shot," but that has a slightly different rhythm. The British say [dahn "quicks-oat"] the same way they do "Don Juan," above.)
DONATH, HELEN	♪	G/E	doh-naht, heh-luhn (American, married to a German: <th> = [t].)
DONIZETTI, GAETANO	✍	I	doh-nee-dzeh-tee, gah-ee-tah-no (In normal speech rhythm 3-syllable [gy-tah-noh]. You often hear [doh-nee-tseh-tee] with <z> as [ts] rather than [dz]. Half-English [dah-nu-zeh-tee] also OK.)

Name			Pronunciation
DORÁTI, ANTÁL	𝄞	H/E	"door"-ah-tee, ahn-tahl (Full-Hungarian stresses the first syllable for ["door"-ah-tee]. However, even Maestro D., himself, seems to prefer half-English ["door-rot"-ee] with stress on the 2nd syllable.)
DORRESTEIN, JOHAN	♪	D	"door"-uh-styn, joh-hahn
DOUATTE, ROLAND	𝄞	F	doo-waht roh-lãhn
DOUGLAS, BARRY	♪	E	duh-gluhs, ba-ree
DOWLAND, JOHN	✍	E	dow-luhnd or "dough"-luhnd (Either as in the chemical company or as in bread. This most English of composers was more likely Irish, and the forms Doolan and Dolan occur in the records.)
DOWN THE RIVER VÁH (Moyzes)	🎸	E/Sk	vahkh (with <h> = [kh])
DRAGON, CARMEN	𝄞	E	As in "Puff, the magic…"
DRAGONETTI, DOMENICO	✍ ♪	I	drah-guh-neh-tee, duh-meh-nih-koh (19th-century virtuoso known as the "Paganini of the double bass." To tag him ♪ here is a historical commentary, since he obvioulsy does not appear as performer on any record.)
DRAHOS, BÉLA	♪	H	drah-hohsh, bay-lah
DRAKE, SUSAN	♪	E	drayk, soo-zuhn
DREYFUS, HUGUETTE	♪	F	dray-füs, ü-geht
DROTTNINGHOLM BAROQUE ENSEMBLE	🪑	E	drah-ting-"home"
DRUCKER, STANLEY	♪	E	druh-ker
DU FOND DE L'ABÎME [*From the Bottom of the Abyss*] (L. Boulanger)	🎸	F	dü-fõhn duh-lah-beem
DUFAY, GUILLAUME	✍	F	dü-fy, gee-yohm
DUKAS, PAUL	✍	F	dü-kah, "pole" (√ "Paul")
DUNSTABLE, JOHN	✍	E	duhn-stuh-bull
DUPHIL, MONIQUE	♪	F	dü-feel, moh-neek
DUPRE, JACQUELINE	♪	E	doo-pray, "jack"-lihn (No accent mark on final <e>. She was British, not French [zhah-kleen dü-pray].)
DUPRÉ, MARCEL	✍ ♪	F	dü-pray, mar-sehl
DURAN, ELENA	♪	E	door-uhn, uh-lay-nuh
DURUFLÉ, MAURICE	✍ ♪	F	dü-rü-flay. moh-rees (√ doo-roo-flay)
DUSSEK, JOHANN	✍	Cz	doo-shehk (Czech <ss> is an old spelling for <š>.)
DUSSEK, MICHAEL	♪	E	doo-sehk (American. Read as plain English.)

Name	Lang.	Pronunciation
DUTILLEUX, HENRI	F	dü-tee-yö, ãhn-ree
DUTOIT, CHARLES	F	dü-twah, sharl
DVOŘÁK, ANTONIN	Cz	dvor-zhahk, ahn-toh-neen (This name is so well known in the West with a [zh] in it that no one even notices whether the haček appears over <ř> = [rzh]. His relatives in the U.S. are almost certain to leave it off and call themselves [dvor-ak].)
DVOŘÁK, JAROSLAV	Cz	dvohr-zhahk, jah-roh-slahv
DVOŘÁKOVÁ, LUDMILLA	Cz	dvohr-zhahk-oh-vah, lood-mee-lah (See Movement 3 for note on men's and women's names in Czech.)

E

Name	Lang.	Pronunciation
EBBINGE, KU	D	eh-bing-uh, kü
ECLAT (Boulez)	F	ay-klah
EDELMANN, OTTO	G	ay-duhl-mahn, oh-toh
EDELMANN, SERGEI	R	ay-del-muhn, sehr-gay (Compared to Otto, just above, the Russian unstressed <mann> is [muhn].)
EDGREN, INGEMAR	Sw	ed-gren, ing-uh-mahr
EFFRON, DAVID	E	"F-run"
EGOROV, YOURI	R	yeh-gor-uhf, yoo-ree (This Russian <e> is [yeh], not [eh]. See under Russian vowels in Movement 4. Note French spelling of <Youri> with <ou> for [oo].)
EIJCK (EYCH), JACOB VAN (See also van Eyck, Jacob)	D	"ike," yah-kohp vuhn
EIN DEUTSCHES REQUIEM [*A German Requiem*] (Brahms)	G/E	yn-doy-chihs reh-kvee-ehm (Announce it by the English title.)
EIN HELDENLEBEN [*A Hero's Life*] (R. Strauss)	G	yn-hehl-den-lay-ben (The German title seems to be more frequent than the English.)
EL AMOR BRUJO [*Love, the Sorcerer*] (de Falla)	S	ehl-ah-"more" broo-khoh
EL SOMBRERO DE TRE PICOS [*The Three-Cornered Hat*] (de Falla)	S	ehl sohm-b"rare"-oh day tray pee-kohs
ELGAR, EDWARD	E	ehl-gahr
ELIAS, ROSALIND	E	uh-ly-us, rah-zuh-lind

ENESCO (ENESCU), GEORGES	𝄞	Rm/F	eh-nes-koh, zhorzh (The Romanians spell him George Enescu. He lived most of his life in Paris and is best known for his Romanian-style compositions.)
ENGELHARD, BRIGITTE	♪	G	eng-uhl-hart, brih-gee-tuh
ENSEMBLE BELLA MUSICA DE VIENNE		F/I	ãhn-sãhm-bluh beh-luh moo-zee-kuh duh vyehn
ENSEMBLE WIEN		G	veen (Read as Vienna Ensemble.)
ENTREMONT, PHILIPPE	♪ 𝄞	F	ãhn-truh-mõhn , fee-leep (√ half-French [ãhn-truh-mõhn].)
EPSTEIN, DAVID	𝄞	E	ehp-styn
EQUILUZ, KURT	♪	G	ay-kvee-loots, koort
ERICKSON, GRETA	♪	E	eh-rihk-suhn, greh-tuh
ERNANI (Verdi)		I	ehr-nah-nee
EROSÃO [*Erosion*] (Villa Lobos)		Pt	eh-roo-zõw (The alternate English title is *The Origin of the Amazon River.*)
ERWARTUNG (Schoenberg)		G	ehr-vahr-toong
ERXLEBEN, MICHAEL	𝄞	E	"irks"-lay-ben, my-kuhl
ESCHENBACH, CHRISTOPH	♪	G	ehsh-en-bahkh, krihst-"off"
ESQUISSES [*sketches*]	◆	F	ehs-kees ([kees] = "peace," ≠ "keys.")
ESSWOOD, PAUL	♪	E	ehs-wood
ESTANCIA (Ginastera)		S	eh-stahn-see-ah
ESTERHAZY	◆	E	eh-ster-hah-zee (Famous family, patrons of the arts in the Austro-Hungarian Empire and employers of several major composers, notably Haydn.)
ESZTERHÁZA	◆	H	eh-stehr-hah-zah (The estate of the Esterhazy family where Haydn worked.)
ET ECCE TERRAE MOTUS (Brumel)		L	eht-eh-chay teh-reh moh-toos (Church Latin <ce> = [chay].)
ÉTUDES D'EXECUTION TRANSCENDANTE [*Transcendental Etudes*] (Liszt)		F	ay-tüd "deck"-seh-kü-syõhn trãhn-sãhn-dãhnt (Always announced in English.)
EUGEN(E) ONEGIN (Tchaikovsky)		R/E	yoo-jeen oh-nay-gihn (Main character of this opera based on a novel in verse by Pushkin. Full-Russian is [yehv-gay-nee ah-nyeh-gihn]. Last name is not full-English ["on-again"].*)

* The tradition of pronouncing German Eugen = [oy-gehn], where <eu>= [oy], is unnecessary. Use either Russian or English without involving a third language.

EVSTATIEVA, STEFKA	♪	R	eh-stah-tyeh-vuh, stehf-kuh (She seems to be Bulgarian, so <e> = [eh], not Russian [yeh], though <ie> = [yeh].)
EWALD, VICTOR	✍	G	ay-vahlt (√ -vahld)
EWERHART, RUDOLF	♪	G	eh-vehr-hart, roo-dohlf
EXERJEAN, EDOUARD	♪	F	ehg-zehr-zhãhn, ehd-wahr

F

FAÇADE (Walton)		E	fuh-sahd
FAERBER, JÖRG (FÄRBER)	𝄞	G	"fair"-ber, yerg
FAGIUS, HANS	♪	G	fah-gee-oos, hahns
FAILONI CHAMBER ORCHESTRA (Budapest)		H	fy-loh-nee
FALLA, MANUEL DE (Also de Falla, M.)	✍	S	fy-yuh, mahn-well duh (See note on the pronunciation of <ll> under de Falla, M.)
FALLETTA, JOANN	𝄞 ♪	E	fuh-leh-tuh, joh-an (Conductor of the Bay Area Women's Symphony, the Virginia Symphony, and several other ensembles. She is also a guitarist and lutenist.)
FALÚ, EDUARDO	♪	Pt	fah-loo, ed-wahr-doo (Portuguese unstressed <o> = [oo].)
FANTASIESTÜCKE [*Fantasy Pieces*] (Schumann)		G	fahn-tah-zee shtü-kuh
FASCH, JOHANN FRIEDRICH	✍	G	fahsh, yoh-hahn free-drihk
FASSBAENDER, BRIGITTE (FAßBÄNDER)	♪	G	fahs-bayn-der, brih-gee-tuh (German has the special letter <ß> for <ss> = [s]. The digraph <ae> is an alternate spelling for <ä>, and both = [ay].)
FAURÉ, GABRIEL	✍	F	foh-ray, gah-bree-ehl
FEDOSEYEV, VLADIMIR	𝄞	R	feh-doh-syehf, vlah-dee-meer
FELLEGI, ÁDÁM	♪	H	feh-lay-gee, ah-dahm
FELTSMAN, VLADIMIR	♪	R	felts-muhn, vlah-dee-meer
FERENC ERKEL CHAMBER ORCHESTRA		H	feh-"rents" ehr-kehl
FERNANDEZ, EDUARDO	♪	S	fehr-nahn-dehs, ehd-wahr-doh
FERRIER, KATHLEEN	♪	E	feh-ree-er
FEUERMANN, EMANUEL	♪	G	foy-er-mahn
FEUILLE D'IMAGES (L. Aubert)		F	föy dee-mahzh (√ foy...)
FEVRIER, JACQUES	♪	F	fehv-ree-yay, zhahk

Name			Pronunciation
FIDELIO (Beethoven)		G/E	fee-day-lee-oh (Garden variety European. √ half-English [fih-day-lee-oh] or [fuh-day-lee-oh].)
FIEDLER, ARTHUR	𝄞	E	"feed"-ler (Conducted Boston Pops for half a century. Think German <ie> = [ee], ≠ English "pie.")
FIERRO, CHARLES	♪	E	fyeh-roh
FIGURE HUMAINE (Poulenc)		F	fee-gür ü-mehn
FINZI, GERALD	✍	E	"fin"-zee
FIRKUŠNÝ, RUDOLF	♪	Cz	feer-koosh-nee, roo-dohlf
FISCHER, EDWIN	♪	G	"fisher," ehd-vihn
FISCHER-DIESKAU, DIETRICH	♪ 𝄞	G	"fisher"-dees-"cow," dee-trihkh
FISTOULARI, ANATOLE	𝄞	F/R	"fist"-oo-lah-ree, ah-nah-"toll" (Read French [ah-nah-"toll"] , although he is Russian [ah-nah-"toe"-lee]. In any case avoid English ["Anna-toll"].)
FLAGELLO, NICOLAS	✍ 𝄞	I	flah-"jello," "nickel-us"
FLAGSTAD, KIRSTEN	♪	N	flahg-stahd, keer-sten
FLEISCHER, LEON	♪	E	fly-sher, lee-ahn
FLOTOW, FRIEDRICH VON	✍	G	"flow -toe," free-drihkh fuhn (≠ [floh-tawv]. German <w> is normally [v], but German names ending in <-ow> are [oh], e.g., von Bülow, above. German trranscriptions of Russian names, of course, have <ow> = ["off"], as in "Tschechow" for "Chekhov." Polish names in <ow> are more often <ów> = [oof]. See under "Kraków," below.)
FONTANAROSA, PATRICE	♪	I/F	fohn-tah-nah-roh-zah, pah-trees (Name looks Italian, but he's French.)
FORRESTER, MAUREEN	♪	E	faw-ruh-ster, maw-reen
FORTE [*loud*]	◆	I	for-tay (≠ "fort," ≠ "40"!)
FORTISSIMO [*very loud*]	◆	I	for-tee-see-moh for-tih-suh-moh
FOSS, LUKAS	✍ 𝄞	E	(= ["toss"])
FOURNET, JEAN	𝄞	F	forn-nay, zhãhn
FOURNIER, ANDRE & PIERRE	♪	F	foor-nyay, ãhn-dray & pyehr
FOX, VIRGIL	♪	E	fahks, ver-juhl
FRA DIAVOLO (Auber)		I	frah-dyah-voh-loh (√ Half-English [frah-dee-ah-vuh-loh].)
FRAGER, MALCOLM	♪	E	fray-ger, mal-kuhm
FRANCESCA DA RIMINI (Rakhmaninov, Tchaikovsky, Zandonai)		I	frahn-"chess"-kah dah-rih-mih-nee (Full-Italian, of course, is [ree-mee-nee]. Rakhmaninov's and Zandonai's are operas. Tchaikovsky's is a symphonic fantasy.)

FRANCESCATTI, ZINO	♪	I/F	frahn-cheh-skah-tee, zee-noh (French violinist with an Italian name.)
FRANCIS, ALUN	𝄞	E	6∂→∆ (Alun is British spelling for Alan.)
FRANCK, CÉSAR	✍	F	frãhnk, say-zar (≠ [see-zer "Frank"]. He was Belgian, just for the record.)
FRANOVÁ, TATJANA	♪	Cz	frah-noh-vah, tah-tyah-nah (More familiar Russian name is stressed on the middle syllable [tah-tyah-nuh], but Czech stresses first syllable.)
FRANSSEN, OLGA	♪	Sw	frahn-sehn, ohl-gah
FRANTZ, JUSTUS	♪	G	frahnts, yoo-stoos
FRATRES (Pärt)		L	frah-"trace"
FRECCIA, MASSIMO	𝄞	I	freh-chah, mahs-see-moh
FRENI, MIRELLA	♪	I	fray-nee, mee-reh-lah (√ half-English [muh-reh-luh freh-nee].)
FRESCOBALDI, GIROLAMO	✍	I	"fresco"- bahl-dee, jee-roh-lah-moh
FRICSAY, FERENC	𝄞	H	free-chy, feh-rents
FROMENT, LOUIS DE	𝄞	F	froh-mãhn, loo-ee duh
FRÜHBECK DE BURGOS, RAFAEL	𝄞	G/S	frü-beck duh boor-gohs, rah-fy-el
FUČIK, JULIUS	𝄞 ✍	Cz	foo-"chick, yoo-lyoos (Bandmaster, composer of that circus standby, *Entry of the Gladiators*.)
FUGHETTA [*short or little fugue*]	◆	I	foo-geh-tah
FUGUE [E/F], FUGE [G], FUGA [I] (type of musical structure)	◆	E/F G/I	E: fyoog, F: füg G: foo-guh, I: foo-gah
FURIOSO [*furiously*]	◆	I	full: foor-yoh-zoh half: "furry"-oh-soh
FÜRTWÄNGLER, WILHELM	𝄞	G	fürt-vehng-ler, vihl-helm (√ [foort-])

G

GABRIELLI, GIOVANNI	✍	I	gah-bree-eh-lee, joh-vah-nee (Full-English ["gab"-] is unnecessary but more comfortable for many people.)
GADE, NIELS	✍	Dn	gah-duh, neels (Full-Danish would be [gah-thuh], as in "the," with [d] becoming voiced [th], see Interlude 1. In this author's opinion, English-speaking announcers need not do this any more than they need recognize the same [d/th] phenomenon in Spanish.)
GAITÉ PARISIENNE (Offenbach)		F	gay-tay puh-ree-zee-ehn (Full-French: pah-ree-zyehn)

Entry			Pronunciation
GALÁNTA (DANCES) [*Dances of Galanta*] (Kodály)		H	gah-lahn-tah (Half-Hungarian [gah-lahn-tah] gives way to half-English [guh-lahn-tah]. Full-Hungarian [gaw-lahn-taw] and full-English [guh-lan-tuh], rhyming with Atlanta, aren't even in the running.)
GAGLIARDE, GALLIARD (=Renaissance dance)	◆	I/E	gah-lyahr-deh, "gal"-ee-yard
GALWAY, JAMES	♪	E	gawl-way, jaymz (Compare English <al> = [awl], as in Walton with German and Italian <al> = [ahl]. See notes under Mahler and Vivaldi.)
GAMBA (viola da...)	◆	I	gahm-buh (≠ [gam] = "lamb." Viola da gamba means "leg viola," a Baroque instrument the size of a cello and held between the knees.)
GAND [F] = GENT [D] = GHENT [E] (city in Belgium)	◆	F/D/E	gehnt (Most Belgian cities have a French and a Flemish name. This one is in the Flemish area. Full-French = [gãhn], Dutch Gent = [khehnt], English Ghent with <gh> = [g].)
GANZAROLLI, WLADIMIRO	♪	I	gahn-dzah-roh-lee, vlah-dee-mee-roh (Italianized Russian first name.)
GARATTI, MARIA TERESA	♪	I	gah-rah-tee, mah-ree-ah teh-ray-zah
GARTEN VON FREUDEN UND TRAURIGKEITEN [*Garden of Joy and Sadness*] (Gubaidulina)		G	gahr-ten fohn froy-duh oont trow-rihkh-ky-ten
GARTENFEST (Mozart)		G	gahr-tuhn-fehst
GASPARD DE LA NUIT (Ravel)		F	gahs-pahr duh-lah-nüee/nwee (√ half-French [duh-lah-noo-ee] in four syllables rather than full-French three.)
GÁTI, ISTVÁN	♪	H	gah-tee, eesht-vahn
GAUCI, MIRIAM	♪	I	gow-chee
GAUK, ALEXANDER	𝄞	G	gowk (= "How now, brown cow?")
GAVOTTE, (=Baroque dance)	◆	F	full: gah-voht half: guh-vaht
GAYNE (also spelled GAYANE, GAYANEH) (Khachaturian)		A/E	gy-nuh, gah-yah-neh (The name of the heroine of this Soviet ballet about an Armenian collective farm. The famous "Sabre Dance" is known as a "Russian" orchestral show stopper, but it is, of course, Armenian.)
GDAŃSK (city in Poland)	◆	P	gdahnsk (Do try for the [gd] cluster. The Germans called this Baltic coast city Danzig = [dahn-tsihkh]. Polish <ń> = Spanish <ñ>, but plain [n] will do.)

Name	Type	Language	Pronunciation
GEBURTSTAG DER INFANTIN [*Birthday of the Infanta*] (Zemlinsky)		G	geh-boorts-tahg dehr ihn-fahn-tin (“Infanta” is a term for princess. See also Ravel’s *Pavane pour une Infante Defunte.*)
GEDDA, NICOLAI	♪	Sw	geh-dah, nih-koh-ly (Full-Swedish <ge> = [ye], but nobody calls him [yeh-dah].)
GELBER, BRUNO-LEONARDO	♪	G/S	gehl-ber, broo-noh lay-oh-nahr-doh (Argentinian, but of apparently German background. Read <ge> here as German [ge], not Spanish [khe].)
GEMER DANCES (Moyzes)		E	geh-mehr
GEMINIANI, FRANCESCO	✍	I	jeh-mee-nyah-nee, frahn-ches-koh
GÊNESIS (Villa Lobos)		Pt	zheh-nay-zihsh (√ English Genesis = [jeh-nuh-sihs].)
GENT [D] = GAND [F] = GHENT [E] (city in Belgium)	◆	D/F/E	gehnt (Full-Dutch = [khehnt], also spelled Ghent in English with <gh> = [g]. See Gand, above.)
GEORGESCU, REMUS	𝄞	Rm	johr-jehs-koo, ray-moos
GERHARDT, CHARLES	𝄞	G	gehr-hart
GERSHWIN, GEORGE	✍ ♪	E	(that is, [ger-], not [jer-])
GESANG DER JÜNGLINGE (Stockhausen)		G	guh-zahng dehr yüng-lih-khuh
GESUALDO, DON CARLO	✍	I	jehz-wahl-doh, dohn-kar-loh
GEWANDHAUS ORCHESTRA (LEIPZIG)		G	guh-vahnt-“house” (lyp-tsihg)
GHENT-GENT-GAND (city in Belgium)	◆	E/D/F	gehnt (See Gent, Gand above.)
GHIAUROV, NICOLAI	♪	R	gyah-oo-ruhf, nih-koh-ly (He is Bulgarian, not Russian. This <ghia> is an Italianesque transcription for [gyah].)
GHITALLA, ARMANDO	♪	I/E	gee-tahl-lah, ahr-mahn-doh
GIANNI SCHICCHI (Puccini)		I	jah-nee skee-kee (Full-Italian with double consonants would be [jahn-“knee” skeek-“key”]. See Il Trittico.)
GIESEKING, WALTER	♪	G	gee-zuh-king, vahl-ter
GIGLI, BENIAMINO	♪	I	jee-lyee, ben-yah-mee-noh
GIGUE [F/E], GIGA [I] (=Baroque dance)	◆	F, I	zheeg, jee-gah
GILBERT AND SULLIVAN (= SIR WILLIAM S. AND SIR ARTHUR)	✍	E	(Lyricist-composer team. Sullivan was the musical half. Both were knighted.)
GILELS, EMIL	♪	R	gih-lelz, eh-meel
GILES, ANNE DIENER	♪	E	jylz, an dee-ner

Name			Pronunciation
GILGAMESH (Martinů)		E	gihl-guh-"mesh" (Title is international, a classic of ancient Babylonian literature. Martinů is Czech.)
GILILOV, PAVEL	♪	R	gih-lee-luhf, pah-vel
GIMSE, HÅVARD	♪	N	yeem-seh, haw-vahr
GINASTERA, ALBERTO	✍	S	khee-nah-steh-rah, ahl-behr-toh (This is one of those names that announcers always seem to disagree on.*)
GIOCOSO [*playfully*]	◆	I	full: joh-koh-zoh half: juh-koh-soh
GISELLE (Adam)		F	zhih-zehl
GIULIANI, MAURO	✍	I	joo-lyah-nee, mow-roh (= "now")
GIULINI, CARLO MARIA	𝄞	I	joo-lee-nee, kar-loh muh-ree-uh
GIULIO CESARE IN EGITTO [*Julius Caesar*] (Handel)		I	English title is the norm without specifying "in Egypt."
GLAETZNER, BURKHARD (GLÄTZNER)	𝄞 ♪	G	glayts-ner, berk-"heart"
GLAGOLITIC MASS (Janáček)		E	gla-guh-lih-tihk (See also *Mše Glagolská.* Sometimes called *Slavonic Mass.***)
GLAZUNOV, ALEXANDER	✍ 𝄞	R	glah-zoo-nuhf (Russian <z> = [z], not German [ts], as one often hears. Since many Russian names came to the west through German transcription, it is easy to assume that German letter-sound correspondences apply, but here it is not so. A German spelling for this name would be <Glasunow>. See note on "Flotow," above.)
GLIÈRE, REINHOLD	✍	R F/G	glee-"air," ryn-hold (A Russian composer with a French last name and German first name.)

---

* Ginastera was from Argentina, so Spanish <gi> = [khee] is expected, though one often hears [jee] or even [gee]. His father was Catalan, in which language <gi> = [jee], but that is not likely to be the source of the confusion. Slonimsky (1992) says A. G. preferred "soft g," but that the usual pronunciation now is with "hard g." This should mean [jee] and [gee], neither of which seems to apply. Robert J. Lurtsema (WGBH, Boston) has a taped interview with the composer pronouncing his own name with full-Spanish <gi> = [khee]. That should settle the controversy.

** Glagolitic was a unique alphabet invented in the mid 9th century by two Byzantine missionaries, Sts. Cyril and Methodius (= [sih-ruhl, muh-thoh-dee-uhs]). It does not resemble any European alphabet. They used it to translate the Gospel into the Slavic language of the Moravians, who occupied a territory more or less in the present-day Czech Republic. (Roman Christianity with its Latin language and script eventually won the Moravians over.) The alphabet known as Cyrillic, based on Greek in honor of St. Cyril, was developed a century or two later for the Slavic languages in the Byzantine cultural sphere, namely, the present-day Macedonians and Bulgarians. Janáček wanted to use an early text from the Moravia-Glagolitic transcription. See the note in Movement 1 on the present-day Slavic languages.

GLINKA, MIKHAIL	✍	R	gleen-kuh, mee-khah-eel (First name is three syllables, not "McHale.")
GLUCK, CHRISTOPH WILLIBALD	✍	G	glook (= "look"), kreest-"off" villy-bahld
GOBBI, TITO	♪	I	goh-bee, tee-toh
GOLOVSCHIN, IGOR	𝄞	R	guh-lahv-sheen, ee-guhr
GOLSCHMANN, VLADIMIR	𝄞	E/R	"goal"sh-mahn, vla-duh-meer (Russian background but made his professional life in U.S., so not Russian [vlah-dee-meer].)
GÖNNENWEIN, WOLFGANG	𝄞	G	gö-nin-"vine", vohlf-gahng (ger-nin-vyn)
GOODE, RICHARD	♪	E	"good"
GOOSENS, EUGENE	𝄞	E	goo-sinz, yoo-jeen (This is also a common Flemish name in Belgium, where it sounds like [khoh-sens].)
GÓRECKI, HENRYK MIKOŁAJ	♪	P	goo-reht-skee, "hen-rick" mee-koh-"why" (Polish <ó> with an accent mark is [oo] and <c> = [ts]; barred <ł> = [w]; <aj> = [y], as in "eye.")
GÖTTERDÄMMERUNG [*Twilight of the Gods*] (Wagner)	🎭	G	gö-ter-deh-muh-roong (√ -roonk)
GOTTSCHALK, LOUIS MOREAU	✍	E	gaht-shawk (= "hawk"), loo-ee muh-roh
GOULD, GLENN	♪	E	goold
GOULD, MORTON	✍ 𝄞	E	goold
GOUNOD, CHARLES	✍	F	goo-noh, sharl
GOYESCAS (Granados)	🎸	S	goy-ehs-kahs
GRAF, MARIA	♪	G	grahf (≠ "graph")
GRAFENAUER, IRENA	♪	G	grah-fuh-"now"-er, ee-reh-nuh
GRAFFMAN, GARY	♪	E	"graph"-muhn, ga-ree
GRAINGER, PERCY	✍	E	grayn-jer, per-see
GRANADOS, ENRIQUE	✍	S	grah-nah-dohs, ehn-ree-kay
GRANDE BRETÈCHE (Claflin)	🎭	F	grãhnd breh-tehsh
GRANDT, MICHAEL	♪	E	"grant"
GRAPPELLI, STEPHANE	♪	I/F	grah-peh-lee, steh-fahn (√ gruh-peh-lee)
GRAZIOSO [*gracefully*]	◆	I	grah-tsyoh-zoh grah-tsee-oh-soh
GRIEG, EDVARD	✍	N	greeg, ehd-vard
GRIMINELLI, ANDREA	♪	E	grih-mih-neh-lee, an-dree-uh
GRISELDA (Bononcini)	🎭	E	gruh-zehl-duh

GROFÉ, FERDE	✍	E	groh-fay, ferdy
GROSZ, EDITH	♪	H	grohs, ay-deet (= "gross," unless she is Polish, in which case: *grohsh*)
GRUBEROVÁ, EDITA	♪	Cz	groo-beh-roh-vah, eh-dee-tah
GRUENBERG, ERICH (GRÜNBERG)	♪	G	grün-behrg, eh-reekh
GRUMIAUX, ARTUR	♪	F	grü-myoh, ahr-tür (√ half-English [groo-mee-oh, ahr-toor])
GRUPO DE MUSICA "ALFONSO X EL SABIO"		S	groo-poh day moo-see-kah ahl-fohn-soh dee-ehs ehl sah-bee-oh
GUARNERI QUARTET		S	gwahr-neh-ree
GUBAIDULINA, SOFIA	✍	R	goo-by-doo-lee-nuh, soh-fyuh (Russian composer of Tatar background.[*])
GUILLAUME TELL [*William Tell*] (Rossini)		F	gee-yohm tehl (An Italian composer's opera written in French about a Swiss hero. Call him William.)
GULDA, FRIEDRICH	♪	G	gool-duh, free-drick
GUNZENHAUSER, STEPHEN	𝄞	E	"guns-in"-how-zer (Not general European ["goon"…].)
GURRELIEDER [*Songs of Gurra*] (Schoenberg)		G	ger-uh-lee-duh (Based on the text of the Danish poet, J.P. Jacobsen.)
GUSCHLBAUER, THEODORE	𝄞	G	goo-shuhl-bower, tay-uh-dor (= "bushel tower")
GUTIERREZ, HORACIO	♪	S	goo-tyeh-rays, oh-rah-see-oh (Western hemisphere <ci> = [see].)

H

HAEBLER, INGRID (HÄBLER)	♪	G	hay-bler, een-grid (German <ä> and <ae> are alternate spellings.)
HAEFLIGER, ERNST (HÄFLIGER)	♪	G	hay-flih-ger, ehrnst (German <ä> = <ae> = [eh, ay].)
HAGEN QUARTET		G	hah-guhn
HAILSTORK, ADOLPHUS	✍	E	hayl-stork, uh-dawl-fuhs

[*] Names can sometimes serve as cultural mini-histories, and Gubaidulina is a good example. The Moslem Turkic peoples of the former Soviet Union (Tatars, Uzbeks, Azerbaidzhanis, etc.) took Islamic last names from Arabic roots and russianized them by adding Russian "-in" or "-ov." The Arabic name Abdallah is "ʕabd + Allah," that is, "servant of God/Allah." (The first sound is a throaty consonant called "ayin." IPA spells it with a reverse question mark and Tatar pronounces it [g].) The diminutive of "ʕabd" is "ʕoo-byd" for "little/humble servant." Here we probably have "Gubaid+ul" from "ʕoo-byd Allah." Adding "-in" makes it Russian, and adding "-a" to that makes it feminine. (See the note on Russian names in Movement 4.)

Name			Pronunciation
HAIMOVITZ, MATT	♪	E/Is	hy-muh-vits
HAITINK, BERNARD	𝄞	D	hy-tink, ber-nahrd
HAJÓSSYOVÁ, MAGDALENA	♪	Cz	hy-yohs-yoh-vah, mahg-dah-leh-nah (The name looks Hungarian, but the suffix <ová> indicates a Czech woman's name.)
HÁLASZ, MICHAEL	𝄞	H	hah-lahs, mee-kah-ehl
HALFFTER, CRISTOBAL	✍	G/S	hahlf-ter, krees-toh-bahl
HALLE ORCHESTRA	🪑	G	hah-lay
HALSTEAD, ANTHONY	♪	E	"haul"-sted
HALSVUO, PEKKA	𝄞	Fn	hahls-voo-oh, peh-kah (Even if you can do the double [k] in ["peck"-kah], there is no need to.)
HALVORSEN, JOHAN	✍	Sw	hahl-vor-sen, yoh-hahn
HAMBURG PHILHARMONIC ORCHESTRA	🪑	G	hahm-boorg (≠ as in "...and fries.")
HAMBURGISCHE KAPITANMUSIK (Telemann)	🎸	G	hahm-boor-gih-shuh kah-pee-tahn-moo-zeek
HAMKE, SONYA	♪	E	hahm-kuh, sohn-yuh (The spelling of Sonya with a <y> suggests she is American, in which case her last name is more likely ["ham-key"].)
HAMMERKLAVIER SONATA (Beethoven)	🎸	G	hah-mer-klah-veer (√ English "hammer.".)
HÄNDEL, GEORGE FREDERIC (HAENDEL)	✍	G	hehn-duhl, gay-org free-drick (Either full-German as given or full-English [jorj freh-drihk "handle"]. Mixtures such as half-English [hahn-duhl] are not justified.[*])
HÄNDL, WALTER	𝄞	E	hen-dull, "wall"-ter
HANSEN, JØRGEN ERNST	♪	N	hahn-sen, yör-gen, ehrnst
HARADA, SADAO	♪	J	hah-rah-dah, sah-dow
HARNARI, JULIA	♪	E	har-nah-ree
HARNASIE (Szymanowski)	💃	P	hahr-nah-sheh
HARNONCOURT, ALICE	♪	G/F	har-"nun"-kort (√ ahr-nõhn-koor)
HARNONCOURT, NIKOLAUS	𝄞	G/F	har-"nun"-kort, "nickel-us" (√ ahr-nõhn-koor)
HARNOY, OFRA	♪	E	har-noy, oh-fruh (Israeli-born, lives in Canada)

---

[*] Handel is often taken as a litmus test of "correct" pronunciation, but it just as often exposes incorrect assumptions based on partial information. The <a> was originally German umlauted <ä> = [eh]. Some people consider "handle" too anglicized, but G.F.H. spent a long time in England, where the umlaut was not written. The sound of English [a] is closer to the German and consistent with English sound/letter correspondences. No need to over-europeanize him to [hahn-duhl].

Entry	Type	Language	Pronunciation
HAROLD EN ITALIE [*Harold in Italy*] (Berlioz)	🎸	F	ah-<u>ruhld</u> ãhn ee-tah-<u>lee</u> (Always announced in full English.)
HARRELL, LYNN (He's a <u>he</u>!)	♪	E	👓→🔔 (= "barrel, Carol")
HARSÁNYI, ZSOLT	♪	H	<u>hahr</u>-sahn-yee, zhohlt
HÁRY JÁNOS (Kodály)	🎸	H	<u>hah</u>-ree <u>yah</u>-nohsh (Name of the main character of this operetta, given in typical Hungarian order: family name first. If he were a performer you would announce him as János Háry.)
HÄUSTER, REGULA	♪	G	<u>hoy</u>-ster, <u>reh</u>-goo-lah (≠ "regular," which with a Boston accent is [<u>reh</u>-gyoo-luh] or [<u>reh</u>-guh-luh]!)
HAUTBOIS (oboe)	◆	F	oh-<u>bwah</u> (But say [<u>oh</u>-boh].)
HAYDN, FRANZ JOSEPH MICHAEL	✍	G	"<u>hide</u>"-uhn, frahnts <u>yoh</u>-zehf/ (√ half-English [frahnz] = "blonds" and English [<u>joh</u>-sehf]. Full-English first name [franz] = "fans" is unnecessary, and English last name [<u>hay</u>-duhn] = fadin' is unthinkable! As for Michael, announcers do both [<u>my</u>-kuhl] and [<u>mee</u>-khah-ehl].)
HE, ZHANHAO	✍	C	hay, <u>jahn</u>-how
HEGEDÜS, ENDRE	♪	H	<u>heh</u>-geh-düsh, <u>ehn</u>-dreh
HEGYI, ILDIKÓ	♪	H	<u>hay</u>-jee, <u>eel</u>-dee-koh
HEIFETZ, DANIEL	♪	E	"<u>high</u>"-fits (no relation to Jascha)
HEIFETZ, JASCHA	♪	R	"<u>high</u>"-fits, <u>yah</u>-shuh (Jascha is a German spelling for Yasha, the nickname for Yakov = [<u>yah</u>-"cuff"].*)
HEISSER, JEAN-FRANÇOIS	♪	G/F	<u>hy</u>-ser, zhãhn-frãhn-<u>swah</u>
HELLENDAAL, PIETER	✍	D	<u>heh</u>-len-dahl, <u>pee</u>-ter
HENZE, HANS WERNER	✍ 𝄞	G	<u>hehn</u>-tsuh, hahnts <u>vehr</u>-ner
HERCEGOVINA or HERZEGOVINA	◆	SC	hehr-tseh-<u>goh</u>-vee-nah (<c> = [ts]. The German spelling Herzegovina with <z> = [ts] also occurs. See also Bosnia-Hercegovina above.)
HÉRODIADE (Massenet)	🎭	F	eh-"rode"-<u>yahd</u>
HEROLD, LOUIS JOSEPH	✍	F	eh-"<u>roll</u>," loo-<u>ee</u> zho-<u>zehf</u>

* Serious Russian performers reserve nicknames for family and friends, not public and professional life. (Politicians such as Boris Yeltsin would never in their wildest dreams appear in public as "Borya," the way our presidents Bill and Jimmy do.) A career in the U.S. often relaxes that behavior. In fact, Americans are fond of these endearing forms and may even encourage Russians to use them. Heifetz came to the U.S. at an early age and the informality may have stuck. The same probably applies to Shura Cherkassky for Alexander. Note, too, full-Russian [<u>khay</u>-fits] has <ei> = [ay], not standard German ["eye"], and Russian often treats German and Yiddish names this way, such as Einstein = [ayn-<u>shtayn</u>]. As for [kh], other families with this name transcribed <ch>, which in turn is pronounced [ch] or [sh], e.g., Hamilton Cheifitz = [<u>shay</u>-fihts] or [<u>chay</u>-fihts].

HEURE ESPAGNOLE (Ravel)	🎭	F	er eh-spahn-yohl
HINDEMITH, PAUL	✍ 𝄞	G	hin-duh-"mitt," pawl ("Paul" or full-German [powl].)
HIPPOLYTE ET ARICIE (Rameau)	🎭	F	ee-poh-leet ay ah-ree-see
HIRSH, ALBERT	♪	E	hersh
HODDINOTT, ALUN	✍	E	hah-duh-naht, a-luhn
HOEPRICH, THEA	♪	D	hoo-prihkh, tay-uh
HOEY, CHOO	𝄞	C	hoy, choo
HOFMANN, JOSEF	✍	G	hohf-mahn, yoh-zef
HOKANSON, LEONARD	♪	E	hoh-kuhn-suhn
HOLIGER, HEINZ	♪	G	"holy"-gehr, hyns (√ hah-lih-ger)
HOLLWEG, WERNER	♪	G	"whole"-vehg, vehr-ner
HOLMÈS, AUGUSTA	✍	F	ohl-mays, oh-güs-tah
HOLST, GUSTAV	✍	E	hohlst (= "hole"st), goo-stahf
HONEGGER, ARTHUR	✍	F	oh-neh-gehr, ar-toor (√ half-French ah-nuh-ger, ar-toor.)
HOOGEVEEN, RONALD	♪	D	hoh-khuh-vayn, "Ronald"
HOOIJEVEEN, GODFRIED	♪	D	hoy-uh-vayn, khawt-freed
HOPF, HANS	♪	G	hohpf, hahns
HORENSTEIN, JASCHA	𝄞	E	hor-in-styn, yah-shuh (See note on Jascha Heifetz.)
HOROWITZ, VLADIMIR	♪	E/R	hor-uh-wits, vla-duh-meer (Russian Jew, but made much of his career in the U.S. No need to re-russianize him to [vlah-dee-meer] or re-yiddishize him to [hor-oh-vihts]. The Russian form is [gor-uh-vihts].)
HORSZOWSKI, MIECZYSŁAW	♪	P	hor-sh"off"-skee, myeh-chih-swahf (Polish <y> = [ih]; barred <ł> is [w].)
HÖSTBALLADER [*Fall Ballads*] (Atterberg)	🎸	Sw	höst bah-lah-der
HOUBART, FRANÇOIS-HENRI	♪	F	oo-bahr, frãhn-swah-ãhn-ree
HOVANHESS, ALAN	✍ 𝄞	E/A	"hoe"-vah-nehs, a-luhn (From Boston, but very strong feeling for his Armenian background. Armenian "Hovan" is equivalent of "John," and the last name is shortened from "Hovanesian," that is, "Johnson." He used to spell it Hovaness.)
HOVE, JOACHIM VAN DEN (See also van den Hove, Joachim)	✍	D	hoh-vuh, yoh-ah-khim vuhn-den
HRVATSKA (REPUBLIKA HRVATSKA)	◆	SC	her-vaht-skah (reh-poo-blee-kah) (The native name for Croatia or the Croatian Republic. Syllabic <r> = [er].)
HUMMEL, JOHANN NEPOMUK	✍	G	hoo-muhl, yoh-hahn nep-uh-mook (both <oo> as in "hook")

HUMPERDINCK, ENGLEBERT		G	hoom-per-dink (<oo> = "hook"), eng-uhl-behrt (Just for eye/ear contrast, recall the American pop singer of the 1960s who took the name and made it full-English [huhm-per-dink, eng-uhl-bert].)
HUWET, GREGOR		D	hü-veht, greh-gor

I

I FIAMMINGHI		I/D	ee-fyah-"ming"-ee (A Flemish-Belgian chamber group. The name is an Italianate version of "the Flemings" or "the Flemish", that is, the people from Flanders, which is the Flemish/Dutch-speaking northern half of Belgium. See Vlaanderen below.)
I FILARMONICI DEL TEATTRO COMUNALE DI BOLOGNA		I	ee-"fill"-ar-moh-nee-chee del tay-ah-troh koh-moo-nah-lay dee boh-"loan"-yuh
I LOMBARDI ALLA PRIMA CROCIATA [*The Lombardians*] (Verdi)		I	ee-lohm-bar-dee ah-lah-pree-mah kroh-chah-tah. (Usually announced as *I Lombardi.*)
I MUSICI		I	ee-moo-zee-chee (One of those Italian words with stress on the third-to-last syllable and not the next-to-last.)
I PAGLIACCI [*The Clowns*] (Leoncavallo)		I	ee-pah-lyah-chee
I PURITANI (Bellini)		I	ee-poo-ree-tah-nee (≠ full-English ["pure"-uh-"tan"-ee])
I SOLISTI DI ZAGREB		I	ee soh-lees-tee dee- zah-greb
I SOLISTI VENETI		I	ee soh-lees-tee veh-neh-tee
I SOLONISTI		I	ee soh-loh-nee-stee
I VESPRI SICILIANI [*Sicilian Vespers*] (Verdi)		I	ee-veh-spree see-chee-lyah-nee
IBERIA (Albeniz)		S	ee-"berry"-uh
IBERT, JACQUES		F	ee-"bare," zhahk
IDOMENEO (Mozart)		I	ee-doh-meh-nay-oh
IEPER [D] = YPRES [F] (city in Belgium)	◆	D/F	ee-per, eepr
IL BARBIERE DI SIVIGLIA [*Barber of Seville*] (Rossini)		I	eel bar-byeh-ray dee see-veel-yah
IL CAMBIALE DI MATRIMONIO [*The Marriage Contract*] (Rossini)		I	"ill" kahm-byah-lay dee-mah-tree-moh-nyoh

Name	Symbol	Language	Pronunciation
IL CAMPANELLO (Donizetti)		I	eel kahm-pah-neh-loh
IL COMBATTIMENTO DI TANCREDI E CLORINDA [*The Combat of T. and C.*] (Monteverdi)		I	"ill" kohm-bah-tee-mehn-toh dee tahn-kray-dee eh kloh-reen-dah
IL CORREGIDOR [*The Magistrate*] (Wolf)		I/G	eel koh-reh-gee-dohr (Italian definite article, but German word "Corregidor" with <gi> = [gee], not [jee].)
IL MATRIMONIO SEGRETO [*The Secret Marriage*] (Cimarosa)		I	eel mah-tree-moh-nyoh seh-gray-toh
IL RE PASTORE [*The Shepherd King*] (Mozart)		I	ihl ray-pah-stoh-ray
IL RITORNO DI ULISSE IN PATRIA [*Ulysses' Return to His Country*] (Monteverdi)		I	ihl-ree-tohr-noh dee-oo-lee-say ihn-pah-tree-ah
IL SIGNOR BRUSCHINO (Rossini)		I	ihl see-nyohr broo-skee-noh
IL TABARRO [*The Cloak*] (Puccini)		I	ihl-tah-bah-roh (See *Il Trittico.*)
IL TRITTICO [*Triptych*] (Puccini)		I	tree-tee-koh (Cycle of one-act operas, listed separately: 1. *Il Tabarro*, 2. *Suor Angelica*, 3. *Gianni Schicchi.*)
IL TROVATORE [*The Troubadors*] (Verdi)		I	eel troh-vah-"tore"-ay
IMAGES (Debussy)		F	ee-mahzh (It means "images," but announce this one in French.)
IN 'T VELD, ASTRID	♪	D	int-vehld, ah-strihd (Literally: "in het Veld," that is, "in the field" with the definite article *het* contracted to *'t*, similarly to Irish names of the "O'Brian" type. The apostrophe carries no sound.)
INBAL, ELIAHU	𝄞	E	ihn-bahl, eh-lee-yah-hoo (Israeli, working in the U.S.)
INCUBUS (Webern)		E	"ink"-yuh-"bus"
IPHIGÉNIE EN TAURIDE (Glück)		F	ee-fee-zhay-nee ãhn-toh-reed
IPPOLITOV-IVANOV, MIKHAIL	✍	R	ee-pah-lee-"tough" ee-vah-nuhf, mee-khah-eel (√ half-English [ih-pah-"lit-off" ee-vahn-"off"].)
ISLAMEY (Balakirev)		R	ihs-lah-may
IVAN (IVO)	◆	Cz, R, E, SC	R: ee-vahn, Cz: ee-vahn, E: "eye"-vuhn, SC: ee-voh (A common first name in several Slavic languages. May also be spelled through German as Iwan.)

IVAN SUSANIN (Glinka)		R	ee-vahn soo-sah-nihn (The Soviet era "ideologically correct" edition of "A Life for the Czar," on which see above.)
IZETBEGOVIĆ, ALIJA (President of Bosnia, 1995)	◆	SC	ee-zeht-beh-goh-vihch, ah-lee-uh (Note that the diamond symbol is stretched here to include "non-musical name.")

J

JABLOKOV, ALEXANDER	𝄞	R	yah-bluh-"cuff" (Either full-Russian, as given, or half-English [yah-bluh-"cough"].)
JACOB, GORDON		E	jay-"cubs"
JALAPA (city in Mexico)	◆	S	(k)hah-lah-pah
JALONS [*Markers*] (Xenakis)		F	zhah-lõhn
JANÁČEK, LEOŠ		Cz	yah-nah-"check," lay-ohsh (The hačeks on <č> and <š> give [ch] and [sh], even if they do not appear in print, and Czech stresses the first syllable. The accent mark on <á> is for length, not stress. (See Interlude 3.) Some announcers read [yah-nah-chehk], perhaps reading <á> as a stress mark. Many Czechs in the U.S. who have this name leave off the diacritics and pronounce [jan-uh-sehk].)
JANCSOVICS, ANTAL	♪	H	yahn-choh-vihch, ahn-tahl
JANDÓ, JENŐ	♪	H	yahn-doh, yeh-nö
JÁNOSKA, ALÁDÁR	♪	H	yah-nohs-kah, ah-lah-dahr
JANOWITZ, GUNDULA	♪	G	yah-noh-vits, goon-doo-lah
JANOWSKI, MAREK	𝄞	P	yah-nawf-skee, mah-rehk
JARDIN AUX LILAS (Chausson)		F	zhahr-dãn oh-lee-lah
JÄRVI, NEEME	𝄞	Es	yehr-vee, nay-meh
JENISOVÁ, EVA	♪	Cz	yeh-nee-soh-vah, eh-vah
JENKINS, NEWELL	𝄞	E	noo-uhl
JENŮFA (Janáček)		Cz	yeh-noo-fah (Stress the first syllable, as is normal in Czech. Original title: *Její Pastorkyňa* = [yeh-yee pah-"store"-keen-yah], *Her Foster Daughter.*)
JERUSALEM, SIEGFRIED	♪	G	yeh-roo-zah-lehm, zeeg-freed (Not English [juh-roo-suh-lehm] or Hebrew [yeh-roo-shah-ly-eem].)
JEUX [*Games*] (Debussy)		F	zhö

JOB, A MASK FOR DANCING (Vaughn Williams)		E	johb (= "robe")
JOCHUM, EUGEN	𝄞	G	yoh-khuhm, oy-gun
JOLIVET, ANDRÉ	✍	F	zhoh-lee-vay, ãhn-dray
JONNY SPIELT AUF [*Johnny Strikes Up (the Band)*] (Křenek)		G	"Johny" shpeelt owf
JOPLIN, SCOTT	✍	E	jah-plihn, skaht
JORDANS, WYNEKE	♪	D	yor-dans, vih-nuh-kuh
JOSEPHSLEGENDE [*Legend of Joseph*] (R. Strauss)		G	yoh-zehfs-leh-gehn-duh
JUNGE LORD (Henze)		G	yoong-uh "lord"
JUNGHÄNEL, KONRAD	♪	G	yoong-hay-nuhl, kohn-rahd

K

K. (plus a number)	◆	G/E	Read as [kay] plus the number. (With Mozart's works, read as "K" or "Köchel," see below. With Domenico Scarlatti's sonatas read as "Kirkpatrick.")
KABALEVSKY, DMITRI	✍	R	kah-bah-lyehf-skee, dmee-tree (√ lehf-skee, and no kidding: dm- cluster together, but "duh-mee-tree will also do.)
KALER, ILYA	♪	H	kah-lehr, eel-yah (Full-Hungarian first name ought to be [ee-yah], but he is probably of Russian background.)
KALISH, GILBERT	♪	E	kay-lish
KALNIŅŠ, ALFREDS	♪	Lv	kahl-neensh, ahl-freds (Latvian, like Czech, reads <š> as [sh]. The n-cedilla <ņ> or <n̦> is the Latvian equivalent of Polish <ń>, Spanish <ñ>, French and Italian <gn>, that is, [n^y].)
KALNIŅŠ, IMANTS	✍	Lv	kahl-neensh, ee-mahnts
KAMARINSKAYA (Glinka)		R	kah-mah-rihn-skuh-yuh (A kind of spritely Russian folk dance. The stress feels odd to English speakers, who would rather not have three unstressed syllables following the stressed one. Nonetheless, it is not [kah-mah-"rinse"-kah-yah] or [kah-mah-rihn-"sky"-uh].)
KAMU, OKKO	𝄞	Fn	kah-moo, oh-koh
KANG, DONG-SUK	♪	K	kahng, dohng-sook
KANTA, LUDOVIT	♪	Cz	kahn-tah, loo-doh-veet

Name			Pronunciation
KARADŽIĆ, RADOVAN [SC] (Leader of Bosnian Serbs, 1995)	◆	SC	kah-rah-jihch, rah-doh-vahn (Try to avoid "carriage itch." He would dispute the "C" part of the SC designation.)
KARAJAN, HERBERT VON (See also von Karajan, H.)	𝄞	G	kah-rah-yahn, hehr-behrt "fun" (Preferable to "carry-on" or "carion." His ancestry is Serbian-Greek.)
KARELIA SUITE (Sibelius)	🎸	Fn	kuh-"rail"-yuh sweet (Orchestral suite. Karelia is a region of eastern Finland, and Karelian is a language related to Finnish. The Finns and Russians have fought over this border many times in history. The full-Finnish name for this area is Karjala = [kahr-yah-lah].)
KÁT'A KABANOVÁ (Janáček)	🎭	Cz	kah-tyah kah-bah-noh-vah (Czech uses apostrophe <t'> or haček <ť> for "palatal [t].)
KATCHEN, JULIUS	♪	E	"catch"-uhn, joo-lee-uhs
KATERINA ISMAILOVA (Shostakovich)	🎭	R	kah-teh-reen-uh ihz-my-luh-vuh (Name of main character in this opera. Full-Russian is [kah-tyih-ree-nuh]. See also *Lady Macbeth of Mtsensk.*)
KATOWICE (city in Poland)	◆	P	kah-toh-vee-tseh
KATSARIS, CYPRIEN	♪	F/E	kah-tsah-res, "sip"-ree-uhn (He is French, though English reading techniques work better.)
KECSKEMET (city in Hungary)	◆	H	kehch-keh-meht
KELEMEN, PÁL	♪	H	keh-leh-mehn, pahl
KELEMEN, ZOLTAN	♪	H	keh-leh-men, zohl-tahn
KEMPE, RUDOLF	𝄞	G	kem-puh, roo-dohlf
KEMPFF, WILHELM	♪	G	kempf, vihl-helm
KERTESI, INGRID	♪	H	kehr-teh-shee
KERTÉSZ, GYÖRGY	♪	H	kehr-tehs, jörj
KERTÉSZ, ISTVAN	𝄞	H	kehr-tehs, eesht-vahn (Hungarian <sz> = [s] and<s> = [sh]!)
KETELBEY, ALBERT W.	✍	E	kuh-tehl-bee
KEVEHÁZI, JENŐ	♪	H	keh-veh-hah-zee, yeh-nö
KEYTE, CHRISTOPHER	♪	E	keet, krihs-tuh-fer
KHACHATURIAN, ARAM	✍ 𝄞	A/R	kah-chah-toor-yahn, ah-rahm (√ ["catch"-uh-toor-ee-uhn, ah-rahm], though Armenian puts the stress on the last syllable. A.K. was Armenian, though he usually numbers among Russian composers because he lived during the Soviet era. See note above on *Gayaneh.*)

Name		Lang.	Pronunciation
KHOVANSHCHINA (Mussorgsky)		R	khoh-vahn-shchee-nuh (Full-Russian is [khah- vahn...], rather than [khoh-vahn...], according to rules of unstressed vowels. This has to do with the Khovansky family. The spelling *Khovantchina* also occurs.)
KIEV, KIEW [R] KYYIV, KYÏV [U]	◆	R/U	R: kee-yehv, U: kih-yeev (All these spellings occur in books and on maps. The Russian name is transcribed first from Russian, then through German. This is the one place where Russian <ie> = [ee-eh] and not [yeh]. Full-Russian is [kee-yehf].) The two Ukrainian transcriptions show the correspondence of Russian <i> = [ee] to Ukrainian <y> = [ih] and of Russian [eh] to Ukrainian <ï> = [yee]. The first of the two syllables is stressed, that is, ≠ [kee-ehv].)
KIKIMORA (Liadov)		R	kee-kee-muh-ruh (A spirit in Russian folklore, subject of a symphonic piece.)
KILANOWICZ, ZOFIA	♪	P	kee-lah-noh-vihch, zoh-fyah
KINDERSZENEN [*Scenes from Childhood*] (Schumann)		G	kihn-ders tsay-nen (German <sz> is the sequence <s> + <z> = [s + ts]. This is not Polish <sz> = [sh] or Hungarian <sz> = [s]. The word is composed of *Kinder* 'children' + *Szenen* 'scenes'.)
KINDERTOTENLIEDER [*Songs of Dead Children*] (Mahler)		G	kin-der-toh-ten-lee-der
KIPNIS, IGOR	♪	E	kihp-nihs, ee-gor
KIRCHNER, LEON	✍	E	kersh-ner, lee-ahn
KISHINEV, KISHINËV = CHIŞINĂU (Captial of Moldova, see above)	◆	R/Rm	kee-shee-nyawf (This Russian name is still frequent.)
KISS, JÓZSEF	𝄞	H	kihsh, yoh-zhehf (almost like "quiche.")
KLAMI, UUNO	✍	Fn	klah-mee, oo-noh
KLEIBER, CARLOS	𝄞	G	kly-ber, kar-lohs
KLEIBER, ERICH	𝄞	G	kly-ber, eh-rik (Full-German = [eh-rihkh].)
KLEMPERER, OTTO	𝄞	G	(= "emperor"), ah-toh (Full-German [oh-toh] is unnecessary.)
KLETZKI, PAUL (KLECKI)	𝄞	P/G	klet-skee, powl (German spelling with <tz> for [ts]. Polish spelling Klecki also occurs with <c> = [ts].)
KLIEN, WALTER	♪	G	"clean," vahl-ter
KLINTCHAROVA, SUSANNA	♪	E	klin-chah-roh-vah, soo-zah-nuh
KLOCKER, DIETER	♪	G	kloh-ker, dee-ter (≠ ["clocker"].)

KMENTT, WALDEMAR	♪	G	kment, vahl-duh-mar
KNAPPERTSBUSCH, HANS	𝄞	G	knah-pehrts-"bush" (<kn> = real [kn])
KOCH, RAMI & ULRICH	♪	G	kohkh, rah-mee & ool-rikh (Ulrich is certainly German. Rami may be Israeli.)
KÖCHEL, LUDWIG (KOECHEL)	◆	G	kö-khuhl, lood-vihg (√ [ker-shuhl]. The fellow who catalogued Mozart's works, as in "K. 106," etc. See "K." above.)
KOCSIS, ZOLTÁN	♪	H	koh-cheesh, zohl-tahn
KODÁLY, ZOLTÁN	✍ 𝄞	H	koh-"dye" *or* "code-eye," zohl-tahn (Surname is two syllables, not three-syllable [koh-"dye"-ee]. First one is stressed. The mark on the <á> is not a stress mark, as in Janáček, above. Hungarian <ly> is a single consonant [y], not the syllable [lee] or [yee].)
KOECHLIN, CHARLES	✍	G/F	kösh-lã̄n, shahrl (The name is Alsatian, hence the German look but French sound. Some people germanize him to [kerk-lihn].)
KOJIAN, VARUJAN	𝄞	A	koh-jyahn, vah-roo-jahn
KOL NIDREI (Bruch)	🎸	G	"call"-nee-dray *or* "coal"-nee-dray (A Hebrew-Aramaic title, literally, "All My Vows," the main prayer of the Jewish Yom Kippur service. Next-to-last-syllable stress is European "Ashkenazi" Hebrew, to which Bruch was most likely exposed. Last-syllable stress is modern Israeli 'Sephardi' Hebrew. Either is fine.)
KOLLO, RENE	♪	G	koh-loh, reh-nay
KOMEN, PAUL	♪	D	koh-men, powl
KONDRASHIN, KIRIL	𝄞	R	kuhn-drah-shin, keer-rill (Full-Russian vowel pattern is [kahn-drah-shihn].)
KÖNIGSKINDER (Humperdinck)	🎭	G	kö-nihks kihn-duh
KOÓ, TAMÁS	𝄞	H	koh, tah-mahsh (Hungarian <oó> is an old spelling for modern <ó> = [oh].)
KOOISTRA, TACO	♪	D	koy-strah, tah-koh
KOOPMAN, TON	♪	D	"cope"-muhn, "tone" (Both <o> and <oo> are [oh] in Dutch. If you want to distinguish them, try first name [tawn] with a clipped [aw].)
KOPPELSTETTER, MARTINA	♪	G	koh-puhl-shteh-tuh, mahr-tee-nah
KÖRMENDI, KLÁRA	♪	H	kör-mehn-dee, klah-rah
KORNGOLD, ERICH WOLFGANG	✍	G	👓→🔔
KOŠICE (city in Slovakia)	◆	Sk	kaw-shee-tseh

Name			Pronunciation
KOŠLER, ZDENĚK	𝄞	Cz	kohsh-lehr, zdehn-yehk
KOSTER, AB	♪	D	koh-ster, ahp
KOUSSEVITZKY, SERGE	𝄞 ♪	R/F	koo-suh-viht-skee, sehrzh (First name is French, rather than full-Russian [sehr-gay]. Spelling of <Kouss> for [koos] is also French. He was also a double bass virtuoso. See note, p. 18.)
KOVÁCS, JANOS	𝄞	H	koh-vahch, yah-nohsh (This person's relatives in the U.S. would certainly be [koh-vaks].)
KOVÁCS, BÉLA	♪	H	koh-vahch, bay-lah
KÖVES, PETER	♪	H	kö-vehsh, pay-tehr
KRAKÓW [P] = CRACOW [E] (city in Poland)	◆	P	krah-koof (The mark on Polish <ó> = [oo] does not usually appear in Western sources, hence the usual English reading ["crack-ow"] often spelled Cracow.)
KRAUS, ALFREDO	♪	S	krows (= "mouse"), ahl-fray-doh
KRAUS, LILI	♪	E/H	krows (= "grouse")
KRAUSE, JANET	♪	E	krows (= "house")
KRAUSE, TOM	♪	Fn	krow-suh, tahm (He no doubt says [tohm] in full-Finnish, but English works here.)
KRCHEK, JAROSLAV	𝄞	Cz	ker-khehk, yah-roh-slahv
KREBBERS, HERMAN	♪	D	kreh-bers, hehr-muhn
KREBS, HELMUT	♪	G	krehps, hehl-moot
KREISLER, FRITZ	✍ ♪	G	"Chrysler"
KREMER, GIDON	♪	R	kray-mer, gee-dohn
KRENEK, ERNST	✍	E/Cz	kreh-"neck," ehrnst (He was born in Vienna of Czech origin and wrote in German. He did spell Křenek = [krsheh-"neck"]. At age 45 he came to the U.S. and stayed the rest of his life. The Czech <ř> eventually yielded to English <r>. Pronounce him in Czech or English.)
KRENN, WERNER	♪	G	krehn, vehr-ner
KREUTZER (sonata by Beethoven)	🎸	G	kroy-tser
KREUZSPIEL [*Cross Play*] (Stockhausen)	🎸	G	kroyts-shpeel ("Kreuz+spiel" creates accidental <zs>, that is, [ts] + [shp], not Hungarian <zs> = [zh].)
KRIPS, JOSEF	𝄞	G	👓→🔔 yoh-zehf
KROEZE, MYRA	♪	D	kroo-zuh, mee-rah
KUBELIK, RAFAEL	𝄞	Cz	koo-beh-"lick," rah-fy-el

Name			Pronunciation
KUIJKEN, BARTOLD- SIGISWALD-WIELAND	♪	D	ky-kehn (with a hint of [koy-kehn]) bar-tohld, sih-gis-wahld, wee-lahnd (Belgian brothers, thus <w> = [w]. If a listener calls up to point out that "correct" Dutch <w> = [v], explain that they are Flemish. Last syllables are given here in half-Dutch with [—d], where full-Dutch would have [t]. As for the vowel sound of <uij> = [y], see Dutch in Movement 4.)
KULLERVO (Sibelius)		Fn	koo-lehr-voh (Name of famous character of Finnish folk legend. Avoid half-English ["cooler"-voh], since the rhythm is quite different.)
KURTZ, EFREM	𝄞	G	koorts, ehf-rehm
KUYPER, ELISABETH	✍	D	ky-per, eh-lee-sah-beht
KWEKSILBER, MARIANNE	♪	G	kvehk-zihl-ber, mah-ree-ah-nuh
KYRKJEBØ, SISSEL	♪	N	sher-shuh-bö, sih-suhl (Norwegian <ky> = [shü], <kje> = [shuh]—more or less.)
KYŠELAK, LADISLAV	♪	Sk	kih-sheh-lahk, lah-dih-slahv

L

Name			Pronunciation
L'AMICO FRITZ (Mascagni)		I	lah-mee-koh frihts
L'ARCHIBUDELLI		I	lar-kee-boo-deh-lee
L'ARLESIANA [*Maid of Arles*] (Cilea)		I	lahr-lay-zyah-nah
L'ARLESIENNE SUITE [*Maid of Arles*] (Bizet)		F	lahr-lay-zyehn (lahr-"lazy"-ehn)
L'ELISIR D'AMORE [*The Elixir of Love*] (Donizetti)		I	leh-lee-zeer dah-moh-ray
L'ENFANCE DU CHRIST [*Childhood of Christ*] (Berlioz)		F	lãhn-fãhns dü-kreest
L'ENFANT ET LES SORTILÈGES [*Child of the Spells*] (Ravel)		F	lãhn-fãhn ay-lay sor-tee-lehzh
L'ESTRO ARMONICO (Vivaldi)		I	lehs-troh ahr-moh-nee-koh
L'HISTOIRE DU SOLDAT [*The Soldier's Tale*] (Stravinsky)		F	lees-twahr-dü-sohl-dah (A morality play with narrator, so the "vocal" designation is applied loosely.)
L'INCORONAZIONE DI POPPEA [*Coronation of Poppaea*] (Monteverdi)		I	leen-koh-roh-nah-tsyoh-nay dee-poh-pay-ah (Take on the [tsy—] cluster bravely or go to half-Italian [tsee-oh-nay] or half-English [naht-see-oh-nee].)

Title			Pronunciation
L'ITALIANA IN ALGERI [*The Italian Girl in Algiers*] (Rossini)		I	lee-tahl-yah-nah ihn ahl-jeh-ree
L. (= Longo. See below.)	◆	I	"long"-oh
LA BATTAGLIA DI LEGNANO [*Battle of Legnano*] (Verdi)		I	lah-bah-tah-lyah dee leh-nyah-noh
LA BELLE HÉLÈNE [*The Fair Helen*] (Offenbach)		F	lah-"bell"-ay-lehn
LA BOHÈME [*Bohemian Life*] (Puccini)		I	lah-boh-ehm
LA BOÎTE À JOUJOUX [*The Toy Box*] (Debussy)		F	lah-bwaht-ah-zhoo-zhoo
LA BOURRÉE FANTASQUE (Chabrier)		F	lah-boo-ray fahn-tahsk (≠Fantastique!)
LA BOUTIQUE FANTASQUE [*The Fantastic Toy Shop*] (Respighi)		F	lah-boo-teek fahn-tahsk (≠Fantastique!)
LA BURRA, MARIA	♪	S	lah-boo-rah, mah-ree-ah
LA CENERENTOLA [*Cinderella*] (Rossini)		I	lah-cheh-neh-rehn-toh-lah
LA CLEMENZA DI TITO [*The Clemency of Titus*] (Mozart)		I	lah-kleh-"mend"-zah dee-tee-toh
LA CRÉATION DU MONDE [*The Creation of the World*] (Milhaud)		F	lah-kray-ah-syõhn dü mohnd
LA DAMNATION DE FAUST [*The Damnation of Faust*] (Berlioz)		F	Announce in English.
LA FANCIULLA DEL WEST [*Girl of the Golden West*] (Puccini)		I	lah-fahn-choo-lah dehl-"west" (sic!)
LA FILLE DU RÉGIMENT [*Daughter of the Regiment*] (Donizetti)		F	lah-fee-dü-reh-zhee-mãhn
LA FILLE MAL GARDÉE (Hérold)		F	lah-fee-mahl-gahr-day
LA FINTA GIARDINIERA [*The Pretended Garden-Girl*] (Mozart)		I	lah-feen-tah jar-dee-nyeh-rah
LA FORZA DEL DESTINO [*The Force of Destiny*] (Verdi)		I	lah-"forts"-ah del-deh-stee-noh (If half-English [luh-forts-uh dehl-duh-stee-noh] slips out, no great harm done.)
LA GAZZA LADRA [*The Thieving Magpie*] (Rossini)		I	lah-gaht-sah lah-drah (Italian <zz> = [ts].)
LA GIOCONDA (Ponchielli)		I	lah-joh-kohn-dah (√ half-Italian [lah-juh-kohn-duh], but avoid English lah-juh-kahn-duh.)
LA GRANDE DUCHESSE DE GÉROLSTEIN (Offenbach)		F	lah-grãhnd dü-shehs-duh zhay-rohl-styn
LA GRANDE MESSE DES MORTS [*Requiem*] (Berlioz)		F	lah-grãhnd mehs day mohr (Just announce as Berlioz' Requiem.)
LA GUIRLANDE OU LES FLEURS ENCHANTEÉS (Rameau)		F	lah-geer-lãhnd

LA MER [*The Sea*] (Debussy)		F	lah-"mare" (Try for this full-French, rather than more English [luh-"mare"].)
LA RONDINE [*The Swallow*] (Puccini)		I	lah-rohn-dee-nay
LA SCALA DI SETA [*The Silken Ladder*] (Rossini)		I	lah-skah-lah dee-say-tah
LA SERVA PADRONA [*The Maid as Mistress*] (Pergolesi)		I	lah-sehr-vah pah-droh-nah
LA SONNAMBULA [*The Sleepwalker*] (Bellini)		I	lah-soh-nahm-boo-luh (Avoid full-English "sun-am"-byuh-luh.)
LA SOURCE		F	lah-soors
LA TRAVIATA [*The Lady Gone Astray*] (Verdi)		I	lah-trah-vee-ah-tuh (Full-Italian [trah-vyah-tah] with 3 syllables is more "correct," though less common, than the 4 syllable half-English. One of those charming inconsistencies in the announcing business.)
LA VIDA BREVE [*Life is Short*] (Falla)		S	lah-vee-dah bray-vay
LA WALLY (Catalani)		F	lah-vah-lee
LA ZINGARA [*The Gypsy Girl*] (Rinaldo di Capua)		I	lah-tseen-gah-rah
LACHIAN DANCES (Janáček)		Cz	lah-khee-uhn (From the Lach = [lahkh] region of what is now the Czech Republic. The Czech title is Lašské Tance = [lahsh-skeh tahn-tseh].)
LACHRIMAE (Dowland)		L/E	lah-kree-may
LADY MACBETH OF MTSENSK (Shostakovich)		E	Do try for the [mts] cluster. (Shostakovich's opera carried the original title of the Russian novella by Nikolai Leskov: [lay-dee mahk-beht mtsehn-skuh-vuh oo-yehz-duh], that is, *Lady Macbeth of the Mtsensk District*, with the Russian stress "Macbeth." Shostakovich got blasted for this work by the Soviet authorities in a now-famous 1936 article in *Pravda* entitled "Chaos Instead of Music." He later "repented" and revamped it in 1961 under the more socialist title *Katerina Izmailova*.)
LAGOYA, ALEXANDRE		S	lah-goy-ah, a-lek-zan-der (French spelling of first name, but usually pronounced as English.)
LAGRIME DI SAN PIETRO (Lassus)		I	lah-gree-may dee-sahn-pyay-troh
LAJOVIC, UROŠ		Sv	"lie"-oh-vuhts, oo-rohsh
LAJTHA, LÁSZLÓ		H	ly-tah, lahs-loh
LAKATOS, ALEXANDER		Gk	lah-kah-tohs (May also be Romanian or even Slovak.)

LAKMÉ (Delibes)		F	lahk-may
LALO, EDOUARD		F	lah-"low," ed-wahr
LAMBOOIJ, HENK	♪	D	lahm-boy, henk
LAMOUREUX ORCHESTRA		F	lah-moo-rö
LANDOWSKA, WANDA	♪	P	lahn-"doff"-skah, vahn-dah (≠ full-English [lan-dow-skuh, wahn-duh]!)
LANGSAM (= *slow*)	◆	G	lahng-zahm
LANIAU, PIERRE	♪	F	lah-nyoh, pyehr
LAREDO, JAIME & RUTH	♪	E/S	luh-ray-doh, jay-mee & rooth (Jaime is not a typo for Jamie. He is from South American, where he assumedly grew up [khy-meh] but came to the U.S. The "&" sign implies no further connection, though they used to be married.)
LARGHETTO [*not as slow as Largo*]	◆	I	lar-geh-toh (≠ lar-"jet"-oh: <gh> = [g])
LARGO [*broad, slow*]	◆	I	lahr-goh
LARRIEU, MAXENCE	♪	F	lah-ryö, mahk-sãhns
LARROCHA, ALICIA DE (See also de Larrocha, A.)	♪	S	lah-"roach"-ah, ah-lee-thee-ah deh (See phonetic remark under de Larrocha.)
LASKINE, LILLY	♪	F	lahs-keen, lee-lee
LATRY, OLIVIER	♪	F	lah-tree, oh-lee-vyay
LAUBENTHAL, HORST	♪	G	low-ben-tahl, horst (<low> = ["cow"].)
LAUSANNE CHAMBER ORCHESTRA		F	loh-zahn
LAUTENBACHER, SUZANNE	♪	G	low-ten-bah-kher, zoo-zah-nuh
LAZAREV, ALEKSANDR	𝄞	R	lah-zuh-rehf, ahl-lek-sahndr (Not a typo. Full-Russian first name is 3 syllables only, with [r] tagged right onto [d]. English 4-syllable [a-leg-zan-der] is fine.)
LE BAISER DE LA FÉE [*The Fairy's Kiss*] (Stravinsky)		F	luh-beh-zay duh-lah-fay
LE BOEUF SUR LE TOIT [*The Ox on the Roof*] (Milhaud)		F	luh-böf sür-luh-twah
LE BOURGEOIS GENTILHOMME [*The Bourgeois Gentleman*] (Lully; R. Strauss)		F	luh-boor-zhwah-zhãhn-tee-"yum" (Lully's is a ballet. Strauss' is an orchestral suite.)
LE CHASSEUR MAUDIT [*The Accursèd Huntsman*] (Franck)		F	luh-shah-ser moh-dee
LE COMTE ORY (Rossini)		F	luh kohmt oh-ree
LE COQ D'OR [*The Golden Cockerel*] (Rimsky-Korsakov)		F	luh-kuhk-"door"
LE MAIR, EVERT	♪	F	luh-mehr, eh-vehr

Name			Pronunciation
LE NOZZE DI FIGARO [*The Marriage of Figaro*] (Mozart)		I	leh-noht-seh dee-fee-gah-roh (√ half-Italian [lay-"notes"-ay dee-"fig-a-row"] Grammatically this is a plural.)
LE QUATTRO STAGIONI [*The Four Seasons*] (Vivaldi)		I	leh-kwah-troh stah-joh-nee
LE QUATUOR POUR LA FIN DU TEMPS [*Quartet For The End of Time*] (Messiaen)		F	luh-kwah-tü-ohr poor lah-fãn dü tãhn
LE SACRE DU PRINTEMPS [*The Rite of Spring*] (Stravinsky)		F	luh-sah-kruh dü-prãn-tãhn (Announced in English or French.)
LE TOMBEAU DE CHATEAUBRIAND (L. Aubert)		F	luh-tohm-boh duh-shah-toh-bree-yãhn
LE TRIOMPHE DE L'AMOUR [*The Triumph of Love*] (Lully)		F	luh-tree-ohmf duh-lah-moor
LEBEDINOE OZERO [*Swan Lake*] (Tchaikovsky)		R	leh-beh-dee-nuh-yuh oh-zyeh-ruh (You might never come across this original Russian title, but just in case...)
LECLAIR, JEAN MARIE	✍	F	luh-klayr, zhãhn mah-ree (He was a he.)
LECUONA, ERNESTO	✍	S	leh-kwoh-nuh, ehr-nes-toh
LEE, NOËL	♪	E	lee, noh-ehl
LEGATO [*connected, smoothly*]	◆	I	full: lay-gah-toh half luh-gah-toh
LEHAR, FRANZ	✍	G	lay-hahr, frahnts
LEHEL, GYÖRGY	𝄞	H	lay-ehl, jerj (just one syllable: <gy> = [j].)
LEHMANN, LOTTE	♪	E/G	lay-mahn, lah-tuh
LEIBOWITZ, RENE	𝄞	P	ly-boh-vits, reh-nay
LEINSDORF, ERICH	𝄞	G/E	"lines"-dorf, eh-rihk (Sometimes full-German [ay-rihkh], though he is most known for his work with the Boston Symphony Orchestra.)
LEIPZIG (city in Germany)	◆	G	lyp-tsihg (Full-German = [lyp-tsihkh], home of the Gewandhaus Orchestra. See above.)
LEISTER, KARL	♪	G	ly-ster, kahrl
LEITNER, FERDINAND	𝄞	G	"light"-ner
LEMMINKÄINEN SUITE (Sibelius)		Fn	"lemon"-ky-nen
LENÁRD, ONDREJ	𝄞	Sk	leh-nard, ohn-dray (This is also a Czech name, but it would be Ondřej = [ohn-jay].)
LENYA, LOTTE	♪	E/G	layn-yuh, lah-tuh
LEONCAVALLO, RUGGERO	✍	I	lay-ohn-kah-vah-loh, roo-jeh-ro
LEONHARDT, GUSTAV	𝄞 ♪	G	lay-ohn-hart, goo-stahf
LEPPARD, RAYMOND	✍	E	leh-pahrd (≠ "leopard": that would be [leh-perd].)

Name			Pronunciation
LES ANNEÉS DE PÈLERINAGE [*Years of Pilgrimage*] (Liszt)		F	lehz-ah-nay duh-pehl-ree-nahzh
LES BICHES (Poulenc)		F	leh-beesh
LES HUGUENOTS (Meyerbeer)		F	lay-ü-guh-noh (≠ lehz-ü…)
LES INDES GALANTES (Rameau)		F	lehz-ãnd gah-lãhnt
LES NOCES [*The Wedding*] (Stravinsky)		F	leh-nohs (Grammatically plural like Italian Le Nozze.)
LES PATINEURS [*The Skaters*] (Waldteufel)		F	leh-pah-tee-nör
LES PÊCHEURS DE PERLES [*The Pearl Fishers*] (Bizet)		F	lay-peh-"sure" duh-pehrl
LES RUSES D'AMOUR (Glazunov)		F	lay-rüz-dah-moor
LES SYLPHIDES (Chopin/Lambert)		F	lay-"sill-feed" (A ballet arranged from Chopin's music by an Englishman, Constant Lambert.)
LES TROYENS [*The Trojans*] (Berlioz)		F	lay-trwah-yãn
LESCHETIZKY, THEODOR		R/G	leh-sheh-tiht-skee, tay-oh-dohr (A Russian who lives in Vienna. Probably born "Fyodor.")
LESLIE, ALAYNE	♪	E	les-lee, uh-layn
LEUVEN [D] = LOUVAIN [F] (city in Belgium)	◆	D	lö-vehn (Dutch <eu> = [ö], not German [oy]. Also known by French name Louvain, see below.)
LEVANT, OSCAR	♪	E	luh-vant, ah-sker
LEVI, YOEL	𝄞	E	leh-vee, yoh-ehl/yoh-ehl (Israeli, works in the U.S. Some Israelis will call him [yoh-ehl]. For other he will be [yoh-ehl]. Your choice.)
LEVINE, JAMES	𝄞 ♪	E	luh-"vine" (≠ luh-veen)
LHEVINNE, JOSEPH	♪	R/E	luh-veen, joh-zuhf (This spelling <lh> is unusual even for Russian.)
LICAD, CECILE	♪	E	lee-kahd, suh-seel
LIEBESFREUD [*Love's Joy*] (Kreisler)		G	lee-bihs-froyt (German <ie> = [ee]; <eu> = [oy].)
LIEBESLEID [*Love's Sorrow*] (Kreisler)		G	lee-bihs-"light" (German <ie> = [ee]; <ei> = [y].)
LIEBESLIEDER WALZER (*Love Song Waltzes*) (Brahms)		G	lee-behs lee-duh vahl-tsuh (√ Eng. "waltzes") (Two instances of <ie> = [ee].)
LIEDER EINES FAHRENDE GESELLEN [*Songs of a Wayfarer*] (Mahler)		G	lee-der y-nehs fah-rehn-duh guh-zeh-len
LIÈGE [F] = LUIK [D] (city in Belgium)	◆	F/D	lyehzh/ "like" (on the way to [loyk])
LIGETI, ANDRÁS	𝄞	H	lih-geh-tee, ahn-drahsh

Name			Pronunciation
LIGETI, GYÖRGY	✍	H	lih-geh-tee, jerj
LIN, CHO-LIANG	♪	C	lin, choh-lang
LINDBERG, JAKOB	♪	G	lind-behrg, yah-kohb
LINDE, HANS-MARTIN	♪	G	"Linda," hahns mahr-tin (Leader of Linde consort.)
LIPATTI, DINU	♪	Rm	lih-pah-tee, dee-noo
LIPOVŠEK, MIRJANA	♪	Sv	lee-poh-shehk, meer-yah-nah (Slovenian <v> before another consonant is [w], thus <ov> = English [oh].)
LISZT, FRANZ (also Ferenc)	✍	H	"list", frahnz (Full-German [frahnts] is overdoing it. Hungarians list him as Ferenc = [feh-rents].)
LITOLFF, HENRY CHARLES	✍	E	lih-tohlf
LIU, ZHUANG	✍	C	lyoo, jwahng
LIVRE DU SAINT-SACRAMENT (Messiaen)	☺	F	leev-ruh dü sãn-sah-kruh-mãhn
LLOYD WEBBER, JULIAN	♪	E	👓→🔔 (Double last name, not hyphenated and not middle. Also listed as Webber, Julian Lloyd.)
LOCATELLI, PIETRO	✍	I	loh-kah-teh-lee, pyay-troh (√ ["lock"-uh-telly].)
ŁÓDŹ (city in Poland)	◆	P	wooch (The marks on <ó> = [oo], <dź> = [j], and the barred <ł > = [w] are usually omitted in western sources, hence the usual English reading = ["lauds"]. See Polish section in Movement 4.)
LOEFFLER, CHARLES MARTIN	✍	G/E	lehf-ler, charlz mar-tin (√ German [löf-ler], but not French [sharl mar-tãn]. He is Alsatian, where French and German co-exist and mix. He moved to the U.S., so first name is full-English.)
LOEILLET, JEAN-BAPTISTE	✍	F	lö-yay, zhãhn bah-teest (Not a typo: French <pt> is only [t]. Same goes for Lully, below.)
LOEVENDIE, THEO	✍	D	loo-vehn-dee, tay-oh
LOHENGRIN (Wagner)	☺	G	loh-ehn-"grin"
LONGO	◆	I	"long"-oh (Or announce as simply "L". He was one of the cataloguers of the sonatas of Domenico Scarlatti. The other is Kirkpatrick, see above.)
LOPEZ-COBOS, JESUS	𝄞	S	loh-pez-koh-bohs, hay-soos (Latin American, so <z> = [s].)
LORENGAR, PILAR	♪	S	lor-en-gahr, pee-lahr
LOTTI, ANTONIO	✍	I	loh-tee, ahn-toh-nee-o

LOUGHRAN, JAMES	𝄞	E	"lock"-run
LOUP [*Wolf*] (Dutilleux)		F	loo
LOUVAIN [F] = LEUVEN [D] (city in Belgium)	♦	F	loo-vãn (Also known by Dutch name, Leuven, see above.)
LT. KIJÉ (Prokofiev)		R/F	loo-"tenant" kee-zhay (Made-up name of main "character" in this spoof on the power of the czar.)
LUBLJANA (capital of Slovenia)	♦	Sv	loo-blyah-nah (√ 4-syllable [loob-lee-ah-nah].)
LUCA, SERGIU	♪	Rm	loo-kah, sehr-joo
LUCERNE FESTIVAL STRINGS		F/E	loo-sern (French is [lü-sehrn], but English is good.)
LUCIA DI LAMMERMOOR (Donizetti)		I	loo-chee-uh dee-lah-mehr-moor
LUCIO SILLA (Mozart)		I	loo-choh sih-lah
LUCREZIA BORGIA (Donizetti)		I	loo-krehts-yah bohr-jah (= "Sorry if I *bored ya*")
LUDWIG, CHRISTA	♪	G	lood-vihg, kris-tuh
LUIK [D] = LIÈGE [F]	♦	D/F	"like"/ lyehzh
LULLY, JEAN-BAPTISTE		F	lü-lee, zhãhn bah-teest (√ loo-lee. See note on Loeillet, above.)
LUPU, RADU	♪	Rm	loo-poo, rah-doo
LUTH (lute)	♦	F	"loot," as in English "lute" (Full- French "lüt" is unnecessary.)
LUTOSŁAWSKI, WITOLD		P	loot-uh-slahf-skee, vee-"told" (This half-Polish is fine, though it would take no extra trouble to let your audience hear full-Polish <ł> = [w] in [loo-toh-swahf-skee, vee-tohlt].)
LVOV, L'VOV [R] LWÓW [P] LVIV, LVIW [U] (city in Ukraine)	♦	R P U	R: [lvohf, luh-vohf] P: [lvoof, luh-voof] U: [lveev, luh-veev] or [lvee-oo], compressed into a single syllable.* (This city in western Ukraine has changed hands several times. In the Austro-Hungarian Empire, it was called Lemberg.)
LYATOSHYNSKY, BORIS		U	lyah-toh-"shin"-skee, boh-rees (Not Russian but Ukrainian. Russian would be [lih-tah-"sheen"-skee]. The subtle visual clue is the Ukrainian spelling <shy> vs. Russian <shi>. See Russian and Ukrainian in Movement 4.)

* All three languages pronounce it as one syllable, but it is all right to break the [lv] cluster into two syllables. The apostrophe in Russian L'vov indicates a "palatalized" [l], not the syllable [luh]. Polish regular <l> = [l], as opposed to barred <ł> = [w]. The two Ukrainian pronunciations represent Eastern (Kiev) and Western (Lviv) Ukrainian pronounciations.

M

MA MÈRE L'OYE [*Mother Goose*] (Ravel)		F	mah-"mare"-lwah
MA NON TROPPO (*But not too much*]	◆	I	mah-nohn-troh-poh (≠ mah-nuhn-trah-poh, like "non-tropical." This phrase serves as a adverb to other tempo markings.)
MÁ VLAST [*My Country/Fatherland*] (Smetana)		Cz	mah-vlahst (The word "vlast" is really more like *native country* than either of the very un-PC terms *father*land or *mother*land. Do what you're comfortable with. Russian has "rodina" = [roh-dee-nuh].)
MA, YO YO	♪	C/E	mah, yoh-yoh (He's a he.)
MAAG, PETER	𝄞	G	mahg, pay-ter
MAASTRICHT (city in Holland)	◆	D	mah-streekht
MAAZEL, LORIN	𝄞	G	mah-zehl, law-rin (He is German, but the name fits French norms better than German. It is neither German [mah-tsuhl] nor English [may-zuhl] or [mah-zuhl].)
MÁCAL, ZDENĚK	𝄞	Cz/E	mah-tsahl, zdeh-nyek (The full-Czech given here may be too correct. He left Czechoslovakia after the Soviet invasion of 1968. Some announcers report he has "gone Western" as [mah-kahl], though not all the way to McCall.)
MACHAUT, GUILLAUME DE	✍	F	mah-"show", gee-yohm duh
MACKERRAS, SIR CHARLES	𝄞	E	muh-ka-russ
MADAMA BUTTERFLY (Puccini)		E	mah-dah-mah (Usually announced as full-English "Madam.")
MAESTOSO [*majestically*]	◆	I	my-stoh-zoh
MAESTRO DI MUSICA (Pergolesi)		I	my-ehs-troh dee-moo-zee-kah
MAGGIO-ORMEZOWSKI, FRANCO	♪	I/P	mah-joh-or-meh-zohf-skee, frahn-koh
MAGNIFICAT (religious vocal piece.)	◆	L/E	mahg-nih-fih-kaht (This is one English pronunciation of Church Latin. Italian [mah-nyee-fee-kaht] with <gn> = [n^y] is an equal option. Half-English is [mag-nih-fuh-kaht] but not all the way to [-"cat"].)
MAGY, SANDOR SOLYOM	♪	H	mahj, shahn-dor sawl-yawm
MAHLER, GUSTAV	✍	G	mah-ler, goo-stahf Neither [may-ler] nor ["mall"-er]. See discussion below of Walton vs. Vivaldi.)

Name			Pronunciation
MAISKY, MISCHA	♪	R/G	my-skee, mee-shuh (Russian born, moved to Israel in the early 1970s. German spelling of <ai> = ["eye"] and <sch> = [sh].)
MAKSYMIUK, JERZY	𝄞	P	mahk-sihm-yook, yeh-zhih (Polish <rz> = [zh]. This does not sound at all like the cotton pullover garment or the state next to New York. The full-Polish vowel at the end is [ih], but half-Polish [yeh-zhee] is good.)
MALGOIRE, JEAN-CLAUDE	𝄞	F	mahl-gwahr, zhãhn-"clawed"
MAMELLES DE TIRÉSIAS (Poulenc)	🎭	F	mah-mehl duh tee-ray-zyahs
MANAHAN, GEORGE	✍	E	"man"-uh-han
MANFREDINI, FRANCESCO	✍	I	mahn-freh-dee-nee, frahn-chess-koh
MANON (Massenet)	🎭	F	mah-nõhn
MANON LESCAUT (Puccini)	🎭	F/I	mah-nõhn lehs-koh
MANUGUERRA, MATTEO	♪	S	mah-noo-geh-rah, mah-tay-oh
MARAIS, MARIN	✍	F	mah-ray, mah-rãn
MARCATO	◆	I	mahr-kah-toh
MARCELLO, ALESSANDRO	✍	I	mar-cheh-loh, ah-leh-sahn-droh
MARKEVITCH, IGOR	𝄞	R/E	mar-kay-vich, ee-gohr (√ mar-kuh-vich)
MAROSSZÉK DANCES (Kodály)	🎸	H	mah-roh-sehk (Both Hungarian <sz> and <ssz> = [s].)
MARRINER, NEVILLE	𝄞	E	"mariner", neh-vuhl
MARTHA (Flotow)	🎭	G	mar-tah
MARTINON, JEAN	✍ 𝄞	F	mahr-tee-nõhn, zhãhn
MARTINŮ, BOHUSLAV	✍	Cz	mahr-tee-noo, boh-hoo-slahf
MASCAGNI, PIETRO	✍	I	mahs-kah-nyee, pyay-troh
MASSENET, JULES	✍	F	mahs-nay, zhül (√ [zhool]. Last name is two syllables or [mah-suh-nay].)
MASUR, KURT	𝄞	G	mah-zoor, koort
MATA, EDUARDO	𝄞	I	mah-tah, ed-wahr-do
MATEAU SANS MAÎTRE (Boulez)	🎸	F	mah-toh sãhn-meh-truh (Full-French has <maître> = [mehtr] in a single syllable.)
MATHIS DER MALER SYMPHONY (Hindemith)	🎸	G	mah-tihs dehr mah-ler
MATHIS, EDITH	♪	F	mah-tees, ay-deet
MAVRA (Stravinsky)	🎭	R/E	mahv-ruh
MEDEA (Cherubini)	🎭	I	meh-day-ah
MÉDÉE (Charpentier)	🎭	F	meh-day

MEDICI STRING QUARTET	🪑	I	meh-dee-chee
MEDIŅŠ, JĀNIS	𝄵 ♪	Lv	meh-deensh, yah-nees (Latvian uses a mācron for [long ah]. Plain [ah] will do.)
MEFISTOFELE (Boito)	🎭	I	meh-fee-stoh-feh-leh
MEHTA, ZUBIN	𝄵	E	may-tuh, zoo-bin (From Bombay, India. His family history goes back to old Persia.)
MEIJERING, CHIEL	✍	D	my-er-ing, kheel
MELOS QUARTET STUTTGART	🪑	G	meh-lohs
MENDELSSOHN, FELIX	✍	G	men-duhl-sohn, fay-liks (√ full-English [mehn-duhl-suhn fee-liks], also full-German [mehn-del-"zone"].)
MENGELBERG, WILLEM	𝄵	G	mengl-behrg, vih-luhm
MENGES, HERBERT	𝄵	E	meng-ihs
MENNIN, PETER	✍	E	meh-nihn
MENOTTI, GIAN CARLO	✍	I/E	muh-"not"-ee, jahn kar-loh (Made his career in the U.S., so full-Italian [meh-"note-tea"] is too correct.)
MENUHIN, YEHUDI	♪ 𝄵	E	mehn-yoo-ihn, yuh-hoo-dee (√ [muh-nyoo-ihn].)
MEPHISTO WALTZ (Liszt)	🎸	E	muh-fihs-toh
MEPPELINK, HIEKE	♪	D	mep-uh-link, hee-kuh
MERCANDANTE, GIUSEPPE	✍	I	mehr-kahn-dahn-tay, joo-zep-pay
MERVILLE, FRANÇOIS	♪	F	mehr-vee, frãhn-swah (Might also be [mehr-veel.)
MESSIAEN, OLIVIER	✍	F	"messy"-ãn oh-lee-vyay
MESTER, JORGE	𝄵	S/E	mehs-ter, jorj (He goes by American [jorj, not Spanish [hohr-hay].)
METAMORPHOSEN [*Metamorphoses*] (R. Strauss)	🎸	G	meh-tah-mohr-foh-zen (English = [meh-tuh-mohr-fuh-sihz].)
METSON, MARIAN RUHL	♪	E	👓→🔔 (rool)
MEYER, BERNHARD VAN DEN SIGTENHORST	✍	D	my-er, behrn-hard vuhn den sihkh-ten-horst
MEYERBEER, GIACOMO	✍	G/I	my-yer-"bare", jah-koh-mo (= "My, you're bare!" German Jew born Jakob Liebmann Beer = ["bear"]. He added Meyer and for professional reasons changed German Jakob to its Italian counterpart Giacomo.)
MEZZO- [*moderately*] (- FORTE, -PIANO, -SOPRANO)	◆	I	meht-soh, mehd-zoh (Prefix for "not as X as Y": not as loud as forte, as soft as piano, as high a range as soprano. This <zz> is, strictly speaking, Italian [dz], since it compares with Latin "medio-" but most people say [ts].)

MIASKOVSKY, NIKOLAI	✍	R	mee-uh-"scoff-ski," nih-koh-ly (Half-Russian as given is fine. Full-Russian is more like ["miss-cough-ski," nih-kah-ly]. Avoid full-English [my-uh-skahf-skee].)
MICHALKOVÁ, ALZBETA	♪	Cz	mee-khal-koh-vah ahlz-beh-tah
MICHEJEW, ALEXANDER	♪	P	mee-khay-ehf (This would be full-Polish, but his first name suggests he is English speaking. In that case there's no telling how his family handles this Polish name. It might be even "Mitch-a-Jew.")
MICHELANGELLI, ARTURO BENEDETTI	♪	I	mee-keh-lahn-jeh-lee, ahr-too-roh beh-neh-"debt"-tee
MIDORI	♪	J	mee-"door"-ree (She goes by the one name. Avoid full-English [muh-"door"-ee] with first syllable shwa. See Interlude 3.)
MIESSEN, MARIJKE	♪	D	mee-suhn, mah-ry-kuh
MIGNON (Thomas)		F/E	meen-yõhn (like the steak)
MIKADO (THE) (Gilbert and Sullivan)		E	muk-kah-doh (Keep this full-English and not pseudo-Japanese [mee-kah-doh].)
MIKROKOSMOS (Bartók)		H/E	mee-kroh-kohs-mohs (Really General European. Half-English = [mee-kruh-kahz-mohs], ≠ full-English [my-kroh-kahz-mohs].)
MIKULÁS, PETER	♪	H	mee-koo-lahsh, pay-tehr
MILAN ANGELICUM ORCHESTRA		I	mee-lahn ahn-jeh-luh-koom
MILHAUD, DARIUS	✍ 𝄞	F	mee-yoh, da-ree-"us"
MILMAN, MIKHAIL	♪	R	mil-muhn, mee-khah-eel (≠ McHale)
MILNES, SHERRILL	♪	E	milnz, sheh-ruhl
MILOŠEVIĆ, SLOBODAN (President of Serbia, 1995)	◆	SC	mih-loh-sheh-vihch, sloh-boh-dahn (A name for news reading rather than for music. Like Radovan Karadžić, above, you would cause an international scene if you referred to him as SC rather than just Serbian. The news media usually leave off the diacritics, so he has become known as [sloh-buh-dahn muh-lah-suh-vihch. You may choose to restore him to near-native pronunciation or not.)
MILSTEIN, NATHAN	♪	E/R	mil-styn, nay-thuhn (From Russia, but Americanized first name. He is often announced as [mee-styn], perhaps because he spend the latter part of his career living in France.)

Name			Pronunciation
MINKOWSKI, MARC	♪	E	meen-"cow"-skee, mark (Looks Polish, which would be ["mean-cough"-skee], but then first name would be full-Polish <Marek>= [mah-rek].)
MINTON, YVONNE	♪	E	👓→🔔, ee-vahn
MINTZ, SHLOMO	♪	R/Is	mints, shloh-moh
MINUET	◆	E	min-yoo-eht (No need for full-French [mãn-ü-eht]. Italian is <minuetto>.)
MIRICIOIU, NELLY	♪	Rm	mee-ree-choy-yoo (Spelling suggests Romanian, but she may be Greek.)
MISSA DEL CID (Weir)	🎭	S	mee-sah del-seed
MISSA ECCE ANCILLA DOMINI (Dufay)	🎭	L	mee-suh eh-chay ahn-chee-lah doh-mee-nee
MISSA GLORIA TIBI TRINITAS (Taverner)	🎭	L	mee-sah "Gloria" tee-bee tree-nee-tahs
MISSA PAPAE MARCELLI (Palestrina)	🎭	L	mee-sah pah-pay mahr-cheh-lee (Classical Latin <ae> = ["eye"], but Church Latin has [eh/ay].)
MISSA SOLEMNIS (Beethoven)	🎭	L/E	mee-sah suh-lehm-nees
MITROPOULUS, DIMITRI	𝄞	Gk	mih-trah-puh-lihs, dih-mee-tree (Like "Metropolis." Full-Greek [mee-troh-poo-loos] goes overboard.)
MLADA (Rimsky-Korsakov)	🎭	R	mlah-duh (Try for that [ml-] cluster, as in "M'Lady," said fast.)
MODERATO (= *moderately*)	◆	I	full: moh-deh-rah-toh (<t> = [t]) half-English: mah-duh-rah-toh (<d>, <t> = [flap)
MOFFO, ANNA	♪	E	mah-foh, "Ann"-uh
MOLINARI-PRADELLI, FRANCESCO	𝄞	I	moh-lee-nah-ree-prah-deh-lee, frahn-chehs-koh
MOLL, PHILLIP	♪	E	"mole"
MÖLLER, WOUTER	♪	D	mö-ler, wow-ter
MOLTER, JOHANN MELCHIOR	✍	G	"mole"-ter, yoh-hahn mehl-kee-ohr
MOLTO [*very*]	◆	I	"mole-toe"
MONDO DELLA LUNA [*World of the Moon*] (Haydn)	🎭	I	mohn-doh deh-lah-loo-nah
MONIUSZKO, STANISŁAW	✍	P	mawn-yoosh-koh, stah-nee-swahf
MONTEUX, PIERRE	𝄞	F	mohn-tö (=ter), pyehr
MONTEVERDI, CLAUDIO	✍	I	mohn-teh-vehr-dee, "cloudy"-oh (√ [mahn-tuh-v"air"-dee], but shun [-ver-dee]. See Verdi, below.)
MORATH, MAX	♪	E	muh-"wrath"

MORAVEC, IVAN	♪	Cz	"more"-ah-vets, ee-vahn (Note Czech stress, ≠ Russian [ee-vahn].)
MORCEAUX [*Pieces*] (various composers)	🎸	F	"more-sew" (both with and without <—x>.)
MORELLI, FRANK	♪	E	muh-reh-lee
MORENO TORROBA, FREDERICO	✍	S	moh-ray-noh tor-roh-bah, freh-deh-ree-koh
MORET, NORBERT	✍	F	moh-ray, nor-behr
MOROSS, JEROME	✍	E	maw-rohs
MOSCHELES, IGNAZ	✍	G	moh-shuh-luhs, ihg-nahts (= "motionless" said with a bad cold.)
MOSCOW (city in Russia or Idaho)		R	mah-skow, mah-skoh (Either is correct for the capital of Russia. Only the latter is a city in Idaho. Full-Russian is [mahsk-vah].)
MOSÈ IN EGITTO (Rossini)	🎭	I	moh-zeh een eh-jee-toh
MOSES UND ARON (Schoenberg)	🎭	G/E	Use English "Moses and Aaron"
MOSONYI, MIHALY	✍	H	moh-shohn^y, mee-"high" (His name was originally German: Michael Brandt, an unusual direction of name change.)
MOSZKOWSKI, MORITZ	✍	P	mohsh-"cough"-skee, moh-rits
MOURET, JEAN JOSEPH	✍	F	moh-ray, zhãhn zho-zef
MOYZES, ALEXANDER	✍	Sk	moy-zehs
MOZART, LEOPOLD	✍	G	moh-tsart, lay-oh-pold
MOZART, WOLFGANG AMADEUS	✍	G	moh-tsart, vohlf-gahng ah-mah-day-oos (= "moat"-sart, with German <z> = [ts]. If "Moe's art" or "Ma's art" slips off your tongue you'll slip into the unemployment line! As for first names, full-English ["wolf-gang" "am-a-day"-iss] is fine.)
MŠE GLAGOLSKÁ MŠA GLAGOLSKAJA [*Glagolitic Mass*] (Janáček)	🎭	Cz	msheh glah-gohl-skah (The Czech name is Mše Glagolská, as given here—even more correct is Hlaholská, since Czech replaces [g] by [h]. The Russian version underneath appears in some sources. In either case, give the [msh—] cluster your best effort and avoid [mush-eh]. See note under the English title for the meaning.)
MUFFAT, GEORG	✍	G	moo-faht, gay-org
MUKK, JÓZSEF	♪	H	mook (= "book"), yoh-zhehf
MUNCH, CHARLES	𝄞	F	münsh, shahrl (√ half-English [charlz moonsh], as in "pull" but not too loudly. Definitely not full-English "munch.")

MUNCHINGER, KARL	𝄞	G	moon-ching-er (French plain <u> is [ü], as in Munch, above, but here German plain <u> is [oo].)
MÜNCHNER BLÄSERAKADEMIE KÖLN		G	münkh-ner blay-zer-ah-kah-day-mee köln
MUND, UWE	𝄞	G	moont, oo-vuh (<oo> ="good"; <oo> = "food.")
MUNICH PRO ARTE ORCHESTRA		G	myoo-nihk proh ahr-tay
MUSGRAVE, THEA	✍	E	muhz-grave, thee-uh (<th> as in think not thee.)
MUSICA ANTIQUA		L	moo-zee-kah ahn-tee-kwa
MUSSORGSKY, MODEST	✍	R	moo-sork-skee, moh-dehst (Full-Russian stresses 1st syllable. More familiar half-Russian is [moo-sork-skee]. The French spelling Mouss- is also frequent.*)
MUTI, RICCARDO	𝄞	I	moo-tee, ree-kar-doh
MUTTER, ANNE-SOPHIE	♪	G	moo-ter, ah-nuh-zoh-fee

N

NABUCCO (Verdi)		I	nah-boo-koh (Italian name for this king of ancient Babylon in the Book of Daniel. Usual English is Nebuchadnezer = [neh-buh-"cud"-neh-zer]. The Hebrew Bible has [nuh-voo-khahd-"nets"-ahr], and we can argue later about the original Assyro-Babylonian.)
NAGY, PÉTER	♪	H	nahj, pay-tehr
NAUSICAA (Glanville-Hicks)		E	"gnaw-sick-a" (A name from Greek mythology, also given as [naw-sick-ay-uh].)
NEIDLINGER, GUSTAV	♪	G	nyd-linger, goo-stahf
NÉMETH, JUDIT	♪	H	nay-meht, yoo-deet

* Transcribing straight from Russian gives Musorgskij with one <s>. The composer himself stressed the first syllable and not the second, although some of his contemporaries did pronounce [moo-sork-skee] or [moo-"soar"-skee] without <g>. The sequence <gs>, according to Russian phonetics, = [ks]. The consonant that begins the second syllable is unmistakably [s] and not [z], as indicated both by Russian spelling <s> = [s] and German spelling <Muss-> with <ss> = [s]. A French reading of <Muss> would be [müs], hence the French spelling <Mouss-> to ensure [moos]. The frequent English pronunciations [moo-zork-skee] or [moo-zorg-skee] are not justified.

NERONE [*Nero*] (Boito)		I	neh-roh-nay
NEUMANN, VÁCLAV	𝄞	G/Cz	noy-mahn, vaht-slahf (German last name with <eu> = [oy]; Czech first name with <c> = [ts] ≠ [k].)
NICOLAI, OTTO	✍	G	nick-oh-ly, ah-toh
NICOLET, AURÈLE	♪	F	nick-oh-lay, oh-rehl
NIGHT ON MT. TRIGLAV (Rimsky-Korsakov)		E/R	tree-glahv (This was an early version of what later became *Night on Bald Mountain* or more properly, *St. John's Night on the Bare Mountain*. Both "bare" and "bald" occur. "Triglav" means "three-head.")
NIJMEGEN (city in Holland)	◆	D	ny-may-gihn
NILSSON, BIRGIT	♪	Sw	nihl-suhn, beer-giht (Swedish <gi> ought to be [yi], but such is the price of international stardom. See Nicolai Gedda, above.)
NIN-CULMELL, JOAQUÍN MARÍA	✍	G/S	neen-kool-mehl, (kh)wah-keen mah-ree-ah
NINA, O SIA LA PAZZA PER AMORE [*Nina or The Lunatic from Love*] (Paisiello)		I	nee-nah oh-syah-lah-paht-sah-pehr-ah-"more"-ay
NINA, OU LA FOLLE PAR AMOUR [*Nina or The Lunatic from Love*] (Persius)		F	nee-nah oo-lah-fuhl-pahr-ah-moor
NISHIZAKI, TAKAKO	♪	J	nee-shee-zah-kee, tah-kah-koh
NOCHES EN LOS JARDINES DE ESPAÑA [*Nights in the Gardens of Spain*] (de Falla)		S	noh-chehs ehn lohs khahr-dee-nehs deh eh-spahn-yah (Always announced in English.)
NOORDT, SYBRAND VAN (See also van Noordt, Sybrand)	✍	D	nort, see-brahnt vuhn
NØRGÅRD, PER	✍	Dn	nör-gohr, pehr
NORMAN, JESSYE	♪	E	(jeh-see)
NOTTURNO (NOCTURNE) (= type of piece)	◆	I, E	noh-toor-noh (= "no-turn"-oh), nahk-tern
NOVÃES, GUIOMAR	♪	Pt	noo-vãhn-ehsh, gee-oo-mar (Portuguese unstressed <o> = [oo]. If nasal [ãhn] is uncomfortable, pronounce plain [ah] with no hint of [n], unlike French.)
NOVÁK, VITEZSLAV	✍	Cz	noh-vahk, vee-teh-slahv
NÜRNBERG SYMPHONY		G	nürn-behrg (The combination <nürn> is very close to English [nern].)

O

OAXACA (city in Mexico)	◆	S	wah-(k)hah-kah
OBBLIGATO (= type of musical structure)	◆	I	full: oh-blee-gah-toh (<t> = [t]) half: ah-bluh-gah-toh (<t> = flap)
OBERFRANK, GÉZA	𝄞	G/H	oh-buh-frahnk, gay-zah
OBERON (Weber)		G	oh-buh-rahn (Full-English is fine. Full-German is [oh-beh-rohn].)
OBERSTADT, FERDINAND	✍	D	oh-ber-staht, fehr-dih-nahnd
OBRAZTSOVA, ELENA	♪	R	oh-brahs-tsoh-vah, yeh-lyeh-nuh (√ full-Russian last name [ah-brahs-tsoh-vuh]; full-English first name [uh-lay-nuh] is unnecessary.)
OCCASIONE FA IL LADRO (Rossini)		I	oh-kah-zyoh-nay fah-eel-lah-droh
OCHMANN, WIESŁAW	♪	P	awkh-mahn, vyeh-swahf
OCKEGHEM, JOHANNES	✍	G	oh-keh-guhm, yoh-hah-ness
OCTANDRE (Varèse)		F	ohk-tahn-druh
ODENSE SYMPHONY		Dn	oh-dehn-suh
OEDIPUS DER TYRANN (Orff)		G	ö-dee-poos dehr tee-rahn (√ E: eh-duh-puhs "the tyrant")
OFFENBACH, JACQUES	✍	G/F	"off"-en-bahkh, zhahk (= ["often-bock"]. German last name, French first name.)
OHLSSON, GARRICK	♪	E	👓→🔔
OISTRAKH, DAVID	♪ 𝄞	R	oy-strahkh, dah-veed (√ [oy-strahk]. No one will complain about full-English [day-vid], either.)
OISTRAKH, IGOR	♪	R	oy-strahkh, ee-gohr (Full-Russian is actually more like "eager.")
OLOMOUC (city in Czech Republic)	◆	Cz	oh-loh-"moats"
ONCZAY, CSABA	♪	H	ohn-tsy, chah-bah
OPALIČ, MARINKO	♪	Sv	oh-pah-leech, mah-reen-koh
OPPENS, URSULA	♪	E	👓→🔔
ORCHESTRA [E, I], ORCHESTRE [F], ORQUESTA [S]	◆	E/I	E: or-kuh-struh, I: or-keh-strah, F: or-kehst(r), S: or-kay-stah
ORCH.. DEL TEATRO ALL SCALA		I	O. dehl tay-ah-troh ahl skah-lah
ORCH.. DE L'ASSOCIATION DES CONCERTS LAMOUREUX		F	O. duh lah-soh-see-ahs-yõhn deh-kohn-sehr lah-moo-rer

ORCH. DE CHAMBRE DE LA FONDATION GULBENKIAN DE LISBONNNE		F	O. duh shahm-bruh duh lah fohn-dah-syõhn gool-behn-kee-uhn duh leez-buhn (Just read as "Gulbenkian Foundation Chamber Orchestra of Lisbon," a French name for an apparently Portuguese outfit apparently funded by an Armenian.)
ORCH. DE CHAMBRE DE LAUSANNE		F	read as "low"-zahn chamber orchestra
ORCH. DE L'OPERA DE LYON		F	read as "lee-õhn opera orchestra
ORCH. DE LA SUISSE ROMANDE (Suisse Romande Orchestra)		F	O. duh lah swees roh-mahnd
ORCHESTRE SYMPHONIQUE D'U.R.S.S.		F	Read as "USSR Symphony Orchestra."
OREBRO CHAMBER ORCHESTRA		S	oh-reh-broh
ORFEO (Monteverdi)		I	or-fay-oh
ORFEO ED EURIDICE (Gluck)		I	or-fay-oh ehd-oo-ree-dee-cheh
ORMANDY, EUGENE	𝄞	E	ohr-muhn-dee, yoo-jeen (An American version of a Hungarian name.)
ORQUESTA DE CONCIERTOS DE MADRID NACIONAL DE ESPAÑA		S	or-kay-stah day kohn-thee-ehr-tohs day mah-dreed nah-thee-oh-nahl day eh-spah-nyah
ORTIZ, CRISTINA	♪	Pt	or-tees, kris-tee-nah
OSTINATO (type of musical structure)	◆	I	full: oh-stee-nah-toh half: ah-stuh-nah-toh
OSTROŁĘKA (city in Poland)	◆	P	aw-stroh-wenk-ah
OŚWIĘCIM (city in Poland)	◆	P	aw-shvehn-cheem (This is the Polish name for the town near Kraków that the Germans called Auschwitz = [ow-shvihts], that notorious site of a World War II conentration camp.)
OUSSET, CECILE	♪	F	oo-say, suh-seel
OYENS, TERA DE MAREZ	✍	D	oy-ehns, tay-rah deh mah-rehz
OZAWA, SEIJI	𝄞	J	oh-zah-wuh, say-jee (same as [oh-zow-uh])

P

PAA VIDDERNE [*On The Heights*] (Delius)		N	paw vih-dehr-nuh (Based on the text of the Norwegian writer, Ibsen.)
PACHELBEL, JOHANN	✍	G	pah-kuhl-bel, yoh-hahn (He is so well known in English that there is no need to restore him to full-German [pah-khuhl-bel].)

Name			Pronunciation
PADBRIE, CORNELIS THIJMENSZOON	✍	D	pahd-bree, kor-neh-lees ty-men-"zone"
PADEREWSKI, IGNACE JAN	♪ ✍	P	pah-deh-rehf-skee, ihg-nahts yahn (Maybe half-English ["pad"-uh-rehf-skee], but never full-English ["pad"-uh-roo-skee].)
PAGANINI, NICCOLÒ	✍	I	pah-gah-nee-nee, nee-koh-loh (√ half-Italian [pah-guh-nee-nee, "nickel-oh"]. You can also get by with half-English [pa-guh-nee-nee] = "bag-o'-," but not full-English [pa-guh-"ninny"].)
PAIK, KUN WOO	♪	K	"peck," koon-woo
PAILLARD, JEAN-FRANCOIS	𝄞	F	"pie-are," zhãhn-frãhn-swah
PAITA, CARLOS	𝄞	S	py-ee-tah (Think of "pie *eater*"—as opposed to "pie *maker*"—with a Boston accent...)
PALESTRINA, GIOVANNI	✍	I	pah-leh-stree-nah, joh-vah-nee (√ [pa-luh-stree-nuh], ["palace"-tree-nuh].)
PALMA, SUSAN	♪	E	pahl-muh
PAN VOYEVODA [*The Leader*] (Rimsky-Korsakov)		R	pahn-voy-uh-voh-duh
PANAMBÍ (Ginastera)		S	pah-nahm-bee
PARADE (Satie)		F	pah-rahd (≠ full-English puh-rayd)
PARAY, PAUL	𝄞	F	puh-ray, "Paul"
PARIS COLLEGIUM MUSICUM		E	kuh-"leggy"-uhm moo-zih-koom
PARKENING, CHRISTOPHER	♪	E	par-kuh-ning
PÄRT, ARVO	✍	Es	pehrt, ahr-voh (Estonian <ä> = [a] in "pat," so try ["parrot"] with the <o> dropped out. The [r] makes it more comfortable for an English speaker to say [pehrt] or ["pair"]+[t]. At any rate, it is not "part.")
PAS D'ACIER (Prokofiev)		F	pah-dah-syay
PAS DE DIX (Glazunov)		F	pah-duh-dees
PASSACAGLIA (type of musical structure)	◆	I	pah-sah-kah-lyah pah-suh-kah-lyuh (≠ ["pass-a-Cal"-yuh] or [..."cag-lee-uh"].)
PÁSZTHY, JULIA	♪	H	pah-stee, yoo-lyah
PAUK, GYÖRGY	♪	H	powk, jörj
PAVANE POUR UNE INFANTE DEFUNTE [*Pavane for a Dead Princess*] (Ravel)		F	pah-vahn poor ün ãn-fãhnt deh-fünt

PAVAROTTI, LUCIANO	♪	I	pah-vah-roh-tee, loo-chah-noh (√ full-Italian [pah-vah-"wrote-tea"] or [oah-vah-"wrought"-tee] is OK but a little heavy-tongued. Half-English [pah-vuh-rah-tee] is frequent, though avoidable. First name is only 3 syllables in Italian with <cia> = [chah]; half-English will squeeze out a fourth: [loo-chee-ah-noh]. This author recommends against full-English [loo-chee-"Ann"-oh pa-vuh-rah-dee].)
PECS (city in Hungary)	◆	H	pehch
PÉDARD, ETIENNE	♪	F	peh-dahr, ay-tyehn
PEERCE, JAN	♪	E	peers, jan (as in "fierce," but ≠ yahn)
PELLEAS UND MELISANDE (Schoenberg)	[illegible]	G	peh-lee-ahs and meh-lee-zahnd (Full-English is fine.)
PELLÉAS ET MELISANDE (Debussy)	[illegible]	F	peh-lee-ahs and meh-lee-zahnd (Full-English is fine.)
PELLERIN, LOUISE	♪	E	[illegible]
PEÑA, PACO	♪	S	"pain"-yah, pah-koh
PENDERECKI, KRZYSZTOF	✍ 𝄞	P	pen-deh-reht-skee, kshihsh-tawf (Honest: [ksh-]! It is the equivalent of "Christopher." The <z>'s won't scare you once you know what their function is. See Polish section in Movement 4.)
PENNARIO, LEONARD	♪	E	peh-nah-ree-o (√ pen-"airy"-oh)
PERAHIA, MURRAY	♪ 𝄞	E	puh-ry-uh (= "pariah"), muh-ree (He is of Sephardic Jewish background, hence the apparently Spanish name. It is probably derived from Hebrew "perah" = [peh-rahkh] meaning "flower.")
PERÉNYI, ESZTER	♪	H	peh-rehn-yee, ehs-tehr
PERESS, MAURICE	𝄞	E	peh-rehs, maw-rees
PERGAMENSCHIKOW, BORIS	♪	R	pehr-gah-myehn-shee-kuhf, "bore"-ihs (This is apparently a German spelling with <sch> approximating Russian [shch].)
PERGOLESI, GIOVANNI	✍	I	pehr-goh-lay-zee, joh-vah-nee (√ half-Italian ["pear"-guh-"lazy"], but not full-English [per-guh-"lazy"], no offense intended!)
PERLEA, JONEL	𝄞	Rm	pehr-lay-uh, yoh-nel
PERLMAN, ITZHAK	♪	E	"pearl"-muhn, yihts-khahk (Israeli, lives in U.S. <tz> = [ts]. Do not think of <zh> = [zh]. The sequence <zh> is only a coincidence: they are separate <z> = [z] and <h> = [kh]. Other variants are ["its"-khahk], [yiht-sahk], but not ["itch"-ahk]!)

Entry		Lang.	Pronunciation
PERSÉPHONE (Stravinsky)		F/E	Use English [per-seh-fuh-nee].
PERSICHETTI, VINCENT	✍	E/I	"purr"-suh-keh-tee, vihn-sent (Full Italian [pehr-see-ket-tee] is more Italian than P. himself says.)
PERTIS, ZSUZSA	♪	H	pehr-teesh, zhoo-zhah
PEŠEK, LIBOR	𝄞	Cz	peh-shehk, lee-"bore"
PETER AND THE WOLF (Prokofiev)		E/R	→ (Literal translation of Russian title *Petya i volk* = [pyay-tyuh ee-vohlk].*)
PETROUCHKA or PETRUSHKA (Stravinsky)		R/E	peh-troosh-kuh (Both the French spelling with <ouch> and English with <ush> give Russian [oosh].)
PETTERSSON, GUSTAF ALLAN	✍	Sw	peh-tehr-suhn, goo-stahf
PFITZNER, HANS	✍	G	pfihts-ner, hahns [yes: pf- , not a typo.]
PHANTASIESTÜCKE [*Fantasy Pieces*] (various composers)		G	fahn-tah-zee shtü-kuh
PIANISSIMO [*very soft*]	◆	I	pee-ah-nee-see-moh pee-uh-nih-suh-moh
PIANO [*soft*]	◆	I	pyah-noh pee-ah-noh (The instrument is [pee-"Anne"-oh].)
PIATIGORSKY, GREGOR	♪	R	pyah-tih-gor-skee, greh-gor (Full-Russian is [pyih-tih-gor-skee], but keep to half-Russian. Unstressed <ia> is Russian [ih], same issue as Miaskovsky, above but not Liadov, where <ia> is stressed [yah].)
PIERLOT, PIERRE	♪	F	pyehr-loh, pyehr
PIERROT LUMAIRE (Schoenberg)		E	pyeh-roh lü-"mare"
PIMPINONE (Telemann)		I	peem-pee-noh-nay
PINNOCK, TREVOR	♪	E	"pin"-uhk, treh-ver
PIQUE DAME [*Queen of Spades*] [R: *Pikovaya Dáma*] (Tchaikovsky)		F/R	peek-dahm (The French title is very frequent—even more correct, since Russian "pee-kee" for "spades" is from French "pique." Full-Russian [pee-kah-vy-uh dah-muh] poses no problem for announcing but is not generally used.)

* This piece is mentioned here only for political-historical interest. English-speaking narrators of this tale refer to "Little Peter." In the Russian text, written during the height of Stalin's purges of cultural figures, he is "Pioneer Peter." The "Young Pioneers" were the Soviets' ideologically-charged answer to the Cub Scouts. No wonder it was so important that this one little Soviet boy could subdue the evil wolf all by himself!

PIÙ MOSSO (= *a little more*)	◆	I	pyoo-moh-soh
PIZZICATO (= *plucked*)	◆	I	full: pee-tsee-kah-toh half: "pits"-uh-kah-toh
PLEIADES (Xenakis)		Gk	Use English plee-uh-deez
PLI SELON PLI [*Fold Upon Fold*] (Boulez)		F	plee suh-lõhn plee
PLOVDIV (city in Bulgaria)	◆	B	plohv-dihv
POLLINI, MAURIZIO	♪	I	poh-lee-nee, mow-ree-tsee-oh (√ half-English [puh-lee-nee, maw-"ritzy"-oh] or [muh-].)
POLOVTSIAN DANCES (Borodin, from opera *Prince Igor*)		E/R	puh-luh-"vets"-ee-uhn (Also appears as "Polovetsian," named for the Polovtsy—R. [puh-lahf-tsih]—a Turkic tribe that the ancient Russians did battle with around the 10th century. A certain Prince Igor took them on, got captured, and was treated to these dances. The English adjective Polovtsian = [puh-lohv-tsee-uhn] is formed straight from the Russian noun. The Russian adjective is [puh-lah-vyeht-skee], whence Polovetsian. Some orchestral recordings of the dances include a chorus.)
PLZEŇ (city in Czech Republic)	◆	Cz	"pill"-zehn[y] (If plain [n] feels better at the end of the word, do it. This is the Czech where pilsner beer comes from.)
POCHISSIMO [*a very little bit*] POCO [*a little bit*]	◆	I	poh-kee-see-moh poh-koh (Note Italian "place preserver" strategy for <co> = [koh] and <chi> = [kee], cf. Italian in Movement 4.)
PONCHIELLI, AMILCARE	✍	I	pohn-kyeh-lee, ah-mil-kah-ray (Three syllables, not four: ["pawn-key-Ellie"].)
POULENC, FRANCIS	✍	F	poo-lenk, frãhn-sees (This half-French seems to be the norm. Full-French is [poo-lãhnk].)
PRAETORIUS, MICHAEL	✍	G	pray-taw-ree-uhs, mee-khah-el (This full-German is fine but less frequent than English [pruh-taw-ree-uhs, my-kuhl.)
PRAGUE [E] = PRAHA [Cz]	◆	E/Cz	prahg, prah-hah (The adjective form is Pražský = [prahsh-skee] with <ž> = voicless [sh] because a voiceless [s] follows it.)
PRAGUE MUSICI		E/I	prahg moo-zee-chee
PRÉ AUX CLERC [*The Scholars' Meadow*] (Hérold)		F	pray oh-klehr

PRÉLUDE À L'APRÈS-MIDI D'UN FAUNE [*Prelude to the Afternoon of a Faun*] (Debussy)		F	pray-<u>lüd</u> ah-lah-preh-mee-<u>dee</u> duhn-"<u>phone</u>" (Announced in French or English. Just note that French "faune" = English "faun," the mythological being. English "fawn" = French "faon" = [fãhn], a young deer. The former is portrayed, for example, in the animated movie *Allegro Non Troppo*.)
PRESTISSIMO [*very fast*]	◆	I	full: preh-<u>stee</u>-see-moh half: preh-<u>stih</u>-suh-moh
PRÊTRE, GEORGES	𝄞	F	<u>preh</u>-truh, zhorzh (If you can squeeze it into one syllable [prehtr], so much the French-er.)
PREVIN, ANDRE	♪	E	<u>preh</u>-vin, <u>ahn</u>-dray (≠ French [preh-<u>vãn</u>, ãhn-<u>dray</u>]!)
PREY, HERMANN	♪	G	pry, <u>hehr</u>-mahn
PRICE, LEONTYNE	♪	E	prys, <u>lay</u>-uhn-teen
PRINZ, ALFRED	♪	G	"prints"
PROHASKA, FELIX	𝄞	G/Cz	<u>pro</u>-hah-skah, <u>fay</u>-lix
PROKOFIEV, SERGEI	✍	R	pruh-"<u>cough</u>"-yehf, sehr-<u>gay</u> (Russian surname is 3 syllables. Half-English [pruh-"<u>coffee</u>"-ehf] with four syllables is fine, but that <i> letter is for the Russian consonant [y] and not for its own syllable. He also appears as French "Serge" = [sehrzh], ≠ "surge." Keep him Russian.)
PSALMUS HUNGARICUS (Kodály)		L	<u>sahl</u>-moos hoon-<u>gah</u>-ree-koos
PUCCINI, GIACOMO	✍	I	poo-<u>chee</u>-nee, <u>jah</u>-koh-moh
PULCINELLA (Stravinsky)		I	"<u>pool</u>"-chee-<u>neh</u>-lah
PURCELL, HENRY	✍	E	"<u>purr</u>"-suhl
PURVIS, WILLIAM	♪	E	"<u>purr</u>"-vihs
PYGMALION (Rameau)		E	English ["pig"-<u>mail</u>"-yuhn] is fine.

Q

QUATUOR MUIR, YSAŸE		F	kwah-tü-<u>ohr</u> myoor, ee-<u>zy</u>-(uh) (This [kw] is a little unexpected. Read as "myoor quartet" and "ee-<u>zy</u> quartet.")
QUINTETTO FAURE DI ROMA		I	kween-<u>teh</u>-toh foh-<u>ray</u> dee <u>roh</u>-mah

R

Name			Pronunciation
RACHMANINOV, SERGEI (Also Rachmaninoff, Rakhmaninov)	✍	R	rahkh-mah-nee-n"off," sehr-gay (Full-Russian is [rahkh-mah-nyee-nuhf], if you wish, but not full-English ["rock-man-un-off"] or ["rock-man-enough"]. He, like Prokofiev, also appears as French Serge, and the spelling with <ch—off> reflects the Russian sound. Nowadays the spelling with <kh—ov>, which reflects the Russian spelling, is gaining currency.)
RADETZKY MARCH (J. Strauss, Sr.)	🎸	G/E	rah-deht-skee (not the same as Berlioz' Rákóczy!)
RAFN, EYVIND	♪	Dn	rah-fin, ay-vin (Combinations such <-nd, -ld, -rd> do not pronounce the <d>.)
RAHBARI, ALEXANDER	𝄞	E	raH-bah-ree (Perhaps Iranian backgound, so you do pronounce the <h> in [raH-] similarly to Arabic names like Rahman = [raH-man], Ahmed = [aH-mehd]. For English it may be easier to substitute [kh] here. Persian and Arabic are not related languages.)
RAIMONDI, RUGGERO	♪	I	ry-mohn-dee, roo-jeh-roh
RÁKÓCZY MARCH (Berlioz)	🎸	H/E	rah-koh-tsee (Half- English is the norm for announcing this piece, not full-Hungarian [rah-koh-tsee]. Hungarian <cz> is an older spelling for modern <cs> = [ts]. Compare Radetzky, above.)
RAMPAL, JEAN-PIERRE	♪ 𝄞	F	rahm-pahl, zhãhn pyehr
RAPPÉ, JADWIGA	♪	F/P	rah-pay, yahd-vee-gah
RAVEL, MAURICE	✍	F	rah-vell, moh-rees (Full-English [ruh-vel] is OK but not [muh-rees] and certainly not "Morris.")
RAYCHEV, ROUSLAN	𝄞	R	ry-chehf, roos-lahn
REDEL, KURT	𝄞	G	ray-duhl, koort
REGER, MAX	✍	G	ray-ger, mahks (√ full-English [maks] but not [ree-ger].)
REICH, STEVE	✍	E	ryk, steev
REINECKE, CARL	✍	G	ry-nuh-kuh
RELÂCHE (Satie)		F	ruh-lahsh
RENNES, CATHARINA VAN (See also van Rennes, Catharina)	✍	D	reh-ness, kah-tah-ree-nah vuhn
RESNIK, REGINA	♪	E	rehz-"nick", ruh-jee-nuh

RESPIGHI, OTTORINO	✍	I	reh-spee-gee, oh-toh-ree-noh (√ ah-tuh-ree-noh)
RETABLO DE MAESE PEDRO (Falla)		S	ray-tah-bloh day-mah-ay-say pay-droh
REZNIČEK, EMIL NIKOLAUS VON	✍	Cz/G	rehz-nih-"check," eh-meel nik-oh-lows fawn (He's listed as German but probably has some Czech in his background.)
REZUCHA, BYSTRÍK	𝄞	Sk	reh-zhoo-khah, bee-streek
RHEINBERGER, JOSEPH	✍	G	ryn-behr-ger, yoh-zef
RICCI, RUGGIERO	♪	I	ree-chee, roo-jeh-roh
RICCIARELLI, KATIA	♪	I	ree-chah-reh-lee, kah-tyah (First name is 2 syllables, not kah-tee-yah.)
RICERCARE (type of musical strucure)	◆	I	ree-chehr-kah-ray (≠ ["richer-car, eh?"])
RICHTER, KARL	♪	G	rihkh-ter
RICHTER, SVIATOSLAV	♪	R	rihkh-ter, svyah-tuh-slahv (Full Russian first name is [svih-tah-slahf]. OK to veer toward English ["Rick"-ter] or [-slahv], but no need to succumb completely to ["sva-tuh-slahv].)
RIDDERBUSCH, KARL	♪	G	rih-der-boosh
RIEGEL, KENNETH	♪	E	"regal"
RIGOLETTO (Verdi)		I	"rig-a-let"-oh (Full-Italian is [ree-goh-leht-toh], if you feel you must.)
RIMSKY-KORSAKOV, NIKOLAI	✍	R	"rim"-skee "course-a-cuff," nih-kuh-ly (Half-English ["nick-a-lie"] or ["nickel-eye"] is the norm. Full-Russian is [nee-kah-"lie"].)
RISE AND FALL OF THE CITY OF MAHAGONNY (Weill)		E	… mah-hah-goh-nee (not like the wood)
RISTENPART, KARL	𝄞	G	"wrist"-in-part
ROBESON, PAUL	♪	E	"robe-sun," pawl
ROBISON, PAULA	♪	E	roh-bih-"sun", "paw"-luh
ROBLES, MARISA	♪	E	roh-buhlz, muh-rih-suh
RODELINDA (Handel)		I	roh-duh-lihn-duh
RODEO (Copland)		E	roh-day-oh (The normal English word is, of course, [roh-dee-oh]. Copland—himself a lifelong city slicker—apparently preferred the version given here.)
ROGG, LIONEL	♪	E	"rogue"
ROMBOUT, ERNEST	♪	F	rohm-boo, ehr-nest

ROMERO, ANGEL	♪	S	roh-"mare"-o, ahn-khell (≠ ayn-juhl!!)
ROMERO, CELEDONIO	♪	Se	roh-"mare"-o, theh-leh-doh-nyoh
ROMERO, PEPE	♪	S	roh-"mare"-o, peh-pay
RONDO (type of musical strucure)	◆	I	rohn-doh rahn-doh
RONTGEN, JULIUS	✍	D	rohnt-khen, yü-lyüs
ROSAMUNDE (Schubert)	🐸	G	roh-zuh-moon-duh (= ["book"])
ROSSINI, GIOACCHINO	✍	I	roh-see-nee, jwah-kee-noh (<gi> = [j], <oa> = [wah], <ch> = [k].)
ROSTROPOVICH, MSTISLAV	♪ 𝄞	R	rah-struh-poh-vihch, mstee-slahf (First name has only 2 syllables. Try your best on the [mst-] cluster and avoid the 3-syllable ["misty"-slahv]. Full-Russian last name is [ruh-strah-poh-vihch]. See notes in Movement 4 on Russian names.*)
ROTH, DANIEL	♪	E	rawth
ROTHENBERGER, ANNALIESE	♪	G	roh-ten-behr-ger, ah-nah-lee-zuh
ROUSSEL, ALBERT	✍	F	roo-sell, ahl-behr
ROUSSET, CHRISTOPHE	♪	F	roo-say, kree-stawf
ROWLAND, GILBERT	♪	E	"row"-luhnd
ROZHDESTVENSKY, GENNADY	𝄞	R	rohzh-dyehst-vehn-skee, geh-nah-dee ([rohzh-] is half-Russian; full Russian is [rahzh-dyehst...]. Stress on second syllable.)
ROZSA, MIKLOS	✍ 𝄞	H/E	roh-zhah, mee-klohsh (This full-Hungarian is an option, though M.R. has been in U.S. since 1940 and usually goes by full-English [roh-zuh, "mick-loss"].)
RSO	◆	E	Read [ahr-ehs-oh] for Radio Symphony Orchestra.
RUBACKYTĖ, MÛZA	♪	Lt	roo-bahts-kee-tay, moo-zah (Lithuanian <c> = [ts], <y> = [ee], dotted <ė> = [ay].)
RUBBRA, EDMUND	✍	E	ruh-bruh
RUBINSTEIN, ANTON	✍	G	roo-bin-shtyn

* Historiographers might find it interesting that Rostropovich's name is absent from Ageenko's 1984 *Slovar udarenii*, the Soviet equivalent of the *NBC Handbook*, listed in Bibliography II. M.R. was stripped of his Soviet citizenship in the early 1970s for supporting the writer Alexander Solzhenitsyn, whose name is also conspicuously missing from that dictionary. These artists officially ceased to exist in the Soviet media, so their names did not appear in their standard reference work. The 1978 *Soviet Encyclopedia of Music* has only a four-line entry on M.R., paraphrased, "Cellist, born Baku. Deprived of Soviet citizenship for defaming the Soviet Union." Both of these artists have now been fully "rehabilitated." In 1993 M.R. and Ignats Solzhenitsyn, the concert pianist son of Alexander, made a highly publicized tour of Russia. The writer has now moved back to Russia. Both names are in Ageenko's 1993 update.

Name			Pronunciation
RUBINSTEIN, ARTUR (Also spelled Arthur)	♪	G/P	<u>roo</u>-bihn-styn, <u>ahr</u>-toor (He was Polish-Jewish, but the last name is usually pronounced as in English. First name is [toor], not [thoor]. German version [<u>roo</u>-bihn-shtyn] is also frequent.)
RÜBSAM, WOLFGANG	♪	G	<u>rüb</u>-zahm, <u>vohlf</u>-gahng
RUDEL, JULIUS	𝄞	E	roo-<u>dehl</u>
RUGGLES, CARL	✍	E	👓→🔔
RUPPE, CHRISTIAN FRIEDRICH	✍	D	<u>roop</u>-puh (=cook)
RUSALKA (Dvořák)	🎭	Cz	roo-<u>sahl</u>-kuh (This half-English is normal. The full-Czech would be [<u>roo</u>-sahl-kah].)
RŮŽIČKOVÁ, ZUZANA	♪	Cz	<u>roo</u>-zheech-koh-vah, <u>zoo</u>-zah-nah (A good example of a Czech "two-layer" word with multiple diacritics.)
RZESZÓW (city in Poland)	◆	P	<u>zheh</u>-shoof

S

Name			Pronunciation
SAAR COLLEGIUM MUSICUM	🪑	G	zahr kuh-"<u>leggy</u>"-uhm <u>moo</u>-zih-koom
SADKO (Rimsky-Korsakov)	🎭	R	sahd-<u>koh</u> (√ either this half-Russian or full-Russian [saht-<u>koh</u>], a merchant in medieval Russia.)
SAINT-SAËNS, CAMILLE	✍	F	sãn-<u>sãhns</u>, kah-<u>mee</u> (The final <s> = [s], and the final <ille> = [ee]. Some sources say the final <s> is silent. Others say it is [z].)
SALERNO-SONNENBERG, NADJA	♪	E	suh-<u>lehr</u>-noh <u>soh</u>-nen-berg, <u>nah</u>-dyuh (American born of Russian-Italian descent)
SALIERI, ANTONIO	✍	I	sah-<u>lyeh</u>-ree, ahn-<u>toh</u>-nee-oh
SALOME (R. Strauss)	🎭	G/E	<u>sah</u>-luh-may (Some announcers go for full-German [<u>zah</u>-loh-may], but audiences may think it funny.)
SALONEN, ESA-PEKKA	𝄞	Fn	<u>sah</u>-loh-nen, <u>eh</u>-sah <u>peh</u>-kah
SALZBURG CAMERATA ACADEMICA	🪑	G	<u>zahlts</u>-boorg kah-muh-<u>rah</u>-tuh ah-kuh-<u>deh</u>-mee-kuh
SALZBURG MOZARTEUM CAMERATA ACADEMICA	🪑	G	<u>zahlts</u>-boorg moh-tsahr-<u>tay</u>-uhm kah-muh-<u>rah</u>-tuh ah-kuh-<u>deh</u>-mee-kuh
SAMAMA, LEO	✍	D	sah-<u>mah</u>-mah, <u>lay</u>-oh

Name			Pronunciation
SAMARTINI, GIOVANNI BATTISTA	✍	I	sah-mar-<u>tee</u>-nee, joh-<u>vah</u>-nee bah-<u>tee</u>-stah (Half-Italian is ["sam-martini"], but no need.)
SAMARTINI, GIUSEPPE	✍	I	sah-mar-<u>tee</u>-nee, joo-<u>zep</u>-pay
SANDERLING, KURT	𝄞	G	<u>zahn</u>-der-ling, koort
SANDOR, GYÖRGY	♪	H/E	<u>shahn</u>-dor, <u>jerj</u>
SANDOR, JANOS	𝄞	H/E	<u>shahn</u>-"door," <u>yah</u>-nohsh
SANTOS, TURIBIO	♪	Pt	<u>sahn</u>-toosh, too-<u>ree</u>-bee-oh
SARABANDE (type of dance)	◆	F	sah-rah-<u>bahnd</u> sah-ruh-"<u>bond</u>" (√ "Sarah Bond," if your "Sarah" sounds like "have a" but not if it sounds like "care a," and definitely ≠ "Sarah Band"!)
SARASATE, PABLO DE	✍	S	sah-rah-<u>sah</u>-tay, <u>pah</u>-bloh deh (No, this is not a something you would expect to see on a skewer in a Thai or Indonesian restaurant.)
SATIE, ERIK	✍	F	sah-<u>tee</u>, <u>eh</u>-"rick"
SATO, HIKARU	♪	J	<u>sah</u>-toh, hee-<u>kah</u>-roo
SAVITRI (Holst)		E	sah-<u>vee</u>-"tree" (Title comes from Sanskrit literature.)
SAWALLISCH, WOLFGANG	𝄞 ♪	G	sah-<u>vah</u>-lish, <u>vohlf</u>-gahng
SCARLATTI, ALESSANDRO	✍	I	skar-<u>lah</u>-tee, ah-leh-<u>sahn</u>-droh (No need for full-Italian ["scar-<u>lot</u>-tee"] with double [tt].)
SCARLATTI, DOMENICO	✍	I	skar-<u>lah</u>-tee, do-<u>meh</u>-nee-koh
SCÈNES DE BALLET (Glazunov)		F	sehn-duh-bah-<u>lay</u>
SCHÁFER, MARKUS	𝄞	G	<u>shay</u>-fer
SCHAT, PETER	✍	D	skhaht, <u>pay</u>-ter
SCHEHERAZADE (Rimsky-Korsakov)		E	sheh-heh-ruh-<u>zahd</u> (The Arabic name for the Persian heroine of the thousand and one *Arabian Nights*. This spelling has elements of French: <zade> = [zahd]; and of German: <sch> = [sh]. The English spelling "Sheherazade" also occurs.)
SCHEIDT, SAMUEL	✍	G	shyt (= "sight")
SCHEIN, JOHANN HERMANN	✍	G	shyn, <u>yo</u>-hahn, <u>hehr</u>-mahn
SCHELLENBERGER, HANSJÖRG	♪	G	<u>sheh</u>-len-behr-ger, hahns-<u>yerg</u>
SCHELOMO (Bloch)		E	<u>shloh</u>-moh (This is the Hebrew name of King Solomon. The 2-syllable pronunciation is modern Israeli Hebrew. You might also hear 3-syllable [shuh-loh-<u>moh</u>] or [shuh-<u>loh</u>-moh], which reflects old European Hebrew pronunciation. Either is fine.)

Name			Pronunciation
SCHERBAKOV, KONSTANTIN	♪	R	shchehr-bah-"cough," kuhn-stahn-teen (The <sch> seems to be a short cut for full-Russian [shch].)
SCHERCHEN, HERRMANN	𝄞	G	shehr-khen, hehr-mahn
SCHERMERHORN, KENNETH	𝄞	E	sher-mer-horn (Bollard's 1993 *Pronouncing Dictionary* gives [sker-] as the name of the conductor but [sher-] as the name of a street in New York.)
SCHERZANDO, SCHERZO [*very fast*]	◆	I	skehr-tsahn-doh, skehr-tsoh (= "scare"-tsoh)
SCHICKELE, PETER	✍	E	shick-uh-lee, pee-ter
SCHIFF, ANDRAS	♪	G/H	shihf, ahn-drahsh
SCHIFF, HEINRICH	♪	G	shihf, hyn-rihkh
SCHIØTZ, AKSEL	♪	Dn	shöts, ak-sehl (The <sch> is a German spelling.)
SCHMEISSER, ANNEMARIE	♪	G	shmy-ser, ah-nuh-mah-ree
SCHMIDT-ISSERSTEDT, HANS	𝄞	G	shmit-ihs-er-shteht, hahns
SCHMIEDER, WOLFGANG	◆	G	shmee-der, "wolf-gang" (The diamond sign here could stand for "musicologist," a cataloguer of the works of J.S. Bach. See also BWV.)
SCHNABEL, ARTUR	♪	G	shnah-buhl, ahr-toor
SCHNEIDER, MISCH	♪	E	shny-der
SCHOENBERG, ARNOLD	✍	G	shön-behrg (√ full-English shern-berg)
SCHOENFELD, PAUL	♪	E	"shone"-feld
SCHOLA CANTORUM BASILIENSIS	🪑	L	skoh-luh kahn-toh-ruhm bah-zee-lyehn-sihs
SCHØNWANDT, MICHAEL	𝄞	Dn	shön-vahnt
SCHRADER, DAVID	♪	E	shray-der
SCHREIER, PETER	♪	G	shry-er, pay-ter
SCHREKER, FRANZ	✍	G	shray-ker, frahnts
SCHUB, ANDRE MICHEL	♪	G/F	shoob, ahn-dray mee-shell (Last name looks German, though he was born in France. The French spelling for this sound would have to be <Choube>. He came to U.S. in infancy, but your eyes need to think of both "G" and "F" to read him without rhyming with "shrub.")
SCHUBERT, FRANZ	✍	G	"shoe"-behrt, frahnts (√ half-English ["shoo-bert, frahnz])
SCHULZ, WOLFGANG	♪	G	shoolts, vohlf-gahng
SCHULZE, THEODORA	♪	G	shool-tsuh, tay-oh-dor-uh
SCHUMAN, WILLIAM	✍	E	"shoe"-muhn, "will"-yuhm
SCHUMANN, ROBERT	✍	G	"shoe"-mahn, roh-behrt

SCHURICHT, CARL	𝄞	G	shur-rikht
SCHÜTZ, HEINRICH	✍	G	shüts, hyn-rihkh (√ [shoots], in case an English CD producer left off the dots on German <ü>.)
SCHWALBE, MICHEL	♪	G	shvahl-buh, mee-shel
SCHWANENGESANG [*Swan Song*] (Schubert)	🎭	G	shvah-nehn-geh-zahng
SCHWARZ, GERARD	♪	E	shworts, juh-rahrd
SCHWARZKOPF, ELISABETH	♪	G	shvahrts-kawpf, "Elizabeth"
SCIMONE, CLAUDIO	𝄞	I	shee-moh-nay, "cloudy"-oh
SCOTTO, RENATA	♪	I	skoht-toh, reh-nah-tah (√ half-English [ruh-nah-tuh skah-toh].)
SCRIABIN, ALEXANDER	✍	R	skryah-bin, a-leg-zan-der (Full Russian last name is only 2 syllables; half-Russian is [skree-ah-bin]. Full-English first name is fine.)
SEBESTYÉN, JÁNOS	♪	H	sheh-beh-styen, yah-nohsh
SECHS MONOLOGE AUS "JEDERMANN" [*Six Monologues from "Everyman"*] (Martin)	🎭	G	zehks moh-noh-loh-guh ows yay-der-mahn
SEEFRIED, IRMGARD	♪	G	zay-freed, eerm-gard
SEGERSTAM, LEIF	𝄞	Sw	seh-ger-stahm, layf (He is based in Finland but the name is Swedish, where <ei> is between [layf] and "life." Americans usually say "leaf.")
SEGOVIA, ANDRES	♪	S	seh-goh-vee-ah, ahn-drays
SEIPENBUSCH, EDGAR	𝄞	G	zy-pehn-boosh
SEMIRAMIDE (Rossini)	🎭	I	seh-mee-rah-mee-day
SEQUOIA STRING QUARTET	🪑	E	suh-kwoy-ah
SERAFIN, TULLIO	𝄞	I	seh-ruh-fin, too-lyoh
SEREBRIER, JOSE	𝄞	S	seh-reh-bree-"air", hoh-say
SERENI, MARIO	♪	I	seh-ray-nee, mah-ree-oh
SERKIN, PETER	♪	E	"sir"-kin, pee-ter
SERKIN, RUDOLF	♪	G	sehr-kin, roo-dohlf
SERSE or XERXES (Handel)	🎭	I/E	zerk-seez (Use full-English, unless you really want to do Italian [sehr-seh].)
SFORZANDO [*suddenly loud*]	◆	I	sfor-tsahn-doh (The <sf> should pose no trouble: think "Sphinx.")
SGOUROS, DIMITRIS	♪	Gk	zgoo-rohs, dee-mee-trees

Name			Pronunciation
SHCHEDRIN, RODION	✍	R	shcheh-dreen, roh-dee-ohn (Also listed above as French Chedrin. Both [shch] and [sh] are OK. Full-Russian is [rah-dyohn).)
SHENG, LIHONG	✍	C	shuhng, lee-hohng
SHOSTAKOVICH, DMITRI	✍ ♪	R	shah-stuh-koh-vihch, dmee-tree (√ [shaw-stuh-koh-vihch]. Full-Russian last name is [shuh-stah-koh-vihch]. See notes on Russian names in Movement 4 for names in "ovich." First name is two syllables with a [dm] consonant cluster. The 3-syllable [duh-mee-tree] is also OK. On a German, Dutch, or Hungarian disk he would appear as Schostakowitsch, Sjostakovitsj, or Sosztakovics.)
SHOSTAKOVICH, MAXIM	𝄞	R	shah-stuh-koh-vich, mahk-seem (Son of Dmitri)
SHVANDA, THE BAGPIPER (Weinberger)	🎭	E/Cz	shvahn-dah (Original Czech is Švanda Dudák, see below. Also occurs in German as Schwanda, der Dudelsackpfeifer = [dehr-doo-dehl-zahk-pfy-fer].)
SIBELIUS, JEAN (also Jan)	✍	Fn/F	sih-bay-lee-uhs, zhãhn (yahn) (He is the essence of Finnish music, though his name, a Latinized form of Sibbe = [sih-beh] does not follow the Finnish pattern of stressing the first syllable. His family was Swedish-speaking, and he preferred French Jean = [zhãhn] to native Jan = [yahn].)
SIEGFRIED (Wagner)	🎭	G	zeeg-freed
SIEPI, CESARE	♪	I	syay-pee, cheh-zah-ray
SILJA, ANJA	♪	G	seel-yuh, ahn-yuh
SILVERSTEIN, JOSEPH	♪	E	sil-ver-styn
SIMON BOCCANEGRA (Verdi)	🎭	I	see-mohn boh-kah-nay-gruh
SIMON, ABBEY	♪	E	sy-muhn
SINDING, CHRISTIAN	✍	N	"sin-ding," krihs-chuhn
SINFONIA DA CAMERA	🪑	I	seen-"phony"-uh dah kah-muh-ruh
SINFONIEORCHESTER DES SÜDWEST	🪑	G	Read as "Southwest Symphony Orchestra."
SINOPOLI, GIUSEPPE	𝄞	I	sih-noh-poh-lee, joo-zep-pay (√ half-English [suh-nah-puh-lee].)
SIPKAY, DEBORAH	♪	H	"ship"-ky
SKROWACZEWSKI, STANISŁAW	𝄞	P	skroh-vah-cheff-skee, stah-nee-swahf (√ half-English [stan-ih-slahv], ≠ full-English [stan-ih-slaw].)
SLOTHOUWER, JOCHEM	✍	D	"slaw-tower," yoh-khuhm

Name			Pronunciation
SLOVÁK, LADISLAV	𝄞	Sk	sloh-vahk, lah-dih-slahv
SLOWICK, KENNETH	♪	E	sloh-wihk
SMETANA, BEDŘICH	✍	Cz	smeh-tah-nah, bay-drihk (Beware: some older sources give [shmeh-tah-nah], apparently over-extending the German idea of <sp> = [shp]. German <sm> = [sm], and [shm] = <schm>. As for <ř> = [rzh], if you can do full-Czech [bay-drzhihkh], please do.)
SOBOL, LAWRENCE	♪	E	"sew"-buhl
SÖDERSTRÖM, ELISABETH	♪	Sw	sö-der-ström
SOKKELUND SANGKOR	🎹	Dn	soh-kuh-loond sahng-kohr
SOLEÁ, MAÑA (MARIA)	♪	S	soh-lay-ah, mah-nyah
SOLER, (PADRE) ANTONIO	✍	S	soh-lair, (pah-dray) ahn-toh-nee-oh [He was a priest.]
SOLIN, HANS	♪	G	zoh-lin, hahns
SÖLLSCHER, GÖRAN	♪	G	zöl-sher, gö-rahn
SOLOMON, YONTY	♪	E	sah-luh-muhn, yahn-tee
SOLTI, GEORG (SIR)	𝄞	H/G	"shoal"-tee, gay-org (American announcers use either [jorj] or German [gay-org]. If spelling is any indication, Sir Georg, knighted British subject though he, seems to prefer German. At least, he does not use Hungarian [jörj].)
SOLUM, JOHN	♪	E	soh-luhm
SONATA (type of musical strucure)	◆	I	soh-nah-tah <t> = [t] suh-nah-tuh <t> = [flap]
SONI VENTORUM WIND QUINTET	🎹	L	soh-nee vehn-toh-ruhm
SÖNSTEVOLD, KNUT	♪	Sw	sön-stuh-vohl, knoot
SOSARME, RÈ DI MEDIA [*Sosarmes, King of the Medes*] (Handel)	🎭	I	soh-sahr-may, ray-dee-meh-dee-ah
SOSNOWIEC (city in Poland)	◆	P	"saw-snow"-vyehts (Polish <w> = [v], as in German; <c> = [ts], as in the haček languages.)
SOUZAY, GERARD	♪	F	soo-zay, zheh-rahr
SPANJAARD, ED	𝄞	D	spahn-yard
SPANOGHE, VIVIANE	♪	D	spah-noh-khuh, vee-vyahn
SPOHR, LUDWIG	✍	G	shpohr, lood-vig (= "look")
SRBIJA, REPUBLIKA SRPSKA	◆	SC	ser-bee-uh, serp-skah reh-poo-blee-kah (The native name of Serbia and the Serbian Republic. Note syllabic [r] and that voiced <b> in <Srb> is spelled <Srp> when followed by voiceless [s].)

ST. MARTIN-IN-THE-FIELDS, ACADEMY OF		E	👓→🔔
STAATSKAPELLE DRESDEN		G	shtahts-kah-peh-luh
STACCATO [*very short notes*]	◆	I	full: stah-kah-toh half: stuh-kah-toh
STAIER, ANDREAS	♪	G	shty-er, ahn-dray-ahs
STAMITZ, CARL	✍	G	shtah-mits
STANCIU, SIMION	♪	Rm	stahn-choo, see-mohn
STANTS, IET	✍	D	stahnts, eet
STARKER, JANOS	♪	H	star-ker, yah-nohsh (In his native Hungary he was no doubt [shtar-ker].)
STEIN, HORST	𝄞	G	shtyn
STENGAARD, FRODE	♪	Dn	stehn-gohr, froh-duh (See note on Niels Gade for Danish <d> after a vowel as [th].)
STICH-RANDALL, TERESA	♪	E	"stick"-ran-duhl, tuh-ree-suh
STIMMEN...VERSTUMMEN... (Gubaidulina)		G	shtih-men fehr-shtoo-men
STIMMUNG [*Mood*] (Stockhausen)		G	shtih-moong
STOCKHAUSEN, KARLHEINZ	𝄞	G	shtohk-"how"-zen, karl-hynts
STOCKHOLM (capital of Sweden)	◆	E/Sw	"stock"-hoh(l)m (Not a German name, so <st> = [st]. Only German <st> = [sht], not Scandinavian.)
STOKOWSKI, LEOPOLD	𝄞	P	stuh-"cough"-skee, lay-uh-pohld (Pronounce in half-Polish as given.*)
STOLTZMAN, RICHARD	♪	E	stohlts-muhn
STOLZE, GERHARD	♪	G	shtohl-tsuh, gehr-hard
STÖLZEL, GOTTFRIED HEINRICH	✍	G	shtöl-tsuhl, goht-freed hyn-rikh (√shtel-tsuhl)
STRADELLA, ALESSANDRO	✍	I	strah-deh-lah, ah-leh-sahn-droh
STRANO, FRANCESCO	♪	I	strah-noh, frahn-ches-kah
STRATTA, ETTORE	𝄞	I	strah-tah, eh-toh-ray
STRAUSS, JOHANN JR.-SR. & JOSEF	✍	G	shtrows, yoh-hahn & yoh-zehf (= ["mouse"])

* Stokowski was born in England. His father was Polish and his mother, British. He might well have grown up as full-English [stuh-"cow"-skee] (as Mickey Mouse called him in the movie *Fantasia*). At the beginning of the 19th century Slavic names were considered "classy" in the arts, and Stokowski apparently restored the Polishness for the sake of his career, even affecting an intermittent Polish accent. Slonimsky recounts the anecdote in his preface to the 6th edition of *Baker's Biographical Dictionary* (1978, reprinted in the 8th edition 1992 listed in Bibliography I) of how he caught Stokowski in the act of being "too Polish" when the maestro recorded his full "Polish" name as Leopold Bolesławowicz Stokowski, with a Russian-style patronymic [boh-leh-swah-voh-vihch] from his father Bolesław = [boh-leh-swahf]. The trouble is that Poles do not use patronymics. Unfortunately, Slonimsky does not go on to relate Stokowski's reaction.

Name		Lang.	Pronunciation
STRAUSS, RICHARD	✍ 𝄞	G	shtrows, rih-kard
STRAVINSKY, IGOR	✍ 𝄞	R	struh-vihn-skee, ee-gohr (Half-English is better here than full-Russian ["eager" strah-veen-skee].)
STRYJA, KAROL	𝄞	P	stree-yah, kah-rohl
STUTTGART (city in Germany)	◆	G	shtoot-gahrt ([shtoot] = "soot," ≠ "suit.")
•BACH COLLEGIUM			bahkh koh-lay-gee-oom
•KIRCHENMUSIKTAGE			keer-khen-moo-zeek-tah-guh
•SOLISTEN			zoh-list-uhn
STUYVESANT QUARTET		E	sty-vuh-suhnt
SUCHOŇ, EUGEN	✍	Sk	soo-khuhn^{y}, eh-oo-gehn
SUISSE ROMANDE ORCHESTRA		F	"Swiss" roh-mahnd ("orchestra")
SUITE PROVENÇALE (Milhaud)		F	"sweet" proh-vãhn-sahl
SUK, JOSEPH	♪	Cz	sook, yoh-zef (= "shook")
SUOR ANGELICA [*Sister Angelica*] (Puccini)		I	"swore" ahn-jeh-lee-kah (The middle opera of the cycle "Il Trittico.")
SURINACH, CARLOS	✍	S	soo-ree-nahk
SUZUKI, HIDEMI & ICHIRO	♪	J	soo-zoo-kee, hee-deh-mee & ee-chee-roh
ŠVANDA DUDÁK (Weinberger)		Cz	shvahn-dah doo-dahk (See Shvanda, above.)
SVÄTOPLUK (Suchoň)		Sk	sva-toh-plook (An opera set in the 9th century, the same ancient time and place as that used by Janáček in his Glagolitic Mass.)
SVETLANOV, YEVGENY	𝄞	R	svet-lah-n"off," yev-gay-nee
SWAROWSKY, HANS	𝄞	P/G	svah-roff-skee, hahns
SWEELINCK, JAN PIETERSZOON	✍	D	svay-link, yahn "Peter's own"
ŚWIERCZEWSKI, MICHEL	𝄞	P/F	shvyehr-chehf-skee, mee-shehl (Polish family, born and raised in France. He may pronounce <ś> as plain [s].)
SZABO, IMRICH	♪	H	sah-boh, eem-reekh
SZABO, MIKLOS	𝄞	H	sah-boh, mee-klohsh
SZECSÓDI, FERENC	♪	H	seh-choh-dee, feh-rehnts
SZEGED (city in Hungary)	◆	H	seh-gehd
SZELECSÉNYI, NORBERT	♪	H	seh-leh-chehn-yee
SZELL, GEORGE	𝄞	H/E	"sell," jorj (Hungarian <sz> = [s]. He is not German [zehl], where <s-> would [z], or Polish, where <sz> = [sh] First name is American [jorj], not German [gay-org] or Hungarian [jerj]. Compare Sir Georg Solti.)
SZERYNG, HENRYK	♪	P	sheh-ring, "hen-rick" (= ["sharing"]: Polish <sz> = [sh].)

SZIGETI, JOSEPH	♪	H	sih-geh-tee, yoh-zef (Be careful to distinguish Polish <sz> = [sh] from Hungarian <sz> = [s] whenever possible.)
SZOKOLAY, BALÁZS	♪	H	soh-koh-ly, bah-lahzh
SZYMANOWSKI, KAROL	✍	P	shih-mahn-"off"-skee, kah-ruhl (≠ "Carol")

T

TACCHINO, GABRIEL	♪	I	tah-kee-noh, gah-bree-ehl
TACHEZI, HERBERT	♪	G	tah-kay-tsee, hehr-behrt
TADDEI, GIUSEPPE	♪	I	tah-day-ee, joo-zep-pay
TAFELMUSIK	🪑	G	tah-fuhl-moo-zeek
TAILLEFERRE, GERMAINE	✍	F	"tie-affair," zhehr-men
TAKÁCS STRING QUARTET	🪑	H	tah-kahch
TALLIS, THOMAS	✍	E	👓→🔔 (As in "Vitalis" hair tonic.)
TANEYEV, SERGEI	✍	R	tah-nay-eff, sehr-gay
TANNHÄUSER (Wagner)	🎭	G	tahn-hoy-zer (Stay clear of any "tan houses.")
TARREGA, FRANCISCO	✍	S	tar-reh-gah, frahn-thees-koh (A Spaniard, but √ Latin American [frahn-sees-koh].)
TARTINI, GIUSEPPE	✍	I	tar-tee-nee, joo-zep-pay
TASHI	🪑	J	tah-shee
TCHAIKOVSKY, PETER ILYICH (TSCHAIKOWKSI, PYOTR/PIOTR)	✍	R	chy-"cough"-skee, pee-ter ihl-yihch *or* pyoh-ter ihl-yihch (This <Tch> spelling follows a French model for [ch]. The German spelling Tschaikowski with <tsch> = [ch] is also frequent. The English spellings Chaikovsky and Chaykovsky are gaining currency. You are free to restore him to full-Russian [pyohtr]. *)
TE KANAWA, KIRI	♪	E	teh-kah-nuh-wah, kee-ree (Of Maori background from New Zealand, but her name is pronounced in "general European.")

* Some authors have strong opinions on retaining <Tch->(e.g., Kennedy, *Oxford Dictionary* 1985) or adopting <Ch-> (e.g., Westrup, Harrison and Wilson *New College Encyclopedia* 1976). On a Dutch or Hungarian CD you might come across Tsjaikovsky or Csajkovszki. Same fellow, same sound. As for the name Peter over Piotr, in addition to the note on page 18 in Movement 1, it is worth conjecturing that Peter arose as a misreading of the transcription of Russian Pëtr = [pyohtr] without the dots. The remaining Petr might have been assumed to be a misprint for Peter.

TEBALDI, RENATA	♪	I	teh-bahl-dee, reh-nah-tah
TEITOV, FRANCES	♪	E	"tie"-tawv
TELEMANN, GEORG PHILIP	✍	G	tay-luh-mahn, gay-org
TELVELA, MARTTI	♪	Fn	tel-veh-lah, mar-tee
TEMIRKANOV, YURI	𝄞	R	teh-meer-kah-noff, yoo-ree
TENNSTEDT, KLAUS	𝄞	G	"ten"-shteht, klows (= "louse," ≠ "claws.")
TER LINDEN, JAAP	♪	D	ter-lihn-den, yahp
TER VELDHUIS, JACOB	✍	D	ter-veld-hys, yah-kohp
TERFEL, BRYN	♪	W	tehr-vuhl, brihn (Welsh <f> = [v].)
TERPSICHORE (various composers)	🎸	E	terp-"sick"-uh-ree
TÉTARD, ALBERT & JEANINE	♪	F	tay-tahr, ahl-behr & juh-neen
THAÏS (Massenet)	🎭	F	tah-ees
THALBERG, SIGISMOND	✍	G	ahl-behrg, zih-gihs-mohnt
THIOLLIER, FRANÇOIS-OËL	♪	F	tyoh-lyay, frãhn-swah-zhoh-ehl
THOMPSON, MICHAEL	♪	E	👓→🔔 (The variants "Thomson/Thompson" are interesting from a language point of view. See Interlude 2 for why <p> should appear in a name that means "Thom's son." Don't ask about the <h>.)
THUNEMANN, KLAUS	♪	G	too-nuh-mahn, klaws
TICHY, GEORG	♪	G	tee-khee, gay-org (His background is probably Czech, in which language *tichý* is the word for "quiet.")
TILL EULENSPIEGEL'S MERRY PRANKS (R. Strauss)	🎸	G	"till" oy-lehn-shpee-"gull" (Actually, Till is a Flemish character named Tijl Uilenspiegel = ["tile," y-luhn-spee-khuhl], a sort of folk hero during the fifteenth century Spanish domination of what is now Belgium.)
TIERKREIS [*Zodiac*](Stockhausen)	🎸	G	teer-krys
TIMIŞOARA city in Romania)	◆	Rm	tee-mee-shwah-rah (Romanian spells [sh] with an underhook on <ş> the way Czech and several other languages use an overhook on <š>.)
TJEKNAVORIAN, LORIS	𝄞	A	"check"-nuh-vor-yahn, loh-rihs (This spelling probably comes from a Dutch disc, where <tj> = [ch].)
TOFTE-HANSEN, JENS	♪	Sw	tohf-tuh-hahn-sen, yehns (= "tense," ≠ "lens")
TOKODY, ILONA	♪	H	toh-kohj, ee-loh-nah
TOKOS, ZOLTÁN	♪	H	toh-kohsh, zohl-tahn

Name			Pronunciation
TOMOWA-SINTOW, ANNA	♪	B	toh-moh-vah seen-tohf, ah-nuh (Full Bulgarian is [toh-moo-vuh seen-toof], with unstressed <o> = [oo]. She, herself, prefers this German spelling.)
TÖNKÖ, AGNES	♪	Fn	tön-kö (= "turn-curr")
TONKUENSTLER (TONKÜNSTLER) ORCHESTRA		G	"tone"-künst-ler (Literally, Tone Artists. German <ue> is alternate spelling for <ü>.)
TORELLI, GIUSEPPE	✍	I	toh-reh-lee, joo-zep-pay
TÖRÖK, FRANTISEK	♪	H	tö-rök, frahn-tee-shehk (First name is Czech František. Hungarian achieves the same sound without a haček since Hungarian <s> = [sh].)
TOSCANINI, ARTURO	𝄞	I	"toss"-kah-nee-nee, ahr-too-roh (√ [tahs-kuh-nee-nee], ["tusk-a-knee"-nee].)
TOTENTANZ [*Dance of Death*] (Liszt)		G	toh-tehn-tahnts
TÓTH, JÁNOS	𝄞	H	"tote," yah-nohsh
TOULOUSE CHAMBER ORCHESTRA		F	too-looz
TOUREL, JENNIE	♪	E	tuh-rehl *or* too-rehl, "Jennie"
TOUVRON, GUY	♪	F	too-vrõhn, gee
TOYOHIKO, SATOH	♪	J	toh-yoh-hee-koh, sah-toh
TOZZI, GIORGIO	♪	I/E	toh-tsee/tah-tsee, jor-joh (He is American. Same issue as Frederica von Stade, below.)
TRAUBEL, HELEN	♪	E	trow-buhl
TRIO FONTENAY		F	fohn-tuh-nay
TRISTAN UND ISOLDE (Wagner)		G/E	trihs-tan "and" ee-zohl-duh (Use English "and.")
TROUTTET, ANDRÉ	♪	F	troo-tay, ãhn-dray
TROYANOS, TATIANA	♪	E/Gk	troy-ah-nohs, tah-tyah-nuh (American singer, Greek father.)
TUDJMAN, FRANJO (president of Croatia, 1995)	◆	SC	tooj-mahn, frahn-yoh (He would greet the "S" part of this designation with hearty disagreement.)
TUMAGIAN, EDUARD	♪	A	too-mah-jyahn, "Edward" (This spelling of Eduard is probably transcribed straight from Russian. French would be Edouard = [ehd-wahr].)
TURANGALÎLA (Messiaen)		E	too-rahn-guh-lee-lah
TURINA, JOAQUIN	✍	S	too-ree-nuh, (kh)wa-keen
TURKOVIĆ, MILAN	♪	SC	toor-koh-vihch, mee-lahn
TUROVSKY, YULI	𝄞	R	toor-"off"-skee, yoo-lee
TURRIZIANI, ANGELO	♪	I	too-ree-tsyah-nee
TYLŠAR, ZDENĚK & BEDŘICH	♪	Cz	teel-shahr, zdehn-yehk & beh-drzhihkh

TZIGANE [*Gypsy*] (Ravel)		F	tsih-gahn (This is the Russian word for "gypsy" borrowed by this French composer for a fiery violin piece. The spelling <tz> = [ts] does not otherwise occur at the beginning of a word. See note on Tzimon Barto, above.)

U

UCHIDA, MITSUKO	♪	J	oo-chee-dah, meets-koh (Silent <u> between voiceless consonants in Japanese.)
UGHI, UTO	♪	I	oo-gee, oo-toh
UIRAPARÚ (Villa Lobos)		Pt	oo-ee-rah-pah-roo (Not really Portuguese, but from a native Brazilian language.)
ULALUME (J. Holbrooke)		E	yoo-luh-loom
UN BALLO IN MASCHERA [*A Masked Ball*] (Verdi)		I	oon-bah-loh een-mahs-keh-rah
UN GIORNO DI REGNO (Verdi)		I	oon-jor-noh dee-rehn-yoh
UNDINE (Henze)		F	"earn"-deen (with a British accent)
UITTENBOSCH, ANNEKE	♪	D	"eye"-ten-bohs, ah-nuh-kuh
UTKIN, ALEXEI	♪	R	oot-kin, ah-lek-say

V

VAJDA, JÓZSEF	♪	Sk/H	vy-dah, yoh-zhehf (Slovak last name, Hungarian first name.)
VAJNAR, FRANTÍŠEK	𝄞	Cz	vy-nar, frahn-tee-shehk
VALENTE, BENITA	♪	E	vuh-len-tee, buh-nee-tuh
VALERIUS, ADRIANUS	✍	D	vah-leh-ree-uhs, ah-dree-ah-nus
VALLET, NICOLAS	✍	D	vah-leht
VALSE TRISTE [*Sad Waltz*] (Sibelius)		F	vahls-treest
VALSES NOBLES ET SENTIMENTALES [*Noble and Sentimental Waltzes*] (Ravel)		F	vahls-noh-bluh ay-sãhn-tee-mãhn-tahl
VAN ASPEREN, BOB	♪	D	vuhn ahs-puh-ruhn, bohp (≠ [bahb]) (See note on Dutch vs. Belgian "van" under "Dutch" in Movement 3.)
VAN BAAREN, KEES (See also Baaren, Kees van)	✍	D	vuhn bah-ren, "case"

VAN BEINUM, EDUARD	𝄞	D	vuhn-by-nuhm
VAN DELDEN, LEX (See also Delden, Lex van)	✍	D	vuhn-del-den
VAN DEN BERGH, GERTRUDE	✍	D	vuhn-den-behrkh, khehr-trood
VAN DEN HOVE, JOACHIM (See also Hove, Joachim van den)	✍	D	vuhn-den-hoh-vuh, yoh-ah-khim
VAN DER LEIST	♪	D	vuhn-der-lyst
VAN DER ZWART, TEUNIS	♪	D	vuhn der zvart, tö-nihs
VAN DOESELAAR, LEO	♪	D	vuhn doo-suh-lahr, lay-oh
VAN EIJCK (EYCH), JACOB (See also Eyck, Jacob van)	✍	D	vuhn-"ike," yah-kohp
VAN NOORDT, SYBRAND (See also Noordt, Sybrand van)	✍	D	vuhn-nort, sy-brahnt
VAN OORTMERSSEN, JACQUES	♪	D	vuhn ort-mer-sen, zhahk
VAN RENNES, CATHARINA (See also Rennes, Catharina van)	✍	D	vuhn-reh-ness, kah-tah-ree-nah
VAN RUTH, FRANS	♪	D	vuhn root, frahns
VAN STRALEN, ESTHER	♪	D	vuhn strah-len
VAN VUERDEN, BERNARD	✍	D	vuhn vür-den, behr-nard
VAN WAAS, GUY	♪	D	vuhn vahs, khee
VANDERNOOT, ANDRE	𝄞	D	vuhn-der-"note," ahn-dray
VÄNSKÄ, OSMO	𝄞	Fn	van-ska, ohs-moh
VARGA, LASZLO	♪	H	var-gah, lahs-loh
VÁRJON, DÉNES	♪	H	vahr-yohn, deh-nehsh
VÁSÁRY, TAMÁS	♪	H	vah-shah-ree, tah-mahsh
VAUGHN WILLIAMS, RALPH	✍	E	vawn-wihl-yuhmz, rayf (= ["dawn"], but ≠ American [ralf]. See note under "What's in a Name?")
VÉGH, SÁNDOR	𝄞	H/F	"vague", shahn-"door"
VERDI, GIUSEPPE	✍	I	vehr-dee, joo-zep-pay (If you let him rhyme with "birdie," start looking for another job.)
VEREBITS, IBOLYA	♪	H	veh-reh-bihts, ee-boy-ah
VERHÖR DES LUKULLUS (Dessau)	🎭	G	fehr-"her" dehs-loo-koo-loos
VERKLÄRTE NACHT [*Transfigured Night*] (Schoenberg)	🎸	G	fehr-klehr-tuh nahkht
VERSAILLES CHAMBER ORCHESTRA	🪑	F	vehr-"sigh"
VETÖ, TAMÁS	𝄞	H	veh-tö, tah-mahsh
VEYRON-LACROIX, ROBERT	♪	F	vay-rõhn lah-krwah (√ kwah), roh-behr
VIAGY, DENNIS	♪	H/E	vyahj
VICTORIA, TOMAS LUIS DE	✍	S	vihk-toh-ree-ah, "toe"-mahs, loo-ees deh

VIER LÄTZTE LIEDER [*Four Last Songs*] (R. Strauss)		G	feer leht-stuh lee-duh
VIERNE, LOUIS	✍	F	vyehrn, loo-ee
VIEUXTEMPS, HENRI	✍	F	vyö-tãhn (√ vyer-tahn), ãhn-ree
VILLA-LOBOS, HEITOR	✍	Pt	vee-lah loh-bohsh, hay-tor (Not Spanish <ll> = [y].)
VIRUMBRALES, LUIS LOZANO		S	vee-room-brah-lays, loo-ees loh-sah-noh (loh-thah-noh)
VISAGE NUPTIAL (Berlioz)		F	vee-zahzh nüp-syahl
VISHNEVSKAYA, GALINA	♪	R	vee-shnyehf-skah-yah, gah-lee-nuh (√ [vih-shnyehf-"sky"-uh, guh-lee-nuh])
VIVALDI, ANTONIO	✍	I	vee-vahl-dee, ahn-toh-nee-oh (√ half-English [vuh-vahl-dee], but resist full-English [vuh-vawl-dee]. Same issue as with Mahler vs. Galway, above, and Walton, below.)
VIVIANI, GIOVANNI BUONAVENTURA	✍	I	vee-vyah-nee, joh-vah-nee bwoh-nah-ven-too-rah
VLAAMS, VLAMING, VLAANDEREN	◆	D	vlahms, vlah-ming, vlahn-duh-rihn (The native Flemish names for the language, the people and the area of Flanders, the northern half of Belgium. See I Fiamminghi, above. Note <aa> = [ah] in closed syllable. There may be a connection to Flamenco in Spain.)
VLADAR, STEFAN	♪	Cz	vlah-dar, steh-fahn
VLTAVA [*The Moldau*] (Smetana)		Cz	vihl-tah-vah (You are welcome to try syllabic [l] in [vl-tah-vah]. This is the section of *Má Vlast* depicting the river flowing through the Czech countryside. It is a wandering tune in Europe. Mozart wrote variations on it, and it is also assumed to be the basis for the Israeli national anthem "Hatikva.")
VON HEUTE AUF MORGEN (Schoenberg)		G	fuhn hoy-tuh awf "more-gun"
VON KARAJAN, HERBERT (See also Karajan, H. von)		G	"fun"-kah-rah-yan, hehr-behrt (Awfully close to "carry-on.")
VON STADE, FREDERICA	♪	E/G	vahn stah-duh, freh-duh-ree-kuh (American singer of German background. √ [vahn shtah-duh].)
VUURSTEEN, FRANS	✍	D	vür-stayn, frahns

W

Name		Lang.	Pronunciation
WÄCHTER, EBERHARD (WAECHTER)	♪	G	vaykh-ter, eh-ber-hart
WAFFENSCHMIED (Lortzing)		G	vah-fehn-shmeet
WAGENAAR, DIDERIK	✍	D	vah-khuh-nahr, dee-duh-"rick"
WAGNER, RICHARD	✍	G	vahg-ner, rick-kard (rih-khard)
WAGNER, SIEGFRIED	✍	G	vahg-ner, zeeg-freed
WALDSTEIN (sonata of Beethoven)		G	vahld-shtyn (≠ "walled"-steen)
WALDTEUFEL, EMIL	✍	G/F	vahl-toy-fuhl, ay-meel (Some sources list him as French Émile. He was born in Strasbourg, and his mother was Bavarian.)
WAŁĘSA, LECH (president of Poland, 1995)	◆	P	vah-wehn-sah, lehkh (Polish <w> = [v], barred <ł> = [w] but plain <l> = [l], <ę> = [ẽhn].)
WALLENSTEIN, ALFRED	𝄞	G/E	"wall"-in-styn
WALLEZ, JEAN-PIERRE	♪ 𝄞	F	vah-lay, zhãhn pyehr
WALLFISCH, ERNST	♪	G	vahl-fish, ehrnst
WALLFISCH, RAFAEL	♪	G/E	"wall"-fish, rah-fy-el
WALPURGISNACHT (Gounod)		G	vahl-poor-gihs-nahkht
WALTER, BRUNO	𝄞	G	vahl-ter, broo-noh
WALTHER, HANS-JÜRGEN	𝄞	G	vahl-ter, hahns-yür-guhn
WALTON, WILLIAM	✍ 𝄞	E	"wall"-tuhn (See note on Vivaldi and <al>.)
WARCHAL, BOHDAN	𝄞	G/Cz	vahr-khahl, bohkh-dahn
WARSZAWA (capital of Poland)	◆	P	vahr-shah-vah (English ["War-saw"] is perfectly good.)
WATTS, ANDRE	♪	E	wahts, ahn-dray
WAXMAN, FRANZ	𝄞	G/E	"wax"-muhn, frahnz
WEBBER, JULIAN LLOYD (See Lloyd Webber, Julian)	♪	E	
WEBER, CARL MARIA VON	✍	G	vay-ber, karl, mah-ree-uh fawn (Yes, he's a he, despite Maria!)
WEBERN, ANTON	✍	G	vay-behrn, ahn-tohn
WEI, XUE	♪	C	way, shway (Some classical music journals have already dubbed him "sure way." That's as good an approximation as the one suggested here.)
WEIGLE, JÖRG-PETER	𝄞	G	vy-guhl, yerg-pay-ter
WEIKL, BERNHARD	♪	G	vy-kuhl, behrn-hart
WEILL, KURT	✍	G	"vile" (="Vait a vile: I'll be right vit you.")

Name			Pronunciation
WEIHNACHTSORATORIUM [*Christmas Oratorio*] (J.S. Bach)		G	vy-nahkhts-oh-rah-toh-ree-oom
WEINBERGER, JAROMÍR	✍	G/Cz	"vine"-behr-ger, yah-roh-meer (A Czech composer with a German last name, like Väclav Neumann.)
WEINGARTNER, FELIX	𝄞	G	"vine"-gart-ner
WEINZWEIG, JOHN	✍	E	"wine"-swyg (And not re-germanized to vyn-tsvyg.)
WEIR, GILLIAN	♪	E	wee-er, jil-ee-in
WEISSENBERG, ALEXIS	♪	E/B	"why"-sen-berg, uh-lek-sis (Pronunciation is full-English, but he is of Bulgarian background.)
WELLER, WALTER	𝄞	G	veh-ler, vahl-ter
WESTERBERG, STIG	𝄞	G	vest-er-behrg, shtihg
WIDOR, CHARLES MARIE	✍	F	vee-dor, sharl mah-ree
WIENER BLUT [*Vienna Blood*] (J. Strauss)		G	vee-ner bloot
WIENIAWSKI, HENRYK	✍	P	vyeh-nyahf-skee, hen-"rick"
WIKLUND, ADOPLH	✍	G	vik-loond, ah-dolf
WILLIAMS, SIONED	♪	E	shaw-nid (First name is Welsh, where <si> = [sh].)
WILMS, JOHAN WILLEM	✍	D	vihlms, yoh-hahn vih-luhm
WINDGASSEN, WOLFGANG	♪	G	vint-gah-suhn, vohlf-gahng
WINSCHERMANN, HELMUT	𝄞 ♪	G	vihn-sher-mahn, hehl-moot
WIRÉN , DAG	✍	Sw	vee-rehn, dahg (Swedish <w> = [v]. Ignore the accent.)
WITTE, GEORGE HENDRIK	✍	D	viht-tuh
WIXELL, INGVAR	♪	Sw	vik-suhl, ing-var
WOLF, HUGO	✍	G	vohlf, hoo-goh
WOLF-FERRARI, ERMANNO	✍	I	vohlf-feh-rah-ree, ehr-mah-noh (German father, and he added his Italian mother's name.)
WOZZECK (Berg)		G	voht-sehk
WROCŁAW (city in Poland)	◆	P	vrawt-swahf (The Germans called it Breslau.)
WUNDERLICH, FRITZ	♪	G	voon-der-lihkh, frihts
WÜRTTEMBERG CHAMBER ORCHESTRA		G	vür-tuhm-behrg

Name			Pronunciation
XIN, HUGUANG	✍	C	sheen, hoo-gwahng
XINJIANG DANCES (Xin)		C	sheen-jyahng

Y

YAKAR, RACHEL	♪	F	yah-kahr, rah-shehl (Sources are inconclusive here. Last name looks Israeli and first name may be.)
YAMASHITA, KAZUHITO & NAOKO	♪	J	yah-mahsh-tah, kah-zooH-toh & nah-oh-koh (Silent <i> between voiceless [sh—t] and [h—t] despite more familiar English [yah-mah-shee-tah"] and [kah-zoo-hee-toh]. [H] = audible [h] at end of syllable.)
YEPES, NARCISO	♪	S	yeh-pays, nar-thee-soh (From Spain, but √ [nar-see-soh].)
YIN, CHENGZONG	✍ ♪	C	yeen, chuhng-zohng
YPRES [F] = IEPER [D] (city in Belgium)	◆	F	eepr, ee-per
YSAŸE, EUGÈNE	𝄞 ♪	F	ee-zy-(uh), ö-zhehn (A Belgian violinist and conductor.)

Z

ZABALETA, NICANOR	♪	S	zah-bah-lay-tah, nee-kah-nor (√ full-Spanish is [sah-. . .].)
ZACCARIA, NICOLA	♪	Gk	zah-kah-ree-ah, nee-koh-lah
ZAGROSEK, LOTHAR	𝄞	G	tsah-groh-sehk, loh-tahr
ZAÏDE (Mozart)		I	tsah-ee-duh
ZAMFIR, GHEORGHE	✍ ♪	Rm	zahm-feer, geh-orh-geh (He goes by Zamfir only.)
ZAMKOCHIAN, BERJ	♪	E/A	zahm-"coach"-yuhn, behrzh
ZAR UND ZIMMERMANN [*King and Carpenter*] (Lortzing)		G	tsahr oont tsih-mer-mahn
ZEHETMEIR, THOMAS	♪	G	tseht-my-er, toh-mahs
ZIGEUNERLIEBE [*Gypsy Love*] (Lehár)		G	tsih-goy-ner-lee-buh
ZIGEUNERWEISEN [*In the Gypsy Manner*] (Sarasate)		G	tsih-goy-ner-vy-zihn
ZIMERMAN, KRYSTIAN	♪	P/E	zih-mer-mahn, krihs-tyahn (He's Polish, but read <zim> as [zihm].)
ZSIGMONDY, DENES	♪	H	zhihg-mohnj, deh-nesh
ZUKERMAN, PINCHAS	♪	E	zook-er-muhn, pin-khahs (= ["booker"]. Israeli living in America. [Peen-khahs], ≠ "Pinkus." Full-Hebrew [tsoo-kehr-mahn] is unnecessary.)
ZWEISTRA, AGEET	♪	D	zvy-struh, ah-khayt

MOVEMENT 3

LANGUAGE LIST

This movement repeats many of the names and terms in Movement 2 organized by language, rather than by alphabet. The aim is to provide training in recognizing each language's standard spelling strategies for making educated guesses at the sound of names that do not occur in these lists. The phonetic spellings now appear under the name so that it is clear which letters represent which sounds in a given language. The additional commentary, most alternate pronunciations, and translations of titles are not repeated. The "type" symbols, composers of pieces, and idenitifcation of geographical places are still given for reference. (People who share a last name are given in the same entry, but this does not necessarily imply a relationship between them.)

Armenian and Greek names have their own sections here, and Greek has a short section in Movement 4. Bulgarian has its own section here and comes together wtih Russian and Ukrainian in Movement 4. Estonian comes together with Finnish here and in Movement 4. The term "haček languages" has been coined here to accommodate the reading techniques of Czech, Latvian, Lithuanian, Serbo-Croatian, Slovak, and Slovenian, and all are included in this movement under Czech. Danish, Norwegian, and Swedish are all listed together as Scandinavian.

ARMENIAN

GAYNE (GAYANEH)
(Khachaturian)
gy-nuh; gah-yah-neh

KHACHATURIAN, ARAM ✍ 𝄞
kah-chah-toor-yahn, ah-rahm

KOJIAN, VARUJAN 𝄞
koh-jyahn, vah-roo-jahn

TJEKNAVORIAN, LORIS 𝄞
"check"-nuh-vor-yahn, loh-rihs

TUMAGIAN, EDUARD ♪
too-mah-jyahn

BULGARIAN

EVSTATIEVA, STEFKA ♪
ehv-stah-tyeh-vuh, stehf-kuh

GHIAUROV, NICOLAI ♪
gyah-oo-ruhf, nih-koh-ly

PLOVDIV ◆
plohv-dihv

TOMOWA-SINTOW, ANNA ♪
toh-moo-vuh seen-toof

CHINESE

Chinese names are normally given in the order "surname-given name." The same is true of Hungarian names. The names below may appear just this way on record jackets. For announcing purposes, however, turn them around to "given name-surname," as with other European names.

CHEN, GANG ✍
chuhn, gahng

CHEN, PI-HSIEN ♪
chuhn, pee-shuhn

CHU, WANHUA ✍
choo, wahn-hwah

HE, ZHANHAO ✍
hay, jahn-how

LIN, CHO-LIANG ♪
lihn, choh-lyang

LIU, ZHUANG ✍
lyoo, jwahng

MA, YO YO ♪
mah, yoh-yoh

SHENG, LIHONG ✍
shuhng, lee-hohng

WEI, XUE ♪
way, shway (= "Sure way")

XIN, HUGUANG ✍
sheen, hoo-gwahng

XINJIANG DANCES (Xin)
sheen-jyahng

YIN, CHENGZONG ✍ ♪
yeen, chuhng-zohng

CZECH AND THE HAČEK LANGUAGES

The term "haček languages" has been coined here as a cover term for the four Slavic languages (Czech, Slovak, Serbo-Croatian, Slovenian) and two Baltic languages (Lithuanian, Latvian) that use that wedge mark on <š, č, ž> for [sh, ch, zh]. (Some people call it caret or chevron, on which see page 222 and the Diacritic Review in the Coda.)They also share a few other reading techniques. The details are in Movement 4. In this list assume a name is Czech unless it is specified in brackets: [Sk.], [SC], [Sv.] and [Lt.], [Lv.].

Note on Last Names

Czech and Slovak surnames have different grammatical endings for men and women. Men have <-(sk)ý> and women have <-(sk)á>. (The accent mark is not a stress mark. Czech and Slovak stress is on the first syllable, and Slovak names may or may not have the accent mark.) For example, Firkušný's wife, sister, or daughter would be Firkušná. Names that end in a consonant are men's, and women add <ová>. The women in Dvořák's family are Dvořáková. Serbo-Croatian names often end in <-(ov)ić>, while Slovenian names end in <-ič>, but for announcing consider them both [ch]. Latvian names tend to end in <s> or <š>, while Lithuanian names tend to end in <as, is>.

BEOGRAD, BELGRAD(E) [SC]
(capital of Serbia)
bay-oh-grahd, "bell-grade"

BOSNIA [SC]
"boss"-nee-ah

BRABEC, EMANUEL
brah-bets, eh-mah-noo-el

BRATISLAVA [Sk.]
(captial of Slovakia)
brah-tih-slah-vah

BRNO (city)
ber-noh (2 syllables)

CÁPOVÁ, SILVIA
tsah-poh-vah, seel-vee-yah

ČIURLIONIS, MIKOLAUS KONSTANTINAS [Lt.]
choor-lyoh-nees, mee-koh-laws kohn-stahn-tee-nahs

CZERNY, CARL
[chehr-nee, kahrl]

DOLEZAL, VLADIMIR
doh-leh-zahl, vlah-dee-meer

DOMARKAS, JUOZAS [Lt.]
doh-mahr-kahs, yoo-oh-zahs

DUSSEK, JOHANN
doo-shehk

DVOŘÁK, ANTONIN/JAROSLAV
dvor-zhahk, ahn-toh-neen/jah-roh-slahv

DVOŘÁKOVÁ, LUDMILLA
dvohr-zhahk-oh-vah, lood-mee-lah

FIRKUŠNÝ, RUDOLF
feer-koosh-nee, roo-dohlf

FRANOVÁ, TATJANA
frah-noh-vah, tah-tyah-nah

FUČIK, JULIUS
foo-"chick, yoo-lyoos

GRUBEROVÁ, EDITA
groo-beh-roh-vah, eh-dee-tah

HAJÓSSYOVÁ, MAGDALENA
hy-yohs-yoh-vah, mahg-dah-leh-nah

HERCEGOVINA
HERZEGOVINA [SC]
"hair"-tseh-goh-vee-nah

HRVATSKA (REPUBLIKA) [SC] her-vahts-kah

JANÁČEK, LEOŠ
yah-nah-"check," lay-ohsh

JENISOVÁ, EVA
yeh-nee-soh-vah, eh-vah

JENŮFA (Janáček)
yeh-noo-fah

KALNIŅŠ, ALFREDS/IMANTS [Lv.]
kahl-neensh, ahl-freds/ee-mahnts

KANTA, LUDOVIT [Sk.]
kahn-tah, loo-doh-veet

KARADŽIĆ, RADOVAN[SC]
(leader of Bosnian Serbs)
kah-rah-jihch, rah-doh-vahn

KÁT'A KABANOVÁ (Janáček)
kah-tyah kah-bah-noh-vah

KOŠICE [Sk.] (city)
koh-shee-tseh

KOŠLER, ZDENĚK
kohsh-lehr, zdehn-yehk

KRCHEK, JAROSLAV
ker-khehk, yah-roh-slahv

KUBELIK, RAFAEL
koo-beh-"lick," rah-fy-el

KYŠELAK, LADISLAV [Sk.]
kih-sheh-lahk, lah-dih-slahv

LACHIAN DANCES (Janáček)
lah-khee-uhn

LAJOVIC, UROŠ [Sv.]
ly-oh-vuhts, oo-rohsh

LENÁRD, ONDREJ [Sk.]
leh-nard, ohn-dray

LIPOVŠEK, MIRJANA [Sv.]
lee-poh-shehk, meer-yah-nah

LUBLJANA [Sv.]
(capital of Slovenia)
loob-lyah-nah

MÁ VLAST (Smetana)
mah-vlahst

MÁCAL, ZDENĚK
mah-tsahl, zdeh-nyek
(also mah-kahl)

MARTINŮ, BOHUSLAV
mahr-tee-noo, boh-hoo-slahf

MEDIŅŠ, JĀNIS [Lv.]
meh-deensh, yah-nees

MICHALKOVÁ, ALZBETA
mee-khal-koh-vah ahlz-beh-tah

MILOŠEVIĆ, SLOBODAN [SC]
(president of Serbia, 1995)
mee-law-sheh-vihch

MORAVEC, IVAN
"more"-ah-vehts, ee-van

MOYZES, ALEXANDER [Sk.]
moy-zehs

MŠE GLAGOLSKÁ (Janáček)
msheh glah-gohl-skah

NEUMANN, VÁCLAV
noy-mahn, vaht-slahf

NOVÁK, VITEZSLAV
noh-vahk, vee-teh-slahv

OLOMOUC (city)
oh-loh-"moats"

OPALIČ, MARINKO (Sv.)
oh-pah-leech, mah-reen-koh

PEŠEK, LIBOR
peh-shek, lee-"bore"

PLZEŇ (Czech city)
"pill"-zehn^{y}

PRAHA (Prague)
prah-hah

PROHASKA, FELIX
pro-hah-skah, fay-lix

RAMOVŠ, PRIMOŽ (Sv.)
rah-mohsh, pree-mohzh

REZUCHA, BYSTRÍK [Sk.]
reh-zhoo-khah, bee-streek

RUBACKYTĖ, MÛZA [Lt.]
roo-bahts-kee-tay, moo-zah

RUSALKA (Dvořák)
roo-sahl-kuh

RŮŽIČKOVÁ, ZUZANA
roo-zheech-koh-vah, zoo-zah-nah

SLOVÁK, LADISLAV [Sk.]
sloh-vahk, lah-dih-slahv

SMETANA, BEDŘICH
smeh-tah-nah, bay-drihkh

SRBIJA, REPUBLIKA SRPSKA
[SC] ser-bee-ah, reh-poo-blee-kah serp-skah

SUK, JOSEPH
sook, yoh-zehf (="shook")

TUDJMAN, FRANJO [SC]
(president of Croatia, 1995)
tooj-mahn, frahn-yoh

TURKOVIĆ, MILAN [SC]
toor-koh-vihch, mee-lahn

TYLŠAR, ZDENĚK & BEDŘICH
teel-shahr, zdehn-yehk & beh-drzhihkh

VAJDA, JÓZSEF [Sk./H]
vy-dah, yoh-zhehf

VAJNAR, FRANTÍŠEK
vy-nahr, frahn-tee-shehk

VLADAR, STEFAN
vlah-dahr, steh-fahn

VLTAVA
(River in *Má Vlast.*)
vihl-tah-vah

DUTCH AND FLEMISH

Two notes on Dutch names with the articles "de, den, der, ter" and the preposition "van":

Sound

<van> = [vuhn] in Belgium, ["fun"] in Holland; ["van"] in the English-speaking world. That little word is not stressed in speech, nor are the articles "de, der, ter, den."

Alphabetical Order

Belgians alphabetize "van" and "de" names under <v, d>. Thus, Jo van den Hauwe would be "van den Hauwe, Jo." Sometimes the <v> is capitalized, thus Andries Van Damme is "Van Damme, Andries." Dutch alphabetize "van" names by the name itself and do not capitalize the "van," thus Cornelis van Schooneveld would be listed as "Schooneveld, Cornelis van." If the last name is all written as a single word, just use the first letter, as in "Vandernoot." English alphabetizing practice of such names is more like Belgian, and the listing in the present movement gives these under <v> or <d>.

ADDRIAENSSEN, EMANUEL
ah-dree-ahn-sen, eh-mah-noo-ehl

AMELING, ELLY
ah-muh-ling, eh-lee

AMSTERDAM LOEKI STARDUST QUARTET
loo-kee

ANDRIESSEN, HENDRIK
ahn-dree-sehn, hehn-drihk

BANK, JACQUES
bahnk, zhahk

BOGAARD, ED
boh-khard, ehd

BOSMANS, HENRIETTE
"boss"-muhns, hen-ree-eh-tuh

BOUR, ERNEST
(="flour"), ehr-nehst

BREDA (city in Holland) ◆
bray-dah

BRUGGE [D] = BRUGES [F] ◆
(city in Belgium)
broozh

BRUNNER, EDUARD ♪
brü-ner, ehd-wahrd

BUYSE, LEONE ♪
"buy"-suh, lay-oh-nuh

BYLSMA (BIJLSMA, BŸLSMA), ANNER ♪
byl-smuh, ah-ner

COENEN, LOUIS ✍
koo-nuhn, loo-ee

CONCERTGEBOUW ◆
kohn-sehrt-guh-"bow"
(-khuh-bow)

DE GROOT, FRANK ♪
duh-khroht, frahnk

DE LEEUW, TON ✍
duh-lay-ü, tohn

DE NEVE, GUIDO ♪
duh-nay-vuh, khee-doh

DE RIJKA, HELENUS ♪
duh-ry-kuh, heh-lay-nüs

DE VRIES, HANS ♪
duh-vrees, hahns

DE WAART, EDO 𝄞
duh-vart, ay-doh

DE ZEEUW, CHANTAL ♪
duh-zay-ü, shahn-tahl

DEKKERS, MINY ♪
"deck"-ers, "mini"

DEVREESE, FRÉDÉRIC ✍ 𝄞
duh-vrayz, freh-deh-reek

DORRESTEIN, JOHAN ♪
"door"-uh-styn, joh-hahn

EBBINGE, KU ♪
eh-bing-uh, kü

GENT [D] = GAND [F] ◆
(Belgium)
gehnt, khehnt

HAITINK, BERNARD 𝄞
hy-tink, ber-nahrd

HELLENDAAL, PIETER ✍
heh-len-dahl, pee-ter

HOEPRICH, THEA ♪
hoo-prihkh, tay-uh

HOOGEVEEN, RONALD ♪
hoh-khuh-vayn, roh-nuhld

HOOIJEVEEN, GODFRIED ♪
hoy-uh-vayn, khawt-freed

HUWET, GREGOR ✍
hü-vet, greh-gor

IEPER [D] = YPRES [F] ◆
(Belgium)
D: ee-per, F: eepr

IN 'T VELD, ASTRID ♪
int-veld, ah-strihd

JORDANS, WYNEKE ♪
yor-dahns, vih-nuh-kuh

KOMEN, PAUL ♪
koh-men, powl

KOOISTRA, TACO ♪
koy-strah, tah-koh

KOOPMAN, TON ♪
"cope"-muhn, "tone"

KOSTER, AB ♪
koh-ster, ahp

KREBBERS, HERMAN ♪
kreh-bers, hehr-muhn

KROEZE, MYRA ♪
kroo-zuh, mee-rah

KUIJKEN (Belgian)
ky-ken (√ koy-kehn)
BARTOLD, SIGISWALD, & WIELAND

bar-tohlt, sih-gihs-wahlt, wee-lahnd

KUYPER, ELISABETH
ky-per, eh-lee-sah-bet

LAMBOOIJ, HENK
lahm-boy, henk

LEUVEN [D] = LOUVAIN [F] (Belgium)
D: lö-vehn, F: loo-vãn

LOEVENDIE, THEO
loo-vehn-dee, tay-oh

LUIK [D] = LIÈGE [F] (city in Belgium)
"like," loyk

MAASTRICHT (city in Holland)
mah-streekht

MEIJERING, CHIEL
my-er-ing, kheel

MEPPELINK, HIEKE
mep-uh-link, hee-kuh

MEYER, BERNHARD VAN DEN SIGTENHORST
my-er, behrn-hard vuhn den sihkh-ten-horst

MIESSEN, MARIJKE
mee-suhn, mah-ry-kuh

MÖLLER, WOUTER
mö-ler, wow-ter

NIJMEGEN (city in Holland)
ny-may-khuhn

OBERSTADT, FERDINAND
oh-ber-staht, fehr-dih-nahnd

OYENS, TERA DE MAREZ
oy-uhns, tay-rah deh mah-rehz

PADBRIE, CORNELIS THIJMENSZOON
pahd-bree, kor-neh-lees ty-men-"zone"

RONTGEN, JULIUS
rohnt-khen, yül-yüs

RUPPE, CHRISTIAN FRIEDRICH
roop-puh

SAMAMA, LEO
sah-mah-mah, lay-oh

SCHAT, PETER
skhaht, pay-ter

SLOTHOUWER, JOCHEM
"slaw-tower," yoh-khuhm

SPANJAARD, ED
spahn-yard, ehd

SPANOGHE, VIVIANE
spah-noh-khuh, vee-vyahn

STANTS, IET
stahnts, eet

STUYVESANT QUARTET
sty-vuh-suhnt

SWEELINCK, JAN PIETERSZOON
svay-link, yahn "Peter's own"

TER LINDEN, JAAP
ter-"linden," yahp

TER VELDHUIS, JACOB
ter-veld-hys, yah-kohp

UITTENBOSCH, ANNEKE
"eye-ten-boss," ah-nuh-kuh

VALERIUS, ADRIANUS
vah-leh-ree-üs, ah-dree-ah-nüs

VALLET, NICOLAS
vah-let, nih-kuh-luhs

VAN ASPEREN, BOB
vuhn ahs-puh-ruhn, bohp

VAN BAAREN, KEES
vuhn bah-ruhn, "case"

VAN BEINUM, EDUARD
vuhn-by-nuhm

VAN DELDEN, LEX
vuhn-dehl-duhn

VAN DEN BERGH, GERTRUDE
vuhn-den-behrkh, khehr-trood

VAN DEN HOVE, JOACHIM
vuhn-den-hoh-vuh, yoh-ah-khim

VAN DER LEIST
vuhn-der-lyst

VAN DER ZWART, TEUNIS
vuhn der zvart, tö-nihs

VAN DOESELAAR, LEO
vuhn doo-suh-lahr, lay-oh

VAN EIJCK, JACOB
vuhn-"ike," yah-kohp

VAN NOORDT, SYBRAND
vuhn-nort, sih-brahnt

VAN OORTMERSSEN, JACQUES
vuhn ort-mer-sen, zhahk

VAN RENNES, CATHARINA
vuhn-reh-ness, kah-tah-ree-nah

VAN RUTH, FRANS
vuhn root, frahns

VAN STRALEN, ESTHER
vuhn strah-luhn

VAN VUERDEN, BERNARD
vuhn vür-den, behr-nard

VAN WAAS, GUY
vuhn vahs, khee

VANDERNOOT, ANDRE
vuhn-der-"note," ahn-dray

VUURSTEEN, FRANS
vür-stayn, frahns

WAGENAAR, DIDERIK
vah-khuh-nahr, dee-duh-"rick"

WILMS, JOHAN WILLEM
vilms, yoh-hahn vil-uhm

WITTE, GEORGE HENDRIK
viht-tuh

ZWEISTRA, AGEET
zvy-struh, ah-khayt

ENGLISH

Some of the really obvious 👓→🔔 names from Movement 2 do not reappear here. If either the surname or given name is obvious, it is given no phonetic spelling.

ABRAVENEL, MAURICE
uh-brah-vuh-nel, maw-rees

ABU HASSAN (Weber)
ah-boo hah-sahn

ADDINSELL, RICHARD
"add-in-sell," rih-cherd

ADELAIDE SYMPHONY ORCHESTRA
a-duh-layd

AEOLIAN
ay-oh-lee-uhn
CHAMBER PLAYERS
QUARTET

AGON (Stravinsky)
ay-gahn

AGRELL, DONNA
uh-grehl, dah-nuh

ALBION ENSEMBLE
"Al"-bee-uhn ahn-sahm-"bull"

ALBUQUERQUE CHAMBER ORCHESTRA
"Al"-buh-ker-kee

ALCESTIS (V. Fine)
ahl-sehs-tihs

ALDWINCKLE, ROBERT
awld-"wink"-uhl, rah-bert

ALWYN, KENNETH
"all-win" (= awl-wihn)

AMADEUS QUARTET
ah-muh-day-uhs

ANGELICUM CHAMBER ORCHESTRA
"Ann"-jeh-lih-koom

ANTHEIL, GEORGE
an-"tile," jorj

ANTIGONAE (Orff)
"Ann"-tih-guh-nee

APOLLO (Stravinsky)
uh-pah-loh

APPALACHIAN SPRING (Copland)
a-puh-lay-"shin"

ARNE, THOMAS
ahrn

AUGER, ARLEEN [F]
oh-zhay, ahr-leen

AULOS ENSEMBLE
"ow"-luhs

AZRUNI, SAHAN (Iranian)
ahz-roo-nee, sah-hahn

BANOWETZ, JOSEPH
ban-uh-"wits," joh-sehf

BARBIROLLI, JOHN
bar-buh-roh-lee

BARENBOIM, DANIEL
"barren"-boym

BARTO, TZIMON
"bar"-toh, tsee-mohn

BEAUTIFUL GALATEA, THE (von Suppé)
ga-luh-tay-uh

BELSHAZZAR'S FEAST (Walton)
"bell"-shuh-zahr,
"bell"-shaht-sahr

BERBERIAN, KATHY
ber-beh-ree-uhn, ka-thee

BERKELEY, LENNOX (British)
"bar"-klee, leh-nuhks

BERNSTEIN, LEONARD
"burn"-styn (≠steen), leh-nerd

BEZNOSIUK, LISA
behz-noh-syook, lee-suh

BILGRAM, HEDWIG
"bill"-gruhm, "head-wig"

BLEGEN, JUDITH
blay-"gun"

BLITZSTEIN, MARC
blihts-styn

BLOMSTEDT, HERBERT
bluhm-steht

BLUM, DAVID
bluhm (="plum")

BLUME, NORBERT
bloom, nor-bert

BOLCOM, WILLIAM
"bowl"-kuhm

BOLERO (Ravel)
buh-"lair"-oh

BONYNGE, RICHARD
bah-ning

BORGUE, DANIEL
borg, da-nyuhl

BOULT, ADRIAN
"bolt," ay-dree-uhn

BOURNEMOUTH (England)
born-muhth

BOWYER, KEVIN
"boy"-yer

BROWN, IONA
"eye"-oh-nuh

BRYMER, JACK
bry-mer

BRYN-JULSON, PHYLLIS
brihn-jool-suhn

BUMBREY, GRACE
bum-bree

BURDICK, JAMES OWEN
ber-dihk, jaymz oh-wen

BYRD, WILLIAM
"bird"

CALLAS, MARIA
kah-lahs, mah-ree-ah

CASALS FESTIVAL ORCHESTRA
kuh-sahlz

CHEIFITZ, HAMILTON
shay-fits

CHENEY, AMY MARCY
chay-nee

CHILINGIRIAN STRING QUARTET
"chillin'-gear"-ee-uhn

CHORZEMPA, DANIEL
kor-zehm-puh

CLARINADE (Gould)
kla-rih-nahd

CLIBURN, VAN
kly-"burn," "van"

COLOGNE (Köln, Germany)
kuh-lohn

CONDIE, RICHARD P.
kahn-"dye"

CONLON, JAMES
kahn-lun

COPLAND, AARON
"cope"-lund, a-ruhn
(= "baron")

CORIGLIANO, JOHN [I]
kor-ree-lyah-noh, jahn

COSTELLO, MARILYN
kah-steh-loh, ma-rih-lihn

COWELL, HENRY
"cow"-uhl

CURZON, CLIFFORD
ker-zuhn, klih-ferd

DAPHNIS AND CHLOË (Ravel)
daf-nihs and kloh-ee

DAVIS, COLIN
kah-lin or kull-in

DAVIS, IVAN
"eye"-vihn

DE PEYER, GERVASE
duh-py-er, jer-vis

DE PRIEST, BRIAN
duh preest

DELIUS, FREDERICK
dee-lee-"us"

DELLO JOIO, NORMAN
deh-luh-joy-oh

DELOS CHAMBER ORCHESTRA
deh-lohs

DIDO AND AENEAS (Purcell)
"die-dough" & "a-knee-us"

DONATH, HELEN [G]
doh-naht, heh-luhn

DOWLAND, JOHN
(√ both "Dow" and "dough.")

DOWN THE RIVER VÁH (Moyzes) ...vahkh

DUPRE, JACQUELINE
doo-pray, "jack"-lihn

DURAN, ELENA
door-uhn, uh-lay-nuh

DUSSEK, MICHAEL
doo-sehk

EFFRON, DAVID
"F-run"

ELIAS, ROSALIND
uh-ly-us, rah-zuh-lind

EPSTEIN, DAVID
ehp-styn

ERICKSON, GRETA
eh-rihk-suhn, greh-tuh

ERXLEBEN, MICHAEL
"irks"-lay-ben, my-kuhl

ESTERHAZY ORCHESTRA
ehs-ter-hah-zee

EUGEN(E) ONEGIN (Tchaikovsky)
yoo-jeen oh-nay-gihn

FAÇADE (Walton)
fuh-sahd

FERRIER, KATHLEEN
feh-ree-er, kath-leen

FIDELIO (Beethoven)
fih-day-lee-oh

FIEDLER, ARTHUR
"feed"-ler

FIERRO, CHARLES
fyeh-roh

FINZI, GERALD
"fin"-zee

FLEISCHER, LEON
fly-sher, lee-ahn

FORRESTER, MAUREEN
faw-rest-er, maw-reen

FOSS, LUKAS
(="toss," loo-"kiss")

FRAGER, MALCOLM
fray-ger, mal-kuhm

FRANCIS, ALUN
(= "Alan")

GALWAY, JAMES
gawl-way, jaymz

GEMER DANCES (Moyzes)
geh-mehr

GILES, ANNE DIENER
jylz, an dee-ner

GILGAMESH (Martinů)
gihl-guh-"mesh"

GLAGOLITIC MASS (Janáček)
gla-guh-lih-tihk

GOLSCHMANN, VLADIMIR
"goal"sh-mahn, vla-duh-meer

GOODE, RICHARD
(="good")

GOOSENS, EUGENE
goo-sinz, yoo-jeen

GOTTSCHALK, LOUIS MOREAU
gaht-shawk (= "hawk"), loo-ee muh-roh

GOULD, GLENN/MORTON
(goold)

GRAINGER, PERCY
grayn-jer

GRIMINELLI, ANDREA
grih-mih-neh-lee, an-dree-uh

GRISELDA (Bononcini)
gruh-zehl-duh

GROFÉ, FERDE
grof-fay, ferdy

GUNZENHAUSER, STEPHEN
("guns-in"-how-zer)

HAIMOVITZ, MATT
hy-muh-vits

HALSTEAD, ANTHONY
"haul"-stehd

HAMKE, SONYA
hahm-kuh, sohn-yuh

HÄNDL, WALTER
hen-dull, "wall"-ter

HARNARI, JULIA
har-nah-ree, jool-yuh

HARNOY, OFRA [Is]
har-noy, oh-fruh

HARRELL, LYNN
ha-ruhl, lihn

HEIFETZ, DANIEL
"high-fits"

HODDINOTT, ALUN
hah-dih-naht, a-luhn

HOKANSON, LEONARD
hoh-kuhn-suhn

HOLST, GUSTAV
hohlst, goo-stahf

HORENSTEIN, JASCHA
hor-in-styn, yah-shuh

HOROWITZ, VLADIMIR
hor-uh-"wits," vla-duh-meer

HOVANHESS, ALAN
"hoe"-vah-nehs, a-luhn

INBAL, ELIAHU [Is]
ihn-bahl, eh-lee-yah-hoo

INCUBUS (Webern)
"ink"-yuh-"bus"

JENKINS, NEWELL
noo-uhl

JOB, A MASK FOR DANCING (Vaughn Williams)
johb

JOPLIN, SCOTT
jah-plihn, skaht

KALISH, GILBERT
kay-lish, "Gilbert"

KATCHEN, JULIUS
"catch"-uhn, joo-lee-uhs

KATSARIS, CYPRIEN [F]
kah-tsah-rees, "sip"-ree-uhn

KETELBEY, ALBERT W.
kuh-tel-bee

KEYTE, CHRISTOPHER
keet, krihs-tuh-fer

KIPNIS, IGOR
kip-nis, ee-gor

KIRCHNER, LEON
kersh-ner, lee-ahn

KLINTCHAROVA, SUSANNA
klin-chah-roh-vah, soo-zah-nuh

KRAUS, LILI
krows (= "grouse")

KRAUSE, JANET
krows

LADY MACBETH OF MTSENSK (Shostakovich)
mtsehnsk

LAREDO, JAIME
luh-ray-doh, jay-mee

LEE, NOËL
lee, noh-ehl

LEHMANN, LOTTE
lay-mahn, lah-tuh

LENYA, LOTTE
layn-yuh, lah-tuh

LEPPARD, RAYMOND
leh-pahrd

LESLIE, ALAYNE
les-lee, uh-layn

LEVANT, OSCAR
luh-vant, ah-sker

LEVI, YOEL [Israeli]
leh-vee, yoh-ehl

LEVINE, JAMES
luh-"vine"

LHEVINNE, JOSEPH
luh-veen, joh-zuhf

LICAD, CECILE
lee-kahd, suh-seel

LITOLFF, HENRY CHARLES
lih-tohlf

LOEFFLER, CHARLES MARTIN
löf-ler, charlz mar-tin

LOUGHRAN, JAMES
"lock"-run

LUCERNE FESTIVAL STRINGS
loo-sern

MACKERRAS, SIR CHARLES
muh-ka-ruhs

MARKEVITCH, IGOR
mar-kay-vich, ee-gor
(√ mar-kuh-vich)

MARRINER, NEVILLE
"mariner," neh-vuhl

MAVRA (Stravinsky)
mahv-ruh

MEHTA, ZUBIN
may-tuh, zoo-bin

MENGES, HERBERT
meng-is, "Herbert"

MENNIN, PETER
meh-nin, "Peter"

MENOTTI, GIAN CARLO
muh-"not"-ee, jahn kar-loh

MENUHIN, YEHUDI
men-yoo-in, yuh-hoo-dee

MEPHISTO WALTZ (Liszt)
muh-fihs-toh

MESTER, JORGE
mehs-ter, jorj

METSON, MARIAN RUHL
("rule")

MIKADO (THE)
(Gilbert and Sullivan)
muk-kah-doh

MIKROKOSMOS (Bartók)
mee-kroh-kohs-mohs

MILNES, SHERRILL
milnz, sheh-ruhl

MILSTEIN, NATHAN
mil-styn, nay-thuhn

MINKOWSKI, MARC
meen-"cow"-skee, mark

MOFFO, ANNA
mah-foh

MOLL, PHILLIP
"mole"

MORATH, MAX
muh-"wrath"

MORELLI, FRANK
muh-reh-lee

MOROSS, JEROME
maw-rohs

MUNICH PRO ARTE ORCHESTRA
myoo-nihk proh ahr-tay
(≠ G: München)

MUSGRAVE, THEA
muhz-"grave," thee-uh

NAUSICAA (Glanville-Hicks)
naw-"sick-a" (-sih-kay-uh)

NIGHT ON MT. TRIGLAV
(Rimsky-Korsakov)
tree-glahv

NORMAN, JESSYE
jeh-see

OHLSSON, GARRICK
ohl-suhn

OPPENS, URSULA
ah-pins

ORMANDY, EUGENE
or-muhn-dee, yoo-jeen

PANITZ, MURRAY
pan-ihts

PELLEAS AND MELISANDE
(Schoenberg)
peh-lee-ahs and meh-lee-zahnd

PENNARIO, LEONARD
peh-nah-ree-oh

PERAHIA, MURRAY
puh-ry-uh (= "pariah"), muh-ree

PERESS, MAURICE
peh-rehs, maw-rees

PERLMAN, ITZHAK [Is]
"pearl"-muhn, yihts-khahk

PERSÉPHONE (Stravinsky)
per-seh-fuh-nee

PINNOCK, TREVOR
"pin"-uhk, treh-ver

POLOVETSIAN DANCES
(Borodin)
puh-luh-"vets"-ee-uhn

PRAGUE
prahg (Cz. is Praha = [prah-hah].)

PREVIN, ANDRE
preh-vin, ahn-dray

PRICE, LEONTYNE
prys, lay-uhn-teen

PURCELL, HENRY
"purr"-suhl

PURVIS, WILLIAM
"purr"-vihs

PYGMALION (Rameau)
"pig"-may-lee-uhn

QUATUOR MUIR
(read as [myoor] quartet)

RADETZKY MARCH
(J. Strauss, Sr.)
rah-deht-skee

RAHBARI, ALEXANDER
raH-bah-ree

REICH, STEVE
ryk, steev

RESNIK, REGINA
rehz-"nick," ruh-jee-nuh

RIEGEL, KENNETH
"regal"

RISE AND FALL OF THE CITY OF MAHAGONNY (Weill)
... mah-hah-goh-nee

ROBESON, PAUL
"robe-sun," pawl

ROBISON, PAULA
roh-bih-"sun," "paw"-luh

ROBLES, MARISA
roh-buhlz, muh-rih-suh

RODELINDA (Handel)
roh-duh-"Linda"

RODEO (Copland)
roh-day-oh

ROGG, LIONEL
"rogue," ly-uh-nuhl

ROTH, DANIEL
rawth

ROWLAND, GILBERT
"row"-luhnd

RUBBRA, EDMUND
"rub"-ruh

RUBINSTEIN, ARTUR
roo-bin-styn, ahr-toor

RUDEL, JULIUS
roo-dehl

SALERNO-SONNENBERG, NADJA
sah-lehr-noh soh-nen-berg, nah-dyuh

SALOME (R. Strauss)
sah-luh-may

SAVITRI (Holst)
sah-vee-"tree"

SCHEHERAZADE (Rimsky-Korsakov)
sheh-heh-ruh-zahd

SCHELOMO (Bloch)
shloh-moh

SCHERMERHORN, KENNETH
sher-mer-horn

SCHICKELE, PETER
shick-uh-lee, pee-ter

SCHNEIDER, MISCH
shny-der, mihsh

SCHOENFELD, PAUL
"shone"-feld

SCHRADER, DAVID
shray-der

SCHUMAN, WILLIAM
"shoe"-muhn

SCHWARZ, GERARD
shworts, juh-rahrd

SEQUOIA STRING QUARTET
suh-kwoy-ah

SERKIN, PETER
"sir"-kin, pee-ter

SERSE or XERXES (Handel)
zerk-seez

SILVERSTEIN, JOSEPH
sihl-ver-styn

SLOWICK, KENNETH
sloh-wihk

SOBOL, LAWRENCE
"sew"-buhl

SOLOMON, YONTY
sah-luh-muhn, yahn-tee

STEINBERG, WILLIAM
styn-berg

STICH-RANDALL, TERESA
"stick"-ran-duhl, tuh-ree-suh

STOLTZMAN, RICHARD
stohlts-muhn

TE KANAWA, KIRI
teh-kah-nuh-wah, kee-ree

TEITOV, FRANCES
"tie"-tawv

TERFEL, BRYN [W]
tehr-vuhl, brihn

TERPSICORE (Praetorius, Handel)
terp-"sick"-uh-ree

TOUREL, JENNIE
tuh-rehl or too-rehl

TRAUBEL, HELEN
trow-buhl

TROYANOS, TATIANA [Gk]
troy-ah-nohs, tah-tyah-nuh

TURANGALÎLA (Messiaen)
too-rahn-guh-lee-lah

ULALUME (J. Holbrooke)
yoo-luh-loom

VALENTE, BENITA
vuh-len-tee, buh-nee-tuh

VAUGHN WILLIAMS, RALPH [Brit]
vawn-wihl-yuhmz, rayf

VON STADE, FREDERICA
vahn stah-duh, freh-duh-ree-kuh

WALLENSTEIN, ALFRED
"wall"-in-styn

WALLFISCH, RAFAEL
"wall"-fish, rah-fy-ehl

WATTS, ANDRE
wahts, ahn-dray

WAXMAN, FRANZ
"wax"-muhn, frahnz

WEINZWEIG, JOHN
"wine"-swyg

WEIR, GILLIAN
wee-er, jih-lee-ihn

WEISSENBERG, ALEXIS
"why"-sehn-berg, uh-lek-sis

WIFE OF MARTIN GUERRE (Bergsma) gehr

WILLIAMS, SIONED
shaw-nid [W]

ZAMKOCHIAN, BERJ [A]
zahm-"coach"-yuhn, behrzh

ZIMERMAN, KRYSTIAN [P]
zih-mer-mahn, krihs-tyahn

ZUKERMAN, EUGENIA & PINCHAS
zook-er-muhn, yoo-jeen-yuh & pin-khahs

FINNISH AND ESTONIAN

HALSVUO, PEKKA
hahls-voo-oh, peh-kah

JÄRVI, NEEME (Es)
yehr-vee, nay-meh

KAMU, OKKO
kah-moo, oh-koh

KLAMI, UUNO
klah-mee, oo-noh

KRAUSE, TOM
krow-suh, "Tom"

KULLERVO (Sibelius)
koo-lehr-voh

LEMMINKÄINEN SUITE (Sibelius)
leh-mihn-ky-nen

PÄRT, ARVO (Es)
pehrt, ahr-voh

SALONEN, ESA-PEKKA
sah-loh-nen, eh-sah peh-kah

SIBELIUS, JEAN (also Jan)
sih-bay-lyuhs, zhãhn (yahn)

TELVELA, MARTTI
tehl-veh-lah, mar-tee

TÖNKÖ, AGNES
tön-kö

VÄNSKÄ, OSMO
vayn-skya, ohs-moh

FRENCH

ADÉLAIDE OU LA LANGAGE DES FLEURS (Ravel)
ah-deh-lehd oo-lah-lãhn-gahj deh flör

ADRIANA LECOUVREUR (Cilea)
ah-dree-ah-nah luh-koov-rör

ALAIN, MARIE-CLAIRE
ah-lãn, mah-ree-klehr

AMÉRIQUES (Varèse)
ah-meh-reek

AMOUR ET SON AMOUR (Franck)
ah-moor ay-sawn-ah-moor

ANDRÉ, MAURICE
ãhn-dray, moh-rees

ANDREA CHÉNIER (Giordano)
ahn-dray-ah shehn-yay

ANIMAUX MODÈLES (Poulenc)
ah-nee-moh moh-dehl

ARBEAU'S ORCHÉSOGRAPHIE
ar-bohz or-keh-zoh-grah-fee

ARNAUD, LÉO
ahr-noh, lay-oh

AUBER, DANIEL FRANÇOIS
oh-"bear," dahn-"yell" frãhn-swah

BACCHUS ET ARIANE
(Roussel)
bah-kűs ay ah-ree-ahn

BACQUIER, GABRIEL
bah-kyay, gah-bree-ehl

BARBOTEU, GEORGES
bar-boh-tö, zhorzh

BARDON, PIERRE
bar-dõhn, pyehr

BASTIEN ET BASTIENNE
(Mozart)
bah-styẽh ay-bah-styehn

BEAUX ARTS TRIO
boh-zahr

BERLIOZ, HECTOR
behr-lee-ohz, ek-tor

BERNARD, ANDRE
behr-nahr, ãhn-dray

BEROFF, MICHEL
beh-rawf, mee-shel

BESNARD, GUY
beh-nahr, gee

BIZET, GEORGES
bee-zay, zhorzh

BLAVET, MICHEL
blah-vay, mee-shel

BOËLLMANN, LÉON
bwehl-mãhn, lay-õhn

BOIELDIEU, FRANÇOIS
bwahl-dyö , frãhn-swah

BOK, HENRI
bohk, ãhn-ree

BOLLING, CLAUDE
"bowling," "clawed"

BOULANGER, LILI/NADIA
boo-lãhn-zhay, lih-lee/nah-dyah

BOULEZ, PIERRE
boo-lehz, pyehr

BOURNE, JEAN-LUC
boorn, zhãhn-lük

BOURRÉ
boo-ray

BRANSLE
brãhn-luh

BRUGES [F] = BRUGGE [D]
(city in Belgium)
broozh

CAMPRA, ANDRÉ
kahm-prah, ãhn-dray

CAPITOLE DE TOULOUSE ORCHESTRA
kah-pee-tohl duh too-looz

CARDILLAC (Hindemith)
kahr-dee-yahk

CASADESUS
GABY, JEAN, ROBERT
kah-sah-duh-sü
gah-bee, zhãhn, roh-behr

CASTOR ET POLLUX
(Rameau)
kah-"store" ay-poh-lüks

CÉPHALE ET PROCRIS OU L'AMOUR CONJUGAL
(Grétry)
seh-fahl ay-proh-kree oo-lah-moor kõhn-zhü-gahl

CHABRIER, EMANUEL
shah-bree-ay, ee-"man"-yoo-el (√ shah-bree-ay)

CHACONNE
shah-kohn
shuh-kahn

CHAILLY, RICCARDO [I]
"shy"-yee, rih-"card"-oh

CHAMBRON, JACQUES
shãhm-brõhn, zhahk

CHAMINADE, CECILE
shah-mee-nahd, suh-"seal"

CHARPENTIER, MARC-ANTOINE
shar-pãhn-tyay, mark ãhn-twahn

CHAUSSON, ERNEST
"show"-sõhn, ehr-nest

CHERRIER, SOPHIE
sheh-ree-ay

CHOÉPHORES (Milhaud)
koh-ay-"four"

CHOPIN, FREDERIC [P]
"show"-pãn, freh-duh-reek

CIRQUE DE DEUX (Gounod)
seerk duh dö

CLAVECIN
klah-vuh-sãn

CLUYTENS, ANDRE
klü-tãhn, ãhn-dray

COCHEREAU, PIERRE
koh-shuh-roh, pyehr

COLLARD, JEAN-PHILLIPE
koh-lahr, zhãhn fee-leep

CONTES D'HOFFMAN (Offenbach)
kõhnt "doff"-mahn

CORBOZ, MICHEL
kor-bohz, mee-shehl

CORRÉ, PHILLIPE
"core"-ay, fee-leep

CORTOT, ALFRED
kor-"toe"

COUPERIN, FRANÇOIS & LOUIS
"cooper"-rãn, frãhn-swah & loo-ee

CRESPIN, REGINE
kres-pãn, reh-zheen

CRIME ET CHÂTIMENT (Honegger)
kreem ay shah-tee-mãhn

CUI, CÉSAR [R]
kü-ee, seh-zahr

D'ANGLEBERT, JEAN HENRI
dãhn-guhl-behr, zhan-ãhn-ree

D'INDY, VINCENT
dãn-dee, vãn-sãhn

DANSES CONCERTANTES (Stravinsky)
dãhns kõhn-sehr-tãhnt

DEBOST, MICHEL
duh-bohs, mee-shel

DEBUSSY, CLAUDE
duh-bü-see (√ deh-byoo-see)

DEGENNE, PIERRE
duh-zhehn, pyehr

DELALANDE, MICHEL-RICHARD
duh-lah-lahnd, mee-shehl ree-shar

DELIBES, LEO
duh-leeb, lay-oh

DEPLUS, GUY
duh-plü, gee

DERVAUX, PIERRE
dehr-voh

DES PREZ, JOSQUIN
deh "pray", zhohs-kãn

DEVIENNE, FRANÇOIS
duh-vyehn, frãhn-swah

DIABLE À QUATRE (Adam)
dyah-bluh ah-kah-truh

DIANE ET ACTÉON (Rameau)
dee-ahn ay ahk-tay-õhn

DON QUICHOTTE (Massenet)
dõhn kee-"shut"

DOUATTE, ROLAND
doo-watt roh-lãhn

DREYFUS, HUGUETTE
dray-füs, ü-geht

DU FOND DE L'ABÎME
(L. Boulanger)
dü-fõhn duh-lah-beem

DUFAY, GUILLAUME
dü-fy, gee-yohm

DUKAS, PAUL
dü-kah, "pole" (√ "Paul")

DUPHIL, MONIQUE
dü-feel, moh-neek

DUPRÉ, MARCEL
dü-pray, mar-sehl

DURUFLE, MAURICE
dü-rü-flay, moh-rees

DUTILLEUX, HENRI
dü-tee-lyö, ãhn-ree

DUTOIT, CHARLES
dü-twah, sharl

ECLAT (Boulez)
ay-klah

ENSEMBLE BELLA MUSICA
DE VIENNE
ãhn-sãhm-bluh beh-luh moo-zee-kuh duh vyehn

ENTREMONT, PHILIPPE
ãhn-truh-mõhn, fee-leep
(√ ãhn-truh-mõhn)

ESQUISSES
ehs-kees

ÉTUDES D'EXECUTION
TRANSCENDANTE (Liszt)
ay-tüd "deck"-seh-kü-syõhn
trãhn-sãhn-dãhnt

EXERJEAN, EDOUARD
eg-zehr-zhãhn, ed-wahr

FAURÉ, GABRIEL
foh-ray, gah-bree-ehl
(√ gah-bree-ehl)

FEUILLE D'IMAGES
(L. Aubert)
föy dee-mahzh

FEVRIER, JACQUES
fehv-ree-yay, zhahk

FIGURE HUMAINE (Poulenc)
fee-gür ü-mehn

FISTOULARI, ANATOLE [R]
"fist"-oo-lah-ree, ah-nah-"toll"

FOURNET, JEAN
forn-nay, zhãhn

FOURNIER, ANDRE & PIERRE
foor-nyay, ãhn-dray & pyehr

FRANCK, CÉSAR
frãhnk, say-zar

FROMENT, LOUIS DE
froh-mãhn, loo-ee duh

GAND [F] = GENT [D]
(Belgian city)
gehnt

GASPARD DE LA NUIT (Ravel)
gahs-pahr duh-lah-nüee/nwee

GAVOTTE
gah-voht
guh-vaht

GIGUE
zheeg

GISELLE (Adam)
zhih-zehl

GOUNOD, CHARLES
goo-noh, sharl

GRANDE BRETÈCHE (Claflin)
grãhnd breh-tehsh

GRAPPELLI, STEPHANE
grah-peh-lee, steh-fahn

GRUMIAUX TRIO
groo-mee-oh

GRUMIAUX, ARTUR
grü-myoh, ahr-toor

GUILLAUME TELL (Rossini)
gee-yohm tehl

HAUTBOIS
oh-bwah = oboe

HÉRODIADE (Massenet)
eh-"rode"-yahd

HÉROLD, LOUIS JOSEPH
eh-"roll," loo-ee zho-zehf

HEURE ESPAGNOLE (Ravel)
er eh-spahn-yohl

HIPPOLYTE ET ARICIE (Rameau)
ee-poh-leet ay ah-ree-see

HOLMÈS, AUGUSTA
ohl-mays, oh-güs-tah

HONEGGER, ARTHUR
oh-neh-gehr, ar-toor

HOUBART, FRANÇOIS-HENRI
oo-bahr, frãhn-swah-ãhn-ree

IBERT, JACQUES
ee-"bare," zhahk

IMAGES (Debussy)
ee-mahzh

IPHIGÉNIE EN TAURIDE (Glück)
ee-fee-zhay-nee ãhn-toh-reed

JALONS (Xenakis)
zhah-lõhn

JARDIN AUX LILAS (Chausson)
zhahr-dãn oh-lee-lah

JEUX (Debussy)
zhö

JOLIVET, ANDRÉ
zhoh-lee-vay, ãhn-dray

KOECHLIN, CHARLES
kösh-lãn, shahrl

L'ARLESIENNE SUITE (Bizet)
lahr-lay-zyehn

L'ENFANCE DU CHRIST (Berlioz)
lãhn-fãhns dü-kreest

L'ENFANT ET LES SORTILÈGES (Ravel)
lãhn-fãhn ay-lay-sohr-tee-lehzh

L'HISTOIRE DU SOLDAT (Stravinsky)
lees-twahr-dü-sohl-dah

LA BELLE HÉLÈNE (Offenbach)
lah-"bell"-ay-lehn

LA BOÎTE À JOUJOUX (Debussy)
lah-bwaht-ah-zhoo-zhoo

LA BOURRÉE FANTASQUE (Chabrier)
lah-boo-<u>ray</u> fahn-<u>tahsk</u>

LA BOUTIQUE FANTASQUE (Respighi)
lah-boo-<u>teek</u> fahn-<u>tahsk</u>

LA CRÉATION DU MONDE (Milhaud)
lah-kray-ah-<u>syõhn</u> dü <u>mohnd</u>

LA DAMNATION DE FAUST (Berlioz)
lah-dahm-nah-<u>syõhn</u> duh-<u>fowst</u>

LA FILLE DU RÉGIMENT (Donizetti)
lah-<u>fee</u> dü-reh-zhee-<u>mãhn</u>

LA FILLE MAL GARDÉE (Hérold)
fee-mahl-gahr-<u>day</u>

LA GAITÉ PARISIENNE (Offenbach)
lah-gay-<u>tay</u> puh-ree-<u>zyehn</u>

LA GRANDE DUCHESSE DE GÉROLSTEIN (Offenbach)
lah-grãhnd dü-<u>shehs</u>-duh zhay-rohl-<u>styn</u>

LA GRANDE MESSE DES MORTS (Berlioz)
lah-grãhnd-<u>mehs</u> day-<u>mohr</u>

LA GUIRLANDE (Rameau)
lah-geer-<u>lãhnd</u>

LA MER (Debussy)
lah-"mare"

LA SOURCE
lah-<u>soors</u>

LA WALLY (Catalani)
lah-vah-<u>lee</u>

LAKMÉ (Delibes)
<u>lahk</u>-may *or* lahk-<u>may</u>

LALO, EDOUARD
lah-"<u>low</u>," ed-<u>wahr</u>

LAMOUREUX ORCHESTRA
lah-moo-<u>rö</u>

LANIAU, PIERRE
lah-<u>nyoh</u>, pyehr

LARRIEU, MAXENCE
lah-<u>ryö</u>, mahk-<u>sãhns</u>

LASKINE, LILLY
lahs-<u>keen</u>, <u>lee</u>-lee

LATRY, OLIVIER
lah-<u>tree</u>, oh-lee-<u>vyay</u>

LAUSANNE CHAMBER ORCHESTRA
loh-<u>zahn</u>

LE BAISER DE LA FÉE (Stravinsky)
luh-beh-<u>zay</u> duh-lah-<u>fay</u>

LE BOEUF SUR LE TOIT (Milhaud)
luh-<u>böf</u> sür-luh-<u>twah</u>

LE BOURGEOIS GENTILHOMME (Lully; R. Strauss)
luh-boor-<u>zhwah</u> zhãhn-tee-"<u>yum</u>"

LE CHASSEUR MAUDIT (Franck)
luh-shah-<u>ser</u> moh-<u>dee</u>

LE COMTE ORY (Rossini)
luh-kohmt oh-<u>ree</u>

LE COQ D'OR (Rimsky-Korsakov)
luh-<u>kohk</u> "<u>door</u>"

LE MAIR, EVERT
luh-<u>mehr</u>, eh-<u>vehr</u>

LE QUATUOR POUR LA FIN DU TEMPS (Messiaen)
luh-kwah-tü-ohr poor lah-fãn dü-tãhn

LE SACRE DU PRINTEMPS (Stravinsky)
luh-sah-kruh dü-prãn-tãhn

LE TOMBEAU DE CHATEAUBRIAND (L. Aubert)
luh-tohm-boh duh-shah-toh-bree-yãhn

LE TRIOMPHE DE L'AMOUR (Lully)
luh-tree-ohmf duh-lah-moor

LECLAIR, JEAN MARIE
luh-klair, zhãhn mah-ree

LES ANNEÉS DE PÈLERINAGE (Liszt)
lehz-ah-nay duh-pehl-ree-nahzh

LES BICHES (Poulenc)
leh-beesh

LES HUGUENOTS (Meyerbeer)
lay-ü-guh-noh

LES INDES GALANTES (Rameau)
lehz-ãnd gah-lãhnt

LES NOCES (Stravinsky)
leh-nohs

LES PATINEURS (Waldteufel)
leh-pah-tee-nör

LES PÊCHEURS DE PERLES (Bizet)
lay-peh-"sure" duh-pehrl

LES RUSES D'AMOUR (Glazunov)
lay-rüz-dah-moor

LES SYLPHIDES (Chopin)
lay-"sill-feed"

LES TROYENS (Berlioz)
lay-trwah-yẽhn

LIÈGE [F] = LUIK [D] (city in Belgium)
lyehzh

LIVRE DU SAINT-SACRAMENT (Messiaen)
leev-ruh dü sãn-sah-kruh-mãhn

LOEILLET, JEAN-BAPTISTE
lö-yay, zhãhn bah-teest

LOUP (Dutilleux)
loo

LOUVAIN [F] = LEUVEN [D] (city in Belgium)
F: loo-vãn D: lö-vehn

LT. KIJÉ (Prokofiev)
loo-"tenant" kee-zhay

LULLY, JEAN-BAPTISTE
lü-lee (√ loo-lee), zhãhn bah-teest

LUTH = lute

MA MÈRE L'OYE (Ravel)
mah-"mare"-lwah

MACHAUT, GUILLAUME DE
mah-"show," gee-yohm duh

MALGOIRE, JEAN-CLAUDE
mahl-gwahr, zhãhn-"clawed"

MAMELLES DE TIRÉSIAS (Poulenc)
mah-mehl duh tee-ray-zyahs

MANON /LESCAUT
mah-nõhn/lehs-koh

MARAIS, MARIN
mah-ray, mah-rãn

MARTINON, JEAN
mahr-tee-nõhn, zhãhn

MASSENET, JULES
mahs-nay, zhül (√ zhool)

MATEAU SANS MAÎTRE (Boulez)
mah-toh sãhn-meh-truh

MATHIS, EDITH
mah-tees, ay-deet

MÉDÉE (Charpentier)
meh-day

MERVILLE, FRANÇOIS
mehr-veel, frãhn-swah

MESSIAEN, OLIVIER
"messy"-ãn oh-lee-vyay

MIGNON (Thomas)
meen-yõhn

MILHAUD, DARIUS
mee-yoh, da-ree-"us"

MONTEUX, PIERRE
mohn-tö (=ter), pyehr

MORCEAU(X)
"more-sew"

MORET, NORBERT
moh-ray, nor-behr

MOURET, JEAN JOSEPH
moh-ray, zhãhn zhoh-zehf

MUNCH, CHARLES
münsh, shahrl

NICOLET, AURÈLE
nick-oh-lay, oh-rehl

OCTANDRE (Varèse)
ohk-tahn-druh

ORCHESTRE (DE CHAMBRE)
or-keh-struh/or-kehst
(duh-shahm-bruh)

ORCH. DE L'ASSOCIATION DES CONCERTS LAMOUREUX
...duh lah-soh-see-ahs-yõhn
deh-kohn-sehr lah-moo-rer

ORCH. DE CH. DE LA FONDATION GULBENKIAN DE LISBONNNE
...duh-lah fohn-dah-syõhn
gool-behn-kee-uhn duh leez-buhn

ORCH. DE CH. DE LAUSANNE
read as "low"-zahn chamber orchestra

ORCH. DE L'OPERA DE LYON
Read as "lee-õhn opera orchestra"

ORCH. DE LA SUISSE ROMANDE
...duh lah swees roh-mahnd

ORCHESTRE SYMPHONIQUE D'U.R.S.S.
"USSR Symphony Orchestra"

OUSSET, CECILE
oo-say, suh-seel

PAILLARD, JEAN-FRANCOIS
py-yahr, zhãhn-frãhn-swah

PARADE (Satie)
pah-rahd

PARAY, PAUL
puh-ray, "Paul"

PAS D'ACIER (Prokofiev)
pah-dah-syay

PAS DE DIX (Glazunov)
pah-duh-dees

PAVANE POUR UNE INFANTE DEFUNTE. (Ravel)
puh-vahn poor ün ãn-fahnt
deh-fünt

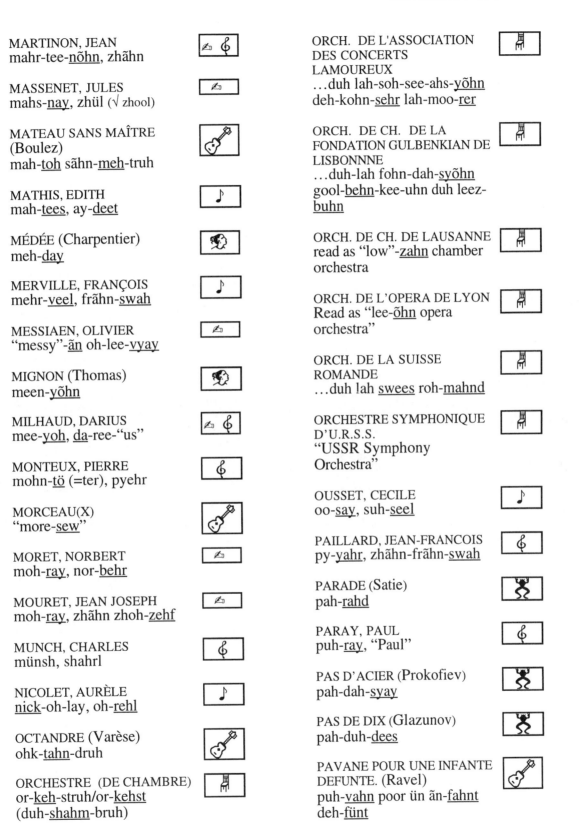

PÉDARD, ETIENNE
peh-dahr, ay-tyen

PIERLOT, PIERRE
pyehr-loh, pyehr

PIERROT LUMAIRE (Schoenberg)
pyeh-roh lü-"mare"

PIQUE DAME (Tchaikovsky)
peek-dahm

PLI SELON PLI (Boulez)
plee suh-lõhn plee

POULENC, FRANCIS
poo-lãnk, frãhn-sees

PRÉ AUX CLERC (Hérold)
pray oh-klehr

PRÉLUDE À L'APRÈS-MIDI D'UN FAUNE (Debussy)
pray-lüd ah-lah-preh-mee-dee dũhn-"phone"

PRÊTRE, GEORGES
preh-truh, zhorzh

QUATUOR YSAŸE
kwah-tü-ohr ee-zy-uh

RAMPAL, JEAN-PIERRE
rahm-pahl, zhãhn pyehr

RAVEL, MAURICE
rah-vehl, moh-rees

RELÂCHE (Satie)
ruh-lahsh

ROMBOUT, ERNEST
rohm-boo, ehr-nest

ROUSSEL, ALBERT
roo-"sell," ahl-behr

ROUSSET, CHRISTOPHE
roo-say, kree-stawf

SAINT-SAËNS, CAMILLE
sãn-sãhns, kah-mee

SATIE, ERIK
sah-tee, eh-"rick"

SCÈNES DE BALLET (Glazunov)
sehn-duh-bah-lay

SCHUB, ANDRE MICHEL
shoob, ahn-dray mee-"shell"

SOUZAY, GERARD
soo-zay, zheh-rahr

SUISSE ROMANDE ORCHESTRA
(= ORCH. DE LA SUISSE ROMANDE)
"Swiss" roh-mahnd orchestra

SUITE PROVENÇALE (Milhaud)
sweet proh-vãhn-sahl

TAILLEFERRE, GERMAINE
"tie-affair," zhehr-mehn

TÉTARD, ALBERT & JEANINE
tay-tahr, ahl-behr & juh-neen

THAÏS (Massenet)
tah-ees

THIOLLIER, FRANÇOIS-JOËL
tyoh-lyay, frãhn-swah-zhoh-ehl

TOULOUSE CHAMBER ORCHESTRA
too-looz

TOUVRON, GUY
too-vrõhn, gee

TRIO FONTENAY
fohn-tuh-nay

TROUTTET, ANDRÉ
troo-tay, ãhn-dray

TZIGANE (Ravel)
tsee-gahn

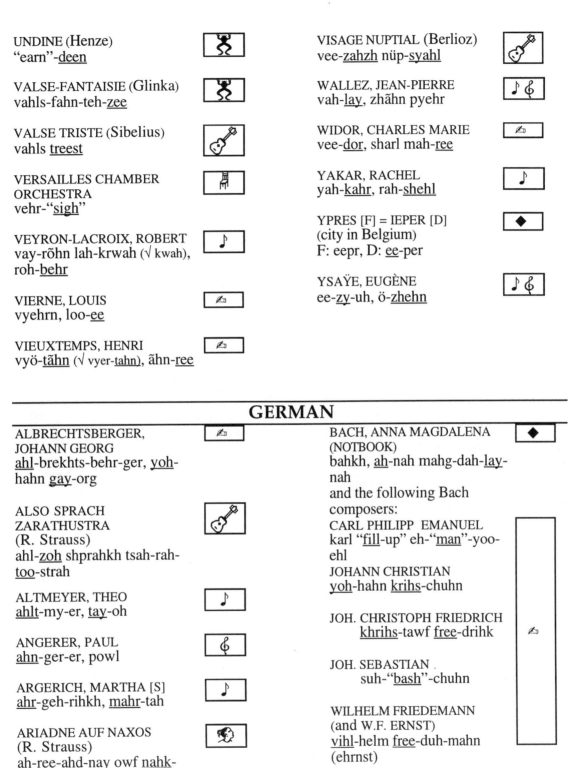

UNDINE (Henze)
"earn"-deen

VALSE-FANTAISIE (Glinka)
vahls-fahn-teh-zee

VALSE TRISTE (Sibelius)
vahls treest

VERSAILLES CHAMBER ORCHESTRA
vehr-"sigh"

VEYRON-LACROIX, ROBERT
vay-rõhn lah-krwah (√ kwah), roh-behr

VIERNE, LOUIS
vyehrn, loo-ee

VIEUXTEMPS, HENRI
vyö-tãhn (√ vyer-tahn), ãhn-ree

VISAGE NUPTIAL (Berlioz)
vee-zahzh nüp-syahl

WALLEZ, JEAN-PIERRE
vah-lay, zhãhn pyehr

WIDOR, CHARLES MARIE
vee-dor, sharl mah-ree

YAKAR, RACHEL
yah-kahr, rah-shehl

YPRES [F] = IEPER [D]
(city in Belgium)
F: eepr, D: ee-per

YSAŸE, EUGÈNE
ee-zy-uh, ö-zhehn

GERMAN

ALBRECHTSBERGER, JOHANN GEORG
ahl-brekhts-behr-ger, yoh-hahn gay-org

ALSO SPRACH ZARATHUSTRA
(R. Strauss)
ahl-zoh shprahkh tsah-rah-too-strah

ALTMEYER, THEO
ahlt-my-er, tay-oh

ANGERER, PAUL
ahn-ger-er, powl

ARGERICH, MARTHA [S]
ahr-geh-rihkh, mahr-tah

ARIADNE AUF NAXOS
(R. Strauss)
ah-ree-ahd-nay owf nahk-sohs

BACH, ANNA MAGDALENA (NOTBOOK)
bahkh, ah-nah mahg-dah-lay-nah

and the following Bach composers:

CARL PHILIPP EMANUEL
karl "fill-up" eh-"man"-yoo-ehl

JOHANN CHRISTIAN
yoh-hahn krihs-chuhn

JOH. CHRISTOPH FRIEDRICH
khrihs-tawf free-drihk

JOH. SEBASTIAN
suh-"bash"-chuhn

WILHELM FRIEDEMANN (and W.F. ERNST)
vihl-helm free-duh-mahn (ehrnst)

BACHWERKEVERZEIGNIS
bahkh vehr-kuh fehr-tsykh-nihs (cf. BWV [E].)

BACKHAUS, WILHELM
bahk-"house," vil-helm

BADEN-BADEN RADIO ORCHESTRA
bah-duhn bah-duhn

BADURA-SKODA, PAUL
bah-doo-rah-skoh-dah, "Paul"

BALLADEN DER LIEBE (Bruch)
bah-lah-duhn dehr lee-buh

BALLI, HEINZ
bah-lee, hynts

BAMBERG PHILHARMONIC
bahm-behrg

BÄR, ALWIN (BAER)
"bare," ahl-vihn

BARGEL, WOLFGANG
bar-guhl, vohlf-gahng

BAUMANN, HERMANN
bow-mahn, hehr-mahn

BAUMANN, JÖRG
bow-mahn, yörg (= yerg)

BAYERN (= Bavaria)
by-ern

BAYREUTH (city in Germany)
by-royt

BEETHOVEN, LUDWIG VAN
bay-toh-vehn, lood-vihg vahn

BERG, ALBAN
behrg, ahl-bahn

BIBER, HEINRICH VON
bee-ber, hyn-rihk fuhn

BIEDERMEIER ENSEMBLE WIEN
bee-der-my-er ahn-sahm-buhl veen

BLOCH, ERNEST
blohkh, ehr-nest
(√ "talk," ≠"block")

BOEHMER, KONRAD
bö-mer, kohn-rahd

BÖHM, KARL
böm (= berm)

BOSKOVSKY, WILLI
"boss-cough"-skee, vih-lee

BRAHMS, JOHANNES [E]
brahmz, yoh-hah-nehs

BRATSCHE
brah-chuh = viola

BREMBECK, CHRISTIAN
brehm-behk

BRENDEL, ALFRED
bren-duhl, al-fred

BROUWER, LEO
brow-er (="tower"), lee-oh

BRUCH, MAX
brookh, maks

BRUCKNER, ANTON
"brook"-ner, ahn-"tone"

BRÜGGEN, FRANS
brü-guhn, frahns
(*Dutch*: brü-khuhn)

BÜHLER, FRANZ
bü-ler, frahnts

BÜLOW, HANS GUIDO VON
bü-loh, hahns gee-doh fuhn

BUSCH, FRITZ
"bush"

BUXTEHUDE, DIETRICH
"book"-stuh-hoo-duh, dee-trihkh

CHÖRE FÜR DORIS (Stockhausen)
kö-ruh für "Doris"

CLEMENCIC, RENÉ
kleh-mähn-seech, reh-nay

DAS GLÜCKLICHE HAND (Schoenberg)
dahs-glük-lih-khuh hahnd

DAS HERZ (Pfitzner)
dahs- hehrts

DAS KLAGENDE LIED (Mahler)
dahs-klah-gehn-duh-leed

DAS LIED VON DER ERDE (Mahler)
dahs-leed-fohn-der-ehr-duh

DAS RHEINGOLD (Wagner)
dahs-ryn-"gold"

DAS WOHLTEMPERIERTE KLAVIER (J.S. Bach)
dahs-vohl-tehm-puh-reer-tuh klah-veer

DAVIDSBÜNDLERTÄNZE (Schumann)
dah-veedz bünd-ler "tents"-uh

DER FERNE KLANG (Schreker)
dehr-fehr-nuh klahng

DER FLIEGENDE HOLLÄNDER (Wagner)
dehr flee-gehn-duh hoh-lehn-der

DER FREISCHÜTZ (Weber)
dehr-fry-shüts (√ shoots)

DER HÄUSLICHE KRIEG (Schubert)
dehr-hoys-lih-khuh kreeg

DER JASAGER (Weill)
dehr-yah-zah-ger

DER MOND (Orff)
dehr-mohnt

DER RING DES NIEBELUNGEN (Wagner)
dehr-ring dehs-nee-beh-loong-uhn

DER ROSENKAVALIER (R. Strauss)
dehr-roh-zehn-kah-vah-leer

DER SCHAUSPIELDIREKTOR (Mozart)
dehr-shaw-shpeel-dee-rehk-tohr

DER WILDSCHÜTZ (Lortzing)
deht-vihld-shoots

DES KNABEN WUNDERHORN (Mahler)
dehs-knah-bihn voon-der-horn

DEUTSCHE WELLE
doy-chuh veh-luh

DICHTERLIEBE (Schumann)
dihkh-tuh-lee-buh

DIE ENTFÜHRUNG AUS DEM SERAIL (Mozart)
dee ehnt-fü-roong ows dehm seh-"rye"

DIE FLEDERMAUS (J. Strauss)
dee-flay-der-mows

DIE FRAU OHNE SCHATTEN (R. Strauss)
dee-frow oh-nuh shah-tuhn

DIE GEZEICHNETEN (Schreker)
dee-guh-tsykh-nuh-tuhn

DIE MEISTERSINGER (Wagner)
dee-my-ster-"zinger"

DIE SCHÖNE MÜLLERIN (Schubert)
dee-shö-nuh mü-luh-rihn

DIE SCHÖPFUNG (Haydn)
dee-shöp-foong

DIE SEEJUNGFRAU (Zemlinsky)
dee-zay-yoong-frow

DIE SIEBEN TODSÜNDEN DER KLEINBÜRGER (Weill)
dee-zee-buhn toht-zün-den dehr-klyn-bür-guh

DIE WALKÜRE (Wagner)
dee-vahl-kü-ruh

DIE WINTERREISE (Schubert)
dee-vihn-tuh-ry-zuh

DIM LUSTRE (R. Strauss)
deem-loo-struh

DITTERSDORF, KARL DITTERS VON
diht-ters-dorf, karl dih-ters fohn

EDELMANN, OTTO
ay-duhl-mahn, oh-toh

EIN HELDENLEBEN (R. Strauss)
yn-hehl-den-lay-ben

ENGELHARD, BRIGITTE
eng-uhl-hart, brih-gee-tuh

ENSEMBLE WIEN
veen

EQUILUZ, KURT
eh-kvee-loots, koort

ERWARTUNG (Schoenberg)
ehr-vahr-toong

ESCHENBACH, CHRISTOPH
ehsh-en-bahkh, kree-stohf

EWALD, VICTOR
ay-vahlt (√ -vahld)

EWERHART, RUDOLF
eh-vehr-hart, roo-dohlf

FAERBER, JÖRG (FÄRBER)
"fair"-ber, yerg

FAGIUS, HANS
fah-gee-oos, hahns

FANTASIESTÜCKE (Schumann)
fahn-tah-zee shtü-kuh

FASCH, JOHANN FRIEDRICH
fahsh, yoh-hahn free-drihk

FASSBAENDER, BRIGITTE (FAßBÄNDER)
fahs-bayn-der, brih-gee-tuh

FEUERMANN, EMANUEL
foyer-mahn

FISCHER, EDWIN
"fisher," ehd-vihn

FISCHER-DIESKAU, DIETRICH
"fisher"-dee-skow (= "cow"), dee-trihkh

FRANTZ, JUSTUS
frahnts, yoo-stoos

FRÜHBECK DE BURGOS, RAFAEL
frü-behk duh boor-gohs, rah-fy-ehl

FÜRTWÄNGLER, WILHELM
fürt-veng-ler, vihl-helm

GARTEN VON FREUDEN UND TRAURIGKEITEN (Gubaidulina)
gahr-ten fohn froy-duh oont trow-rihkh-ky-ten

GARTENFEST (Mozart)
gahr-tuhn-fehst

GAUK, ALEXANDER
gowk (= "cow")

GEBURTSTAG DER INFANTIN (Zemlinsky)
geh-boorts-tahg dehr ihn-fahn-tin

GERHARDT, CHARLES
gehr-hart

GESANG DER JÜNGLINGE (Stockhausen)
guh-zahng dehr yüng-lih-khuh

GEWANDHAUS ORCHESTRA (Leipzig)
lyp-tsihg guh-vahnt-"house"

GIESEKING, WALTER
gee-zuh-king, vahl-ter

GLAETZNER, BURKHARD (GLÄTZNER)
glayts-ner, berk-"heart"

GLUCK, CHRISTOPH WILLIBALD
glook (= "look"), kree-stoff villy-bahld

GÖNNENWEIN, WOLFGANG
gö-nin-"vine," vohlf-gahng

GÖTTERDÄMMERUNG (Wagner)
gö-ter-deh-muh-roong

GRAF, MARIA
grahf, mah-ree-uh

GRAFENAUER, IRENA
grah-fuh-now-er, ee-reh-nuh

GRUENBERG, ERICH (GRÜNBERG)
grün-behrg, eh-reekh

GULDA, FRIEDRICH
gool-duh, free-drihkh

GURRELIEDER (Schoenberg)
ger-uh-lee-duh

GUSCHLBAUER, THEODORE
goo-shul-bower, tay-uh-dor (="bushel-tower")

HAEBLER, INGRID (HÄBLER)
hay-bler. een-grid

HAEFLIGER, ERNST (HÄFLIGER)
hay-flih-ger, ehrnst

HAGEN QUARTET
hah-guhn

HALFFTER, CRISTOBAL
hahlf-ter, krees-toh-bahl

HALLE ORCHESTRA
hah-lay

HAMBURG PHILHARMONIC ORCHESTRA
hahm-boorg

HAMBURGISCHE KAPITANMUSIK (Telemann)
hahm-boor-gih-shuh kah-pee-tahn-moo-zeek

HAMMERKLAVIER SONATA (Beethoven)
hah-mer-klah-veer

HÄNDEL, GEORGE FREDERIC
G: hen-duhl, gay-org free-drihk
E: "handle," jorj freh-drihk

HARDEN, WOLF
hahr-dehn, vohlf

HARNONCOURT, ALICE
har-"nun"-kort

HARNONCOURT, NIKOLAUS
har-"nun"-kort

HÄUSTER, REGULA
hoy-ster, reh-goo-lah

HAYDN, FRANZ JOSEPH
"hide"-uhn, frahnts yoh-zehf

HAYDN, MICHAEL
"hide"-uhn, mee-khah-ehl

HEISSER, JEAN-FRANÇOIS [F]
hy-ser, zhãhn-frãhn-swah

HENZE, HANS WERNER
hehn-tsuh, hahnts vehr-ner

HINDEMITH, PAUL
hin-duh-"mitt," pawl

HOFMANN, JOSEF
hohf-mahn, yoh-zehf

HOLIGER, HEINZ
"holy"-ger, hynts

HOLLWEG, WERNER
"whole"-vehg, vehr-ner

HOPF, HANS
hohpf, hahns

HUMMEL, JOHANN NEPOMUK
hoo-muhl, yoh-hahn neh-puh-mook

HUMPERDINCK, ENGLEBERT
hoom-per-dink (<oo> = "hook"), eng-uhl-behrt

JANOWITZ, GUNDULA
yah-noh-vihts, goon-doo-lah

JERUSALEM, SIEGFRIED
yeh-roo-zah-lem, zeeg-freed

JOCHUM, EUGEN
yoh-khuhm, oy-gun

JONNY SPIELT AUF (Krenek)
"Johny" shpeelt owf

JOSEPHSLEGENDE (R. Strauss)
yoh-zehfs-leh-gehn-duh

JUNGE LORD (Henze)
yoong-uh "lord"

JUNGHÄNEL, KONRAD
yoong-hay-nuhl, kohn-rahd

KARAJAN, HERBERT VON
kah-rah-yahn, hehr-behrt fuhn

KEMPE, RUDOLF
kem-puh, roo-dohlf

KEMPFF, WILHELM
kempf, vihl-helm

KINDERSZENEN (Schumann)
kihn-duhs-tsay-nen

KINDERTOTENLIEDER (Mahler)
kin-duh-toh-ten-lee-der

KLEIBER, CARLOS & ERICH
kly-ber, kar-lohs & eh-rihk

KLEMPERER, OTTO
(= "emperor," ah-toh

KLETZKI, PAUL
kleht-skee, "Paul"

KLIEN, WALTER
"clean," vahl-ter

KLOCKER, DIETER
kloh-ker, dee-ter

KMENTT, WALDEMAR
kment, vahl-duh-mar

KNAPPERTSBUSCH, HANS
knah-pehrts-"bush"

KOCH, RAMI & ULRICH
kohkh, rah-mee & ool-rihkh

KÖCHEL, LUDWIG
(KOECHEL)
kö-khuhl

KOL NIDREI (Bruch)
"call-need-ray" *or* "coal"-nee-dray

KOLLO, RENE
koh-loh, reh-nay

KÖLN = köln, kerln
(See also Cologne.)

KÖNIGSKINDER
(Humperdinck)
kö-nihks kihn-duh

KOPPELSTETTER, MARTINA
koh-puhl-shteh-tuh, mahr-tee-nah

KREBS, HELMUT
krehps, hehl-moot

KREISLER, FRITZ
"Chrysler"

KRENEK, ERNST
kreh-"neck," ehrnst

KRENN, WERNER
krehn, vehr-ner

KREUTZER (sonata of Beethoven)
kroy-tser

KREUZSPIEL (Stockhausen)
kroyts-shpeel

KRIPS, JOSEF
krihps, yoh-zehf

KURTZ, EFREM
koorts, ehf-rem

KWEKSILBER, MARIANNE
kvehk-zihl-ber, mah-ree-ah-nuh

LANGSAM
lahng-zahm

LAUBENTHAL, HORST
low-ben-tahl, horst
(<low> = "cow.")

LAUTENBACHER, SUZANNE
low-ten-bah-kher, zoo-zah-nuh

LEHAR, FRANZ
lay-hahr, frahnts

LEINSDORF, ERICH [E]
"lines"-dorf, eh-rihk

LEIPZIG (city)
lyp-tsihg

LEISTER, KARL
ly-ster, kahrl

LEITNER, FERDINAND
"light"-ner

LEONHARDT, GUSTAV
lay-ohn-hart, goo-stahf

LESCHETIZKY, THEODOR
leh-sheh-tiht-skee, tay-oh-dohr

LIEBESFREUD (Kreisler)
lee-bihs-froyd

LIEBESLEID (Kreisler)
lee-bihs-"light"

LIEBESLIEDER WALZER
(Brahms)
lee-behs lee-duh vahl-tsuh

LIEDER EINES FAHRENDE
GESELLEN
(Mahler)
lee-der y-nehs fah-rehn-duh guh-zeh-len

LINDBERG, JAKOB
lind-behrg, yah-kohb

LINDE, HANS-MARTIN
lin-duh, hahns mahr-tin

LOHENGRIN (Wagner)
loh-ehn-"grin"

LUDWIG, CHRISTA
lood-vihg, krihs-tuh

MAAG, PETER
mahg, pay-ter

MAAZEL, LORIN
mah-zehl, loh-rin

MAHLER, GUSTAV
mah-ler, goo-stahf

MAISKY, MISCHA [R]
my-skee, mee-shah

MARTHA (Flotow)
mar-tah

MASUR, KURT
mah-zoor, koort

MATHIS DER MALER SYMPHONY (Hindemith)
mah-tihs dehr mah-ler

MELOS QUARTET STUTTGART
meh-lohs

MENDELSSOHN, FELIX
men-duhl-sohn, fay-liks

MENGELBERG, WILLEM
meng-uhl-behrg, vih-luhm

METAMORPHOSEN (R. Strauss)
meh-tah-mohr-foh-zen

MOLTER, JOHANN MELCHIOR
"mole"-ter, yoh-hahn mehl-kee-or

MOSCHELES, IGNAZ
moh-shuh-luhs, ihg-nahts

MOSKAU (= Moscow)
mohs-"cow"

MOZART, LEOPOLD & WOLFGANG AMADEUS
moh-tsart, lay-oh-pold & vohlf-gahng ah-mah-day-oos

MUFFAT, GEORG
moo-faht, gay-org

MUNCHINGER, KARL
moon-ching-er

MÜNCHNER BLÄSERAKADEMIE KÖLN
münkh-ner blay-zer-ah-kah-day-mee köln

MUND, UWE
moont, oo-vuh

MUNICH PRO ARTE ORCHESTRA
myoo-nihk proh ahr-tay

MUTTER, ANNE-SOPHIE
moo-ter, ah-nuh-zoh-fee

NEIDLINGER, GUSTAV
nyd-linger, goo-stahf

NICOLAI, OTTO
nick-oh-ly, ah-toh

OBERON (Weber)
oh-buh-rahn

OCKEGHEM, JOHANNES
oh-keh-guhm, yoh-hah-nehs

OEDIPUS DER TYRANN (Orff)
ö-dih-poos dehr tee-rahn

OFFENBACH, JACQUES
"off"-en-bahkh, zhahk

PACHELBEL, JOHANN
pah-kuhl-bel, yoh-hahn

PFITZNER, HANS
pfihts-ner, hahns

PHANTASIESTÚCKE
fahn-tah-zee shtü-kuh

PRAETORIUS, MICHAEL
preh-taw-ree-uhs, my-kuhl

PREY, HERMANN
pry, hehr-mahn

PRINZ, ALFRED
"prints"

REDEL, KURT
ray-dul, koort

REGER, MAX
ray-ger, mahks

REINECKE, CARL
ry-nuh-kuh

REZNIČEK, EMIL NIKOLAUS VON
rehz-nih-chehk, eh-meel nik-oh-lows "fun"

RHEINBERGER, JOSEPH
ryn-behr-ger, yoh-zef

RICHTER, KARL
rihkh-ter

RIDDERBUSCH KARL
rih-der-boosh

RISTENPART, KARL
"wrist"-in-part

ROSAMUNDE (Schubert)
roh-zuh-moon-duh

ROTHENBERGER, ANNALIESE
roh-ten-behr-ger, ah-nah-lee-zuh

RUBINSTEIN, ANTON
roo-bin-shtyn, ahn-"tone"

RÜBSAM, WOLFGANG
rüb-zahm, vohlf-gahng

SAAR COLLEGIUM MUSICUM
zahr kuh-"leggy"-uhm moo-zih-koom

SALZBURG MOZARTEUM
zahlts-boorg moh-tsahr-tay-uhm

SANDERLING, KURT
zahn-der-ling, koort

SAWALLISCH, WOLFGANG
sah-vah-lish, vohlf-gahng

SCHEIDT, SAMUEL
shyt (="sight")

SCHEIN, JOHANN HERMANN
shyn, yoh-hahn, hehr-mahn

SCHELLENBERGER, HANSJÖRG
sheh-len-behr-ger, hahns-yerg

SCHERCHEN, HERRMANN
shehr-khen, hehr-mahn

SCHIFF, HEINRICH
shihf, hyn-rihkh

SCHMEISSER, ANNEMARIE
shmy-ser, ah-nah-mah-ree

SCHMIDT-ISSERSTEDT, HANS
shmit-is-er-shtet, hahns

SCHMIEDER, WOLFGANG
shmee-der

SCHNABEL, ARTUR
shnah-buhl, ahr-toor

SCHOENBERG, ARNOLD
shön-behrg (√ shern-berg)

SCHREIER, PETER
shry-er, pay-ter

SCHREKER, FRANZ
shray-ker, frahnts

SCHUBERT, FRANZ
"shoe"-behrt, frahnts

SCHULZ, WOLFGANG
shoolts, vohlf-gahng

SCHULZE, THEODORA
shool-tsuh, tay-oh-dor-uh

SCHUMANN, ROBERT
"shoe"-mahn, "Robert"

SCHURICHT, CARL
shur-rikht

SCHÜTZ, HEINRICH
shüts, hyn-rihkh

SCHWALBE, MICHEL
shvahl-buh, mee-"shell"

SCHWANENGESANG (Schubert)
shvah-nehn-geh-zahng

SCHWARZKOPF, ELISABETH
shvahrts-kawpf

SECHS MONOLOGE AUS "JEDERMANN" (Martin)
zehks moh-noh-loh-guh ows yay-der-mahn

SEEFRIED, IRMGARD
zay-freed, eerm-gard

SEIPENBUSCH, EDGAR
zy-pehn-boosh

SERKIN, RUDOLF
sehr-kin, roo-dohlf

SIEGFRIED (Wagner)
zeeg-freed

SILJA, ANJA
seel-yuh, ahn-yuh

SINFONIEORCHESTER DES SÜDWEST
Read: Southwest Symphony Orchestra

SOLIN, HANS
zoh-lin, hahns

SÖLLSCHER, GÖRAN
zöl-sher, gö-rahn

SPOHR, LUDWIG
shpohr, lood-vihg (= "look")

STAATSKAPELLE DRESDEN
shtahts-kah-peh-luh

STAIER, ANDREAS
shty-er, ahn-dray-ahs

STAMITZ, CARL
shtah-mits

STEIN, HORST
shtyn

STIMMEN...VERSTUMMEN... (Gubaidulina)
shtih-men fehr-shtoo-men

STIMMUNG (Stockhausen)
shtih-moong

STOCKHAUSEN, KARLHEINZ
shtohk-"how"-zen, karl-hynts

STOLZE, GERHARD
shtohl-tsuh, gehr-hard

STÖLZEL, GOTTFRIED HEINRICH
shtól-tsuhl, goht-freed hyn-rikh

STRAUSS
shtrows (= "mouse")

JOHANN (Jr.&Sr.)
yoh-hahn

JOSEF yoh-zehf

RICHARD rih-kard

STUTTGART (city)
shtoot-gahrt

KIRCHENMUSIKTAGE
... keer-khen-moo-zeek-tah-guh

SOLISTEN
shtoot-gahrt zoh-"list"-uhn

TACHEZI, HERBERT
tah-kay-tsee, hehr-behrt

TAFELMUSIK
tah-fuhl-moo-zeek

TANNHÄUSER (Wagner)
tahn-hoy-zer

TELEMANN, GEORG PHILIP
tay-luh-mahn, gay-org

TENNSTEDT, KLAUS
"ten"-shtet, klows (="louse")

THALBERG, SIGISMOND
tahl-behrg, zih-gihs-mohnt

THUNEMANN, KLAUS
too-nuh-mahn, klaws

TICHY, GEORG
tee-khee, gay-ohrg

TIERKREIS (Stockhausen)
teer-krys

TILL EULENSPIEGEL
(R. Strauss)
"till" oy-lehn-shpee-guhl

TONKUENSTLER
(TONKÜNSTLER)
ORCHESTRA, VIENNA
nord-oh-stuh "tone"-künst-ler

TOTENTANZ (Liszt)
toh-ten-tahnts

TRISTAN UND ISOLDE
(Wagner)
trihs-tahn oont ee-zohl-duh

VERHÖR DES LUKULLUS
(Dessau)
fehr-"her" dehs loo-koo-loos

VERKLÄRTE NACHT
(Schoenberg)
fehr-klehr-tuh nahkht

VIER LETZTE LIEDER
(R. Strauss)
feer leht-stuh lee-duh

VON HEUTE AUF MORGEN
(Schoenberg)
fuhn hoy-tuh awf "more-gun"

WÄCHTER, EBERHARD
(WAECHTER)
vaykh-ter, eh-ber-hart

WAFFENSCHMIED (Lortzing)
vah-fehn-shmeet

WAGNER
vahg-ner

FRIEDERIKE
free-duh-ree-kuh

RICHARD rih-khard

SIEGFRIED zeeg-freed

WALDSTEIN
(sonata of Beethoven)
vahld-shtyn

WALDTEUFEL, EMIL
vahl-toy-fuhl, ay-meel

WALLFISCH, ERNST
vahl-fish, ehrnst

WALPURGISNACHT (Gounod)
vahl-poor-gihs-nahkht

WALTER, BRUNO
vahl-ter, broo-noh

WALTHER, HANS-JÜRGEN
vahl-ter, hahns-yür-guhn

WARCHAL, BOHDAN
vahr-khahl, bohkh-dahn

WEBER, CARL MARIA VON
vay-ber, karl, mah-ree-uh "fun"

WEBERN, ANTON
vay-behrn, ahn-tohn

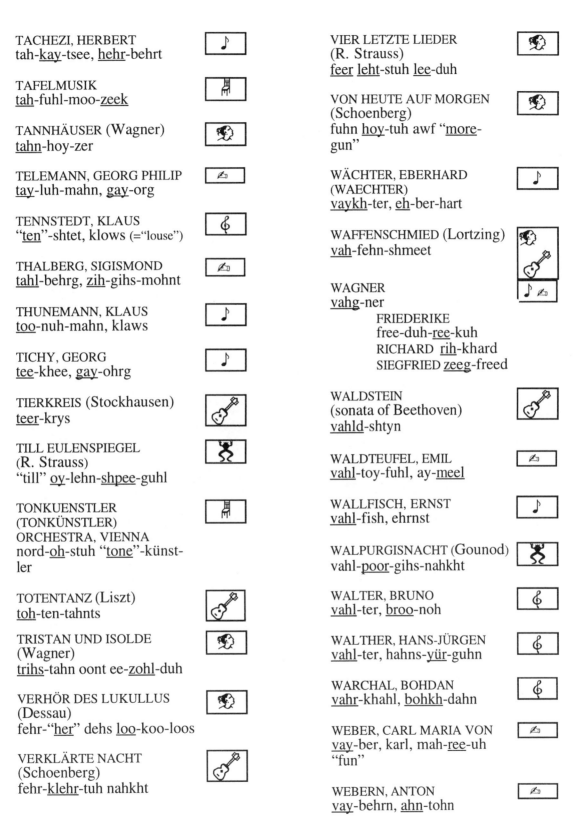

WEIGLE, JÖRG-PETER
vy-guhl, yerg-pay-ter

WEIHNACHTSORATORIUM (J.S. Bach)
vy-nahkhts-oh-rah-toh-ree-oom

WEIKL, BERNHARD
vy-kuhl, behrn-hart

WEILL, KURT
"vile"

WEINBERGER, JAROMÍR
"vine"-behr-ger, yah-roh-meer

WEINGARTNER, FELIX
"vine"-gart-ner

WELLER, WALTER
veh-ler, vahl-ter

WERTHER (Massenet)
vehr-tuh

WESTERBERG, STIG
vest-er-behrg, shtihg

WIENER BLUT (J. Strauss)
vee-ner bloot

WIKLUND, ADOPLH
vihk-loond, ah-dolf

WINDGASSEN, WOLFGANG
vint-gah-suhn, vohlf-gahng

WINSCHERMANN, HELMUT
vihn-sher-mahn, hel-moot

WOLF, HUGO
vohlf, hoo-goh

WOZZECK (Berg)
voht-sehk

WUNDERLICH, FRITZ
voon-der-lihkh, frits

WÜRTTEMBERG CHAMBER ORCHESTRA
vür-tuhm-behrg

ZAGROSEK, LOTHAR
tsah-groh-sehk, loh-tahr

ZAÏDE (Mozart)
tsah-ee-duh

ZAR UND ZIMMERMANN (Lortzing)
tsahr oont tsih-mer-mahn

ZEHETMEIR, THOMAS
tseht-my-er, toh-mahs

ZIGEUNERLIEBE (Lehár)
tsih-goy-ner-lee-buh

ZIGEUNERWEISEN (Sarasate)
tsih-goy-ner-vy-zihn

GREEK

BALTSA, AGNES
bahl-tsah, ag-nihs

LAKATOS, ALEXANDER
lah-kah-tohs

MITROPOULUS, DIMITRI
mih-trah-puh-luhs, dih-mee-tree

SGOUROS, DIMITRIS
zgoo-rohs, dee-mee-trees

ZACCARIA, NICOLA
zah-kah-ree-ah, nee-koh-lah

HUNGARIAN

ANDA, GÉZA
ahn-dah, gay-zah

ANTÁL, MÁTYÁS
ahn-tahl, mah-tyahsh

BALOGH, JÓZSEF
bah-lohg, yoh-zhehf

BARSONY, LÁSZLÓ
bahr-shohn^{y}, lah-"slow"

BARTÓK, BÉLA
bar-tohk, bay-lah
(√ "bar-talk" but not "bell"-uh)

BENYACS, ZOLTÁN
ben-yahch, zohl-tahn

BERKES, KÁLMÁN
behr-kehsh, kahl-mahn

BIRET, IDIL
bee-reht, ee-"dill"

BOTVAY, KÁROLY
boht-vy, kah-roy

BUDAPEST (capital city)
boo-dah-pehsht

CSER, PÉTER
chehr, pay-tehr

CZIDRA, LÁSZLÓ
tsee-drah, lahs-loh

DEBRECEN (Debreczen)
deh-breh-tsehn

DOHNANYI, CHRISTOPH VON/ERNST VON
dohkh-nah-nyee, kree-stawf "fun"/ehrnst

DORÁTI, ANTÁL
"door"-ah-tee, ahn-tahl

DRAHOS, BÉLA
drah-hohsh, bay-lah

ESZTERHÁZA
ehs-ter-hah-zah

FAILONI CHAMBER ORCHESTRA
fy-loh-nee

FELLEGI, ÁDÁM
feh-leh-gee, ah-dahm

FERENC ERKEL CHAMBER ORCHESTRA
feh-"rents" ehr-kel

FRICSAY, FERENC
free-chy, feh-rents (= "China.")

GALÁNTA (DANCES) (Kodály)
gah-lahn-tah

GÁTI, ISTVÁN
gah-tee, eesht-vahn

GROSZ, EDITH
grohs, eh-deet

HÁLASZ, MICHAEL
hah-lahs, mee-kah-ehl

HARSÁNYI, ZSOLT
hahr-shahn-yee, zhohlt

HÁRY JÁNOS (Kodály)
hah-ree yah-nohsh

HEGEDÜS, ENDRE
heh-geh-düsh, ehn-dreh

HEGYI, ILDIKÓ
hay-jee, eel-dee-koh

JANCSOVICS, ANTAL
yahn-choh-vihch, ahn-tahl

JANDÓ, JENŐ
yahn-doh, yeh-nö

JÁNOSKA, ALÁDÁR
yah-nohs-kah, ah-lah-dahr

KALER, ILYA
kah-lehr, eel-yah

KECSKEMET (city)
kehch-keh-meht

KELEMEN, PÁL & ZOLTÁN
keh-leh-mehn, pahl & zohl-tahn

KERTESI, INGRID
kehr-teh-shee

KERTÉSZ, ISTVAN/GYÖRGY
kehr-tehs, eesht-vahn/jörj

KEVEHÁZI, JENŐ
keh-veh-hah-zee, yeh-nö

KISS, JÓZSEF
kihsh, yoh-zhehf

KOCSIS, ZOLTÁN
koh-cheesh, zohl-tahn

KODALY QUARTET
"code-eye"

KODÁLY, ZOLTÁN
koh-"dye"-ee, zohl-tahn

KOÓ, TAMÁS
koh, tah-mahsh

KÖRMENDI, KLÁRA
kör-mehn-dee, klah-rah

KOVÁCS, BÉLA
koh-vahch, bay-lah

KOVÁCS, JANOS
koh-vahch, yah-nohsh

KÖVES, PETER
kö-vehsh, pay-tehr

LAJTHA, LÁSZLÓ
ly-tah, lahs-loh

LEHEL, GYÖRGY
lay-ell, jerj

LIGETI, ANDRÁS/GYÖRGY
lih-geh-tee, ahn-drahsh/jerj

LISZT, FRANZ (also Ferenc)
"list," frahnz

MAGY, SANDOR SOLYOM
mahj, shahn-dor sawl-yawm

MAROSSZÉK DANCES (Kodály)
mah-roh-sehk

MIKULÁS, PETER
mee-koo-lahsh, pay-tehr

MUKK, JÓZSEF
mook, yoh-zhehf

NAGY, PÉTER
nahj, pay-tehr

NÉMETH, JUDIT
nay-meht, yoo-deet

OBERFRANK, GÉZA
oh-buh-frahnk, gay-zah

ONCZAY, CSABA
ohn-tsy, chah-bah

PÁSZTHY, JULIA
pah-stee, yoo-lyah

PAUK, GYÖRGY
powk, jörj

PECS (city)
pehch

PERÉNYI, ESZTER
peh-rehn-yee, ehs-tehr

PERTIS, ZSUZSA
pehr-teesh, zhoo-zhah

RÁKÓCZY MARCH (Berlioz)
rah-koh-tsee

ROZSA, MIKLOS [E]
roh-zhah, mee-klohsh
(√ roh-zuh, "meek-loss")

SANDOR, GYÖRGY
shahn-dor, jerj

SANDOR, JANOS
shahn-“door,” yah-nohsh

SCHIFF, ANDRAS [G]
shihf, ahn-drahsh

SEBESTYÉN, JÁNOS
sheh-beh-styehn, yah-nohsh

SIPKAY, DEBORAH
“ship”-ky

SOLTI, GEORG (SIR)
“shoal”-tee, jorj

STARKER, JANOS
star-ker, yah-nohsh

SZABO
sah-boh
IMRICH eem-reekh
MIKLOS mee-klohsh

SZECSÓDI, FERENC
seh-choh-dee, feh-rehnts

SZEGED (city)
seh-gehd

SZELECSÉNYI, NORBERT
seh-leh-chehn-yee

SZELL, GEORGE
“sell,” jorj

SZIGETI, JOSEPH
sih-geh-tee, yoh-zef

SZOKOLAY, BALÁZS
soh-koh-ly, bah-lahzh

TAKÁCS STRING QUARTET
tah-kahch

TOKODY, ILONA
toh-kohj, ee-loh-nah

TOKOS, ZOLTÁN
toh-kohsh, zohl-tahn

TÖRÖK, FRANTÍSEK
tö-rök, frahn-tee-shehk

TÓTH, JÁNOS
toht, yah-nohsh

VAJDA, JÓZSEF
vy-dah, yoh-zhehf

VARGA, LASZLO
var-gah, lahs-loh

VÁRJON, DÉNES
vahr-yohn, deh-nehsh

VÁSÁRY, TAMÁS
vah-shah-ree, tah-mahsh

VÉGH, SÁNDOR
“vague,” shahn-“door”

VEREBITS, IBOLYA
veh-reh-beets, ee-boy-ah

VETÖ, TAMÁS
veh-tö, tah-mahsh

VIAGY, DENNIS [E]
vyahj, deh-nihs

ZSIGMONDY, DENES
zhihg-mohnj, deh-nesh

ITALIAN

ABBADO, CLAUDIO
ah-bah-doh, “cloudy”-oh

ACCADEMIA DI SANTA CECILIA, ROME
ahk-kah-day-mee-ya dee sahn-tah cheh-chee-lyah

ACCADEMICI DI MILANO
ahk-kah-day-mee-chee dee mee-lah-noh

ACCARDO, SALVATORE
ah-"card"-oh, sahl-vah-toh-ray

ADAGIETTO
ah-dah-jeh-toh (<t> = [t])
uh-dah-jee-eh-toh (<t> = [flap])

ADAGIO
ah-dah-joh
uh-dah-jee-oh

ALBANESE, LICIA
ahl-bah-nay-zay, lee-chah

ALBINONI, TOMASO
ahl-bee-noh-nee, "toe"-mah-soh

ALCINA (Handel)
ahl-chee-nah

ALLEGRETTO
ah-leh-greh-toh (<t> = [t])
ah-luh-greh-toh (<t> = [flap])

ALLEGRO
ah-lay-"grow"
"a-leg-row"

ALVA, LUIGI [S]
ahl-vah, loo-ee-jee

ANDANTE
ahn-dahn-tay

ANDANTINO
ahn-dahn-tee-noh

APPASSIONATA (Beethoven)
ah-pahs-yuh-nah-tuh

ARICO, FORTUNATO
ah-ree-koh, for-too-nah-toh

ARLECCHINO (Busoni)
ahr-leh-kee-noh

ASSAI
ah-sy
uh-"sigh"

AYO, FELIX
"eye"-o, fay-"licks"

BALLO DELLE INGRATE (Monteverdi)
bah-loh deh-lah-een-grah-tay

BARBIERI, FEDORA
bar-byeh-ree, feh-"door"-ah

BARTOLI, CECILIA
"bar"-toh-lee, cheh-chee-lyah

BEATRICE DI TENDA (Bellini)
bay-ah-tree-chay dee-tehn-dah

BELLINI, VINCENZO
beh-lee-nee, veen-chehn-(d)zoh

BENVENUTO CELLINI (Berlioz)
behn-veh-noo-toh cheh-lee-nee

BERGANZA, TERESA
behr-gahn-dzah, teh-ray-zah

BERIO, LUCIANO
beh-ree-oh, loo-chah-no

BOCCHERINI, LUIGI
boh-keh-ree-nee, loo-ee-jee

BOLOGNA (city)
boh-"loan"-yuh

BONFIGLIO, ROBERT [E]
bohn-fee-lyo, rah-bert

BOTTESINI, GIOVANNI
boh-teh-zee-nee, joh-vah-nee

BRUSON, RENATO
broo-zohn, reh-nah-toh

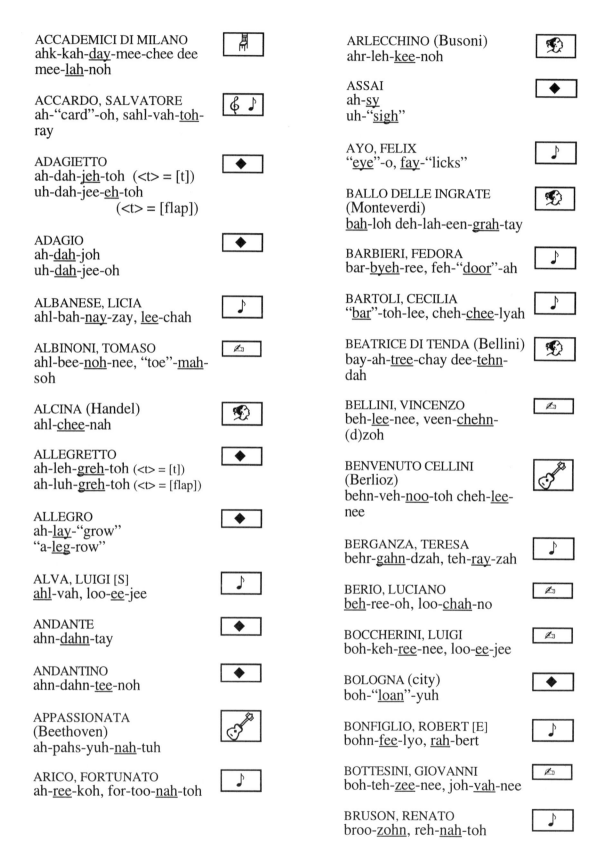

BUSONI, FERRUCIO
boo-zoh-nee, fehr-roo-choh

CANTATA
kahn-tah-tah (<t> = [t])
kuhn-tah-tuh (<t> = [flap])

CANINO, BRUNO
kah-nee-noh, broo-noh

CANTABILE
kahn-tah-bih-lay

CANTELLI, GUIDO
kahn-teh-lee, gwee-doh

CAPPRICCIO
kah-pree-choh
kuh-"preachy"-oh

CARMIRELLI, PINA
kar-mee-reh-lee, pee-nah

CARUSO, ENRICO
kah-roo-zoh, en-ree-koh

CASTELNUOVO-TEDESCO, MARIO
kah-stel-nwoh-voh-teh-deh-skoh, mah-ree-oh

CAVALLERIA RUSTICANA (Mascagni)
kah-vah-leh-ree-ah roo-stee-kah-nah

CECCATO, ALDO
cheh-kah-toh, ahl-doh

CHERUBINI, LUIGI
keh-roo-bee-nee, loo-ee-jee

CICCOLINI, ALDO
chick-oh-lee-nee, ahl-do

CIMAROSA, DOMENICO
chee-mah-roh-za, doh-meh-nih-koh

CLEMENTI, MUZIO
kleh-men-tee, moo-tsee-oh

CON BRIO
kohn bree-oh (≠"con" or kahn)

CON FUOCO
kohn fwoh-koh

CON MOTO
kohn-moh-toh

CONCERTO
kohn-chehr-toh
Pl. concerti, concertos
Pl.: -tee, "toes"

CONTINUO
kuhn-"tin-you"-oh

CORELLI, ARCANGELO
koh-reh-lee, ark-ahn-jeh-loh

CORELLI, FRANCO
koh-reh-lee, frahn-koh

COSÌ FAN TUTTE (Mozart)
koh-zee fahn too-tay

CRESCENDO
kruh-shehn-doh

D'AMORE (oboe, viola)
dah-"moray"

DA CAPO CHAMBER PLAYERS
dah-kah-poh

DA CHIESA
dah-kyay-sah
duh-kee-ay-zuh

DALLAPOZZA, ADOLF
dah-lah-poh-tsah, ah-dohlf

DE GAETANI, JAN [E]
duh-gy-uh-tah-nee, jan

DE SABATA, VICTOR
deh sah-bah-tah

DEL TREDICI, DAVID [E]
del treh-dih-chee (day-vid)

DI BONAVENTURA, ANTHONY [E]
dee-boh-nah-ven-too-ruh, an-thuh-nee

DI STEFANO, GIUSEPPE
dee-steh-fah-noh, joo-zep-pay

DIMINUENDO
duh-mihn-yoo-end-oh

DOLCE
"dole"-chay

DON CARLO (Verdi)
dohn-kahr-loh

DON GIOVANNI (Mozart)
dohn-joh-vah-nee

DON PASQUALE (Donizetti)
dohn-pah-skwah-lay

DONIZETTI, GAETANO
doh-nee-dzeh-tee, gah-eh-tah-noh

DRAGONETTI, DOMENICO
drah-guh-neh-tee, duh-meh-nih-koh

ERNANI (Verdi)
ehr-nah-nee

FLAGELLO, NICOLAS
flah-"jello," "nickel-us"

FONTANAROSA, PATRICE [F]
fohn-tah-nah-roh-zah, pah-trees

FORTE
for-tay (≠ "40"!)

FORTISSIMO
for-tee-see-moh
for-tih-suh-moh

FRA DIAVOLO (Auber)
frah-dyah-voh-loh

FRANCESCA DA RIMINI (Rakhmaninov, Tchaikovsky, Zandonai)
frahn-"chess"-kah dah rih-mih-nee

FRANCESCATTI, ZINO [F]
frahn-cheh-skah-tee, zee-noh

FRECCIA, MASSIMO
freh-chah, mahs-see-moh

FRENI, MIRELLA
fray-nee, mee-reh-lah

FRESCOBALDI, GIROLAMO
"fresco"- bahl-dee, jee-roh-lah-moh

FUGHETTO
foo-geh-toh

FUGA [I], FUGE [G]
FUGUE [E,F]
I: foo-gah, G: foo-guh,
E: fyoog, F: füg

FURIOSO
foor-yoh-zoh
fyer-ee-oh-soh

GABRIELLI, GIOVANNI
gah-bree-eh-lee, jo-vah-nee

GAGLIARDE [I]
GALLIARD [E]
I: gahl-yahr-deh
E: "gal"-ee-yard

GAMBA (viola da gamba)
gahm-buh

GANZAROLLI, WLADIMIRO
gahn-dzah-roh-lee, vlah-dee-mee-roh

GARATTI, MARIA TERESA
gah-rah-tee, mah-ree-ah teh-ray-zah

GAUCI, MIRIAM
gow-chee

GEMINIANI, FRANCESCO
jeh-mee-nyah-nee, frahn-ches-koh

GESUALDO, DON CARLO
jehz-wahl-doh, dohn-kar-loh

GHITALLA, ARMANDO
gee-tah-lah, ahr-mahn-doh

GIANNI SCHICCHI (Puccini)
jah-nee skee-kee

GIGLI, BENIAMINO
jee-lyee, ben-yah-mee-noh

GIOCOSO
joh-koh-zoh
juh-koh-soh

GIULIANI, MAURO
joo-lyah-nee, mow-roh

GIULINI, CARLO MARIA
joo-lee-nee, kar-loh muh-ree-uh

GOBBI, TITO
goh-bee, tee-toh

GRAZIOSO
grah-tsyoh-zoh
grah-tsee-oh-soh

GUARNERI
gwahr-neh-ree

I FIAMMINGHI
ee-fyah-"ming"-ee

I FILARMONICI DEL TEATTRO COMUNALE DI BOLOGNA
ee-"fill"-ar-moh-nee-chee del tay-ah-troh koh-moo-nah-lay dee boh-"loan"-yuh

I LOMBARDI ALLA PRIMA CROCIATA (Verdi)
ee-lohm-bar-dee ah-lah-pree-mah kroh-chah-tah

I MUSICI
ee-moo-zee-chee

I PAGLIACCI (Leoncavallo)
ee-pah-lyah-chee

I PURITANI (Bellini)
ee-poo-ree-tah-nee

I SOLISTI DI ZAGREB
ee soh-lees-tee dee- zah-greb

I SOLISTI VENETI
ee soh-lees-tee veh-neh-tee

I SOLONISTI
ee-soh-loh-nees-tee

I VESPRI SICILIANI (Verdi)
ee-veh-spree see-chee-lyah-nee

IDOMENEO (Mozart)
ee-doh-meh-nay-oh

IL BARBIERE DI SIVIGLIA (Rossini)
"ill" bar-byeh-ray dee see-veel-yah

IL CAMBIALE DI MATRIMONIO (Rossini)
"ill" kahm-byah-lay dee-mah-tree-moh-nyoh

IL CAMPANELLO (Donizetti)
eel kahm-pah-neh-loh

IL COMBATTIMENTO DI TANCREDI E CLORINDA (Monteverdi)
"ill" kohm-bah-tee-mehn-toh dee tahn-kray-dee eh kloh-reen-dah

IL CORREGIDOR (Wolf) [G]
eel koh-reh-gee-dohr

IL MATRIMONIO SEGRETO (Cimarosa)
eel mah-tree-moh-nyoh seh-gray-toh

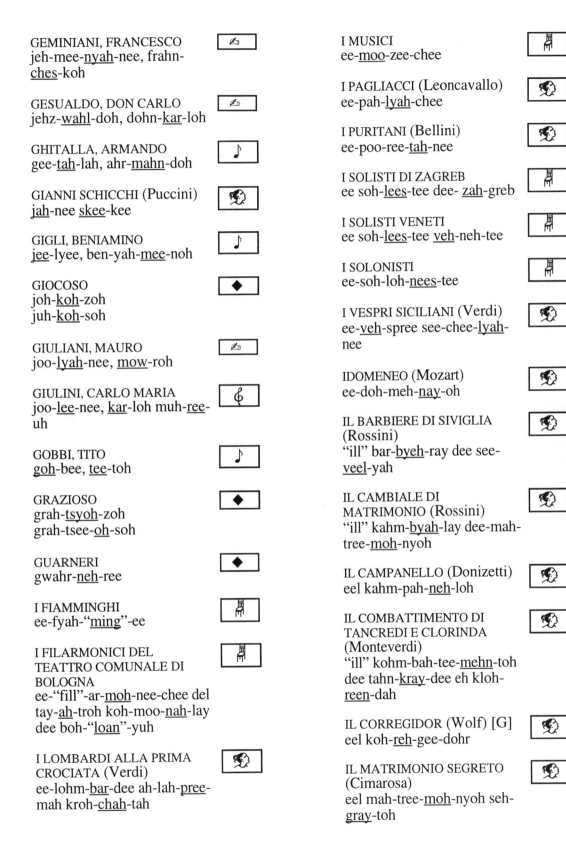

IL RE PASTORE (Mozart)
ihl ray-pah-stoh-ray

IL RITORNO DI ULISSE IN PATRIA (Monteverdi)
ihl-ree-tohr-noh dee-oo-lee-say ihn-pah-tree-ah

IL SIGNOR BRUSCHINO (Rossini)
ihl see-nyohr broo-skee-noh

IL TABARRO (Puccini)
ihl-tah-bah-roh

IL TRITTICO (Puccini)
ihl-tree-tee-koh

IL TROVATORE (Verdi)
eel troh-vah-"tore"-ay

L'AMICO FRITZ (Mascagni)
lah-mee-koh frihts

L'ARCHIBUDELLI
lar-kee-boo-deh-lee

L'ARLESIANA (Cilea)
lahr-lay-zyah-nah

L'ELISIR D'AMORE (Donizetti)
leh-lee-zeer dah-moh-ray

L'ESTRO ARMONICO (Vivaldi)
lehs-troh ahr-moh-nee-koh

L'INCORONAZIONE DI POPPEA (Monteverdi)
leen-koh-roh-naht-syoh-nay dee-poh-pay-ah

L'ITALIANA IN ALGERI (Rossini)
lee-tahl-yah-nah ihn ahl-jeh-ree

LA BATTAGLIA DI LEGNANO (Verdi)
lah-bah-tah-lyah dee leh-nyah-noh

LA BOHÈME (Puccini)
lah-boh-ehm

LA CENERENTOLA (Rossini)
lah-cheh-neh-rehn-toh-lah

LA CLEMENZA DI TITO (Mozart)
lah-kleh-"mend"-zah dee-tee-toh

LA FANCIULLA DEL WEST (Puccini)
lah-fahn-choo-lah dehl-"west"

LA FINTA GIARDINIERA (Mozart)
lah-feen-tah jar-dee-nyeh-rah

LA FORZA DEL DESTINO (Verdi)
lah-"forts"-ah del-deh-stee-noh

LA GIOCONDA (Ponchielli)
lah-joh-kohn-dah

LA RONDINE (Puccini)
lah-rohn-dee-nay

LA SCALA DI SETA (Rossini)
[lah-skah-lah dee-say-tah]

LA SERVA PADRONA (Pergolesi)
lah-sehr-vah pah-droh-nah

LA SONNAMBULA (Bellini)
lah-soh-nahm-boo-luh

LA TRAVIATA (Verdi)
lah-trah-vee-ah-tuh

LA ZINGARA (Rinaldo di Capua)
lah-tseen-gah-rah

LAGRIME DI SAN PIETRO (Lassus)
lah-gree-may dee-sahn-pyay-troh

LARGHETTO
lar-geh-toh

LARGO
lahr-goh

LE NOZZE DI FIGARO (Mozart)
leh-"note -say" dee-fee-gah-roh

LE QUATTRO STAGIONI (Vivaldi)
leh-kwah-troh stah-joh-nee

LEGATO
lay-gah-toh (<t> = [t])
luh-gah-toh (<t> = [flap])

LEONCAVALLO, RUGGERO
lay-ohn-kah-vah-loh, roo-jeh-roh

LOCATELLI, PIETRO
loh-kah-teh-lee, pyay-troh

LONGO
"long"-oh

LOTTI, ANTONIO
loh-tee, ahn-toh-nee-oh

LUCIA DI LAMMERMOOR (Donizetti)
loo-chee-uh dee-lah-mehr-moor

LUCIO SILLA (Mozart)
loo-choh sih-lah

LUCREZIA BORGIA (Donizetti)
loo-krehts-yah "bore"-jah

MA NON TROPPO
[*not too much*]
mah-nohn-troh-poh

MAESTOSO
my-stoh-zoh

MAESTRO DI MUSICA (Pergolesi)
my-ehs-troh dee-moo-zee-kah

MAGGIO-ORMEZOWSKI, FRANCO
mah-joh-or-meh-zohf-skee, frahn-koh

MANFREDINI, FRANCESCO
mahn-freh-dee-nee, frahn-"chess"-koh

MARCATO
mahr-kah-toh

MARCELLO, ALESSANDRO
mar-cheh-loh, ah-leh-sahn-droh

MASCAGNI, PIETRO
mahs-kah-nyee, pyay-troh

MATA, EDUARDO
mah-tah, ed-wahr-do

MEDEA (Cherubini)
meh-day-ah

MEDICI STRING QUARTET
meh-dee-chee

MEFISTOFELE (Boito)
meh-fee-stoh-feh-leh

MERCANDANTE, GIUSEPPE
mehr-kahn-dahn-tay, joo-zep-pay

MEYERBEER, GIACOMO [G]
my-yer-"bare," jah-koh-moh

MEZZO- (-FORTE, -PIANO)
met-soh. . .

MICHELANGELLI, ARTURO BENEDETTI
mee-keh-lahn-jeh-lee, ahr-too-roh beh-neh-"debt"-tee

MILAN ANGELICUM ORCHESTRA
mee-lahn ahn-jeh-luh-koom

MINUET
min-yoo-eht

MODERATO
moh-deh-rah-toh
mah-duh-rah-toh

MOLINARI-PRADELLI, FRANCESCO
moh-lee-nah-ree-prah-del-lee, frahn-ches-koh

MOLTO
"mole-toe"

MONDO DELLA LUNA (Haydn)
mohn-doh deh-lah-loo-nah

MONTEVERDI, CLAUDIO
mohn-teh-vehr-dee, "cloudy"-oh

MOSÈ IN EGITTO (Rossini)
moh-zeh een eh-jee-toh

MUTI, RICCARDO
moo-tee, ree-kar-doh

NABUCCO (Verdi)
nah-boo-koh

NERONE (Boito)
neh-roh-nay

NINA, O LA PAZZA PER AMORE (Paisiello)
nee-nah oh-lah-paht-sah-pehr-ah-"more"-ay

NOTTURNO (nocturne)
noh-toor-noh
nahk-tern

OBLIGATO
oh-blee-gah-toh
ah-bluh-gah-toh

OCCASIONE FA IL LADRO (Rossini)
oh-kah-zyoh-nay fah-eel-lah-droh

ORCHESTRA DEL TEATRO ALL SCALA
or-keh-strah dehl tay-ah-troh ahl skah-lah

ORFEO (Monteverdi)
or-fay-oh

ORFEO ED EURIDICE (Gluck)
or-fay-oh ehd-oo-ree-dee-cheh

OSTINATO
oh-stee-nah-toh
ah-stuh-nah-toh

PAGANINI, NICOLÒ
pah-gah-nee-nee, nee-koh-loh

PALESTRINA, GIOVANNI
pah-leh-stree-nah, joh-vah-nee

PASSACAGLIA
pah-sah-kah-lyah

PAVAROTTI, LUCIANO
pah-vah-roh-tee, loo-chah-noh

PERGOLESI, GIOVANNI
pehr-goh-lay-zee, joh-vah-nee

PERSICHETTI, VINCENT [E]
"purr"-suh-keh-tee, vihn-sent

PIANISSIMO
pee-ah-nee-see-moh
pee-uh-nih-suh-moh

PIANO
pyah-noh (volume)
pee-a-noh (instrument)

PIMPINONE (Telemann)
peem-pee-noh-nay

PIÙ MOSSO
pyoo-moh-soh

PIZZICATO
pee-tsee-kah-toh
"pits"-uh-kah-toh

POCHISSIMO, POCO
poh-kee-see-moh, poh-koh

POLLINI, MAURIZIO
poh-lee-nee, mow-ree-tsee-oh

PONCHIELLI, AMILCARE
pohn-kyeh-lee, ah-mil-kah-ray

PRESTISSIMO
preh-stee-see-moh
preh-stih-suh-moh

PUCCINI, GIACOMO
poo-chee-nee, jah-koh-moh

PULCINELLA (Stravinsky)
"pool"-chee-neh-lah

QUINTETTO FAURE DI ROMA
kween-teh-toh foh-ray dee roh-mah

RAIMONDI, RUGGERO
ry-mohn-dee, roo-jeh-roh

RESPIGHI, OTTORINO
reh-spee-gee, oh-toh-ree-noh

RICCI, RUGGIERO
ree-chee, roo-jyeh-roh

RICCIARELLI, KATIA
ree-chah-reh-lee, kah-tyah

RICERCARE
ree-chehr-kah-ray

RIGOLETTO (Verdi)
"rig-a-let"-oh

RODELINDA (Handel)
roh-duh-"Linda"

RONDO
rahn-doh

ROSSINI, GIOACCHINO
roh-see-nee, jwah-kee-noh

SALIERI, ANTONIO
sah-lyeh-ree, ahn-toh-nee-oh

SAMARTINI, GIOVANNI BATTISTA
sah-mar-tee-nee, joh-vah-nee bah-tee-stah

SAMARTINI, GIUSEPPE
sah-mar-tee-nee, joo-zep-pay

SARABANDE
sah-ruh-bahnd

SCARLATTI, ALESSANDRO
skar-lah-tee, ah-leh-sahn-droh

SCARLATTI, DOMENICO
skar-lah-tee, do-meh-nee-koh

SCHERZANDO
skehr-tsahn-doh

SCHERZO
skehr-tsoh (= "scare"-tsoh)

SCIMONE, CLAUDIO
shee-moh-nay, "cloudy"-oh

SCOTTO, RENATA
skoht-toh, reh-nah-tah

SEMIRAMIDE (Rossini)
seh-mee-rah-mee-day

SERAFIN, TULLIO
seh-ruh-fin, too-lyoh

SERENI, MARIO
seh-ray-nee, mah-ree-oh

SFORZANDO
sfor-tsahn-doh

SIEPI, CESARE
syay-pee, cheh-zah-ray

SIMON BOCCANEGRA (Verdi)
see-mohn boh-kah-nay-gruh

SINFONIA DA CAMERA
seen-“phony”-uh dah kah-muh-ruh

SINOPOLI, GIUSEPPE
sih-noh-poh-lee, joo-zep-pay

SONATA
soh-nah-tah (<t> = [t])
suh-nah-tuh (<t> = [flap])

SOSARME, RÈ DI MEDIA (Handel)
soh-sahr-may, ray-dee-meh-dee-ah

STACCATO
stah-kah-toh (<t> = [t])
stuh-kah-toh (<t> = [flap])

STRADELLA, ALESSANDRO
strah-deh-lah, ah-leh-sahn-droh

STRANO, FRANCESCO
strah-noh, frahn-chehs-kah

STRATTA, ETTORE
strah-tah, eh-toh-ray

SUOR ANGELICA (Puccini)
“swore” ahn-jeh-lee-kah

TACCHINO, GABRIEL
tah-kee-noh, gah-bree-ehl

TADDEI, GIUSEPPE
tah-day-ee, joo-zep-pay

TARTINI, GIUSEPPE
tar-tee-nee, joo-zep-pay

TEBALDI, RENATA
teh-bahl-dee, reh-nah-tah

TORELLI, GIUSEPPE
toh-reh-lee, joo-zep-pay

TOSCA (Puccini)
“toss”-kuh

TOSCANINI, ARTURO
tohs-kah-nee-nee, ahr-too-roh

TOZZI, GIORGIO
toh-tsee, jor-joh

TURANDOT (Puccini)
toor-ahn-doht

TURRIZIANI, ANGELO
too-ree-tsyah-nee

UGHI, UTO
oo-gee, oo-toh

UN BALLO IN MASCHERA (Verdi)
oon-bah-loh een mahs-keh-rah

UN GIORNO DI REGNO (Verdi)
oon-johr-noh dee-“rain”-yoh

VENERE E ADONE (Scarlatti)
vehn-“air”-ay ay-ah-doh-nay

VERDI, GIUSEPPE
vehr-dee, joo-zep-pay

VIVACE
vee-vah-chay
vih-vah-chee

VIVALDI, ANTONIO
vee-vahl-dee, ahn-toh-nee-oh

VIVIANI, GIOVANNI BUONAVENTURA
vee-vyah-nee, joh-vah-nee bwoh-nah-ven-too-rah

WOLF-FERRARI, ERMANNO
vohlf-feh-rah-ree, ehr-mah-noh

JAPANESE

AKIYAMA, KAZUYOSHI
ah-kee-yah-mah, kah-zoo-yoh-shee

ARITA, CHIYOKO
ah-ree-tah, chee-yoh-koh

ARITA, MASAHIRO
ah-ree-tah, mah-sah-hee-roh

HARADA, SADAO
hah-rah-dah, sah-dow

MIDORI
mee-“door”-ee

NISHIZAKI, TAKAKO
nee-shee-zah-kee, tah-kah-koh

OZAWA, SEIJI
oh-zah-wuh, say-jee

SATO, HIKARU
sah-toh, hee-kah-roo

SUZUKI, HIDEMI & ICHIRO
soo-zoo-kee, hee-deh-mee & ee-chee-roh

TASHI
tah-shee

TOYOHIKO, SATOH
to-yoh-hee-koh, sah-toh

UCHIDA, MITSUKO
oo-chee-dah, meets-koh

YAMASHITA, KAZUHITO & NAOKO
yah-mahsh-tah, kah-zoo-hee-toh & nah-oh-koh

KOREAN

CHANG, HAE-WON
chahng, hay-wohn

CHUNG, KYUNG WHA
chuhng, kyuhng-wah

HOEY, CHOO
hoy, choo

KANG, DONG-SUK
kahng, dohng-sook

PAIK, KUN WOO
“peck,” koon-woo

YIP, WING-SIE
yeep, “wing”-syeh

LATIN

These names are mostly Medieval or Church Latin, though a few names of groups are more “antique” sounding.

ANTIQUA MUSICA ORCHESTRA
an-tee-kwuh moo-zee-kuh

ARS REDIVIVA
ars “ready”-vee-vuh

CAMERATA ACADEMICA DES MOZARTEUMS SALZBURG
kah-muh-rah-tah ah-kah-day-mee-kah dehs moh-tsahr-tay-ooms zahlts-boorg

CANTUS (Pärt)
kahn-toos

CAPELLA kah-peh-lah
CLEMENTINA ISTROPOLITANA
kleh-men-tee-nah ee-struh-puh-lee-tah-nah

CARMINA BURANA (Orff)
kahr-mee-nuh boo-rah-nuh

COLLEGIUM
koh-lay-gee-oom
C. AUREUM
aw-ree-oom
C. MUSICUM
moo-zee-koom

CONCENTUS MUSICUS VIENNA
kohn tsen-toos moo-zee-koos

CONSORTIUM MUSICUM
kuhn-"sore"-tee-uhm moo-zee-koom

ET ECCE TERRAE MOTUS (Brumel)
eht-eh-chay teh-reh moh-toos

FRATRES (Pärt)
frah-trays

LACHRIMAE (Dowland)
lah-kree-may

MAGNIFICAT
mahg-nih-fih-kaht

MISSA ECCE ANCILLA DOMINI (Dufay)
mee-suh eh-chay ahn-chee-lah doh-mee-nee

MISSA GLORIA TIBI TRINITAS (Taverner)
mee-sah "Gloria" tee-bee tree-nee-tahs

MISSA PAPAE MARCELLI (Palestrina)
mee-sah pah-pay mahr-cheh-lee

MISSA SOLEMNIS (Beethoven)
mee-sah suh-lehm-nees

MUSICA ANTIQUA
moo-zih-kuh ahn-tee-kwah

PSALMUS HUNGARICUS (Kodály)
sahl-moos hoon-gah-ree-koos

SCHOLA CANTORUM BASILIENSES
skoh-luh kahn-toh-ruhm bah-see-lyehn-suhs

SONI VENTORUM WIND QUINTET
soh-nee vehn-toh-ruhm

TABULA RASA (Pärt)
tah-boo-lah rah-sah

POLISH

Note on Polish last names

Polish last names ending in <(ow/ew)ski> = ["off"-skee, (y)ehf-skee] belong to men, while those in <(ow/ew)ska> belong to women. There are no diacritics, as compared with Czech <(sk)ý, (sk)á>. If the name stem ends in <t>, the result is <-ecki, -icki> = [eht-skee, eet-skee] (Polish Americans are usually [eh-kee, ih-kee].) Stems that end in <an> yield <ański>. The other typical Polish endings are <-ów> = [oof] and <-owicz, -ewicz> = [oh-vihch, (y)eh-vihch], and they are unisex. (Compare Russian <-ov, -ovich> in Movement 4. See also the footnote on Stokowski in Movement 2.)

ALPERYN, GRACIELA ♪
ahl-peh-rihn, grah-tsyeh-lah

BIAŁYSTOK (city) ◆
byah-wih-stohk

BOROWSKA, JOANNA ♪
boh-rohf-shak, yoh-ah-nah

BYDGOSZCZ (city) ◆
"bid"-gohshch

CZĘSTOCHOWA (city) ◆
chehn-stoh-khoh-vah

GDAŃSK (city) ◆
gdahnsk

GÓRECKI, HENRYK MIKOŁAJ ♪
goo-reht-skee, "hen"-rihk mee-koh-"why"

HARNASIE (Szymanowski)
hahr-nah-sheh

HORSZOWSKI, MIECZYSŁAW ♪
hor-sh"off"-skee, myeh-chih-swahf

JANOWSKI, MAREK 𝄞
yah-nawf-skee, mah-rek

KATOWICE (city) ◆
kah-toh-vee-tseh

KILANOWICZ, ZOFIA ♪
kee-lah-noh-vihch, zoh-fyah

KLETZKI, PAUL (KLECKI) 𝄞
klet-skee, powl

KRAKÓW [P] = CRACOW [E] ◆
(city) krah-koof

LANDOWSKA, WANDA ♪
lahn-"doff"-skah, vahn-dah

LEIBOWITZ, RENE 𝄞
ly-boh-vits, reh-nay

ŁÓDŹ (city) ◆
wooch

LUTOSLAWSKI, WITOLD ✍
loot-uh-slahf-skee, vee-"told"

MAKSYMIUK, JERZY 𝄞
mahk-sihm-yook, yeh-zhee

MICHEJEW, ALEXANDER ♪
mee-khay-ehf

MONIUSZKO, STANISŁAW ✍
mohn-yoosh-koh, stah-nee-swahf

MOSZKOWSKI, MORITZ ✍
mohsh-"cough"-skee, moh-rits

OCHMANN, WIESŁAW ♪
okh-mahn, vyeh-swahf

OSTROŁĘKA (city) ◆
aw-stroh-wenk-ah

OŚWĘCIM (city) ◆
aw-shvehn-cheem

PADEREWSKI, IGNACE JAN ♪ ✍
pah-deh-reff-skee, ihg-nahts yahn

PENDERECKI, KRZYSZTOF ✍ 𝄞
pen-deh-rets-skee, kshih-shtawf

RAPPÉ, JADWIGA ♪
rah-pay, yahd-vee-gah

RZESZÓW (city) ◆
zheh-shoof

SKROWACZEWSKI, STANISŁAW 𝄞
skroh-vah-cheff-skee, stah-nee-swahf

SOSNOWIEC (city)
"saw-snow"-vyehts

STOKOWSKI, LEOPOLD
stuh-"cough"-skee, lay-uh-pohld

STRYJA, KAROL
stree-yah, kah-rohl

SWAROWSKY, HANS
svah-roff-skee, hahns

ŚWIERCZEWSKI, MICHEL
shvyehr-chef-skee, mee-shel

SZCZECIN (city)
shcheh-cheen

SZERYNG, HENRYK
sheh-ring, "hen-rick"

SZYMANOWSKI, KAROL
shih-mahn-"off"-skee, kah-ruhl

WAŁĘSA, LECH
(President of Poland, 1995)
vah-wehn-sah, lehkh

WARSZAWA (capital city)
vahr-shah-vah (= Warsaw)

WIENIAWSKI, HENRYK
vyeh-nyahf-skee, hen-"rick"

WROCŁAW (city)
vroht-swahf

PORTUGUESE

ALMEIDA, ANTONIO DE
ahl-may-duh, ahn-toh-nee-oh day

AMAZONAS (Villa Lobos)
ah-mah-zoh-nuhsh

ASSAD, SERGIO & ODAIR
ah-sahd, sehr-jee-oo & oh-dah "ear"

BACHIANAS BRASILEIRAS (Villa Lobos)
bahk-yah-nahsh brah-zeel-"air-ish"

CHÔROS (Villa Lobos)
shoh-roosh

COSTA, SEQUEIRA
kohsh-tuh, seh-kway-ruh

DANÇA DOS MOSQUITOS (Villa Lobos)
dahn-sah dohsh moo-skee-toosh

DANÇAS AFRICANAS (Villa Lobos)
dahn-sahsh ah-free-kah-nahsh

EROSÃO (Villa Lobos)
eh-roo-zõw

FALÚ, EDUARDO
fah-loo, ed-wahr-doo

GÊNESIS (Villa Lobos)
zheh-nay-zihsh

NOVÃES, GUIOMAR
noo-vãh-ehsh, gee-oo-mar

ORTIZ, CRISTINA
or-tees, kris-tee-nah

SANTOS, TURIBIO
sahn-tohsh, too-ree-bee-oh

UIRAPURÚ (Villa-Lobos)
oo-ee-rah-poo-roo

VILLA-LOBOS, HEITOR
vee-lah loh-boosh, hay-tor

ROMANIAN

ANDREESCU, HORIA
ahn-dray-ehs-koo, hohr-yah

BACIU, ION
bah-choo, yohn

BALANESCU QUARTET
bah-luh-nehs-koo

BREDICEANU, MIHAI
bray-dee-chah-noo, mee-"high"

CELEBIDACHE, SERGIU
chel-leh-bih-dah-keh, sehr-joo

CHIŞINĂU (Moldova)
= KISHINEV, KISHINËV
kee-shee-now

CLUJ-NAPOCA (city)
kloozh-nah-poh-kah

COMISSIONA, SERGIU
koh-"missy"-oh-nah, sehr-joo

CONTA, IOSIF
kohn-tah, yoh-seef

ENESCO, GEORGES
eh-nes-koh, zhorzh

GEORGESCU, REMUS
johr-jehs-koo, ray-moos

LIPATTI, DINU
lih-pah-tee, dee-noo

LUCA, SERGIU
loo-kah, sehr-joo

LUPU, RADU
loo-poo, rah-doo

MIRICIOIU, NELLY
mee-ree-choy-yoo

PERLEA, IONEL
pehr-lay-uh, yoh-nel

STANCIU, SIMION
stahn-choo

TIMIŞOARA (city)
tee-mee-shwah-rah

ZAMFIR, GHEORGHE
zahm-feer, geh-or-geh

RUSSIAN AND UKRAINIAN

See "Notes on Names" under Russian and Ukrainian in Movement 4.

ALEKO
(Tchaikovsky; Rachmaninov)
ah-leh-koh

ALEXANDROV, BORIS
ah-lehk-sahn-druhf, boh-rihs

ANICHANOV, ANDRÉ
ahn-nee-chah-nuhf, ahn-dray

ARENSKY, ANTON
ah-ren-skee, ahn-"tone"

ASHKENAZY, VLADIMIR
ahsh-keh-nah-zee, vlah-dee-meer

BABA YAGA (Liadov)
bah-buh yah-gah

BALAKIREV, MILY
bah-lah-kee-rehf, mee-lee

BEREZOVSKY, BORIS
beh-reh-zohf-skee, boh-rihs

BERMAN, LAZAR
behr-muhn, lah-zahr

BEZRODNY, SERGEI
byez-rohd-nee, sehr-gay

BISENGALIEV, MARAT
bih-sehn-gah-lyehf, mah-raht

BOLSHOI THEATRE ORCHESTRA
bahl-shoy (√ "bowl"-shoy)

BORIS GODUNOV (Mussorgsky)
bah-rees guh-"dune-off"

BORODIN, ALEXANDER
"bore-a-dean"

BYCHKOV, SEMYON
"bitch-cough," seem-yohn

CHALIAPIN, FEODOR
shah-lyah-pin, fyoh-der

CHERKASSKY, SHURA
"chair"-kahs-skee, shoo-ruh

CHISTYAKOV, ANDREI
chee-styah-"cough," ahn-dray

DAVIDOVICH, BELLA
dah-vee-doh-vihch, beh-luh

DILETSKY, NIKOLAI
dih-leht-skee, nih-koh-ly
(U/P: Dylecki, Mikołaj)

DMITRY DONSKOY (Rubinstein)
dmee-tree dahn-skoy

EDELMANN, SERGEI
ay-del-muhn, sehr-gay

EGOROV, YOURI
yeh-gor-uhf, yoo-ree

FEDOSEYEV, VLADIMIR
feh-doh-syeff, vlah-dee-meer

FELTSMAN, VLADIMIR
felts-muhn, vlah-dee-meer

GILELS, EMIL
gih-lelz, eh-meel

GILILOV, PAVEL
gih-lee-luhf, pah-vel

GLAZUNOV, ALEXANDER
glah-zoo-nuhf

GLIÈRE, REINHOLD [G]
glee-"air," ryn-hold

GLINKA, MIKHAIL
gleen-kuh, mee-khah-eel

GOLOVSCHIN, IGOR
guh-lahv-sheen, ee-guhr

GUBAIDULINA, SOFIA
goo-by-doo-lee-nuh, soh-fyuh

HEIFETZ, JASCHA
"high"-fits, yah-shuh

IPPOLITOV-IVANOV, MIKHAIL
ee-pah-lee-"tough" ee-vah-nuhf, mee-khah-eel

ISLAMEY (Balakirev)
ihs-lah-may

IVAN SUSANIN (Glinka)
ee-vahn soo-sah-nihn

JABLOKOV, ALEXANDER
yah-bluh-"cuff"

KABALEVSKY, DMITRI
kah-bah-lyef-skee, dmee-tree

KAMARINSKAYA (Glinka)
kah-mah-reen-shah-yah

KATERINA ISMAILOVA (Shostakovich)
kah-teh-reen-uh ihz-my-luh-vuh

KHOVANSHCHINA (Mussorgsky)
khoh-vahnsh-chee-nuh

KIEV, KIEW [R] kee-yehv
KYYIV, KYÏV [U] kih-yeev

KIKIMORA (Liadov)
kee-kee-muh-ruh

KISHINEV, KISHINËV = CHIŞINĂU
kee-shee-nyawf

KONDRASHIN, KIRIL
kohn-drah-shin, keer-rill

KOUSSEVITZKY, SERGE
koo-suh-vit-skee, sehrzh

KREMER, GIDON
kray-mer, gee-dohn

LAZAREV, ALEKSANDR
lah-zuh-reff, ahl-lek-sahndr

LEBEDINOE OZERO (Tchaikovsky)
leh-beh-dee-nuh-yuh oh-zyeh-ruh

LVOV, L'VOV [R]: lvohf
LWÓW [P]: lvoof
LVIV, LVIW [U]: lveev
(city in Ukraine)

LYATOSHYNSKY, BORIS [U]
lyah-toh-"shin"-skee, boh-rees

MILMAN, MIKHAIL
mil-muhn, mee-khah-eel

MLADA (Rimsky-Korsakov)
mlah-duh

MUSSORGSKY, MODEST
moo-sork-skee, moh-dest

OBRAZTSOVA, ELENA
oh-brahs-tsoh-vah, yeh-lyeh-nuh

OISTRAKH, DAVID & IGOR
oy-strahkh, dah-veed & ee-guhr

PAN VOYEVODA (Rimsky-Korsakov)
pahn-voy-uh-voh-duh

PERGAMENSCHIKOW, BORIS
pehr-gah-myehn-shee-kuhf, "bore"-ihs

PETRUSHKA / PETROUCHKA (Stravinsky)
peh-troosh-kuh

PIATIGORSKY, GREGOR
pyah-tih-gor-skee, greh-gor

PROKOFIEV, SERGEI
pruh-"cough"-yef, sehr-gay

RAKHMANINOV, SERGEI (RACHMANINOFF)
rahkh-mah-nee-n"off," sehr-gay

RAYCHEV, ROUSLAN
ry-chef, roos-lahn

RICHTER, SVIATOSLAV
rihkh-ter, svyah-tuh-slahf

RIMSKY-KORSAKOV, NIKOLAI
rim-skee kor-suh-"cuff," nih-koh-ly

ROSTROPOVICH, MSTISLAV
rah-struh-poh-vihch, mstee-slahf

ROZHDESTVENSKY, GENNADY
rohzh-dyest-ven-skee, geh-nah-dee

SADKO (Rimsky-Korsakov)
saht-koh

SCHERBAKOV, KONSTANTIN (SHCHERBAKOV)
shchehr-bah-"cough," kuhn-stahn-teen

SCRIABIN, ALEXANDER
skryah-bin, a-leg-zan-der

SHCHEDRIN, RODION
shcheh-dreen, roh-dee-ohn

SHOSTAKOVICH, DMITRI
shah-stuh-koh-vihch, dmee-tree

SHOSTAKOVICH, MAXIM
shah-stuh-koh-vich, mahk-seem

STRAVINSKY, IGOR
struh-vihn-skee, ee-gor

SVETLANOV, YEVGENY
svet-lah-noff, yev-gay-nee

TANEYEV, SERGEI
tah-nay-eff, sehr-gay

TCHAIKOVSKY, PYOTR ILYICH (TSCHAIKOWSKI)
chy-"cough"-skee, pee-ter il-yich (pyohtr il-yich)

TEMIRKANOV, YURI
teh-meer-kah-noff, yoo-ree

TUROVSKY, YULI
toor-"off"-skee, yoo-lee

UTKIN, ALEXEI
oot-kin, ah-lek-say

VISHNEVSKAYA, GALINA
vee-shnyehf-skah-yah, gah-lee-nuh

SCANDINAVIAN

Swedish, Danish, and Norwegian are all included here. Assume Swedish, unless marked [D] or [N].

ALFVÉN, HUGO
ahl-fin, hyoo-goh

ATTERBERG, KURT
ah-ter-behr, koort

AUSTBØ, HÅKON [N]
owst-bö, haw-kohn

BERG, GUNNAR [D]
behr, goo-nahr

BERWALD, FRANZ [G]
behr-vahlt, frahnts

BIRKELAND, ØYSTEIN [N]
beer-kuh-lahn, öy-stihn

BJOERLING, JUSSI
byör-ling, yoo-see (=byer-)

EDGREN, INGEMAR
ed-gren, ing-uh-mahr

FLAGSTAD, KIRSTEN [N]
flahg-stahd, keer-sten

FRANSSEN, OLGA
frahn-suhn, ohl-gah

GEDDA, NICOLAI
geh-dah, nih-koh-ly

GIMSE, HÅVARD [N]
yeem-seh, haw-vahr

GRIEG, EDVARD [N]
greeg, ehd-vard

HALVORSEN, JOHAN
hahl-vor-sen, yoh-hahn

HANSEN, JØRGEN ERNST [N]
hahn-sen, yör-gen, ehrnst

HÓSTBALLADER (Atterberg)
höst-bah-lah-der

NILSSON, BIRGIT
nihl-suhn, beer-giht

NØRGÅRD, PER [D]
nör-"gohr," pehr

ODENSE SYMPHONY [D]
oh-dehn-suh

PAA VIDDERNE (Delius) [N]
paw-vih-dehr-nuh

PETTERSSON, GUSTAF ALLAN
peh-tehr-suhn, goo-stahf

RAFN, EYVIND [D]
rah-fin ay-vin

SCHØNWANDT, MICHAEL [D]
shön-vahnt

SEGERSTAM, LEIF
seh-ger-stahm, "leaf"

SINDING, CHRISTIAN [N]
sihn-ding

SÖDERSTRÖM, ELISABETH
sö-der-strohm

SOKKELUND SANGKOR [D]
soh-kuh-loon sahng-kohr

SÖNSTEVOLD, KNUT
sohn-steh-vohld, knoot

STENGAARD, FRODE [D]
stehn-gohr, froh-duh

TOFTE-HANSEN, JENS
tohf-tuh-hahn-sen, yens

WAGNER, BØRGE [D]
vahg-ner, "burger"

WIRÉN , DAG
vee-rehn, dahg

WIXELL, INGVAR
vik-suhl, ing-vahr

SPANISH

The transcription of <ci, ce, z> in the Western Hemisphere as [see, seh, s] vs. Eastern Hemisphere as [thee, theh, th] suggests the origin of a relevant name, but both varieties of Spanish are good Spanish.

AGUADO, DIONYSIO
ah-gwah-doh, dee-oh-nee-syoh

ALBENIZ, ISAAC
ahl-bay-neeth, ee-sahk

ANGELES, VICTORIA DE LOS
ahn-kheh-lehs, vihk-toh-ree-ah deh-lohs

ANIEVAS, AGUSTIN
ah-nyeh-vahs, ah-goo-steen

ARAIZA, FRANCISCO
ah-rah-ee-sah, frahn-sees-koh

ARRAU, CLAUDIO
ah-row, klow-dee-oh

ARRIAGA, JUAN CRISOSTOMO
ah-ree-ah-gah, (kh)wahn kree-soh-stoh-moh

ARROYO, MARTINA
ah-roy-oh, mahr-tee-nah

BATIZ, ENRIQUE
bah-tees, ehn-ree-kay

BOITO, ARRIGO
bo-ee-"toe," ah-ree-go

BOLET, JORGE
boh-leht, jorj

BONELL, CARLOS
boh-nehl, kar-lohs

CABALLE, MONTSERRAT
kah-by-ay, mohn-seh-raht

CANTILENA
kahn-tee-lay-nah

CASALS, PABLO
kah-sahlz, pah-bloh

CHAVEZ, CARLOS
chah-vehs

CONCIERTO DE ARANJUEZ (Rodrigo)
kohn-thyehr-toh day ah-rahn-khwayth

CUATRO SOLES (Chavez)
kwah-troh soh-lays

DE FALLA, MANUEL
duh-fy-yuh, mahn-well

DE LA TOMASA, JOSÉ
deh-lah-toh-mah-sah, hoh-say

DE LARROCHA, ALICIA
deh-lah-"roach"-ah, ah-lee-thee-ah

DE LOS ANGELES, VICTORIA
deh-lohs-ahn-kheh-lehs, vihk-toh-ree-uh

DE PALMA, PIERO
deh-pahl-mah, pyay-roh

DOMINGO, PLACIDO
doh-meen-goh, plah-see-doh

EL AMOR BRUJO (de Falla)
ehl-ah-"more" broo-khoh

EL SOMBRERO DE TRE PICOS (de Falla)
ehl sohm-b"rare"-oh day tray pee-kohs

ESTANCIA (Ginastera)
eh-stahn-see-ah

FALLA, MANUEL DE
fy-yuh, mahn-well duh

FERNANDEZ, EDUARDO
fehr-nahn-dehs, ed-wahr-doh

GELBER, BRUNO-LEONARDO [G]
gehl-ber, broo-noh lay-oh-nahr-doh

GINASTERA, ALBERTO
khee-nah-steh-rah, ahl-behr-toh

GOYESCAS (Granados)
goy-ehs-kahs

GRANADOS, ENRIQUE
grah-nah-dohs, ehn-ree-kay

GRUPO DE MUSICA "ALFONSO X EL SABIO"
groo-poh day moo-see-kah ahl-fohn-soh dee-ehs ehl sah-bee-oh

GUTIERREZ, HORACIO
goo-tyeh-rays, oh-rah-see-oh

IBERIA (Albeniz)
ee-"berry"-uh

JALAPA (city in Mexico)
(k)hah-lah-pah

KRAUS, ALFREDO
krows (="house"), ahl-fray-doh

LA BURRA MARIA
la-boo-rah, mah-ree-ah

LA VIDA BREVE (de Falla)
lah-vee-dah bray-vay

LAGOYA, ALEXANDRE
lah-goy-ah, a-lek-zan-der

LECUONA, ERNESTO
leh-kwoh-nuh, ehr-nes-toh

LOPEZ-COBOS, JESUS
loh-pehs-koh-bohs, hay-soos

LORENGAR, PILAR
lor-en-gahr, pee-lahr

MANUGUERRA, MATTEO
mah-noo-geh-rah, mah-tay-oh

MISSA DEL CID (Weir)
mee-sah del-seed

MORENO TORROBA, FEDERICO
moh-ray-noh tor-roh-bah, feh-deh-ree-koh

MORENO, ALFONSO
mor-ray-noh, ahl-fohn-soh

NIN-CULMELL, JOAQUÍN MARÍA
neen-kool-mehl, (kh)wah-keen mah-ree-ah

NOCHES EN LOS JARDINES DE ESPAÑA (de Falla)
noh-chehs ehn lohs khahr-dee-nehs deh-eh-spahn-yah

OAXACA (city in Mexico)
wah-(k)hah-kah

OREBRO CHAMBER ORCHESTRA
oh-reh-broh

ORQUESTA DE CONCIERTOS DE MADRID
or-kay-stah day kohn-thee-ehr-tohs day mah-dreed

ORQUESTA NACIONAL DE ESPAÑA
or-kay-stah nah-thee-oh-nahl day eh-spah-nyah

PAITA, CARLOS
py-ee-tah, "car"-lohs

PANAMBÍ (Ginastera)
pah-nahm-bee

PEÑA, PACO
"pain"-yah, pah-koh

RETABLO DE MAESE PEDRO (de Falla)
ray-tah-bloh day-mah-ay-say pay-droh

ROMERO, ANGEL
roh-"mare"-oh, ahn-khell

ROMERO, CELEDONIO & PEPE
roh-"mare"-oh, theh-leh-doh-nyoh & peh-pay

SARASATE, PABLO DE
sah-rah-sah-tay, pah-bloh deh

SEGOVIA, ANDRES
seh-goh-vee-ah, ahn-drays

SEREBRIER, JOSE
seh-reh-bree-"air", hoh-say

SOLEÁ, MAÑA (MARIA)
soh-lay-ah, mah-nyah

SOLER, (PADRE) ANTONIO
soh-lair, (pah-dray) ahn-toh-nee-oh

SURINACH, CARLOS
soo-ree-nahk

TARREGA, FRANCISCO
tar-reh-ga, frahn-thees-koh

TONADAS (Nin-Culmell)
toh-nah-dahs

TURINA, JOAQUIN
too-ree-nuh, (kh)wa-keen

VICTORIA, TOMAS LUIS DE
vihk-toh-ree-ah, "toe"-mahs, loo-ees deh

VIRUMBRALES, LUIS LOZANO
vee-room-brah-lays, loo-ees loh-sah-noh

YEPES, NARCISO
yeh-pays, nar-thee-soh

ZABALETA, NICANOR
zah-bah-lay-tah, nee-kah-nor

ZAPATEADO (Granados)
sah-pah-tay-ah-doh

FIVE INTERLUDES FOR TONGUE AND LARYNX

These short sketches present some terms and concepts that announcers will find useful for juggling sounds and letters, for talking about language issues with other announcers, and for mentioning them to listeners—not to mention for defending your choice of pronunciation against attack from those "know better." Familiarity with these terms will also make the individual language explanations in Movement 4 more understandable. Readers with a background in linguistics will recognize references to larger principles of that discipline, but theoretical issues will be side-stepped and phonetic particulars will be glossed over.

Interlude 1. The Voicing Principle

As was mentioned in Movement 1, several Latin letters represent the same consonant sounds in most European languages. The letters <b, p, f, m, n, k, t, d, r, l>, then, are also the symbols for the sounds [b, p, f, m, n, k, t, d, r, l].[*] This first interlude brings to announcers' attention a property of sound that is useful for sorting out spelling discrepancies in several languages.

Two Kinds of Consonants

VOICING is a property of speech sounds that states whether your vocal chords are vibrating or not as you produce them.

> A *voiced* consonant is one that you pronounce with your vocal chords vibrating. You feel a "buzz" if you place your open hand on top of your head as you say

[*] Treat <r> and <l> as in English. The German and French have throat-roll [r] and Spanish, Italian, Polish, and Russian have tongue-tap or trilled [r]. In this author's opinion these have no place in English-speaking broadcasting. As for [l], English has two automatic variants: a so-called "light" one pronounced *before* a vowel and a so-called "dark" pronounced *after* a vowel, that is, before a consonant or at the end of a word. You may not hear it, but the [l]'s in such word pairs as "lid-dill, loss-Saul" are different. German and French have only "light-l", sometimes called "continental-l." Similarly, Scottish English has only "dark-l." (Pronouncing English words with light-l at the end or with "dark-l" at the beginning are typical marks of a German, French, or Scottish accent in American English.) Russian has both kinds. Unlike English, both can occur independently before and after vowels. (The light one is written <l'>.)

them. The letters <b, d, j, g> and <v, z> always represent *voiced* consonants in English. The consonants represented by <m, n, r, l> and all vowels are also voiced. Note that <s> can represent either a voiced consonant [z] or voiceless [s].

A *voiceless* consonant is one you produce without setting your vocal chords a-flutter. The letters <p, f, t, k> always represent *voiceless* consonants in English. the letter combinations <ch, sh> also represent voiceless consonants.

In the following pairs of English words notice the pronunciation of the *final* consonant *sound*. Pay attention only to sound and ignore spelling:

GROUP I	cab	cad	crag	calve (verb)	teethe (verb)	lose
GROUP II	cap	cat	crack	calf (noun)	teeth (noun)	loose

Listen to the *first* consonant sound of these words (ignore spelling):

GROUP I	zoo	this-that-Thy	jigger-gill -Jew
GROUP II	sue	thistle-thatch-thigh	chigger-chill-chew

Isolate the *middle* consonant in these (use your ears, not your eyes):

GROUP I	resort-design	northern	treasure-erosion	bridges
GROUP II	rescind-decide	North Pole	pressure-emission	britches

Group I consonants are *voiced* and Group II consonants are their *voiceless* counterparts. This voicing principle sets apart eight pairs of consonants: b/p, v/f, d/t, z/s, th(is)/th(istle), j/ch, zh/sh, g/k. (The consonant [m, n, r, l, y, w] are always voiced and have no voiceless pair.) Two interesting incongruities of English spelling obscure certain distinctions that may become issues for announcers: the fact that <z> is always a visual signal for a *voiced* consonant (mostly [z] in "zero" but occasionally [zh] in "azure"), while the *sound* [z] in English is represented by either <z> or <s>. The combination <th> is the only way to spell both the voiced and voiceless consonants.

Add <s> to the words in the first chart group. What does it *sound* like?

GROUP I	cabs	cads	crags	calves (pl. noun/sg. verb)	teethes (sg. verb)
GROUP II	caps	cats	cracks	calf's (possessive)	tooth's (possessive)

In Group I <s> = [z] (voiced) because all the words you add it to end in a *voiced* consonant. This is also true of words that end in vowels ("law/s" = [law/z]), nasals ("can/s" = [kar/z]), liquids ("car/s, call/s" = [kahr/z, kawl/z]), and glides ("cow/s" = [kow/z]). In Group II <s> = [s] (voiceless) because all the words you add it to end in a *voiceless* consonant. In the phonetic spelling in Movement 2, [s] means only [s], and you will have to keep yourself from treating the language-neutral sound [s] like the English letter <s> (which is either [s] or [z]). This is why, for example, Brahms and Casals come out in normal English as [brahmz] and [kuh-sahlz]. If they were spelled Brahmce and Casalce no one would have trouble saying the "correct" German [brahms] and Spanish [kah-sahls]. The sound, itself, is not the issue, just the difference between English spelling and the language-neutral phonetic symbol. The overwhelming majority of [z]-sounds in English are spelled with the <s>-letter, rather than <z>. (In written English, only Winnie the Pooh and Madison Avenue advertisers are allowed the privilege of using <z> for [z], as in "Pleez knock" and trade names like "Cheez Whiz.")

This awareness makes the letter-sound correspondences less chaotic. Here are some other points that will help you get oriented. Many of these schematic statements will recur in Movement 4.

The <s> in Latin and Spanish is always [s] (voiceless), while in Italian, French, and Portuguese the same <s> represents [s] (voiceless) at the beginning of a word and [z] (voiced) between vowels. In German <s> is voiced [z] at the beginning of a word and between vowels, but always voiceless [s] at the end of a word. The letter <z> in Spanish represents only a *voiceless* consonant: either [s], as in American Spanish, or voiceless [th] as in "think" in European Spanish, as in "Albeniz." In Italian and German the <z> letter represents a voiceless consonant *cluster*, namely, [ts] in Italian "pizzicato" and German "Mozart." (See Interlude 2 for the term *affricate*.) In Italian it can also represent the *voiced* consonant cluster [dz], as in "Donizetti."

Interlude 2. Consonants on Paper and in the Mouth

The four major "points of contact" in the mouth from the front to the back are lips, upper teeth, hard palate (roof of mouth), and soft palate (downslope back part of palate). Either your lips close or your tongue hits the back of the upper teeth, the roof of the mouth, or the back of it. The following consonant sounds are associated with one of these parts of the mouth, regardless of how English or another language spells them. In English they come in both voiced and voiceless pairs. (An additional set of terms is introduced below.) Imagine this diagram as a side view of mouth facing leftward.

	Front of mouth		**Roof of mouth**	**Back of mouth**
	LIP(S)	UPPER TEETH	HARD PALATE	SOFT PALATE
VOICED	[b, v]	[d, z, th] (Thy)	[j, zh]	[g]
VOICELESS	[p, f]	[t, s, th] (thigh)	[ch, sh]	[k, kh]
OTHER	[m] [w]	[n] [l] [r]	[ñ] [y]	[ng]

The points of contact go by slightly technical aliases. Consonants produced with the lip(s) are called *labial* = [lay-bee-uhl]. The "teeth" consonants are called *dental.* The "hard palate" consonants [sh, zh, ch, j] are called *palatals.* Since the anatomical term for the soft palate is *velum* = [vee-luhm], the consonants [k, g, kh] are *velar* = [vee-ler]. It is worth the effort to get familiar with these terms because it simplifies describing individual sounds and relations among sounds. Given that the consonants [m, n, ñ, ng] are *nasal*, then [m] is a *labial nasal*, and [n] is a *dental nasal.* All the languages in this book have at least those two nasals. English and German have a *velar nasal* spelled <-ng>—that is, there is no real [g] sound, just the semblance of one because the velum is involved. IPA has the symbol "stretched-n" called *engma*: [ŋ], more on which under "Catch" below. The consonants [l, r] are called *liquid*, and [w, y] are called *glides* (sometimes *semivowels*). Nasals, liquids, and glides as a group are always voiced in English and in the other languages in this book.

English has many pairs of words that illustrate how these sounds interact. They are not just changes in spelling, but "switched-on" vs. "switched-off" vocal cords without changing the point of contact. Here are some typical sound relationships across related words, whether the spelling shows it or not:

Change of voicing, no change of place

VOICELESS	[f] leaf	[s] close (call)	(No) use	advice	[th] teeth [θ]
↓	↓ ↓	↓ ↓	↓	↓	↓ ↓
VOICED	[v] leaves	[z] close (the door)	use (soap)	advise	[th] teethe [ð]
	Labial	*Dental*			

Other word pairs show "change of contact point" with no change in voicing: either they are both voiceless or both voiced. The change of place is sometimes reflected in English spelling, but more often than not the change is invisible.

All voiceless, but change of place

DENTAL	[s]	face	space	press	[t]	emote	emit
↓	↓	↓	↓	↓	↓	↓	↓
PALATAL	[sh]	facial	spatial	pressure	[sh]	emotion	emission*

All voiced, but change of place

DENTAL	[z]	seize	close	please	[d]	erode	divide
↓	↓	↓	↓	↓	↓	↓	↓
PALATAL	[zh]	seizure	closure	pleasure	[zh]	erosion	division**

Some Terminology for Types of Sounds

A few more terms will help to describe consonants and give announcers more precise ways of exchanging notes and impressions. (If ever you consult other book on singing diction or general phonetics you will find at least these terms and probably several others, but these will be plenty for now.) The voiced consonants [b, d, g] and the voiceless consonants [p, t, k] are called *stops* or *plosives* because you produce them by blocking the

---

* In English many nouns that have a dental consonant exchange it for a palatal consonant when forming an adjective. Many verbs do the same when forming related nouns.

** In all these examples the verb has a dental consonant, while the related noun has a palatal consonant. Note, too, that in "please-pleasure" there is not only an audible but invisible change of place of consonant but also an audible but invisible change of vowel: [ee] to [eh].

air and then letting it out with a bang. The voiced consonants [v, z, th, zh] and the voiceless consonants [f, s, th, sh] are called *fricatives* = [frih-kuh-tihvz] or *spirants* = [spy-rihnts] because you squeeze the air through a narrow opening with a hiss or hush. Thus, [f] is a *voiceless fricative*—specifically a *voiceless labial fricative*. Similarly, [d] is a *voiced stop*—specifically a *voiced dental stop*. The two consonants [ch, j] have characteristics of both stops and fricatives. (Recall that they are the combinations of [t+sh] and [d+zh].) For this reason they are called *affricates* = [a-fruh-kihts], so [ch] is a *voiceless affricate* and [j] is a *voiced affricate*. Both these affricates are *palatal affricates*. (For reference, the [ts] spelled by German and Italian <z> and by Czech and Polish <c> is a *voiceless dental affricate*. Italian <z> can also spell the *voiced dental affricate* [dz].) Here are a few consonants with their full linguistic appellation:

[b] = *voiced labial stop*
[f] = *voiceless labial fricative*
[ch] = *voiceless palatal affricate*
[k] = *voiceless velar stop*

[t] = *voiceless dental stop*
[z] = *voiced dental fricative*
[sh] = *voiceless palatal fricative*
[g] = *voiced velar stop*

So-called Hard and Soft Consonants

The impressionistic terms "hard" and "soft" apply to several different kinds of consonant contrasts. The terminology just introduced can now serve to sort them out.

THE TWO PRONUNCIATIONS OF <C> AND <G>. In "cat, get" the sounds [k, g] are said to be "hard," while in "cite, gem" the [s, j] are called "soft."

[k]	electric	conviction	[g]	legal	regal
↓	↓	↓	↓	↓	↓
[s]	electricity	convince	[j]	legitimate	regicide

Both sounds of <c> are voiceless and both sounds of <g> are voiced, so "hard" and "soft" here really refer to a change of contact place in the mouth. Given the terminology just introduced, it is possible to recast this use of hard-soft:

> [k] → [s] is a jump from soft palate to upper teeth, that is, "hard-c" is a *voiceless velar stop* [k], while "soft-c" is a *voiceless dental fricative* [s]. One of the functions of the letter <c> in English spelling is to signal the word sets where this shift can occur. (In English these jumps usually occur in words of Latin or French origin, and similar kinds of changes occur in all the Romance languages. See Movement 4.)

> [g] → [j] is a shorter trip: from soft palate to hard palate, that is, "hard-g" is a *voiced velar stop*, while "soft-g" is a *voiced palatal affricate*. English spelling has only the single letter <g> to play both roles. (English <j> always spells the *voiced palatal affricate*.)

Several languages experience similar consonant "place shifts." French <c> works like English, namely, <c> = [k] before <a, o, u> and [s] before <i, e>. Under the same circumstances, French <g> represents both [g] and [zh], according to the same principle as English [g] and [j], though the details are slightly different. (French moves the *voiced velar stop* [g] to a *voiced palatal fricative* [zh] compared with the English affricated [j].) Italian is more "symmetrical," that is, <c, g> represents a *voicelesss-voiced* pair of *velar stops* [k, g] and *palatal affricates* [ch, j]. See the next section for the Spanish usage of "hard/soft-g" and the German section in Movement for "hard/soft-ch" in Bach vs. ich.

THE TWO PRONUNCIATIONS OF <B-V> AND <D>. Another frequent use of the terms "hard" and "soft" is in reference to the pronunciation of Spanish <b-v> and <d> by many Spanish speakers. The "hard" pronunciations are [b] (for both <b> and <v>) and [d], that is, *voiced stops* (a *voiced labial stop* and a *voiced dental stop*, respectively. "Soft" <b-v> is a sort of [v] in many varieties of Spanish, and the "soft" variant occurs after a vowel. "Soft" [d] is [th], that is, *voiced dental fricative* [ð] as in "then".[*] Sometimes this term is applied to Spanish <g> in its two guises as "hard" *voiced velar stop* [g] in Miguel and "soft" *voiceless velar fricative* [kh] in Ginastera.

By way of comparison with <c, g>, it is clear now that that pair involves both a place shift (velar → dental, velar → palatal) and a type shift (from stop → fricative, stop → affricate). This Spanish usage of "hard-soft" means only a shift from stop to fricative but no place shift.

PALATALIZED CONSONANTS. This term appears mostly in connection with the Slavic languages, especially Russian. "Hard" and "soft," as applied to Russian consonants means "non-palatalized" and "palatalized." Palatalization means, roughly, raising the middle of the tongue toward the roof of the mouth while producing the consonant. Some varieties of Engish have palatalized consonants before the vowel [oo] in word pairs like "two lips" vs. "tulips," "do" vs. "dew," "loot" vs. "lute," "noodle" vs. "Newt'll..." Russian has this contrast for most of its consonants. The feature is transcribed in several ways:

an apostrophe after the letter:	<t'>
a kind of cedilla at the bottom:	<ţ>
a tilde over or next to it, modeled on Spanish ñ:	<t~>
a superscript "y" after the letter:	<t^{y}>

The last one is meant to suggest the *qualities* of the consonant [y], that is, raising the tongue toward the roof of the mouth but not blocking any air while doing it. This does not

* Strictly speaking this [th] is called an *interdental* because you produce it by sticking your tongue between your teeth. See also Danish in Movement 4. The term *spirantization* is sometimes used to describe the exchange of a stop for a fricative (spirant) without changing point of contact. It is stated in several places in this book that English speaking announcers need not try to incorporate this feature of Spanish into their announcing. Nonetheless, it comes up in conversation often enough that announcers ought to be able to talk about it consistently.

mean to pronounce a full [y]. (See Russian in Movement 4 for further remarks on the transcription and non-transcription of this quality.) It is a question for people who study English phonology whether words like "few, view, beauty, pure, cute" begin with palatalized [f^y, v^y, b^y, p^y] or the consonant clusters [[fy-, vy-], etc. In this book phonetic spellings like [fy-, vy-] indicate consonant clusters when a vowel follows them. Occasionally there is a raised "y," e.g, [n^y], as in French Bourgogne = [boor-<u>gohn</u>^{y}] or Polish Gdańsk = [gdahn^{y}sk]. (See "Cluster Reprise" below.)

Flap, Catch, Shift

In the section above, generally accepted linguistic terminology replaced vague terminology. The terms *flap, catch, shift* are semi-technical terms deliberately introduced here to fill a gap, describing sound distinctions that English speakers may be aware of but have no way to spell, particularly to variant pronunciations of <t> and <d>. Since English treats these consonants differently from most of the other languages in this book, people often point to these as signs of anglicizing. Whether this is good or bad, encouraged or discouraged, is not at issue. It is just useful to have a way of talking about them.

At the beginning or end of an English word, the letters <t> and <d> normally represent a voiceless dental stop [t] and a voiced dental stop [d], respectively. In the middle of an English word these two letters have variations that English has no way to spell. To English speakers the variations are unconscious and automatic.

FLAP. Recall the first time you heard the following popular song text from 1943:

> "Mairzy doats and dozey doats and liddle lamzie divey.
> A kiddlie divey, too, wouldn't you?"

These apparently nonsensical lines were adapted from a children's nursery rhyme and made into a hit song by Milton Drake, Al Hoffman, and Jerry Livingston.* The standard English spelling, is, of course:

> "Mares eat oats and does eat oats and little lambs eat ivy.
> A kid will eat ivy, too, wouldn't you?"

Regardless of its literary merit, this text illustrates a typical feature of American English: <t> and <d> between vowels "merge": they are both pronounced as a sound that is neither [t] nor [d]. It is more like the [r] in British "Larry" or the "tapped-r" in Spanish, Italian, or Russian. This sound is called a *flap*, because the tongue does not quite make contact with the upper teeth the way it does with either [t] or [d]. Nonetheless, it is a voiced sound, like [d]. This is why "Mairzy dotes" spells it with <d>. (This distorted spelling is a device often

---

* Actually, the idea came from Livingston's daughter, who brought home the following text from nursery school: Cowzy tweet and sowzy tweet and liddle sharkzy doysters.

used to represent speech—usually coarse speech—as in "whadaya want?") IPA recognizes that this sound is "r"-like by using a rounded or hooked [ɾ].

The unconscious rule that almost all speakers of American English follow is to make <t> and <d> into a flap when it occurs *between vowels*. This is especially clear when the vowel *before* the <t, d> is stressed. If the vowel immediately following <t, d> is stressed, flap does not usually occur. The <t, d> in "deter, reduce" are the regular stops [t, d] because the stressed vowel *follows* them. The <t, d> in "Peter, reader" are flaps because they *follow* the stressed vowels. Similarly, the difference between <t> and <d> is preserved in spelling but masked in speech in "latter-ladder," "liter-leader," "betting-bedding," "putting-pudding." (This is often a big stumbling block for children learning to spell.) This phenomenon occurs both within a word and across words. When a word that ends with [t, d] is followed by a word beginning with a vowel, it is pronounced as a flap. The <t> in "eat oats" and "eat ivy" and the <d> in "kid'll" all have this flap sound.

Pronouncing a flap is a typical feature of anglicizing* and one of the main factors that led the author of this book to introduce the terminology "full-Italian," "half-Italian," etc. in Movement 2. A "full-native" version has [t, d] as dental stops, while a "half" version may have flap, even though it is not explicit in the phonetic spellings. (The author assumed that native readers would do this intuitively, and sometimes there is an explicit note on it, as under Pavarotti. Here are some typical examples in which an American radio announcer can hardly imagine making any sound but flap:

- Scarlatti and similar Italian names, such as Pavarotti, Menotti,
- Italian terms such as "moderato," where both <d> and <t> are flaps; "adagietto," (where only <tt> is a flap but not <d>); but not "adagio."
- Spanish names like Aguado (See Spanish section in Movement 4 for the Spanish treatment of <d> under the same circumstances) or German names like Dittersdorf.
- Russian names like Katerina and Sviatoslav, but not Modest.

Notice that flap can also occur when neither of the vowels is clearly stressed, that is, when the stressed vowel of the word is neither immediately preceding nor immediately following the <t, d>, as in Katerina.

In IPA, then, the Mairzy dotes text, broken into syllables,would look something like this:

[mer-zi-ɾots-ən do-zi-ɾots-ən lɪ-ɾəl læm-zi-ɾaj-vi].

The other examples are [skar-la-ɾi, ma-ɾə-ra-ɾo, dɪ-ɾərz-dorf], and so forth.

---

* Some people consider the flap a mark of sloppiness or laziness on the part of American English speakers, probably because it does not match the letters <t, d>. It is not lazy. From a linguistic point of view, the flap is no sloppier or lazier than the Spanish pronunciation of <d> after vowels as [ð]—a pronunciation on which the same people would probably insist because school textbooks say to do it.

CATCH. This is another pronunciation of <t> between vowels, but specifically when the consonant after the second vowel is <n>. This happens only to <t>, not to <d>. This seems fussy, but it is a linguistic fact of American English. (Many regional varieties of British English have it, too.) Say aloud: "She's ridden all over town and written about her experiences." The <d> in "ridden" is a flap, but for many (though not all) speakers of American English the <t> in "written" is a sound called *glottal stop* or *catch* because the consonant catches the air in the throat. (For some speakers both these words do, indeed, have a flap.) Other common examples of flap vs. catch are "a bitter pill" vs. "a flea-bitten animal," "Mr. Cotter has a cotton shirt," "Butter a button." Sometimes this catch is symbolized by an apostrophe, as in Cockney "bo'l, ki'in" = "bottle, kitten." IPA spells this catch as an undotted question mark [ʔ]. These pairs, then, can be transcribed:

[bɪɾər]   [kaɾər]   [bʌɾər]
[bɪʔən]   [kaʔən]   [bʌʔən].

Compare with "forbidden fruits, four bitten fruits," where <d> and <t> are followed by <n>, but the first is a flap and the second is a catch. (There are still other variations.)

Notice, too, that <t> becomes a catch when the <n> involved is *dental* [n] but not *velar* [ng] (IPA *engma*: [ŋ]). For speakers who pronounce "sitting, kidding" with [ng], the <t, d> in these words remain flap:

The baby sitter was [sitting / sittin'] on the couch.

sɪɾər   sɪɾɪŋ
        sɪʔən

I'm not [kidding: / kiddin':] the kitten needs a bath.

kɪɾɪŋ   kɪʔən
kɪɾən

An announcer may choose "full-foreign" pronunciation by preserving such <t, d> as [t, d] or anglicize them to flap and catch.* Many even choose Smetana = [smeh-ʔuh-nuh].

SHIFT. Another variation on <t, d> is their shift from the dental stops [t, d] to the palatal affricates [ch, j]. This happens regularly when <t, d> follow a vowel and are

* One grammatical/sociological polemic: people who pronounce <-ing> as [ihn] are accused of being sloppy, of "dropping the <g>," as the popular spelling <-in'> indicates. Actually, the <g> is not "missing," since it was not there in the first place. There is simply a difference in English between the velar nasal [ng] as part of a root, as in "sing, rung, fang"—which everybody pronounces—and the grammatical ending <-ing> that forms participles and verbal nouns. The truth is that there are simply two variations of that ending. One is [ing]; one is [ihn]. Some authors would go one step further and say that some speakers of English have [-ng] only in *stressed* syllables, that is, [sing] but [mornin'], even though this <ing> is not a grammatical ending.

followed by <u> = [oo]. In addition, the [oo] vowel, since it is unstressed, is usually pronounced [uh] (see shwa in Interlude 3). Compare flap vs. shift in "futile-future" = [fyoo-tyl, fyoo-tuhl] (with flap)-[fyoo-cher], "edify-educate" = [eh-dih-fy]-[eh-joo-kayt] (more likely [eh-juh-kayt]). The same applies to the dental fricatives [s, z] that shift to palatal fricatives [sh, zh] as illustrated in the chart above in "press-pressure" and "seize-seizure." This consonant shifting is another feature that distinguishes American English from British.

Suffice it to say, the terms "hard" and "soft" have in common that they capture English speakers' intuition that *stops* are somehow "hard" sounds, while *fricatives* and *affricates* are "soft" sounds. There is, indeed, some physiological basis for this perception. A slightly closer look gives a certain group of professionals a firmer handle to grasp.

Doubles and Dub Bulls

English spelling includes many double consonant letters even when English speech has only one consonant sound. In words like "letter, miss, Hobbit" = [leh-ter, mihs, hah-biht] there is only one [t, s, b], respectively. Doubling the consonant letter has special function in English spelling, but it has to do with the pronunciation of the previous *vowel* letter, as in "later-latter" = [lay-ter, la-ter].

English can sometimes produce a double sound when a word ends with the same consonant with which the next word begins. A word with a single [t] (actually, a flap) like "mighty" sounds different from a phrase like "Arnold Palmer *might tee* off at 2:00." You might misunderstand the following two fellows' names if you only heard them and did not see them written out: "I am Ike. I am Mike." A single [m] sounds slightly different from a double [mm]. In "wanton act" vs. "I want ten acts," it is possible to force a single vs. double [t]. The same applies to the [b] in "doubles" and the [bb] in "dub bulls," odd though that phrase is. There is no space, no hesitation between these two identical consonants. They act like a single "long" consonant. English, then, can distinguish single from double consonants, but is does so only across words, not within a single word.

Italian, Finnish, and Hungarian are noted for distinguishing single from double consonants within a word. These three languages spell that difference with a single or double consonant letter. In Italian Corelli, the [ll] is held literally twice as long as that the [l] in Gabrieli. (The vowel quality of the <e> is also different: <elli> = [ehl-lee], <eli> = [ay-lee].) In full-Italian the [t] in Scarlatti is twice as long as in "gelato." This sound feature contributes to the staccato rhythm many people associate with Italian. English-speaking announcers are under no obligation to do this, but those who choose that path should pronounce a single long [t] and not two separate [t]'s. The transcription tries to suggest such a doubling for "full-native" but usually offers a single consonant for "half-native." Scarlatti is either [skahr-laht-tee] (and no flap) or [skahr-lah-tee] (with [t] or flap), dependng on whether a given announcer hears the difference and chooses to make it. For Pavarotti, most American announcers are unlikely to pronounce [pah-vah-"wrote"-tee] differently from [pah-vah-"row"-tee], or [pah-vah-"wrought"-tee] differently from [pah-vah-raw-tee] (not to mention that the [t] is a flap in any case). In Finnish, Kullervo has double [ll], while each [l] in Kalevala is single. Hungarian also spells and pronounces single vs. double consonants. Those single consonants already spelled with two letters, such as <sz> = [s] or <gy> = [j], show the double sound by doubling the first of the letters. Thus, <sz, ssz> is the spelling for [s, ss], as in, "I miss you" with [s] and "I miss Sue" with [ss]. The same holds in principle for <ggy> = [jj].*

Consonant Cluster Reprise

No English speaker has trouble pronouncing consonant clusters in stop, drop, or flop. English also has the clusters [-ts, -dz] but only at the end of a word (cats, cads) and not at the beginning, as in German Zauberflöte = [tsow-ber-flö-tuh] and Italian "zucchero" = [dzoo-keh-roh] (sugar). Clusters like Russian Dmitri, Mstislav and Polish Krzysztof, Gdańsk present a special challenge.Try to capture them in a single attack and not to separate them into two syllables.

English has hidden consonant clusters of which the second consonant is [y], though it is not represented in spelling. The vowel following these is always [oo]. There were several examples in the Palatalization section above, namely, [byoo-] in beauty, [kyoo-] in cute, and others in Movement 1. In many of the languages in this book such clusters occur before other vowels, such as full-French Pierre = [pyehr], full-Italian Siciliana = [see-chee-lyah-nah], full-Russian Feoder [fyoh-duhr]. English speakers tend to separate these clusters into two syllables, as in [pee-ehr, sih-"chilly"-ah-nuh], and the "half-native" transcriptions in Movement 2 often suggest just that. This is one of the reasons for giving such variants as three-syllable half-Russian Prokofiev = [pruh-"cough"-yehf] vs. four-syllable half-English [pruh-"coffee"-ehf]. Some very well known names are left as half-English instead of half-native on just this basis, such as Traviata = [trah-vee-ah-tuh], rather than full-Italian [trah-vyah-tah] and Khachaturian = ["catch-a-tour-ee-uhn"], rather than [khah-chah-too-ryahn]. One way to transcribe these is to end one syllable with the first consonant and begin the next syllable with [y], something like Pagliacci, Moniuszko = [pahl-yah-chee, mohn-yoosh-koh]. However, such a spelling lets the reader think the two consonants are separate. By transcribing [pah-lyah-chee, moh-nyoosh-koh] the reader is encouraged to push the consonants together, but it takes practice.

The same applies to clusters of which the second consonant is [w]. English has sweet, tweet, thwart, quick = [kw-] but not [bw-] as in Italian buono, fuoco = [bwoh-noh,

---

* Doubling a [j] is actually not so simple. In a contrived English phrase like, "Did Judge Jim judge him?" the two [j]'s in [juhj-jihm] can hardly help but be pronounced with a slight separation because of the complex nature of [j] = [d+zh]. So, [jj] = [d+zh+d+zh]. Hungarian and Italian double [jj] are more accurately composed of [dd+zh], prolonging only the first part of the affricate: the *stop* part. The veteran announcer George Jelinek (WQXR, New York) is Hungarian. His name (actually a Czech name [yeh-lee-nehk]) in America is [jorj jeh-lih-nehk] with a break between the two [jj]'s. In his otherwise flawless English he introduces himself in purely Hungarian style as [jorddzheh-lih-nehk] with no break between the two [jj]'s. In a recent telephone conversation with the author, Mr. Jelinek admitted that he only recently became aware of this phonetic habit.

fwoh-koh] and Portuguese João = [zhwõw]. Keep an eye/ear out for these, too, and keep from separating them into [boo-ay-noh], etc.

Interlude 3. Vowels in "General European" vs. English

Vowels in the Mouth

Vowel sounds can be described in terms of how widely your lower jaw is open, how rounded or spread your lips are, and whether the tip of your tongue or the back of it is involved. An open jaw brings the tongue down. These are "low" vowels. A closed jaw brings the tongue up. These are "high" vowels. In most of Europe, spread lips correlate with the tip of the tongue in the "front" of the mouth. Rounded lips go together with the "back" of the tongue. Below is a rough "triangle" scheme used by phoneticians to map the vowel sounds in the mouth. As with the consonant charts in Interlude 2, imagine a side view of a mouth facing leftward.

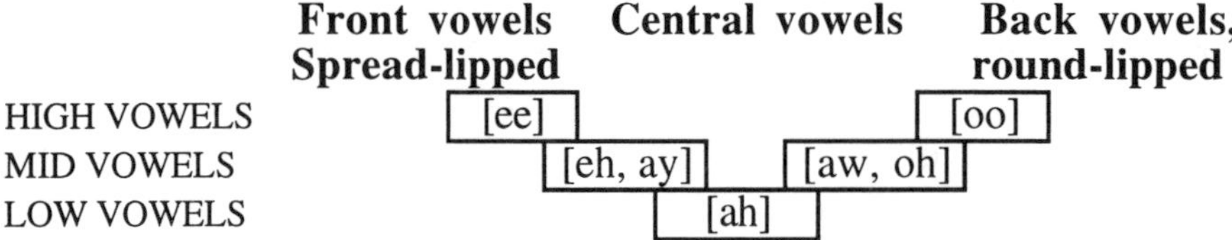

Thus, [ee] is *high front vowel*, and [oo] is a *high back vowel.* Similarly, [eh] and [ay] are varieties of *mid front vowels*, while [aw] and [oh] are *mid back vowels.* The *low central vowel* is [ah].

In the European and Asian languages included in this book it is most likely that the letters <i, e, a, o, u> represent the sounds [ee, eh/ay, ah, oh/aw, oo], but the transcription in this book is based, for better or worse, on English spelling. The hope of this book is that once you have worked your way through it the vowels of Italian, Hungarian, and Polish will be able to be their own transcription and there will be no need to filter them through English practice.

Other Vowel Sounds

Many languages have more vowel sounds but they can all be described in terms of the triangle above. Here is a complementary triangle that, given a little artistic imagination, could be superimposed on the triangle above.

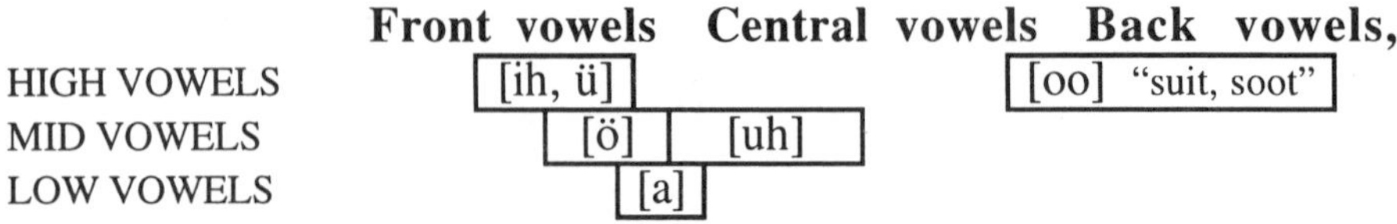

English [ih] is a kind of [ee], that is, also a *high front vowel.* The second guise of [oo] as in "soot" is a *high back vowel.* English [a] is *low front vowel.* The vowel [uh] called *shwa* (see below) is a *mid central vowel.* it may be clearer now than it was in Movement 1 why [ü, ö] are called front rounded vowels: they combine the tongue features of front vowels with the lip features of back vowels.

Of Diphthongs and Digraphs

A *diphthong*—that is, [dihf-thawng], ≠ ["dip"-thawng]—is a complex sound consisting usually of "vowel+y" or "vowel+w." The English vowel in "loud" is a diphthong, namely, [ow] or [ah+w, a^w] pronounced as a single unit. Similarly, the vowel in "lied" (= told a lie) is also a diphthong, namely, [y] or [ah+y, a^y, a^j] pronounced as a single unit.* The vowels in "maid" and "mode" are, strictly speaking, also diphthongs: [eh+y, e^y, e^j], [oh+w, o^w] and usually occur here in the form [ay, oh].

A *digraph* is a group of (usually two) letters. Together they may spell either a single sound, as in "lead" (the metal), where the digraph <ea> spells the simple vowel [eh]. The digraph <ou> in "loud" spells the diphthong [ow]. In "mice" the vowel sound is the diphthong [ah+y, a^y], but English spells it with a single letter <i>. The schoolbook definition of a diphthong is "two vowels together," but the weakness of such a formulation should now be apparent: that definition refers only to vowel *letters*, and the connection between sound and letter is incidental. The <ea> of "lead" is not a diphthong.

In the realm of consonants, it is possible to speak of clusters vs. digraphs. English uses digraphs <th, sh> to spell the single sounds that IPA represents as [ð, š]. It also uses the single letter <j> to spell what is essentially a consonant cluster [d+zh]. (There is often debate among linguistic theoreticians whether the affricates [ts, dz, ch, j] count as clusters or single complex sounds.)

"Long" and "Short"

The English vowels called "long" are those in "hay, he, high, hoe, who?" The vowels in "hat, head, hit, hot, hut, hood" are usually called "short." In dictionary phonetics these eleven sounds are [hā, hē, hī, hō, ho͞o; hă, hĕ, hĭ, hŏ, hə, ho͝o]. Given the above chart of vowels in the mouth, it is clear that these are actually different vowel sounds produced with a different mouth shape. In most European languages, the terms "long" and "short" refer only to the actual time that the vowel sound is held. In Czech, for example, <a> is a short [ah], and <á> is also [ah] pronounced literally for a few milliseconds longer. In Dutch a single <a> may be long or short, and <aa> is only long. Hungarian has not only short <u>and <ü> but also long <ú> and <ű>. Announcers need not try to reproduce this distinction, and audiences may even perceive it as a hesitation or affectation. (In historical perspective, the terms long and short vowels used to have this sense for English until

* A few English verbs form their present and past tenses by exchanging these diphthongs, viz., find-found and wind, bind, grind. Two nouns have [ow] in the singular and [y] in the plural, namely, mouse-mice, louse-lice.

approximately the fifteenth century. The vowels that English now calls long and short are developments of formerly long and short vowels. The pronouncing dictionary by Noory listed in Bibliography II has a brief summary of this "Great Vowel Shift," as does any history of the English language or introductory linguistics textbook.)

"Broad" and "Flat"

The terms "broad-a" and "flat-a" mentioned in Movement 1 can now be recast in terms of placement of the tongue in the mouth. "Broad-a" as [ah] is a low central vowel, while "flat-a" as [a] is a low front vowel. English has much more of a tendency to assign the sound value [a] to the letter <a>, while the rest of Europe assigns the value [ah] to that letter. (It is like sliding the bass/treble or the volume lever on the stereo: more front tongue to less front tongue.) This is why one of the typical marks of "anglicizing" is to pronounce "Scarlatti" as ["scar"-la-tee] (= "laddie"), rather than Italian [skahr-lah-tee], Paganini as [pa-guh-nee-nee], rather than [pah-guh-nee-nee]. This letter/sound discrepancy is what allowed the Swingle Singers in the later 1960s to title an album "Back to Bach," which they assumed would be pronounced [bak too bak] by most people and not [bak too bahk(h)]. All these languages have the sound [ah], but they spell it differently. The same goes for <o>. Both English and Italian have an [ah], but Italian spells it <a>, while English spells it <o> most of the time. This is why Pavarotti comes out [pah-vuh-rah-tee].

Shwa

In the rhythm of normal English speech, the values of the vowels letters mentioned above are valid when the vowel in question is stressed in a word. Almost any vowel that is *not* stressed is pronounced as a quick [uh]. This is especially true of the vowel in the syllables right before the stressed one and right after it. Compare, for example, the stressed and unstressed vowels in a word pair like "major" = [may-juhr] and "majority" = [muh-jaw-ruh-tee] or [muh-jaw-rih-tee]. The two words *sound* quite different from each other—that is, stressed vowels are replaced by shwa when they are not stressed—but English speakers are barely aware of that because spelling keeps them *looking* similar. The same goes for a pair of words like "compete, competition" = [kuhm-peet, kahm-puh-tih-shuhn]. Even though English spelling seems irregular to many people, it actually does you the favor of spelling the unstressed [uh]-sound with the letter that represents the full sound when the stress falls on it. This [uh] vowel has its own name: "shwa," also spelled "schwa," a term from Hebrew for a similar phenomenon.*

Most European languages do not have the shwa sound in their repertoire. Applying the rules of English "shwa" to another language,then, is another of the classic marks of anglicizing. (Note that this is not just an example of English "sloppiness," as many people

---

* Note that common Hebrew words in English, e.g., the organization B'nai B'rith = [buh-nay buh-rihth (or brihth)] spell this quick vowel with an apostrophe. Nowhere in Europe, however, does apostrophe suggest a vowel sound. Read right through it: French l'histoire = [lees-stwahr], Italian d'amore = [dah-"more"-ay].

assume.) The alternate pronunciations in the alphabetical list in Movement 2 and the term "half-English" reflect this natural accommodation. Full-Italian "Pavarotti" casts both <a> letters as [ah]. An English mouth will make the second one [uh], since it is right before the stressed syllable: [pah-vuh-roh-tee] or [pah-vuh-raw-tee]. Here are some other common names in their full-native and half-/full-English versions with shwa (spelled IPA [ə] and flap (spelled IPA [ɾ]):

Paganini	**Albinoni**	**Górecki**	**Casals**
[pah-gah-nee-nee]	[ahl-bee-noh-nee]	[goo-rehts-kee]	[kah-sahls]
[pah-gə-nee-nee]	[ahl-bə-noh-nee]	[gə-rehts-kee]	[kə-sahls]
moderato	**Galina**	**Prokofiev**	**Jaroslav**
[moh-deh-rah-toh]	[gah-lee-nə]	[prah-"cough"-yehf]	[jah-roh-slahv]
[mah-ɾə-rah-ɾoh]	[gə-lee-nə]	[prə-"coffee"-yehf]	[jah-rə-slahv]
Corelli	**Gewandhaus**	**allegro**	**capriccio**
[koh-rehl-lee]	[geh-vahnt-hows]	[ah-leh-groh]	[kah-pree-choh]
[kə-reh-lee]	[gə-vahnt-hows]	[ə-leh-groh]	[kə-pree-chee-oh]

Interlude 4. Stress Management

Which syllable gets the emphasis? Word stress and phrase stress are some of the most important elements in human speech, yet not a single writing system has a consistent way of marking these features. (Note that in this book the term *stress* is used where may people use *accent*. Either is fine.) This is one of the subtle ways that the language designation in the lists can give you a nudge in the right direction. In sóme publicátions an áccent mark is wrítten óver the apprópriate vówel létter. ´Ma-ny ´dic-tion-ar-ies use a ´stress mark at the be-´gin-ning of the ap-´pro-pri-ate ´syl-la-ble. O´-thers put the mark af´-ter that syl´-la-ble. Some books use UPper and LOWer case LETters to show ACcented and UNaccented SYLlables. (Some people find this mix very distracting.) Just so there is no misunderstanding, in the transcriptions in this book the accented syllable is always underlined. Furthermore, some languages consistently stress a certain syllable of each of its words. (See Mawson 1934, pp. xl-xliii in Bibliography II for a list.) Here are the briefest of guidelines of *tendencies*:

CZECH, HUNGARIAN, and FINNISH always stress the *first* syllable		
Cz: Janáček = yah-nah-chehk Smetana = smeh-tah-nah Vltava = vuhl-tah-vah	Fn: Kalevala = kah-leh-vah-lah Helsinki = "hell-sink"-ee Salonen = sah-loh-nehn	H: Kodály = koh-dy Dorati = doh-rah-tee Dohnányi = dohkh-nah-nyee*

* You also hear [yah-nah-chehk], [dohkh-nah-nyee], [doh-rah-tee]. Just remember that the accent mark on <á> is not a stress mark in these systems. See note under Sibelius for his non-first-syllable stress.

GERMAN, DUTCH: first or second syllable		FRENCH: *final* syllable	
1st		Henri =	ãhn-ree
Heinrich =	hyn-rihkh	Ravel =	rah-vel
Albrecht =	ahl-brehkht	Albert =	ahl-behr
Bertold=	behr-told	Debussy =	duh-bü-see
2nd (unstressed prefix)		Couperin =	koop-uh-rãn *or* koo-prãn
Gewandhaus =	guh-vahnt-"house"		
Verzeichnis =	fehr-tsykh-nihs	Cassadesus =	kah-sah-duh-sü *or* kah-sahd-sü
Gesellschaft =	guh-zehl-shahft		
Concertgebouw =	(kohn-sehrt) khuh-bow (compound word)		

The German and Dutch grammatical prefixes <ge-, be-, er-, ver-> are never stressed. This is why the last three examples are stressed on the second syllable. When the letter sequence, e.g, <ge-> is part of the word and not a prefix the first syllable gets the stress, as in German Gerhard = [gehr-hahrt] and Dutch Gerritt = [kheh-riht].

ITALIAN and POLISH: next-to-last or third-to-last syllable			
Next to last		Third to last	
ITALIAN			
Donizetti =	doh-nee-dzeh-tee	Giacomo =	jah-koh-moh
Cavarodossi =	kah-vah-roh-doh-see	Girolamo =	jee-roh-lah-moh
Bononcini =	boh-nohn-chee-nee	Carissimi=	kah-ree-see-mee
Rossini = and all the names that end in *-ini*.	roh-see-nee		
POLISH			
Szymanowski =	shih-mah-noff-skee	muzyka =	moo-zih-kah
Lutosławski =	loo-toh-swahf-skee		

SPANISH: last or next-to-last syllable, sometimes third-to-last		
Last	Next to last	Third to last
Casals	de la Rocha	Tarrega
	Romero	
	Federico	
	Segovia [seh-goh-vyah]	

Spanish and Italian mark stress only if it falls on an *un*expected syllable. Spanish indicates this with an acute accent, as in Simon Bolívar = [see-mohn boh-lee-bar] and verb forms like past tense "habló" = [ah-bloh] (he spoke) vs. "hablo" = [ah-bloh] (I speak). Italian uses a grave accent, especially on the *last* syllable, as in verb forms like "vincerò" = [veen-cheh-roh (I will win, from the Nessun Dorma aria in Puccini's *Turandot.*). (Some Italian words are written with either a grave or an acute, such as "più, così" and "piú, cosí." When the final vowel is <e> some, but not all, speakers make a difference between <è> = [eh] and <é> = [ay].

Polish has no marking for stress, but the words that are most likely to have third-from-the-end stress are Latin and Greek words like "muzyka, gramatyka." Names of people and places will always be stressed on the next-to-last. See Movement 4 for details.

English can stress virtually any syllable: first in "object" (noun), second in "object" (verb), "objective," and "objectivize," and fifth out of six (that is, next to last) in "objectivization." There is a tendency to stress the first syllable, which is probably why English speakers often say [deh-byoo-see], ["bore-a-dean"], and [gor-buh-chev], even though there is no linguistic reason why the French [deh-byoo-see], Russian [buh-rah-deen] and [guhr-bah-ch"off"] would present difficulty. Terms from other languages also move stress to the first syllable, as in "prelude" = [pray-lood] and "etude" = [ay-tood] from French [pray-lüd, ay-tüd].

At the same time, there is also a tendency for English speakers to associate final stress or next-to-final stress with "foreign" names—maybe because of the association with French or Italian. This feeling might underlie the shift of Antal Dorati, who would be ["door"-ah-tee] according to the rules of Hungarian, to [doh-rah-tee], which he, himself, now appears to accept as normal.

Interlude 5. Hints on Reading Key Signatures

Titles of pieces often include the key signature, which is composed of three elements read in this order: the name of the key, "sharp" (#) or "flat" (♭), "major" or "minor" (the indication of the two principle "modes" of western classical music, which mean "big" and "small"). Imported records often have this information in two or three languages. English and German use letters for keys. French and Italian use the do-re-mi system. Here is a chart for recognizing the symbols and their names in English, German, Italian, and French so that you can announce them all in English.

	NOTE/KEY							#/♭	MODE
ENG.	C	D	E	F	G	A	B	# = sharp; ♭ = flat	major-minor
GER.	C	D	E	F	G	A	B-H	#: Cis Dis Fis Gis ♭: Ces Des Es Ges As	dur-moll
IT.	Do	Re	Mi	Fa	Sol	La	Si	# = diesis; ♭ = bemolle, e.g., Do-diesis, Mi-bemolle	maggiore-minore
FR.	Ut							# = dièse; ♭ = bémol, e.g., Ut-dièse, Mi-bémol	majeur-mineur

ENGLISH. Read the keys as the plain letters: [see-dee-ee-ehf-jee-ay-bee]. Add "sharp, flat," or neither. Read C# as C-sharp, E♭ as E-flat. (Plain C, E are called "natural" but the word is not usually used as part of the key name. Read just [see, ee].) Add "minor" (marked "minor" or just "m"). "Major" is often left unmarked and unspoken. F# = F-sharp (major), and F#m = F-sharp minor.

GERMAN. The territory of English "B" is divided into two. "B" is only for B-flat, and "H" = [hah] is only for B-natural. The B-minor mass of J.S. Bach will appear on a German recording as "H moll" = [hah mohl], but announce it as "B-minor." The sharp and flat symbols are expressed by the syllables "is" = [ihs] and "es" = [ehs] attached to the letter. If you read the resulting compressed words Cis, Dis, Fis, Gis in German they are [tsihs, dihs, fihs, gihs], but translate them into C#, D#, F#, G#. The flat keys are German Des, Es, Ges, As" = [dehs, ehs, gehs, ahs], but announce them as D♭, E♭, G♭, A♭. Thus, read As-dur as A-flat (major) and Cis-moll as C#m. Just for the record, Dutch in Belgium has a do-re-mi and translates the Latinate terms major and minor into "groot, klein" ([khroht, klyn]), which mean "big" and "small." Belgian classical announcers announce the key of C as "Do groot."

ITALIAN AND FRENCH. Both use the the "do-re-mi" system for naming notes and keys. The difference is that French has *Ut* = [üt] for Italian *Do* = ["dough"]. Announce both as C. (The English do-re-mi system taught in schools has "ti" for "si," as the well-known song from the movie, *The Sound of Music* illustrates: "Doe, a deer, a female deer" all the way up to "Tea, a drink with jam and bread." Announce it as "B," in any case.) The sharp-flat terms are French [dee-ehz, beh-mohl] and Italian [dee-eh-zees, beh-moh-lay]. The terms for major and minor are cognates. Example: Read French "Si-bémol mineur" as "B-flat minor."

MOVEMENT 4

LETTER AND SOUND IN THE LANGUAGES OF EUROPE AND EAST ASIA

This movement gives the visual and audible characteristics of thirty-three European and Asian languages. (See Charles Allen, *Manual of European Languages for Librarians*, listed in Bibliography III, for a complete visual treatment of all European written languages.) The languages are arranged loosely by linguistic family (Romance, Germanic, Slavic, Finno-Ugric) and more by similarity of reading techniques and spelling strategies.

Romance	Classical Latin, Church Latin-Italian-Romanian, French-Portuguese, Spanish
Germanic	English, German, Dutch and Flemish, Scandinavian (Danish-Norwegian-Swedish)
Slavic and Baltic	Polish; a group including four Slavic (Czech, Slovak, Serbo-Croatian, Slovenian) and two Baltic (Latvian and Lithuanian); Russian (with Ukrainian and Bulgarian)
Finno-Ugric	Finnish, Estonian, Hungarian
Other European	Albanian, Greek, Turkish, Welsh, Irish
East Asian	Korean, Japanese, Chinese (not genetically related)

General Remark on Accent Marks and Diacritics

Many of these languages "adjust" their inherited Latin letters by adding dots, dashes, and other diacritics. If the difference in sound between the plain and the adjusted letter does not have an equivalent in English speech it will usually be mentioned but not insisted on. For example, Hungarian <o> is "short," while <ó> is "long" (in the European sense of physical duration as in Interlude 3), but English speakers need not reproduce it. Polish plain <o>, on the other hand, is [oh], while accented <ó> = [oo], which English speakers can easily accomplish.

ROMANCE LANGUAGES

LATIN

Classical Latin

These are the basic letter/sound correspondences typical of Julius Caesar and Marc Antony in the days B.C. The only time you will need this for announcing purposes is for some musical organizations with deliberately "antique" names, like Collegium Musicum, or perhaps the titles of some pieces. (Even there you get variation: some keep classical [koh-lay-gee-oom moo-zee-koom] and others go to full-English [kuh-lee-jee-uhm myoo-zih-kuhm]. Latin words in the language of lawyers and doctors also tend to be fully assimilated into English.)

The five vowel letters have their "general European" values, as discussed in Interlude 3, above: <a, e, i, o, u> = [ah, eh, ee, oh, oo]. After all, this is the language that gave the rest of Europe *its* sound values for those letters. The combinations <ae, au> are more or less the sums of their parts: [y] and [ow]. The vowel combination <oe> is [eh, ay] in normal pronunciation and sometimes [eh] or [ee] in Greek names, such as Oedipus.

The main consonant issues involved are the letters <c> and <g>. The Romans pronounced them [k] and [g], and the combination <qu> spelled the sound combination [kw]. (The only time <kw> occurs in English is in commerical names like Kwik Kopy.) The letter <s> was always voiceless [s] and not voiced [z], and <v> was [w]. In modern practice it is fine to pronounce <s> and <v> according to English rules.

<LETTER(S)>	[SOUND]	EXAMPLE	TRANSCRIPTION
<c>	[k]	Caesar Cicero	ky-sahr kee-keh-roh (English "sis-a-row" is fine.)
<qu>	[kw]	Antiqua	ahn-tee-kwuh
<g>	[g]	Collegium	koh-lay-gee-uhm (√ koh-"leggy"-uhm)
<v>	[w] ([v] is fine for announcing.)	Veni, vidi, vici	way-nee wee-dee wee-kee (J. Caesar's famous quotation.)
<s>	[s]	Caesar Ars	ky-sahr ars (√ half-English "arz")

Medieval (Church) Latin

By the Middle Ages, the pronunciation of spoken Latin was already quite different from Caesar's. The Latin used in the Christian church of that time shows a change of the sequences <ci, ce> all over Europe and of <gi, ge> in most of Europe. In the Italian pronunciation of Church Latin these are [chee, cheh] and [jee, jeh], as in modern Italian. French and English pronounce these as in those languages, namely, [see, seh] and [zhee/jee, zheh/jeh]. German says [tsee, tseh] and [gee, geh]. Church Latin pronunciation is mostly what announcers need for masses, cantatas, motets, and other religious pieces. In fact, one of the organizational principles of the whole of Movement 4 is the way the languages of Europe use <c> and <g>. Classical Latin did not have the sounds [ch, j, sh, zh] and some others. Most of the languages of Europe developed these sounds over the course of history, but no European country made up new letters for them. They just reevaluated the consonant letters they had inherited from Rome and in some cases "adjusted" those letters with accents and diacritics. The other major difference is that the <v> letter moved from a [w] to a [v].

<LETTER(S)>	[SOUND]	EXAMPLE	TRANSCRIPTION
<c+i, e, œ>	[ch] [ts] (German style)	Regina Coeli [Queen of Heaven) Concentus Musicus	reh-jee-nah chay-lee kohn-tsehn-tuhs moo-zih-kuhs (Viennese group)
<-ti->	[ts]	gratius	grah-tsee-oos
<g+a, o, u> <g+i, e>	[g] [jee, jeh/jay]	Regina Cœli Gaudeamus Igitur (medieval student song)	reh-jee-nah chay-lee gaw-day-ah-moos ee-gee-toor (The reading [ee-gee-toor] occurs among German speakers.)
<gn>	[n^y] (Not a syllable, like Spanish <ñ>.)	Agnus Dei magnum	ahn-yoos day-ee (part of the mass) mahn-yoom (and also [mahg-noom])
<v>	[v]	Veni, vidi, vici	vay-nee vee-dee vee-chee (A medieval pronunciation of an ancient phrase. Perfectly acceptable.)

ITALIAN

Vowels

The vowel letters have their general European values. The vowel <e> can be either [eh] or [ay], and <o> can be either [aw] or [oh]. Corelli vs. Gabrieli was discussed in Interlude 2 under double consonants and [koh-rehl-lee] with <e> = [eh] but [gah-bree-ay-lee] with <e> = [ay]. English speakers do not usually distinguish these in half-English [koh-reh-lee] and [gah-bree-eh-lee], both with [eh]. In, for example, "maestoso," <o> = [oh], while in "concerto grosso," <o> = [aw]. Most English speakers pronounce [oh] for both [my-stoh-zoh] and ["grow-so"].

A grave accent indicates word stress on all five vowel letters: "così" = [koh-zee], Nicolò = [nee-koh-loh]. The same goes for <à> and <ù>. Stressed <è, ò> vs. <é, ó> are in principle, [eh, aw] vs. [ay, oh], though not always in practice.

The sequences <ai>, <au>, <oi> are separate vowels: Aida = [ah-ee-dah], Gaetano = [gah-eh-tah-noh] (which at normal speed comes out [gy-tah-noh]), paesano = ["pie"-zah-noh]. Ciao = [chah-oh], at normal speed = [chow]. The combinations <ua>, <oa> both come out [wah], and <uo> = [woh], as in buono = [bwoh-noh] (good).

Consonants

SHIFTERS AND PRESERVERS. As discussed in Interlude 2, Italian hard vs. soft <c, g> are the velar stops [k, g] vs. the palatal affricates [ch, j]. The letters <i> and <e> are both "place shifters," moving the velars to palatals, and the vowels [ee, eh]. Before <a, o, u>, the same <i> is a place shifter only. Thus, <ci> = [chee], but <cia> = [chah]. Conversely, <h> functions as a "place preserver," keeping <c, g> as velars [k, g] before <i, e>. Thus, <ci> = [chee], and <chi> = [kee]. The other function of <i> is to signal the consonant [y] after <ch>. Thus, <ca, chi> = [kah, kee], and <chia> = [kyah]. See the Coda for a chart typical Italian sound sequences and their spellings.

<LETTER(S)>	[SOUND]	EXAMPLE	TRANSCRIPTION
<ci, cci>	[chee]	Puccini	poo-chee-nee
		Ricci	ree-chee
		Cimarosa	chee-mah-roh-za
		fettucine	feh-too-chee-nay
<ce, cce>	[cheh]	concerto	kohn-chehr-toh
		cello	cheh-loh
		Francesco	frahn-cheh-skoh
<cia, cio, ciu>	[chah, choh, choo]	Luciano	loo-chah-noh
	(<i> keeps <c> = [ch])	ciao	"chow" (= goodbye)
		cacciatore	kah-chah-toh-ray (full-Eng. "catch-a-Tory")
<ch, cch>	[k]	Cherubini	keh-roo-bee-nee
	(<h> keeps <c> = [k])	Boccherini	boh-keh-ree-nee
		Ponchielli	pohn-kyeh-lee
		zucchini	tsoo-kee-nee (Eng. [zoo-])
<ch+i+a, o, u>	[kyah, kyoh, kyoo]	chianti	kyahn-tee (√ kee-ahn-tee)
		chiuso	kyoo-zoh ("closed")
<qu>	[kw]	Questa o quela	kweh-stah oh kweh-lah
	(<u> = [w])	(aria from *Rigoletto*)	
<sci, sce>	[shee, sheh]	Scimone	shee-moh-nay
		crescendo	kreh-shehn-doh
<scia, scio, sciu>	[shah, shoh, shoo]	lasciate mi	lah-shah-tay-mee
		prosciutto	proh-shoo-toh
<sch>	[sk]	scherzo	skehr-tsoh
(= <s> +<ch>)		Gianni Schicchi	jah-nee skee-kee

<gi, ggi> <ge, gge>	[jee], [jeh]	Luigi Geminiani Ruggero	loo-ee-jee (lwee-jee) jeh-mee-nyah-nee roo-jeh-roh
<gia, gio, giu>	[jah, joh, joo] (<i> is place shifter)	Giovanni Giorgio Giuseppe Giulini	joh-vah-nee jor-joh joo-sep-pay joo-lee-nee
<gh>	[g] (<h> is place preserver)	Respighi larghetto spaghetti	reh-spee-gee lar-geh-toh spah-geh-tee
<gu> + consonant <gu> + vowel	[goo] ([g]+[oo]) [gw] (unlike Fr. <gu> = [g])	Guglielmo Guido linguine	goo-lyehl-moh gwee-doh ling-gwee-nay
<gn> + vowel <gli>	$[n^y]$ (not a syllable) $[l^y]$ (not a syllable)	Mascagni Bologna gnocchi Pagliacci passacaglia	mahs-kah-nyee boh-loh-nyah (√ "loan-ya") nyohk-kee pah-lyah-chee pah-sah-kahl-yuh

Note that <s> serves for both voiceless [s] and voiced [z] and that <z> is never [z], but rather the voiceless dental affricate [ts] or voiced dental affricate [dz]. Double <-ss-> is only voiceless [s].

<s-> <-s-> <-ss->	[s] [z] [s]	Samartini Sinopoli Scarlatti Busoni Pergolesi Pisa Giuseppe Cimarosa Rossini Carissimi	sah-mar-tee-nee sih-noh-poh-lee skar-lah-tee boo-zoh-nee pehr-go-"lazy" pee-zah (cf., Leaning Tower) joo-zep-pay chee-mah-roh-zah roh-see-nee kah-ree-see-mee

<z->	[ts, dz]	zucchini ziti	tsoo-kee-nee tsee-tee (normal Eng. is [zoo-, zee-])
<-z->	most often [dz], but sometimes [ts] (no good rule for this; on a per-word basis)	Donizetti canzone stazione scherzo	doh-nee-dzeh-tee kahn-dzoh-nay stah-tsyoh-nay "scare"-tsoh
<zz>	[ts, dz]	mezzo pizzicato pizza	mehd-zoh, meht-soh "pits"-uh-kah-toh pee-tsah (≠ Pisa!)
<j> (old spelling for<i>)	[y]	Benjamino (old) Beniamino (new)	behn-yah-mee-noh

ON DOUBLE CONSONANTS. See Interlude 2 for the notion of a single letter for a single consonant and a double letter for a double consonant. To pronounce full-Italian vs. half-Italian "staccato," compare the transcriptions ["stock"-kah-toh] and [stuh-kah-toh] or ["stuck Otto"]. English can force, for example, double [ss] in "Pete's supplies of pencils" versus single [s] in "Pete supplies me with pencils." Similarly, the full-Italian double [tt] in "spaghetti" is like ["get tea"], while the full-English single [t] in "Getty" is not only single, but a flap. "Don Giovanni" has a double [nn] in full-Italian, as in ["on knee"], while normal English has only a single [n] in ["a knee"]. For announcing purposes, full-Italian doubling is usually too correct.

ROMANIAN

Romanian is a Romance, and not a Slavic, language despite its geographical position among Slavic countries (Bulgaria, Serbia, Ukraine). The native spelling is România = [roh-"mini"-uh] and the spellings Rumania and Roumania also occur. Moldova—known during the Soviet period by the Russian name Moldavia—is the continuation of eastern Romanian, and its language is virtually the same as Romanian. Moldavian was written in Cyrillic letters, but independent Moldova is now reverting to Latin script.

Vowels

The vowels are general European. In addition, there are also circumflex (pointing up) <â> and <î>, both of which have the sound [ih], as in România. The crescent on <ă> = [uh]. The combination <ea> is literally [eh-uh] run together.

Consonants

Place shifters and preservers are as in Italian: <ci, ce, gi, ge> = [chee, cheh, jee, jeh]. The place preserver before <i, e> is <h>, as in Italian. The place shifter before <a, o,

u> is also <e>, that is, <ca> = [kah], but <cea> = [chah]. Surnames in ending in <-ici> are normally one syllable [eech]. "Adjusted" <ş> (with an under-hook like a French *cedilla*) = [sh] and under-hooked <ţ> = [ts].

<LETTER(S)>	[SOUND]	EXAMPLE	TRANSCRIPTION
<c+i, e>	[ch] (as in Italian)	Stanciu Comenici (Nadia) Ceaucescu	stahn-choo koh-meh-neech (Names ending in <-ci> are just [ch] with no final vowel.) chow-"chess"-koo (deposed Romanian dictator)
<g+i, e>	[j] (as in Italian)	Sergiu	sehr-joo
<ch, gh>	[k, g] (like Italian)	Celebidache Gheorghe	cheh-leh-bee-dah-kay geh-or-geh
<ş> (under-hook)	[sh]	Timişoara Bucureşti	tee-mee-shwah-rah (city in western Romania) boo-koo-rehsh-tee (native name for the captial Bucharest = [boo-kuh-"rest"].)
<ţ> (under-hook)	[ts]	Constanţa	kohn-stahnt-sah (city on the Black Sea)

FRENCH

Vowels

The French vowel letters and sequences are presented by these symbols:

a, â	è, ê ais, ait	é, et ai, eil	e	i, î, y ie, il, ille	o, ô, ot au(t), eau	ou
↓	↓	↓	↓	↓	↓	↓
[ah]	[eh]	[ay]	[uh]	[ee]	[oh]	[oo]

ail	u, û	eu oeu	an	on	in	en
↓	↓	↓	↓	↓	↓	↓
[y]	[ü]	[ö]	[ãhn]	[õhn]	[ãn]	[ẽhn]

NASALS AND ACCENT MARKS. The spelling of nasal vowels was discussed in Movement 1. There is no special letter, only the configuration of "vowel+m/n+another consonant or end of the word." All five vowel letters can also occur with a circumflex <â, ê, î, ô, û>, which does not affect their reading for broadcasting purposes. (Note the difference with Romanian <â, î>.) The <é> with an acute accent is [ay], while <è> with a grave accent is [eh]. The transcription in Movement 2 is sometimes flexible on this point. English [ay] is just different enough from French [ay] to sound exaggerated in unstressed syllables and is sometimes better given by [eh] as an English approximation. Unstressed <e> with no accent at all is [uh], so names such as de la Fontaine, Le Claire, and Debussy are [duh lah fõhn-tehn], [luh-klehr], and [duh-bü-see]. As the last letter of a word it is silent but signals that the consonant letter before is audible: François, Françoise = [frãhn-swah, frãhn-swahz].

SINGLE VOWEL LETTERS AND COMBINATIONS. The <u> alone is [ü], that is, "[oo] with rounded lips while making your tongue do [ee]," as discussed in Movement 1 and in Interlude 3. (Regular [oo] is a perfectly good substitute for half-French or half-English broadcasting.) It takes the letter combination <ou> to spell plain [oo]. Roussel = [roo-"sell"]; Couperin = [koo-puh-rãn] (√ "cooper"-ran); but: Dukas = dü-kah (√ doo-kah); Lully = [lü-lee] (√ loo-lee).

The sound [oh] is spelled <o>, as in Gounod = [goo-noh] and by the combinations <au>, as in Machaut = [mah-shoh], and <eau> as in the Beaux Arts Trio = [boh-zahr]. The combination <ai>, occasionally spelled <ay>, gives [ay], as in Paul Paray = [pohl pah-ray]. With a following silent consonant, as in <ais, ait>, it is [eh]: Marin Marais = [mah-rãn mah-reh].

The <oi> combination is [wah] as in François = [frãhn-swah], and the ever-popular "croissant" = [krwah-sãhn]. (A reasonable compromise on the [krw] cluster is [kruh-sahnt], but not [kroy-suhnt].) The old spelling <oy> also occurs, as in La Mère L'Oye = [lah-"mare"-lwah] (Mother Goose).

Count <il, ille> as the vowel [ee]. Guillaume = [gee-yohm], Camille = [kah-mee], and Milhaud = [mee-yoh]. The combination <ail> gives [ah+ee] = [y], as in Tailleferre = [ty-uh-"fair"]; <eil> = [eh+ee] = [ay], as in Marseille = [mahr-say]. These are [eel] in the following common words: il (pronoun "he"), fil (wire), tranquil (calm), mille (thousand), ville (town).

Consonants

Reading French differs from Italian in the following important ways:

		ITALIAN	FRENCH
<ci, gi>	=	[chee, jee]	[see, zhee]
<ce, ge>	=	[cheh, jeh]	[seh/suh, zheh/zhuh]
<qu, gu>	=	[kw, gw]	[k, g]
<ch>	=	[k]	[sh]
<j>	=	(not used)	[zh]

See the comparative chart in the Coda section.

SHIFTERS AND PRESERVERS. The place shifters are: for <c>, the underhook called *cedilla* = [suh-dee-yuh], namely, <ç>. The syllables [see, seh, sah, soh, soo] are spelled

<ci, ce, ça, ço, çou>. The place shifter for <g> is <e>, but <j> is always [zh]. The syllables [zhe, zheh, zhah, zhoh, zhoo] are spelled <gi, ge, gea or ja, geo or jo, geou or jou>. Conversely, the syllables <gi, ge, ga, go, gu> = [zhee, zheh, gah, goh, gü]. The place preserver for [k] before <i, e> = <qu>. The place preserver for <g> is <gu>. Final <e> after <c, g> is silent shifter, as in Maurice = [moh-rees].

French final consonant *letters* are mostly silent. Final consonant *sounds* are often signaled with a final silent <e> after a consonant. (Almost all Italian words end in a vowel.)

<-et>: Bizet = [bee-zay]
Blavet = [blah-vay] (hence English "ballet, filet")
<-er>: Boulanger = [boo-lãhn-zhay]
Bacquier = [bah-kyay]
but Auber = [oh-behr]
<-ert>: Robert, Ibert = [roh-behr, ee-"bare"]
<-ez>: des Prez = [deh-pray]
but Boulez = [boo-lehz]
Berlioz = [behr-lee-ohz] ("barely-owes")

<LETTER(S)>	[SOUND]	EXAMPLE	TRANSCRIPTION
<ci, ce> <-ce>	<see; seh, suh> [-s]	Cecile César Maurice	suh-seel seh-zahr moh-rees
<ce + vowel> <ç> (with tail)	[s] [s]	morceau François Besançon (city) façade	mohr-soh frãhn-swah buh-zãhn-sõhn fah-sahd
<qu>	[k] [kw]	Jacques Josquin Bacquier quatre quatuor	zhahk zhohs-kãn bah-kyay (√ kee-ay) kahtr, kah-truh kwah-tü-or (unusual)
<ch>	[sh]	Chausson Charles Michel Munch	shoh-sõhn shahrl mee-"shell" (√mih-, muh-) münsh (√ moonsh)
<tch>	[ch] (as in Russian names)	Tchaikovsky	chy-kohv-skee
<gi, gy>	[zhee]	Gilbert Regine Gymnopédies	zheel-behr (√ zhihl-) ruh-zheen zheem-noh-peh-dee
<ge, gé>	[zheh]	Germaine Gérard	zhehr-mehn zheh-rahr
<ge+n>	[zhãhn]	Gentilhomme	zhãhn-tee-uhm (as in Le Bourgeois —)
<ge+ vowel>	[zh] (<e> keeps <g> = [zh])	Georges	zhorzh <geo-> = [joh], <-ges> = [j]

<gui, guy> <-gue>	[gee]; [geh] (<u> keeps <g> as [g] and not [zh]. [g]	Guy Guillaume Huguette Hugue	gee gee-yohm ü-geht (√ hyoo-"get") üg (√ hyoog)
<gou> <gu>	[goo] [gü]	Gounod aigu (acute accent)	goo-noh ay-gü
<gn> <-gne>	[n^y] (not a syllable)	Avignon (city) Bourguignon (filet) mignon cognac Bourgogne	ah-veen-yõhn boor-geen-yõhn mee-nyõhn koh-nyahk boor-gohn^y (—goh-nyuh, —gun-yuh)
<j>	[zh]	Jean, Jacques Jesus	zhãhn, zhahk zhay-zü
<s-> <-s-> <-s >	s z (sometimes [s]) [silent]!	Satie Jesus Casadesus Paris français	sah-tee zhay-zü kah-sah-deh-sü pah-ree frãhn-seh
<z-, -z-> <-z>	[z] mostly silent: except:	zéro Wallez verbs in <-ez> Berlioz Boulez	zeh-roh vah-lay -ay behr-lee-ohz boo-lehz
<-x> names in <-ix> other oddities	[silent] [eeks] [s]	Monteux paix Astérix Aix en Provence dix	mõhn-tö peh (= "peace") ah-steh-reeks (the Gaul) ehks ãhn proh-vãhns dees
<ll, lh>	[y] (cons.) [l] in a few words	Guillaume Milhaud ville, mille	gee-yohm mee-yoh veel, meel (see above)
<h>	[silent, smooth] [silent, break]	Henri L'Histoire (du soldat) Le Havre	ãhn-ree "lease"-twahr (dü "soul"-dah) luh ahvr (uh)

There is no [h] sound in French, but vowels before <h> either drops as in the definite article *le* → *l'* (called here "silent, smooth") In some cases, the vowel remains, as in the city of Le Havre (called here "silent, rough").

PORTUGUESE

The letter/sound correspondences in Portuguese are in several respects more like those of French or Italian than of its geographical neighbor (in both hemispheres), Spanish.

Vowels

Rules for general European apply. Like French (also German and Dutch), Portuguese pronounces unstressed <e> as [uh]. Stressed <o> is [oh], while *un*stressed <o> is [oo]. The name Sergio = [sehr-zhoo] and the Brazilian Villa Lobos is [vee-lah loh-boosh] (with <ll> = [l], and not Spanish [y]). As in Italian but not as in French, <u> is [oo]. The combination <eu> is the quick sum of its parts, namely, [ay-oo], as in the wine Mateus = [mah-tay-oosh]. (Americans call it [muh-toos]). As for <ai>, it is [y] when stressed and [eh] when unstressed. Vowels can have a circumflex, e.g., <â, î, ê>, but that does not change the sound. Similarly to French, there are nasal vowels spelled <vowel+m/n>. The distinctive visual feature of Portuguese vowels is the a-tilde <ã> in the combination <ão> for nasal [ãhn+oo] = [õw] and <ães> = [ãhn+ehsh] in a single syllable.

Consonants

Reading Portuguese is like reading French with regard to <ci, ce> and <gi, ge>. The digraph <qu> is [k] before <i, e>, as in French and Spanish, but [kw] before <a, o>, as in Italian. Similarly to French and Italian, <s> between vowels is [z] (compare Spanish <s> = [s]) and at the ends of syllables and words <s> = [sh]. Note that <x> = [sh] (like medieval Spanish, not modern). Palatal [n^y] and [l^y] are spelled <nh, lh>.

One of the differences between European and Brazilian Portuguese that might arise in broadcasting is that <ti, te> = European [tee, teh], Brazilian [chee, cheh]; <di, de> = European [dee, deh], Brazilian [jee, jeh]. The European values are always safe.

<LETTER(S)>	[SOUND]	EXAMPLE	TRANSCRIPTION
<g + i, e>	[zh]	Sergio	sehr-zhoo
<j>	[zh]	Jobim (Antonio Carlos, bossa nova king) fejoada (Brazilian rice dish)	zhoo-been feh-zhwah-duh
<s-> <-s-> <-s>	[s] [z] [sh]	senhor casa Villa Lobos	"sane"-yohr (cf. Sp. "señor") kah-zuh (like Italian, but unlike Sp. kah-sah) vee-lah loh-bohsh (boosh) (<ll> = [l], unlike Spanish)
<lh, nh>	[l^y, n^y]	Cunha senhor melhor ("better")	koon-yuh seh-nyohr mehl-yohr
<x>	[sh] (unlike Sp.!)	Texeira	teh-shay-ruh

SPANISH

Spanish is a major language on the European continent and in the western hemisphere. European Spanish differs from Latin American Spanish most audibly in the reading of <ci, ce> and <z>, on which, see the chart in the Coda. Both varieties are legitimate, and in the opinion of this author, if an English speaking radio announcer speaks Latin American, then the Spaniard Alicia de la Roccha will not be offended if such an announcer calls her [ah-lee-see-ah] instead of [ah-lee-thee-ah]. If an announcer is comfortable with European Spanish, then any piece with "concierto" in the title can be [kohn-thyehr-toh] whichever hemisphere produced it. American announcers do not "British up" their speech for British names (with the possible exception of Lennox Berkley, as discussed in Movement 1).*

The names of musicians and places below are supplemented by familiar Mexican food items as a reminder of letter/sound correspondences.

Vowels

Vowels are general European. Acute accent on <á, é, í, ó, ú> marks the stressed syllable. (Compare the grave accent in the same function in Italian. See also Czech for comparison of names such as Spanish Tomás = [toh-mahs], where the accent *is* a stress mark, and Czech Tomáš =[toh-mahsh], where the accent mark is *not* a stress mark.) Vowel combinations with <i> or <u> as the second letter are the sum of its parts: <ai> = [ah + ee] = [y] in quick speech, <ei> = [eh+ee] = [ay], <au> = [ah + oo] = [ow]. (Whether these are one or two syllables depends on speed.) Combinations with <i> or <u> first, as in <ie>, <ue>, <ua> = single syllables [yeh], [weh], [wah]. The city of Buenos Aires demonstrates both types: [bweh-nohs-"I race"] and not English ["air-ease"].** The common expression *adios* (goodbye) is two syllables in full-Spanish [ah-dyohs] and three syllables in full-English [ah-dee-ohs]. Another instance of [w] is the diaresis that distinguishes <gue> = [geh] from <güe> = [gweh]. The adjective form of Nicaragua = [nee-kah-rah-gwah] is Nicaragüense = [nee-kah-rah-gwehn-say]. (Without the dots it would read [nee-kah-rah-gehn-say].)

Consonants

SHIFTERS AND PRESERVERS. In Latin American Spanish <c> works as in French, that is, represents [k] before <a, o, u> and [s] before <i, e>. Note that <z> is [s] all the

---

* The question of variants within Latin American and Spain naturally arises, particularly with respect to Argentina, where <ll> = [zh], Puerto Rico, where <y> = [j], and Cuba, where final <-s> is often not pronounced. Such people as de Falla are known in music circles as [duh-fy-uh], and listeners might wonder who [duh-fah-zhah] is. Without offending any speaker of any variety, the norm for North American radio is Spanish where both <ll> <y> = [consonant y].

** The town of Buena Vista, VA in the Blue Ridge Mountains = [byoo-nuh vihs-tuh].

time in the Americas and voiceless [th] all the time in Europe. (There is no [z] sound in Spanish. Replacing [z] by [s] is a typical feature of Hispanic accent in English.) In European Spanish, then, <ci, ce> = [thee, theh] (θi, θe, voiceless), and <za, zo, zu> = [thah, thoh, thoo]. In all Spanish, <g> is [g] before <a, o, u> and [kh] before <i, e>. (Compare this with French and Portuguese [g, zh] and Italian [g, j].) As in French, <qu> is [k] before <i, e>, and it is never [kw], as in Portuguese. The sound [kw] is spelled <cu>, as in *cuanto, cuando* (how much, when). The <u> keeps <g> as [g] in the combinations <gui, gue>. Both <j> and <x>are always [kh], and <ch> is always [ch]. See the chart in the Coda.

As for <gue> and <güe> discussed above, it is worth adding to the "[g] + vowel" column the spelling of "[gw] + vowel," namely, [gwee, gweh, gwah, gwoh] are <güi, güe> with dots and <gua, guo> without dots. The other distinctive visible property of Spanish consonants is the tilde on <ñ> = [n^y], as in "canyon."

OTHER ANNOUNCERS' PITFALLS, EAST AND WEST. Double <ll> is the consonant [y] in much of American Spanish and in some places in Spain. Some areas in Spain pronounce <ll> as [l^y], as in "million," (cf. Portuguese <lh>, Italian <gli>). Some sources prescribe that names from Spain like de Falla be pronounced [deh fahl-yah]. Almost all native speakers of Spanish accept [deh-fy-yah]. Announcers may choose either one as long as they are consistent with language and country. (Recall that Portuguese and Italian have this [l^y] and spell it <lh>, and <gli>, respectively. See the footnote above on Argentina.) There are two smaller issues discussed under "hard/soft" in Interlude 2, namely, when <v> = [b] and <b> = [v] and when <d> after a vowel = English voiced [th]. The word Dio = [dee-oh] (God) contributes to the expression Adios = [ah-thyohs] (goodbye), but normal English is [ah-dyohs] or three-syllable [ah-dee-ohs]. These points are noted here more for the protection of announcers against listeners who "know better" and call in to correct phonetic details. The chart below contrasts Western Hemisphere <ci, ce, z> = [see, seh, s] and Eastern Hemisphere <ci, ce, z> = [thee, theh, th] in common names and words.

<LETTER(S)>	[SOUND]	EXAMPLE	TRANSCRIPTION
<c + i, e> <z>	Latin America [s] Spain [th] (voiceless= think) (whichever you are comfortable with)	Names:	
		Francisco	frahn-see-skoh frahn-thee-skoh
		Alicia	ah-lee-see-ah, -syah ah-lee-thee-ah, -thyah
		Lopez	loh-pehs loh-pehth
		Chavez	chah-vehs chah-vehth
		Perez	peh-rehs peh-rehth
		Albeniz	ahl-bay-"niece" ahl-bay-neeth
		Zaragoza	"Sara-go"-sah [sah-rah-] thah-rah-goh-thah

		Terms: cinco concierto zarzuela	 "sink"-oh "think"-oh kohn-syehr-toh kohn-thyehr-toh sahr-sway-lah thahr-thway-lah

Otherwise, consider the two hemispheres alike:

<s>	[s] (never [z])	Granados Jose Rosa	grah-nah-dohs (k)hoh-say roh-sah (≠ as in Ital. roh-zah!)
<g + i, e> <g+a, o, u>	[khee, kheh] [g]	Geraldo Los Angeles gaspacho	kheh-rahl-doh lohs ahn-kheh-lehs gahs-pah-choh
<gu + i, e> <gü + i, e> <gu + a, o>	[gee, geh] [gwee, gweh] [gwah, gwoh]	Guevara Mayagüez Nicaragua	geh-vah-rah my-ah-gwehs, gways nih-kuh-rah-gwuh
<qu>	[k] (as in French, not [kw] as in Italian)	Enrique quesadilla	ehn-ree-kay keh-sah-dee-yah
<ch>	[ch] (as in English, unlike French, Italian, German)	Chile	chee-lay
<ñ>	[n^y]	cañon jalapeño	kah-nyohn (k)hah-lah-"pain"-yoh
<ll>	[y] (Maybe be [l^y] in some words in Europe.)	de Falla Medellín tortilla, villa pollo (chicken) relleño (filled)	deh-fy-yah (deh-fahl-yah) meh-deh-yeen (Colombia) tohr-tee-yah, vee-yah poy-oh ray-ayn-yoh
<d> (after a vowel)	[d] (voiced [th] is "correct" but not for announcing)	Madrid Abbado ciudad ("city")	mah-dreeth (= "Ma, breathe!) ah-bah-"though"/"dough" syoo-thahth (-ðahð)
<b, v>	[b] (but <b> = [b], <v> = [v] is normal for announcing.)	Ventura Valencia	behn-toor-uh/vehn… bah-lehn-thee-uh/vah-lehn-see-uh (or combination thereof. Like the <d> issue].)
<j, x>	Both are [kh] or [h] (though in Juan the <w> takes over: (k)hwahn/wahn.)	Juan, Jose Jesus Jorje, Jaime fajita Oaxaca Xalapa Xavier	(k)hwahn, (k)hoh-say (k)hay-soos (k)hor-(k)hay, (k)hy-meh fah-(k)hee-tah wah-khah-kah (Mexico) khah-lah-pah (Mexico) (k)hahv-yehr (khahv-vee-"air," U.S. [zay-vee-er or ehk-zay-vee-er])

GERMANIC LANGUAGES

ENGLISH

English is basically a Germanic language insofar as grammar is concerned, and its vocabulary has a strong influence from French and Latin. Many English letter/sound correspondences, notably of <c, g, s>, are more like French or Italian than they are like German. Here is a recap of what has already been said in part in several places above. Use it for further practice in reading phonetic spellings. This general overview is not a full-scale account of the spelling and phonetic idiosyncracies of English.

Vowels

The five vowel letters of English serve double and triple duty to represent the fourteen distinct vowel sounds of English. Many English dictionaries illustrate this with a "long" mark, for example, [ā] called macron, or a "short" mark on [ă], called breve. (See Interlude 3 for the notions of long and short.)

When

a	e	i	o	u

are "long," as in

ā	ē	ī	ō	ū
hay fatal café weigh great	he, wee lead machine retrieve receive	high why pie	hoe whoa flow	huge few!

they are transcribed in this book as

[ay]	[ee]	[y]	[oh]	[(y)oo]

When they are "short," as in

ă	ĕ	ĭ	ŏ	ŭ
hat	hen any	hit, busy English pretty women	hot bottle	hut love flood young

they appear here as

[a]	[eh]	[ih]	[ah]	[uh]

Other typical dictionary symbols, such as

o͝o	o͞o	aw	ow	ə

put woman wood could	toot do, move crew youth	call, talk off thought caught	how house	about enough connect suspect

are represented here by

[oo]		[aw]	[ow]	[uh]

(As noted in Movement 1, [oo] can represent either of these sounds, and English word hints are usually provided for clarification.)

Note these standard spellings and the way this book represents their vowel sounds:

by buy bite	bit busy pretty women	bat ban	bay bait weigh great	bet bread any bury	Bert dirt hurt work
↓	↓	↓	↓	↓	↓
[y]	[ih]	[a]	[ay]	[eh]	[er]
↓	↓	↓	↓	↓	↓
by byt	biht bih-zee prih-tee wih-mihn	bat ban*	bay bayt way grayt	beht eh-nee beh-ree	bert dert hert werk

but love young	good, put could woman	food move crew	boy boil	bow house	law call caugh
↓	↓		↓	↓	↓
[uh]	[oo]**		[ay]	[eh]	[er]
↓	↓		↓	↓	↓
buht luhv yuhng	good woo- muhn shood	food moov croo	boy boyl	bow hows	law cawl cawf

Consonants

As discussed in Interlude 1 on voicing and Interlude 2 on the terms hard and soft, here is another way of thinking about English spelling of consonants.

<c> = voiceless, whether "hard" [k] (velar stop) or "soft" [s] (dental fricative) (as in French)

* Your ear will tell you that these two [a]s are not quite the same. This is an automatic variation that occurs before [n]. There is no special symbol for it, since English speakers will do it unconsciously.

** This symbol serves for both the"long" o͞o in "suit, hoot, lute" and the "short" o͝o in "soot, hood, look."

<g> = voiced, whether “hard” [g] (velar stop) or “soft” [j] (palatal affricate)
(as in Italian)

<LETTER(S)>	[SOUND]	EXAMPLE	TRANSCRIPTION
<c + i, y, e>	[s] (usually)	Cindy Cynthia Cecile Maurice	sihn-dee sihn-thee-uh suh-seel maw-rees
	[sh] (see <-ci-> below)	special	speh-shuhl (See below.)
<ch>	[ch] [sh] [k]	Charles Charlotte Christ	chahrlz shahr-luht kryst
<g + i, e>	[g] in some words	Gilbert, give, get	gihl-bert, gihv, geht
	[j] in others	Gerald, Gene George giblet, gem	jeh-ruhld, jeen jorj jihb-let, jehm
<-ger>	[ger, jer] in German names	Kissinger	kih-sihn-jer “kissing”-er
	[zhay] in French names	Auger	oh-zhay

<s> = always fricative
[s, sh] (voiceless dental and voiceless palatal) or
[z, zh] (voiced dental and voiced palatal)
<z> = always voiced fricative
[z, zh] (dental and palatal)
<th> = always interdental fricative, whether voiced or voiceless (except in names like Thomas)

<LETTER(S)>	[SOUND]	EXAMPLE	TRANSCRIPTION
<s->	[s]	sign sound	syn sownd
<-s-, -s>	[s] or [z]	design, designs resound, resounds Denise, Chinese Ives desert	duh-zyn, duh-zynz ruh-zownd, ruh-zowndz duh-nees, chy-neez yvz deh-zert, duh-zert
	These pairs of words differ in the voicing of the last consonant, regardless of its spelling:	close (call) close (the door) excuse (me) (no) excuse advice (is cheap) advise (me) “bus us” “as is”	klohs klohz ek-skyooz ek-skyoos ad-vays ad-vayz (spelling helps here) buhs uhs az ihz

<s(u)-> <-(s)su-> <-(s)sion>	[sh] [sh] [zh]	sugar sure pressure, erasure pleasure, measure impression erosion	shoo-ger (= "shook") sher preh-sher, uh-ray-sher pleh-zher ihm-preh-shuhn ee-roh-zhuhn (uh-roh-zhuhn)
<-ci-> <-ti-> (sometimes)	[sh] (in alternation with [-s], [-t].)	face, space facial, spatial emit, elated emission, elation	fays spays fay-shuhl spay-shuhl ee-miht, ee-lay-tihd ee-mih-shuhn, ee-lay-shuhn
<th>	voiceless (θ), as in voiced (ð), as in	thin, thought, breath, teeth, booth this, though, breathe, teethe, smooth	(No good way for English to represent this. See Movement 1 and Interlude 1.)

GERMAN

Two Notes on Visual Impressions

CAPITAL LETTERS. The most unusual feature of German spelling for English eyes is that all nouns—not just proper names like Mozart, Haydn, and Bach—always begin with a capital letter whether they are the first word in the sentence or not. (Just imagine a text such as "Over the River and through the Woods to Grandmother's House we go.")

APPARENTLY IMPOSSIBLY LONG WORDS. German and English both have the ability to create long strings of nouns. The difference is that German usually writes them as a single visual word, while English does this only sometimes: bedroom-dining room, teaspoon-soup spoon. Imagine writing diningroom and soupspoon and extend this to noun groups.

E, *separated*	Bach works catalogue	theater director	magic (wonder) horn
E, *together*	Bachworkscatalogue	theaterdirector	wonderhorn
G	Bachwerkeverzeichnis	Schauspieldirektor	Wunderhorn

English "of"-phrases need to be turned back into strings of nouns:

E, *separated*	Scenes of Childhood	Dances of the League of David
E, *together*	childhoodscenes	David'sleaguedances
G	Kinderszenen	Davidsbündlertänze

This noun compounding strategy does not exclude the possibility of prepositional phrases as in "Das Lied von der Erde." You can recognize these and pull them apart in direct proportion to the size of your German vocabulary.

Vowels

German vowel letters may signal long or short vowel sounds, but a following <h> ensures a long reading (in the sense of Interlude 3). English speakers need not try to reproduce this quality, except perhaps for [eh, ay]. Following are the charts of single letters and sequences, both plain and umlauted (on which see below).

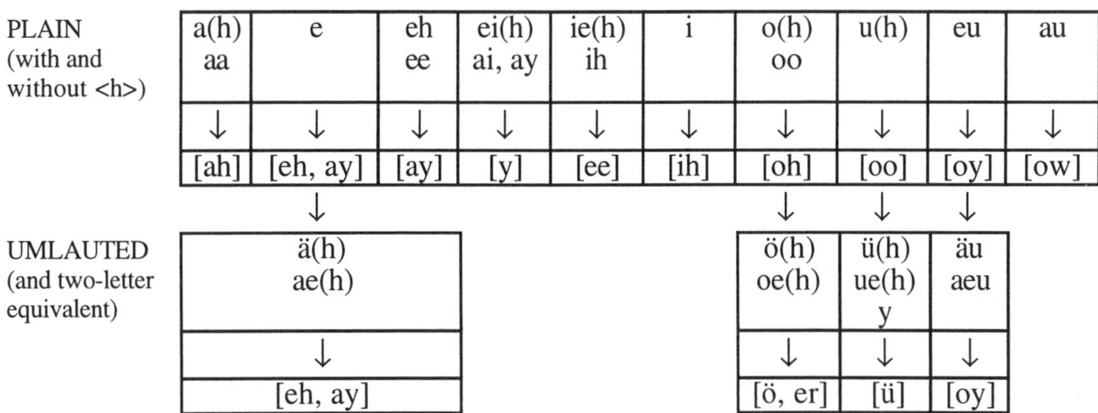

PLAIN (with and without <h>)	a(h) aa	e	eh ee	ei(h) ai, ay	ie(h) ih	i	o(h) oo	u(h)	eu	au
	↓	↓	↓	↓	↓	↓	↓	↓	↓	↓
	[ah]	[eh, ay]	[ay]	[y]	[ee]	[ih]	[oh]	[oo]	[oy]	[ow]
		↓					↓	↓	↓	

UMLAUTED (and two-letter equivalent)	ä(h) ae(h)	ö(h) oe(h)	ü(h) ue(h) y	äu aeu
	↓	↓	↓	↓
	[eh, ay]	[ö, er]	[ü]	[oy]

Unstressed <e> = shwa = [uh], as in Interlude 3. Pachelbel = [pah-khuhl-bel], Reinecke = [ry-nuh-kuh]. Those who know German may prefer a quick [eh], as in [ry-neh-keh], but pronouncing it risks being "too correct." At the end of a word <er> is either shwa, reminiscent of British or Bostonian English, or [er], as in Biber, Wagner, Reger = [bee-buh, vahg-nuh, ray-guh] or [bee-ber, vahg-ner, ray-ger].

The letter <i> by itself is usually [ih], as in Fritz = [frihts], while the combinations <ie> and <ih> are [ee], as in "Stihl" = [shteel] (the company). Both occur in Dietrich Fischer-Dieskau = [dee-trihkh fih-shuh dees-"cow"].

The letter <y> is the front rounded vowel [ü] in mid-word, but [ee] at the end: "Physiker" = [fü-zih-kuh] (physicist), Willy = [vih-lee].

The combinations <au> and <ai, ay> are literally the sum of their parts, namely, [ah + oo], [ah+ee] in a single syllable, given here as [ow, y]: Klaus = ["louse"], Haydn = [hy-duhn], Kaiser = [ky-zuh]. Popular German food items reinforce this: sauerkraut = [zow-uh-krowt], braunschweiger = [brown-shvy-guh]. The spelling <ei> = [y], then, is *not* the sum of its parts: Heinz = [hynts], (the German name), but [hynz] is the American ketchup. Weinberger = ["vine"-behr-ger], Leipzig = [lyp-tsihg] (or [lyp-tsihkh], if you are in the mood), Kapellmeister (choir director) = [kah-pehl-my-stuh].

The combination <eu> = [oy] as in "boy." So Neumann = [noy-mahn], Waldteufel = [vahl-toy-fuhl], Deutsch = [doych], and of course, Freud = [froyd].

UMLAUTS. Three German vowel letters <u, o, a> can occur with two over-dots called "umlaut," discussed in Movement 1). These dots move the rounded back vowels [oo, oh] to rounded *front* vowels [ü, ö] and [ah] from a low central vowel to a mid front vowel [eh, ay]. (See Interlude 3.) The umlauted <ü, ö, ä> can also be spelled <ue, oe, ae>, and all of them can occur with a following silent <h>. Thus, <ü> = <ue> = [ü], <ö> =

<oe> = [ö]. The same person Böhm on one CD jacket might be Boehm on another similarly for Bühler or Buehler, Händel or Haendel = ["hen"-duhl]. Since <ä> = [eh] and <eu> = [oy], it follows that <äu> = <eu> = [oy]: Fräulein = [froy-lyn] ≠ [fraw-lyn].* (The spelling Fraeulein is less common but possible.)

LONG AND SHORT. Double vowel letters <aa, ee, oo> and the sequence "vowel + <h>" indicate "long vowel," in the physical sense of Interlude 3: Saar, Beethoven, Das Boot = [zahr], [bay-toh-vuhn], [dahs boht]. English-speaking announcers need not try to pronounce long and short. (Vocabulary note: German Boot is "boat," not "boot." See the reprise on this question under Dutch, below.)

Note on Names, Letters, and Immigration

German names ending in <stein> would be [shtyn] in German. Jewish names in Europe were pronounced in Yiddish, a language very closely related to German, as [shtayn], like "stain." Many Jews who came to America at the beginning of the 20th century anglicized that to [styn] or [steen]. Some people are very insistent which one they want, but the spelling leaves you clueless as to which one they chose. Most American-born Jews in the arts—just an impression, not a statistical study—seem to prefer the [styn] variant, as do Leonard Bernstein, Marc Blitzstein, Joseph Silverstein. (Their foreparents most likely came through Ellis Island as [behrn-shtayn, blitz-shtayn, zihl-ber-shtayn].) Other such <-ein> names, like Weiner = German [vy-ner], come into English as [wy-ner], although some families prefer [wee-ner]. The common name Klein seems always to be [klyn], never "clean," and some families even spell it "Kline." This is different from the name of the pianist Walter Klien = [vahl-tuh kleen].

Consonants

The main pitfalls are <z> = [ts], <ch> = [kh], <j> = [y], <w> = [v], and the special letter <ß> = [s]. Strictly speaking, there are two varieties of [kh]. English dictionaries usually use Bach or "Scottish loch" as the example of the "hard" one after <a, o, u>. The "soft" on is almost [sh] when following the vowels <i, e, ü, ö>. (That's right: front vowels.) IPA and several of the books in the bibliography transcribe this second variety as <ç>—this is *not* French <ç> = [s]—but if announcers produce something in between [kh] and [sh] for all German <ch>, almost everybody will be satisfied. And as has been said before, [k] is perfectly acceptable as a substitute.

---

* Note that the beer Löwenbräu = [lö-vehn-broy] is now bottled in the U.S. and has lost its umlauts on the trip overseas, so it is now Lowenbrau = [loh-uhn-brow], which is what people were calling it, anyway. If you are "too correct" at your local watering hole you'll get only strange looks and no beer.

<LETTER(S)>	[SOUND]	EXAMPLE	TRANSCRIPTION
<g>	[g]	Georg, Reger Gieseking Gewandhaus	gay-org, ray-ger gee-zuh-king guh-vahnt-hows
<-ig>	[ihk] or [ihkh]	Leipzig	lyp-tsihkh
<c + a, o, u> and <-ck>	[k]	Carl (variant of Karl) Gluck Reinecke	kahrl glook (= "look") ry-nuh-kuh
<c + i, e>	[ts] (German pronunciation of Church Latin)	Cis (= C#)	tsihs
<j>	[y] (consonant as in "yes")	Johann Josef, Jorg Jerusalem Jesu, Jacob	yoh-hahn yoh-zehf, yorg yeh-roo-zah-lem yay-zoo, yah-kohp
<s> + a vowel	[z]	Sigfried Salzburg Saar Joseph langsam gesellschaft	zihg-freed zahlts-boorg zahr yoh-zef lahng-zahm guh-zehl-shahft
<s> at end of syllable or word)	[s]	Klaus Gewandhaus Haas	klows (="grouse") guh-vahnt-hows hahs
<ss>, <ß>	[s]	Strauss mässig (= mäßig)	shtrows (= "louse") may-sihkh (√ -"sick")
<sp, st> at the beginning of a syllable	[shp, sht]	Stephan, Stein Strauss, Stuttgart Stamitz, Spohr Gestalt	shteh-fahn, shtyn shtrows, shtoot-gart shtah-mihts, shpohr guh-shtahlt
<sch>	[sh]	Schumann Schultz geschwind	shoo-mahn shoolts guh-shvint
<schm, schl> (Like <sp->, <st->, but the [sh] part is spelled out. The sequences <sm> and <sl> are mostly in foreign words.)	[shm-, shl-]	Schlitz schmerz	shlihts shmehrts (= pain)
	[sm-, sl-]	Slaven Smetana (See Movement 2.)	slah-vuhn (= "Slavs") smeh-tah-nah
<tsch>	[ch] (literally t+sch)	deutsch Deutsche Welle Tschaikowsky (and other Russians)	doych doy-chuh veh-luh chy-"cough"-skee

<z, tz> (A word can end with <z> or <tz>, but it can only begin with <z>. Both can occur in the middle.)	[ts] (just as in Italian <z>)	Mozart Heinz Franz zigeuner Verzeichnis Konzert Graz	moh-tsahrt hynts frahnts tsih-goy-nuh (=gypsy) fehr-tsykh-nihs kohn-tsehrt grahts (city)
<w> but: <-ow> at end of last name	[v] [oh]	Wolfgang Weber Werner Wagner Wanda Berwald Flotow (This does not apply to German spelling of Russian names, where <ow> = [ohv] or "off," cf., Tschaikowsky.)	vohlf-gahng vay-ber vehr-ner vahg-ner vahn-dah "bear"-vahld (though he is a Swede) floh-toh
<v>	[f]	Verzeichnis	fehr-tsykh-nihs (One of those "too correct" areas. [v] is acceptable.)
<pf>	[pf]	Kempf Pfitzner	just as it looks
<ch>	[kh] (See note on the two varieties above and in Movement 1.)	Bach Pachelbel Richard Köchel Friedrich	bahkh pah-khuhl-"bell" rih-khard (√ -shard, "card") ker-khuhl (√ -shuhl) free-drihkh (√ -drihsh)

Voicing Reprise

Recall that English <s> can be both voiceless [s] and voiced [z]. One important difference between reading English and German is that German <s> is always *voiced* at the beginning of a word and always *voiceless* at the end. In German and Dutch syllables can only end in a *voiceless* consonant. A voiced consonant in that position is pronounced as its *voiceless* counterpart, cf. the charts in Interlude 1. This is why German characters in many Hollywood movies pronounce "Jakob, give me some good bread" as "Ya-kop, giff me zahm goot brett." Other German names like Bernd and Gerhard are [behrnt] and [gehr-hahrt], and you can decide for yourself how closely you want to observe this process, which is called *devoicing*. Note also the Gewandhaus orchestra is [geh-vahnt-hows] (voiced [d] becomes voiceless [t]), and the common first name Hans is full-German [hahns], half-German [hahnz]. Despite this regularity, some names are so well accepted in English that it is unnecessary to "re-germanize" them. Brahms is [brahmz]. Radio audiences might find full-German [brahms]—replacing final voiced [z] by voiceless [s], according to the rules of German—quite odd.

DUTCH AND FLEMISH

Dutch is a Germanic language closely related to German and English. It is the language not only of Holland (The Netherlands) but also of its neighbor to the south, Belgium. The northern half of Belgium and the coast are called Flanders (Vlaanderen = [vlahn-duh-ruhn]) and the people and the language are called Flemish (Vlaams = [vlahms]). The southern half of Belgium, called Wallonia, is French-speaking. Dutch letter/sound correspondences are quite different from those of German, though the resulting sound will be very much like German. Other spelling strategies resemble those of French.

Vowels

General European applies, more or less. Here are the other issues in reading Dutch vowels.

a aa ae	e ee	-en	ie (y)	i	o oo	eu	oe	u uu	ui uy	ij (ÿ) ei
↓	↓	↓	↓	↓	↓	↓	↓	↓	↓	
[ah]	[eh, ay]	[uh]	[ee]	[ih]	[oh]	[ö]	[oo]	[ü]	[y]	

SHWA. Unstressed <e> is [uh], as in de Groot = [duh-khroht], Brugge = [brü-khuh]. The ending <-en>, which marks the infinitives of verbs and the plurals of nouns, is also shwa in full-Dutch, that is, the final <n> is silent, as in the city of Antwerp: Antwerpen = [ahn-twehr-puh] (Flemish) or [ahn-tvehr-puh] (Dutch). Probably the most famous Dutch musician is Frans Brüggen, who despite his German spelling, sounds like [brü-khuh]. The more entrenched pronunciation is [broo-gihn].

SINGLE AND DOUBLE VOWEL LETTERS. As in German, there are both single and double vowel letters: <a, aa> - [ah], <o, oo> = [oh], <e, ee> = [eh, ay], <u, uu> = [ü]. Note that Dutch uses no umlauts. (There is no double <ii>. Only Finnish has that sequence.) The city of Den Haag = [den-hahkh] (the Hague); the names Pieterszoon = [pee-tehr-zohn], Vuursteen = [vür-stayn]. As in German <i> = [ih] and <ie> = [ee]. Older spellings include <ae> = <aa>, <ue> = <uu>, and <ey, uy> = <ei, ui>, thus, <van Stralen> and <van Straelen> are both [strah-lihn].

OPEN AND CLOSED SYLLABLES. Open syllables end in a vowel sound, and closed syllables end in a consonant sound. English "butter," in terms of sounds, is composed of an open syllable and a closed one: [buh-ter]. (Remember that <tt> is a double letter, not a double sound, cf., Interlude 2.) English "butler," with the same number of letters, is composed of two closed syllables: [buht-ler]. Single <a> in Dutch closed syllables is more like [uh] than [ah], while in an open syllable it is [ah]. Double <aa> = [ah]. In the Dutch sentence, "Wat is water?" = [vuht ihs vah-ter] ("What is water?" where English "what" = [wuht], too), "wat" has <a> in a closed syllable, while "wa-ter" has <a> in an open syllable. Similarly, names with <van> are [vuhn] or [fuhn]. This is different from both English "van" (as in the vehicle) and "general European" [vahn]. You are still safe saying [ah]. Dutch single <e> in a closed syllable is [eh], while in open syllables it is [ay], as in the sentence "Dit bed is beter" = [diht beht ihs bay-ter] ("This bed is better").

ON <U>, <EU> VS. <OE>, <OU>. As in French, <u> by itself = [ü], not German [oo]. Dutch <eu> is [ö], as in French, not as in German [oy]. Dutch <oe> = [oo], which is neither French <oeu> for [ö], nor German <oe> as an alternate spelling for <ö> = [ö]. An English word like "boot" transcribed into "phrendly phrench phonetics," for example, would be <boute>. In German it would be spelled <But> or <Buht> (with a captial letter, if it is a noun), and in Dutch it would be spelled <boet>. The sound is the same, [boot], but to read it aloud you have to know what system it was written in. Similarly, if you saw the word "boet" you would not know whether to pronounce it [boot], as in Dutch, or [böt], as in German, unless you knew what language system you were in. (The German title "Das Boot" sounds like [boht] and not [boot].)

OTHER TYPICAL DUTCH FEATURES. The combinations <ij> and <ei> are both [y] = "eye." IPA would represent this sound as [æʲ], but the [y] of "five, bite" (Dutch "vijf, bijt") is as close as the silence of the English printed page can come. Dutch printing sometimes collapses <ij> into a single <y> letter and sometimes it preserves the dots of both <i> and <j>, giving an umlauted <ÿ>. Genuine <y> sometimes appears as [ee].)

Similarly, the combination <ui> and its variant spellings <uy, uij, uÿ> are a sound somewhere between [ow], [oy], and [y] (= "eye"). For the purposes of radio announcing this author suggests [y] for <ui, uy>, and <ij, ei>: Huis, Kuyper, Klein, Sijmon = [hys, ky-per, klyn, sy-mohn]. If you are going to speak Dutch you will have to learn to distinguish these two sounds, but for announcing you are safe with [y]. The next closest English approximation [hoys, koy-per] is too far from the original. Note <-ooij> in the names <Booij>, <Kooij> = "boy" and "coy."*

Consonants

Five features make Dutch consonants different from German: Dutch <g> = [kh] and not [g]; <sch> = [skh], not [sh], and [sk] is a good substitute; <sp, st> = [sp, st], not [shp, sht]; <s> = [s], not [z]; <z> = [z], not [ts]. Some Dutch musicians have become better known by a German-sounding reading because so many announcers in the past have assumed that German letter/sound correspondences work for Dutch, too.

---

* You could explain this <ij, ui> problem to your listening audience, if you like, and the Dutch speakers among them will be pleased that you took the trouble to find this out. Robert J. Lurtsema (WGBH, Boston) relates that when he interviewed the Kuijken brothers on the air, they discoursed extensively on the subtlety of that pronunciation. You are welcome to say [y].

<LETTER(S)>	[SOUND]	EXAMPLE	TRANSCRIPTION
<g>	[kh] (most distinctive feature of Dutch spelling. Usually √ [g] in announcing .)	Frans Brüggen Gouda Concertgebouw	brü-khen (He is so well known around Europe with [g] that it might even be odd to "re-hollandize" him to [brü-khuh].) khow-duh (City famous for cheese. English speakers known it by the French reading, [goo-dah].) kohn-sehrt-khuh-bow (Literally, "concert building." As with Frans Brüggen, you risk giving your listening audience the impression that you are sloppy or pretentious because they are more familiar with [guh-bow].)
<w>	[v] (before vowel) (This is one of the differences between Dutch and Flemish: Flemish <w> is [w], but you are always safe generalizing to [v].)	Willem de Waart Sigiswald	vih-luhm duh-vahrt sih-khihs-vahlt/-wahlt
<-uw>	[ü]	Leeuw	lay-ü (√ -oo) (means "lion")
<v>	[f/v] (Dutch has [f], and Flemish has [v]. Dutch [f] is always safe.)	Vuursteen	vür-stayn
<sch> but: -sch(e) (in adjective endings for countries)	[skh] (substitute: [sk]) [s]	Schat school belgisch(e) (= Belgian) russisch(e) (= Russian)	skhaht skhohl (Yes, it means "school.") behl-khihs(uh) rü-sihs(uh)
<j> (See above on <ij>, <ooij>.)	[y] (consonant)	Jaap Joris Johan	yahp yoh-rihs yoh-hahn (Dutch usu. one <n>; Ger. usu has two)
<sj, tj/tsj, zj> (Many Dutch names end in <-tje>= [chuh], also in spelling of Russian names.)	[sh, ch, zh]	—tje (a common ending for nouns) Sjorsj, Zjorzj Russians: Sjostakovitsj Tsjaikovski Poesjkin Brezjnjev	---chuh shorsh, zhorzh (occasional spellings for "George") Shostakovitch Tchaikovsky Pushkin Brezhnev

SCANDINAVIAN

The three main Scandinavian languages are Danish, Norwegian, Swedish, and they are related to English, German, and Dutch. In geography, cuisine, and tourism the term Scandinavian sometimes includes Finnish, but that language belongs to an entirely different language group, cf. Finno-Ugric, below. In this section the three Germanic Scandinavian languages are treated together and sometimes compared to German and Dutch so that announcers can more easily identify which language is which. (Note that Icelandic is also a Germanic language and can also be considered Scandinavian, but it is mentioned here for only a few details.)

Vowels

General European applies for <a, e, i, o, u>. It is useful to compare the other vowel letters in these languages with German and Dutch as a way of identifying—or failing to identify—which language is which.

[ö]	
Dn-N:	<ø>
G-Sw:	<ö>
D:	<eu>

[ü]	
Dn-N-Sw:	<y>
G:	<ü>
D:	<u, uu>

If the [ü] sound is uncomfortable, substitute [ee] or [ih] for Scandinavian [ü]. In the German section above it was suggested that [oo] was a good replacement for German and Dutch [ü]. This is part of the reason that Grieg's well-known "Peer Gynt" suite is pronounced [gihnt]. (The English-speaking world is more likely to connect <y> with [ee, ih] than with [oo], but see Consonants below for the other part of the reason.)

All five of these Germanic languages have double <aa>. Recall that German and Dutch use it for [ah]. Scandinavian can spell either <aa> or over-circled <å>, and its sound is [aw] or [oh], as in Danish Århus and Norwegian Håkon. The spelling <aa> is considered older, but surnames are often just the places that preserve older spellings. Danish and Norwegian make occasional use of the piggy-back letter <æ> for [a] or [eh]. It is worth mentioning that <ei> = [ay], unlike German and Dutch ["eye"].

Some Swedish names ending in <en> use an acute accent, but it sounds no different from the letter without the mark, as in Alfvén, Wirén. Otherwise, only Icelandic uses acute accents regularly for long vowels <á, é, í, ó, ú>, as opposed to unaccented short one.

Consonants

PLACE SHIFTERS. Recall the shift in Italian from <g> = [g] to <g> = [j] before the vowels <i, e>. The same phenomenon occurs in Norwegian and Swedish, except that the shift is from <g> = [g] to <g> = consonant [y]: <gi, ge> = [yee, yeh], as in Gimse, Gedda, Birgit. Add to the list <gy> = [yü] and <gj> is just the consonant [y], making <gja> = [yah]. Swedish <gö> and Norwegian <gjø> both spell [yö]. The full-Norwegian title of Peer Gynt, cited above, is ["pair" yünt]. The usual English [peer gihnt] applies English standards of <g>. Danish does not experience this shift: <g> remains [g] before these same vowels.

For Danish, Norwegian, and Swedish consider final <g> as silent, especially in names that end in <-berg> = [behr, "bear"]. Some sources suggest that this <g> becomes a quick consonant [y], something like "berry," but this is an exaggeration. (This is reasonable given the English spelling of Edinburgh, where the final <g> does become a syllable in [eh-dihn-buh-roh], but Scandinavian actually merges that sound with the preceding [r] in a way that English-speaking announcers can just leave alone.) The city of Göteburg = half-Swedish [yö-tuh-boor], while the English name Gothenburg = [gah-thehn-berg].

As in most of northern Europe, <j> is [y], and it also contributes to draw consonants up to the hard palate. Danish, Norwegian, and Swedish have <sj> = [sh], as in Dutch. Norwegian and Swedish have <kj> and <skj> = [sh], as well. (Here again, some sources will point out that the [sh] sound of <kj> is different from the one spelled <sj>, but they will not describe the <kj> in a way that announcers would want to say into a microphone. English [sh], while not exact, is the closest there is.

Another consonant issue is Danish <d>. After a vowel it is similar to voiced [th] as in "the," although the quality is not quite English [th]. (Recall the similar phenomenon for Spanish <d> after vowels.) The Danish composer Niels Gade is full-Danish [gah-thuh], though on the air it is fine to say [gah-duh]. (Just be prepared to explain that to Danish speakers who call the station to offer a more accurate version.) The only unfamiliar consonant letters are Icelandic <Þ> and <ð> for voiceless [th] (cf,. thigh, teeth) and voiced [th] (cf., Thy, teethe), respectively. These letters were also part of the Old English alphabet until the Norman conquest. (See note under [th] in Sound Symbols in Movement 1.)

SLAVIC AND BALTIC LANGUAGES

The Slavic languages (also known by the British term "Slavonic") are treated in this section. Lithuanian and Latvian form a separate group of languages called Baltic and will also be mentioned briefly. These groups are geographical neighbors and distant linguistic relatives. Of immediate importance for this book is the fact that the reading techniques for these Baltic languages are similar to Czech and a few others, and all of them are gathered together as the "haček" languages. Romanian has already been treated with the Romance languages, and Hungarian and Finnish will come below in the Finno-Ugric section.

On Language, Religion, and Alphabet

Several Slavic peoples (Poles, Slovaks, Croats, Slovenes, Czechs) and the Baltic peoples (Lithuanians and Latvians) are Roman Christians. They all write their languages in the Roman alphabet they inherited along with their religion. The other Slavic peoples—the Serbs, Macedonians, Bulgarians, Ukrainians, Russians and Belarussians*—belong to the Eastern Orthodox Church and write in the Cyrillic alphabet, which is based on Greek. (See the discussion in Movement 2 on Janáček's *Glagolitic Mass* and in Movement 1 for the political-linguistic situation in the former Jugoslavia.) This movement deals with the reading techniques for the adjusted Latin letters used by these groups and of transcribing Cyrillic names and titles.

POLISH

Polish has the undeserved reputation of being frighteningly unpronounceable to westerners. Actually, Polish spelling is very systematic—"phonetic," as it were, just not in an obvous one-letter-to-one-sound way. Western European printers do themselves a disservice by leaving out the accent marks that make Polish quite manageable. Announcers should learn to recognize Polish names both with and without their graphic plumage.

Vowels

General European applies. In addition, <y> = [ih], while <i> = [ee], and [ie] = [yeh], as in Szymanowski = [shih-mah-n"off"-skee], "Krzysztof" = [kshih-sht"off"], Mieczysław = [myeh-chih-swahf]. The quality of the <o> vowel tends more toward English [aw], but this is not vital for announcing. As was discussed in Movement 1, there are two nasal vowels indicated by under-hooked <ę> = [ẽhn] and <ą> = [õhn], as in "Wałęsa" = [vah-wẽhn-sah] and "Dąbrowski" = [dõhm-brawf-skee]. (You actually hear the consonants [m] or [n] more than in the comparable French nasal vowels in "Entremont" = [ãhn-truh-mõhn].) The only other Polish vowel diacritic is the acute over <ó> = [oo], as in "Górecki" = [goo-reht-skee] and the cities of "Kraków" = [krah-koof] and Łódź= [wooch].

Consonants

It is worthwhile to begin with the sounds of <c> to put Polish in perspective with the rest of the languages covered thus far. Polish plain <c> = [ts]. Thus, <cy, ce, ca, co, cu> = [tsih, tseh, tsah, tsoh, tsoo]. Watch for <i>: the sequence <ci> = [chee]. Any

* Belarussian is the language of the republic of Belarus = [byeh-lah-roos], meaning White Russia. When this country was a Soviet republic it was known by the Russian name, Byelorussia(n). The two languages are very similar. See also Moldavian (Moldovan) under Romanian.

following vowel = [ch + that vowel], as in Italian. In both Polish and Italian, then, <cia, cio, ciu> = [chah, choh, choo]. The difference is that this includes Polish <cie> = [cheh], while <ce> = [tseh]. (Compare Italian <ce> = [cheh].)

To spell [ch] when not followed by a vowel, Polish uses an acute accent: <ć> = [ch]. The combination <cz> is also [ch], strictly speaking, a "darker" [ch] sound, thus <czy, cze, cza, czo, czu> = [chih, cheh, chah, choh, choo]. If you plan to speak Polish you have to learn to distinguish these two kinds of [ch], but for radio announcing English [ch] is fine. The same pattern holds true for the spellings of both <ś> and <sz> = [sh], and <ź> and <ż> (with an overdot rather than an additional <z>) = [zh]. Besides that, note the combination <rz> = [zh]. (Compare Czech <ř> = [rzh] below.) Barred <ł> = [w], and as in German, <w> = [v] and <j> = [y].

VOICING. Polish has the same kind of voicing principle as German and Russian: "Replace (potential) final voiced consonant with corresponding voiceless pair." This is why the names in <owski> are ["off"-skee]. "Witold" is, strictly speaking, [vee-tohlt]. The city of "Łódź" is [wooch] with final [j] (voiced) becoming [ch] (voiceless).

<LETTER(S)>	[SOUND]	EXAMPLE	TRANSCRIPTION
<g>	[g] (always, as in German)	Górecki	goo-rehts-kee
<c> (with no accent mark plus any consonant or any vowel but <i>)	[ts]	Katowice Sosnowiec Wrocław Penderecki	kah-toh-vee-tseh (city) "saw-snow"-vyehts (city) vraw-tswahf (Ger. Breslau) pen-deh-reht-skee (and dozens of names in -ecki, really -et+skee)
<ć> (accent mark and no vowel following)	[ch]	czytać mówić	chih-tahch (= to read) moo-veech (= to speak)
<c + i> (with no other vowel following)	[chee]	Oświęcim	oh-shvyehn-cheem (See note in Movement 2.)
<ci> + other vowel	[ch]+that vowel	ojciec Wojciech	oy-chets (= father) voy-chehkh
<cz>	[ch]	Mieczysław Czesław	myeh-chih-swahf cheh-swahf
<ch>	[kh]	Wojciech Częstochowa	voy-chehkh chehn-stoh-khoh-vah

<ś> (accent mark and no vowel following)	[sh]	Oświęcim Śląsk śpiewać	oh-shvyehn-cheem shlõhnsk (= Silesia) shpyeh-vahch (= to sing)
<s + i> (with no other vowel following)	[shee]	Zanussi	zah-noo-shee (film director)
<si> + other vowel	[sh] + that vowel	Harnasie	har-nah-sheh
<sz>	[sh]	Szymanowski Szeryng Warszawa Moniuszko	shih-mah-n"off"-skee sheh-ring (= "sharing") vahr-shah-vah moh-nyoosh-koh
<ź> (accent mark and no vowel following)	[z]	Ździsław	zhjee-swahf, a first name
<z + i> (with no other vowel following)	[zhee]	Brzezinski Kazimierz	bzheh-zhin-skee kah-zhee-myehsh
<zi> + any other vowel	[zh] + that vowel	Ziemia Obiecana	zhehm-yah oh-byeh-tsah-nah (*The Promised Land*, a film by Andrzej Wajda)
<ż> (over-dot instead of double <zz>)	[zh, j]	Żywiec (city) Ziębice (city)	zhih-vyehts zhehm-bee-tseh
<rz> Same sound as <ż>	[zh] (= voiceless [sh] when following a voiceless consonant: <prz> = [psh], <krz> = [ksh].)	Jerzy (George, Cz. Jiří) Andrzej (= Andrew) Brzezinski Rzeszów Grzegorz Krzysztof	yeh-zhih* ahn-jay (<drz> = [dzh] = [j]) bzheh-zheen-skee zheh-shoof (city) gzheh-gawsh (Note that at the end of a word <rz> = [sh] because of the same rule that devoices all [zh] to [sh].) kshish-tohf (The cluster <krz> = [ksh], that is, [zh] becomes [sh] after voiceless [k].)

* Poles in America usually give up trying to convince English speakers that there is a [zh] in such names. The author Jerzy Kosinski, for instance, is full-English [jer-zee kuh-zihn-skee] and not full-Polish Jerzy Kosiński = [yeh-zhih koh-sheen-skee]. The news media in the 1970s announced President Carter's national security advisor, Zbigniew Brzezinski, as [z-big-nyoo ber-zihn-skee] more often than as [zbihg-nyehf bzheh-zheen-skee].

<dź, dż> (with acute or dot) <dz + i> (with no other vowel following)	[j] literally [d + zh] [jee]	Łódź (city) Włodzimierz Ździsław	wooj (really *wooch* : voiceless at end of word) vwoh-jee-myehsh zhjee-swahf
<ść> (with accent mark and no vowel following) <ści> +other vowel <szcz>	[shch] literally [sh + ch] [shch] + that vowel [shch]	solidarność Kościuszko Bydgoszcz Szczecin	soh-lee-dahr-nohshch (the Solidarity movement) kawsh-choosh-koh "bid"-gohshch (city) shcheh-cheen (city)
<ń> (accent mark) <ni + other vowel>	[n^y] (Fr., It. <gn>, Sp. [ñ]) [n^y + that vowel]	Poznań (city) Gdańsk Gdynia	poh-znahn^y gdahn^{y}sk (if you dare!) gdihn-yah (city)
<w>	[v] (also [f] at end of a word and before ski in names with <-owski, -ewski>	Wanda Landowska Wojciech Witold -owski -ewski Zbigniew Kraków	vahn-dah lahn-"doff"-skah voy-chehkh (<cie>= [cheh]) vee-told (also -tolt, observing voicing principle) -"off"-skee -ehf-skee zbihg-nyehf "krah"-koof
<j>	[y] (consonant)	Jan Jacek Wajda	yahn yah-tsehk vy-dah
<ł> ("barred-l") <l> (unbarred)	[w] [l]	Stanisław Wrocław Łódź Landowska Note first <l> is unbarred and second barred: Lech Wałęsa Karol Wojtyła	stah-nee-swahf vroht-swahf wooch lahn-"doff"-skah lehkh vah-wen-sah kah-"role" voy-tih-wah (Pope John Paul II)

THE HAČEK LANGUAGES

SLAVIC: Czech (Cz.), Slovak (Sk.), Serbo-Croatian (SC), Slovenian (Sv.)
BALTIC: Lithuanian (Lt.), Latvian (Lv.)

"Haček" [hah-"check"] is the standard linguistic designation for the little "v" diacritic on top of a letter. (In Czech it means "little hook." Its invention is usually credited to Jan Hus = [yahn hoos], the leader of the Czech Protestant Reformation in the 15th century. IPA sometimes calls it a wedge.) The term "haček languages" is not standard linguistic usage but has been coined here to group together the languages that use it on <š, ž, č> for [sh, zh, ch]. They also share with Polish and Hungarian (see below) the use of <c> for [ts].

Vowels

General European applies. In addition, Czech, Slovak, and Lithuanian have both <i> and <y> = [ee]. (Recall that Polish <i> = [ee], but that <y> = [ih].) Czech and Slovak mark long vowels with an acute on <á, é, í-ý, ó, ú>. For announcing, consider them the same as [ah, eh, ee, oh, oo]. (Compare the Spanish example of Tomás = [toh-mahs], where the accent *is* a stress mark, and Czech Tomáš =[toh-mahsh], where the accent mark is *not* a stress mark.) Czech also has both <ú> and <ů> = [oo]. Some sources recommend <e> = [eh], <é> = [ay], but [eh] for both is acceptable. A haček over <ě> gives [yeh], and the combination <ou> = [oh+oo] in one syllable, and English [oh] suffices here. (Compare French <ou> = [oo] and Dutch <ou> = [ow].) Slovak has umlauted <ä> for [a] and <ia> = [yah]. The Baltic languages also have long and short vowels. Latvian has long marks on <ā, ē, ī, ō, ū> = [ah, eh, ee, oh, oo]. Lithuanian has hooks on <ą ę į ǫ ų> = [ah, eh, ee, oh, oo], and plain <e> = [eh], while dotted <ė> = [ay].

Consonants

All six of these languages have <š, č, ž> = [sh, ch, zh]. The upper case forms are <Š, Č, Ž>, although in Latvian the haček can be displaced to the right on <Sˇ Cˇ Zˇ>. Czech and Slovak also have <ň, tˇ, dˇ> = [n^{y}, t^{y}, d^{y}], and only Czech has <ř> = [rzh], on which, see below. The upper cases for all these are < Ň, Ť, Ď, Ř>. As in Polish, plain <c> is [ts]. As in the rest of northern and eastern Europe, <j> is [y].

MORE HAČEKS AND OTHER VISUAL CUES. Czech and Slovak put a haček on <ň> for [n^{y}]. Compare some other languages' visual techniques for this sound: Spanish <ñ>, Polish, <ń>, Latvian, <ņ>, Serbo-Croatian and Slovenian <nj>, French and Italian <gn>, and Portuguese <nh> (which is also in Vietnamese, although it has not otherwise been mentioned).

Czech <ř> is the simultaneous pronunciation of [rzh] (not [zhr]). Between syllables it is easy to split into [r] and [zh], as in Dvořák, Jiří = [dvor-zhahk, yeer-zhee]. Within a syllable, as in Bedřich, you can either squeeze it all in or cut it back to [zh], rather than [r], but do not create another syllable: [beh-drzhihkh] or [behd-zhihkh] but not [beh-der-zhihkh].

Serbo-Croatian spells the combinations <dž, dj> = [j]. It also has the special cross-bar <đ>. The upper-case versions of these are <Dž, Dj, Đ>.

Czech and Slovak <ť ď> are also written with a plain apostrophe instead of a haček: <t', d'> in Kat'a = [kah-tyah]. (At the end of a word, plain [t] and [d] are fine for announcing. If listeners who know these languages call up to correct you, just thank them very much and tell them you'll try harder next time.) Slovak also has <l'> = [l^y].

SYLLABIC <R> AND <L>. In Czech, Slovak, and Serbo-Croatian <r> and <l> with no vowels around them function as the vowel in that syllable. English has a syllabic [l] at the end of a word like "table" = [tay-bl], though it is easier to transcribe a full vowel in [tay-buhl]. English's closest answer to syllabic [r] is [er]. Czech, Slovak, and Serbo-Croatian all have syllabic <r>, and the first two have syllabic <l>, as well. The Czech river Vltava is three-syllable [vuhl-tah-vah]. The city of "Brno" is two- syllable ["burn"-oh], and the Croatian island of Krk is [kerk].* In Slovak you might also meet acute accents over "long syllabic" <ŕ, ĺ> but you need not try to hold them doubly long.

Latvian uses an under-mark (resembling a comma or cedilla) for palatalized consonants. That information merely helps you identify a written text as Latvian, but you need not try to pronounce these differently from their plain partners, for example, <t> and <ṭ>, <d> and <ḍ>, <s> and <ṣ>.

Serbo-Croatian and Slovenian, as was said above, both have <č> = [ch]. Slovenian names typically end in <-ič>. Serbo-Croatian has, in addition, an accented <ć> = [ch], as does Polish, and Serbo-Croatian names end in <-ić>.

<LETTER(S)>	[SOUND]	EXAMPLE	TRANSCRIPTION
<c>	[ts] (like Polish)	Václav (Cz.) Hercegovina (SC) (also in German spelling Herzegovina: <z> = [ts].)	vaht-slahv hehr-tseh-goh-vee-nah (also hehr-tseh-goh-vee-nah. For newscasting "hurts-ago"-vee-nuh is also OK.)
<č> and SC <ć>	[ch]	Janáček Smetaček Karadžić (SC) Milošević (SC) Opalič (Sv.) Čiurlionis (Lt.)	yah-nah-chek smeh-tah-chek kah-rah-jihch mee-loh-sheh-vihch oh-pah-leech choor-lyoh-nees
<š> (with haček)	[sh]	Leoš Firkušný Kalniņš (Lv)	lay-ohsh feer-koosh-nee kahl-neensh

* Czech is famous for having a sentence, albeit a silly one, with "no vowels," that is, no vowel letters: Strč prst skrz krk = Stick (your) finger through (your) throat. All the vowels are syllabic [r].

<ž> (with haček)	[zh]	Goražde	gaw-rahzh-deh (city in Bosnia)
<ň> (Cz. with haček as Polish uses <ń>. SC, Sv. use <nj>.)	[n^y]	Plzeň (Cz. city: Ger. Pilsen: pilsner beer) Franjo	"pill"-zehn^y frahn-yoh
<ř> (Cz. only)	[rzh] (Do your best!)	Dvořak Jiří Bedřích	dvor-zhahk yeer-zhee beh-drzhihkh (yup!)
<l, r> surrounded by other consonants	["ill, er"] ("syllable [l] and [r]")	Vltava Plzeň Brno (city)	vihl-tah-vah, vuhl- "pill"-zehn^y "burn-oh"
<lj> (SC, Sv.)	l^y	Kralj	krahl^y
<j>	[y]	Jiří Janáček Sarajevo	yeer-zhee yah-nah-chehk sah-rah-jeh-voh
<Đ, đ, dj> (SC)	[j]	Tudjman (Franjo)	tooj-mahn
v (Sv., after a vowel)	[w]	Ramovš	rah-mohsh

RUSSIAN-UKRAINIAN-BULGARIAN

The following contemporary Slavic languages are written in the Cyrillic alphabet and profess Eastern Orthodox Christianity: Russian, Ukrainian, Belarussian, Serbian, Bulgarian, Macedonian.* Names in any one of these languages will look different when transcribed into Latin letters, since the Germans, French, and English transcrible according to their own sound/letter correspondences. The book of Russian songs by Piatak in Bibliography III gives an acceptable introduction to the letters and transcriptions. See also Movement 1 for notes on the closely related Ukrainian and notions of Post-Soviet "PC."

Vowels

GENERAL NOTES AND [IH]. General European applies for <i, e, a, u> = [ee, eh, ah, oo]. Russian and Ukrainian, like Polish, have both <i> = [ee] and <y> as [ih]. Russian [ih], strictly speaking, has the lip position of [ih] but the tongue position of [oo], a sound that occurs in American dialects of the southern Appalachians, as in "When did you git to Tennesee?" Use standard English [ih] for announcing. Russian and Ukrainian may have the same name, but Russian will have <i> = [ee], where Ukrainian will have <y> = [ih]:

* The main non-Slavic languages of the former Soviet Union written in Cyrillic are the Turkic languages (Azerbaijani, Turkmen, Uzbek, Kazakh, Kirghiz) and Tajik, which is related to Persian. On Moldavian, see Romanian. Outside Slavic or former Soviet territory, only Mongolian has adopted the Cyrillic alphabet.

Dmitrii (R), Dmytro (U) = [dmee-tree, dmih-troh]; Vladimir, Volodymir = [vlah-dee-meer, voh-loh-"dim-ear"]; and see the entry for Kiev in Movement 2. The Russian dancer Baryshnikov = half-Russian [bah-rihsh-nee-"cuff"], half-English [buh-rihsh-nih-"cough"]; the composer Dargomyzhsky = [dar-goh-mihzh-skee], and the author Solzhenitsyn = [sohl-zhuh-nee-tsihn]. (Recall that in Czech and Slovak both <y> and <i> = [ee], as in the Czech last name Bílý = [bee-lee]. The rest of the Slavic group has only <i> = [ee].) In some books the symbol <ï> after a consonant = [ih], as in Dargomïzhsky. IN Ukrainian <ï> after a vowel = [yee], as in Kyïv. Transcriptions of Bulgarian have <ă> = [uh], which resembles Romanian.

UNSTRESSED <O> AND <A>. This is an issue for full-Russian and full-Bulgarian and an optional one for announcing. First, in Bulgarian unstressed <o> = [oo] (similar to Portuguese), and unstressed <a> = [uh], as in Tomowa-Sintow = [toh-moo-vuh-seen-toof]. The quality of Russian stressed [oh] is more like [aw] with a hint of a [w], something like [^{w}aw]. Plain English [oh] will do the job.*

The rules for full-Russian unstressed <o, a> are the opposite of the English rules. Start with the stressed syllable. When <o> and <a> are in the syllable *immediately before the stress*, both are [ah]. English <o, a> are normally shwa under the same circumstances, as was illustrated in Interlude 3.

	↓	↓	↓
	Pro-ko-fiev	**Kon-dra-shin**	**Ga-li-na**
R:	prah-"cough"-yehf	kahn-drah-shihn	gah-lee-nuh
E:	pruh-"coffee"- ehf	kuhn-drah-shihn	guh-lee-nuh

In the syllable *after* the stress, both English and Russian have <o> and <a> = [uh]: Galina = [gah-lee-nuh] (English [guh-lee-nuh]), Ostankino = [ah-stahn-kee-nuh] (the Moscow radio-television station, [aw-stahn-kee-noh]. The same is true in longer words *two* syllables before the stress:

	↓	↓
	Ro-stro-po-vich	**Sho-sto-ko-vich**
R:	ruh-strah-poh-vihch	shuh-stah-koh-vihch
E:	rah-struh-poh-vihch	shah-stuh-koh-vihch

See the entries on these names in Movement 2 for announcing options.

THE "-YE-" FACTOR. English transcriptions of Russian names often differ in the presence or absence of the letter <y> = consonant [y]. When <y> appears before a vowel it

---

* English [oh] is a diphthong . The lips are rounded at the beginning and come even closer together at the end of the vowel. It might more accurately be transcribed [oh^W]. The Russian sound is the mirror image: it *starts* with more rounded lips and spreads them out slightly, something like [^{W}oh], as in some neighborhoods in Brooklyn: "toss the ball" or "talk over a cup of coffee." English announcing can be content with [oh].

is the consonant [y]: Yalta, Yeltsin, and the women's last names ending in <skaya> = ["sky"-uh] or [skah-yuh].

Russian Cyrillic has two letters: <э> = [eh] and <e> = [yeh] after a vowel but [eh] after a palatalized consonant. Different transcriptions into Latin letters either recognize or ignore this phonetic fact. The names Evgeny and Egor = [yehv-"gay-knee"], [yeh-gohr]. Only rarely is this [y] spelled out, as in Yevgeny, Yegor. This [y] also occurs between vowels, as in the various spellings of

Dostoevsky	Nikolaev	Sergeev
Dostoyevsky	Nikolayev	Sergeyev.

This [y] is often spelled <i> after a consonant or in the <skaia> names, that is, <ia, iu> = [yah, yoo]. Typical first names like Katya, Tanya also appear as Katia, Tania. Both are two syllables [kah-tyuh, tah-nyuh], not three-syllable [kah-tee-uh, tah-nee-uh]. The singer [fyoh-duhr shah-lyah-"pin"] is spelled in both French Fiodor Chaliapin and English Fyodor Shalyapin. The composer Miaskovsky may also appear as Myaskovsky. This is three-syllable full-Russian [myih-"scoff"-skee], though four-syllable half-Russian [mee-uh-"scoff"-skee] or half-English [myahs-"cough"-skee] is also good. (Do avoid half-English [my-uh-"scoff"-skee].)

ON <E> AS [YOH], AND NAMES IN <-EV, -OV>. Russian Cyrillic has the letters <e> = [yeh] and <o> = [oh], there is also dotted <ë> = [yoh] (or [oh] after a palatalized consonant, cf. Interlude 2). These dots are neither an umlaut, nor a dieresis, and to keep things interesting, Russian printing normally omits the dots since Russian speakers are assumed to know which <e> represents [yeh] and which represents [yoh]. This is why names such as Khrushchev, Gorbachev, Fedor, Petr may occasionally appear in print with dots as Khrushchëv, Gorbachëv, Fëdor, Pëtr to reflect the audible fact that they are [khroo-shchawf, gor-buh-chawf, fyoh-der, pyotr]. Spellings such as Fyodor and Pyotr are more common. Song lyrics transcribed from Russian sources often do not print <ë>. Singers had better check with a Russian speaker on which <e> is [yeh] or [yoh].

Consonants

Like Polish, Russian also has some imposing consonant clusters: [shch] in Khrushchev, Shchedrin; [mst] in Mstislav; [dm] in Dmitri(i); [vs] in Vsevolod. Do your best to keep little vowel sounds from breaking the clusters up, as in ["misty"-slahf], [duh-mee-tree ("dumb-eat-tree")], etc. Russian has no [w] sound, but Ukrainian does. A <w> in a Russian name and in some Ukrainian names is usually a mark of German spelling for [v].

ON VOICING. Like Polish and German, Russian also has a voicing rule: *voiced* consonants must be pronounced *voiceless* at the end of a word or before another voiceless consonant. This is why stereotypical Russian characters in bad Hollywood movies are famous for such statements as, "Oh, darlink, I lahf you!" (with [f] for expected [v]). Russians who need money will ask, "Can you lent me two bocks?" (with [t] for expected [d]). If they find bugs (= [buhgz]) distasteful they'll exclaim, "I can't stant bocks!" (with the final cluster [gz] devoiced to [sk]). Sometimes this comes across in different spellings of Russian names, especially those that end in <ov, ow>, <ev, ew>, <ovsky, owsky>, and <evsky, ewsky>. You find both Rachmaninov and Rachmaninoff, though hardly ever Tchaikoffsky. Of course for all those Russians whose names we have inherited through German-style spellings with <ow>, which is German [v], you still get [chy-"cough-ski"], never [chy-"cow-ski"]. In Ukrainian, though, pronounce consonants as you see them.

ON <I, E>, APOSTROPHE, AND PALATALIZED CONSONANTS. Most Russian consonants, when followed by <i, e> or an apostrophe are palatalized, that is, <ti, te, t'o> = [tyee, tyeh, t^{y}oo]. In a musicological work you might find a word such as "muzykal'nyj" = [moo-zih-kahl^{y}-nee] for "musical." A few place names might show it, as in Kazan' = [kah-zahn^{y}] or Chernobyl' = [chehr-noh-bihl^{y}]. (Recall from Interlude 2 that English <u> plays a similar trick after some consonants, as in "music, cute, bureau.") Many reference works on Russian for non-specialists give the impression that palatalization means "consonant followed by quick [y]." It is not: it is the consonant articulated simultaneously with the *qualities* of [y].) Cyrillic Russian spelling shows this palatalizing by the spelling of the following vowel: <la, lia> or <mu, miu>. This guide sometimes shows this consonant character in the pronunciation column—more often before the vowel [eh] than before the vowel [ee] because it comes out clearer. The spelling Galina Vishnevskaya reflects Russian letters, but to English eyes it masks full Russian [gah-lyee-nuh vyee-shnyehf-skuh-yuh]. Half-English gives the palatalized consonant in the stressed syllable but not the unstressed syllables: [gah-lee-nuh vee-shnyehf-skuh-yuh]. Full English follows the Russian letters as if they were English: [guh-lee-nuh vih-shnehf-"sky"-uh]. Borodin = full Russian [buh-rah-dyeen] with stress on the end. The usual full-English version is, of course, ["bore-a dean"] with the stress moved to the beginning. Brezhnev (although not a musical name) = full-Russian [bryehzh-nyehf], full-English [brehzh-nehv]. Kabalevsky = [kah-bah-lyehf-skee] or [kah-bah-lehf-skee]. This accounts for the optional Rakhmaninov = [rahkh-mah-nyee-nuhf], [rahkh-mah-nih-nuhf], since this is a case where pronouncing this [y] (that is, palatalizing the [n]) before [ee] gets unwieldy.

<LETTER(S)>	[SOUND]	EXAMPLE	TRANSCRIPTION
<ch>	[ch]	Chekhov (author) Gorbachev	cheh-khuhf (√ "-off") guhr-bah-ch"off"
(The same name can be spelled <kh> or <ch> in different sources.)	[kh]	Rachmaninov, Rakhmaninov	rahkh-mah-nyee-n"off"
	[sh] (If the spelling comes from through French.)	Chaliapin	shah-lyah-"pin"
<tch, tsch>	ch (in French and German spellings)	Tschaikowsky, Tchaikovsky (German-style spelling; a more English-looking Chaikovsky is becoming more frequent.)	chy-"cough"-skee

<shch>	[sh]+[ch] (In a single sweep, like Polish <szcz>.)	Khrushchev	khroosh-ch"off"
<v> or <w>	<v, f> (voicing principle) Ukr: [v] before a vowel; [w] after a vowel	-ov, -off, -ow (but not German <ow>, as in Flotow) Kyiv Ivanivna, Iwaniwna Lviv, Lviw (city in western Ukraine)	"off" kih-yeew ee-vah-neew-nah luh-veew
<z>	[z] not German [ts] (if the spelling is English-based.)	Glazunov Karamazov	glah-zoo-n"off" (See note in Movement 2.) kah-rah-"ma's off" (from the Dostoevsky novel)
<-sky, -skii, -skij> <-skaya, -skaia, -skaja>	[skee] [skah-yuh] (See Names below.)	Glazunov Karamazov	glah-zoo-n"off" (See note in Movement 2.) kah-rah-"ma's off"

A Guide to Russian Last Names and Middle Names

MEN'S AND MOMEN'S LAST NAMES. Three endings are typical of Russian last names: <-in> = [een], as in Borodin, <-ov> = ["off"] with variants <-ev, -ëv>, as in Chekhov, and <-y> = [ee], as in Bely. This last one is most often added to stems that have a <sk>, as in Mussorgsky, etc. All such names are masculine. The first two have automatic feminine variants ending in <-a>: <ina> and <ova> (including <-eva>, <-ëva>). For example, the sisters, wives, daughters, or mothers of Pushkin and (full-Russian) Borodin would be Pushkina and Borodina. (Note that stressed <in> has the feminine form <ina>.) Similarly, men named Chekhov, Nikolaev (= [nee-kah-ly-ehf], Sergeev (= [sehr-gay-ehf], Brezhnev, Gorbachov, or Khrushchov are associated with women named Chekhova, Nikolaeva, Sergeeva, Brezhneva, Gorbachova, Khrushchova. Anna Karenina is married to Karenin. Raskolnikov's sister would be Raskolnikova, etc., (Stressed <ov> has the feminine <ova> without changing the stress.)

The masculine ending <y> is really two letters in Russian <ий>, and they are transcribed variously as <i, ij, iy, yj, yi>. The feminine is <aya> = ["eye"-uh], Russian <ая>, also transcribed <aia>, <aja>. Therefore, "he" is Bely-Byely-Byelyj-Byelyi; "she" is Belaya-Byelaya-Byelaja. Names with <-sky> may appear as <ski, skii, skij, skiy> with feminine forms <skaya, skaia, skaja> = ["sky"-uh]. The feminine of Tchaikovsky is Tchaikovskaya; of Mussorgsky, Mussorgskaya. The masculine of Vishnevskaya is Vishnevsky. (Note, too, that the ending <sky> when following a <t> often has a German spelling <tzky> or <zky> = [tskee]. Polish spells this <cki>.)

Two visual cues keep Russian and Ukrainian names distinct. Ukrainian has an apostrophe in <s'ky> (for palatalized [s]), though it does not usually survive into Western transcription and would sound no different for announcing if it did survive. The final vowel in Ukrainian can be <s'kyj> or <s'kyi>, while Russian has <skij> or <skii>. The

Ukrainian <s'ky> may be stressed or unstressed, and see the next paragraph for Russian stress. The Ukrainian feminine is a single syllable <s'ka, ska>, as opposed to Russian two-syllable <skaya>. Compare with Latin-letter Slavic: Czech has accent marks on <ský-ská>. Polish has no marks on <ski-ska>. When you find plain <ska> on western liner notes look for other clues as to the woman's ethnicity.

MORE ON RUSSIAN STRESS. When <(sk)y> is stressed it is <(sk)oy>. This spelling automaticallyl means that the feminine form is <(sk)aia, (sk)aya, (sk)aja>. Note the pairs Tolstoy-Tolstaya, Donskoy-Donskaya, Rutskoy-Rutskaya, Trubetzkoy-Trubetzkaya. English normally adjusts this stress to the first syllable in familiar names like Tolstoy and the Bolshoi (ballet) = [tohl-stoy] and either ["bowl"-shoy] or ["bowl"-shoy]. (See the entry on Bolshoi for the grammatical side of that term.) The reverse is not true: the feminine spelling <(sk)aya> does not by itself show whether it is stressed or not. Knowing whether "she" is related to a <(sk)y> or a <(sk)oy> tells the story, if that information is available.

OUTSIDE RUSSIA. Russian women who left Russia when they were children often do not maintain the <sky-skaya> distinction and become <sky>. Moslem Turkic peoples under the czars and in the Soviet period added <in> or <ov> to their names: the composer, Sofia Gubaidulina (Tatar background), Chinghiz Aytmatov (the Kirghiz writer). Ukrainian last names typically end in <enko>, <ko>, and <uk>. A typical Armenian last name marker is <ian>, usually stressed as [yahn]. Names in <shvili> = [shvee-lee] and <dze> = [dzeh] are Georgian.

<OVICH>. Last names in <ovich> = [oh-vihch] are normally stressed on the <o>: Shostakovich, Rostropovich, Davidovich, Rabinovich. (This is how you know it is not Shostakovich, but see "patronymics" below.) Such Russian names are thought to be of Polish origin, as the next-to-last-syllable stress suggests, cf. <-owicz>. In addition, they are unisex. English spellings, especially of Jewish names from this area, are mostly <-owitz>, cf. Horowitz, Rabinowitz. The German spelling is <owitsch>.

MIDDLE NAMES (PATRONYMICS). Russians and Ukrainians regularly use middle names formed from the father's name (hence "patronymic"), and a full name is Given Name, Patronymic, Surname. The ending <-ovich, -evich> indicates "son of" and Russian <-ovna, -evna>, Ukrainian <ivna> means "daughter of." (This is not the same as the unisex last names in <ovich> just discussed.) Thus, the father of the great Russian poet Alexandr Sergeevich Pushkin was obviously Sergei. If he had had a daughter, say Vera, she would have been Vera Alexandrovna Pushkina. Adults who do not know each other or are business associates but not friends address each other by first and middle name, that is, "Hello, Alexandr Sergeevich. Please convey my regards to Vera Alexandrovna." In Ukrainian, the fictitious daughter, Tetiana, of their great poet, Taras Shevchenko, would be Tetiana Mikhailivna Shevchenko. (Names in <enko> are unisex.) If such names come through German or Polish transcription they are spelled <iwna> or <owich>. Note that these are stressed on the same syllable as in the name they are added to, and *not* on <o> as last names are: Sergey or Sergei has the patronymics Sergeevich, Sergeevna (four syllables each). Nikolai gives Nikolaevich, Nikolaevna (five syllables each).

There are some exceptions. The patronymic from Pyotr is Petrovich, Petrovna with stressed <o>. Three-syllable Mikhail = [mee-khah-eel] compresses two of those syllables into [mee-khyl] before adding <ovich>, though that does not come across in the usual spelling Mikhailovich, Mikhailovna = [mee-khy-luh-vihch, mee-khy-luhv-nuh]. A few men's names end in <-a>, and they form patonymics in <ich> and <ichna>: Nikita gives Nikitich-Nikitichna; Ilya gives Ilyich and the unusual Ilyinichna. All this becomes a moot point in Western liner notes and in music reference books, since the patronymics are often left off. Russians who travel extensively outside Russia often drop it, as well. See the entry on Heifetz in Movement 2 on the further notion of "endearing" names.

FINNO-UGRIC AND OTHER EUROPEAN LANGUAGES

FINNISH, ESTONIAN, HUNGARIAN

Finnish and Estonian are closely related to each other and distantly related to Hungarian. Together they form a distinct group called Finno-Ugric which in linguistic terms is not related to the other languages of Europe. Finnish is entirely distinct from Swedish and the Scandinavian languages (although it is sometimes classed as Scandinavian because of similarities in culture and geography). Estonian is totally different from its Balti neighbors Lithuanian and Latvian. Hungarian is completely different from the Slavic languages and from Romanian that border it. Finland was under the rule of Sweden for a long time and under the Russian czars after that. It has been independent since 1905, and there is still a large Swedish population in western Finland. Swedish is the official second language of Finland. From World War II till the early 1990s, Estonia was a Soviet republic, and Hungary was part of the Soviet bloc.

Vowels

General European applies. In addition, all three languages have umlauts. All three have <ö> = [ö], as in German and Swedish. Finnish and Estonian have <ä> = [a] or [eh], and Estonian and Hungarian have <ü> for [ü]. Finnish uses plain <y> for [ü], as do Danish, Norwegian, and Swedish. The sound of <ä> is more like the [a] of Swedish, but the [eh] of German is usually a more convenient substitute for English speakers. The Finn Neeme Järvi and the Estonian Arvo Pärt are best announced as [jehr-vee] and [pehrt]. Umlauted vowels in Finnish and Estonian can be double for the long varieties of these vowels just as other vowels, including <ii>. They both have <ää, öö>. Estonian has <üü>, and Finnish has <yy>.[*] Hungarian distinguishes regular umlaut <ö, ü> for short [ö, ü] from "long umlaut" <ő, ű> for long [ö, ü], but do not try to do this in announcing Jenő Jandó = [yeh-nö yahn-doh]. Only Estonian has <õ> and long <õõ>, which is a vowel more like [uh] than like [oh]. (This squiggle is not a tilde and does not mean "nasal," as it does for Portuguese <ão>.)

In Hungarian, a single accent on <á, é, í, ó, ú> indicates "long vowel." In full-Hungarian, strictly speaking, the qualities of long and short are somewhat different. Short <e> = [a] as in "fat," while long <é> = [ay], as in "fate." For half-Hungarian, treat them both as [eh]. In Movement 2 some Hungarian names with <é> are transcribed as [ay], but no names with <e> are transcribed as [a]. In full-Hungarian, short <a> = [aw] in "taut" or British Robert, while long <á> is like the [ah] as in American "tot." The lists always give both <a, á> = [ah]. Compare the following chart with the one on page 216 so that the vowel diacritics in these languages can serve as visual markers for identifying the language:

	long	**umlaut**	**long umlaut**	**special**
H	á-é-í-ó-ú	ö-ü	ő-ű	
Es	aa-ee-ii-oo-uu	ö-ü-ä	öö-üü-ää	õ, õõ = [uh]
Fn			öö-yy-ää	

Consonants

Finnish and Estonian have general European consonants, and they occur singly or doubly. These two languages have no special consonant problems or diacritics.

The chart below focuses on Hungarian, where several letter combinations require an announcer's attention. The <dzs> = literally [d+zh] = [j]. The combinations <dy> and <gy> are also [j]. Some sources give these two as [d^y], as in the British pronunciation of "dune," but this author considers [j] a more natural equivalent for speakers of American English. (Czech has this sound, too, and it is spelled <ď> with a haček. In the Czech section, above, the recommended substitute was plain [d].) Hungarian <y> ≠ [ee]. It serves as a place shifter, that is, <dy>, <gy> = the single consonant [j], not the syllable [jee]; <ty> = [ch], not [chee]; <ny> = [n^y], not [nee]; <ly> = the consonant [y], not [lee] (similar to Spanish <ll> = [y]). The syllable [n^yee] = <nyi> and [yee] = <lyi>.

[*] Either both letters are umlauted or neither is. A commercial name like Haägen Dazs, with a mixed sequence, gives itself away as made up, probably an attempt to resemble Scandinavian. No European language has <aä>. (German <äu> has different vowels.) As for <zs>, it does not occur in Scandinavian, and if it is supposed to be Hungarian [zh], it is not—and Hungarian does not use double vowels.

<LETTER(S)>	[SOUND]	EXAMPLE	TRANSCRIPTION
<sz>	[s]	Szell -szki (in Russian names)	"sell" skee
<zs>	[zh]	Rozsa Zsigmondy	roh-zhah zheeg-mohnj
<s>	[sh]	Solti Budapest János	shohl-tee boo-dah-pesht yah-nohsh
<c> (<cz> old spelling)	[ts] (like Czech, Polish)	Debrecen (city)	deh-breh-tsen
<cs>	[ch]	Kocsis Csajkovszki	koh-cheesh Tchaikovsky
<z>	[z]	Zoltan	zohl-tahn
<gy>	[j] (single consonant, not a syllable)	György Magyar (Hung. for "Hungarian")	jörj (jerj) mah-jahr
<ny>	[n^y] (not a syllable, cf. Fr. <gn>, Sp. <ñ>)	Masony	mah-shohn^y
<ly>	[y]	Kodaly	koh-"dye"

FROM THE ENDS OF EUROPE

These brief remarks on some other European languages—Albanian, Greek, and Turkish from the southeastern periphery and Welsh and Irish from the western periphery—are intented to help in identifying the language.

Albanian

VOWELS. The only unusual one is <ë> = [uh].

CONSONANTS. <c> = [ts], <ç> = [ch], <ş> = [sh]. The most common "adjuster" is <h>: <t, th> is the relation of voiceless [t, θ] and <d, dh> is the relation of voiced [d, ð]. This dental fricatives <s, z> = [s, z] are made palatals, as nowhere else in Europe, besides English: <sh> = [sh], <zh> = [zh]. In addition, <x> = [dz] (voiced dental affricate), <xh> = [j] (voiced palatal affricate). The <q> is basically [k]. The Albanian name for the country is Shqipëria = [shkee-puh-ree-uh], and its captial is Tiranë = [tee-rah-nuh].

Greek

There is a lot to say on transcribing and reading modern Greek. The following minimal points will suffice here.

VOWELS. General European. The digraphs <ai, ou> = [eh, oo] as in French. The modern Greek diphthongs <ei, oi> = [ee].

CONSONANTS. There is one unusual feature. At the beginning of word <mp> = [b] and <nt> = [d]. (The well-known letters "beta" <β> and "delta" <δ> in modern Greek are [v] and [th].) To represent the [b] (voiced labial stop) Greek joins the otherwise voiceless labial stop [p] with the labial nasal [m], which is voiced, cf. Interlude 1. Similarly the voiceless dental stop [t] combines with the dental nasal [n], which is voiced, to form the voiced dental stop [d]. A typical example is the loan word "bank" = Greek <mpank>.

Turkish

VOWELS. Plain and umlaut as in German: o-ö, u-ü. Upper and lower case dotted <İ, i> = [ee]. Upper and lower case undotted <I, ı> = [ih].

CONSONANTS. <c> = [j], <ç> = [ch], <ş> = [sh], <j> = [zh]. The crescent <ğ> occurs only after a vowel. It is best left silent, as in the surname suffix <-oğlu> = [oh-loo].

Welsh and Irish

These languages are notorious for their inefficent spelling systems. Welsh is more manageable than Irish, but this short section gives only the absolute minimum on reading these languages.

VOWELS. The most striking feature is the Welsh use of <y> = [ee, uh] and <w> = [oo]. With circumflex they are <ŷ> = long [ee] and <ŵ> = long [oo]. Irish vowels are short without an acute accent and long with one (<a, á>, etc.), but not for announcing.

CONSONANTS. Both Welsh and Irish have <ch> = [k(h)]. Note Welsh single and double consonants: <d, t> = [d, t], but <dd, th> = voiced/voiceless [th (ð/θ)]; <f> = [v], but <ff> = [f], e.g., Dafydd = [dah-vihth] (David). In addition, <l> = [l], but <ll>, as in Lloyd, Llewelyn, is [hl] with heavy breath. (Do not attempt this at home.) As in Polish, <si> = [sh]. Irish <b, m> = [b, m], while <bh, mh> = [v].

EAST ASIAN LANGUAGES

Chinese, Japanese, and Korean are linguistically unrelated to each other, though they have all been in close cultural contact for centuries. (There is a theory that Japanese and Korean are distantly related to each other and that they descend from the same prehistoric ancestor as the Turkic and Finno-Ugric languages. This is interesting but not very helpful for reading contemporary names.) Not only does each of these East Asian languages have a different writing system, but their sounds are next to impossible to describe for Westerners on the silent page. The few hints given here are not meant to make you sound like a speaker of these languages, just to make sense of the several ways that people use Latin letters to approximate the sounds.

JAPANESE AND KOREAN

A good rule of thumb is to think of the vowels as having their "general European" values and of the consonants as having their English values. This makes Seiji Ozawa = [say-jee oh-zah-wah] with <j> = [j] and <w> = [w]. Korean <u> = English [uh], not [oo]. This is why Kyung Wa Chung = [kyuhng, chuhng] and need not be "Europeanized" to [kyoong, choong]. The Korean combination <eo> is also [uh], and <ae> is [eh].

Japanese Stress and Vowel Skipping

English speakers often read Japanese as they read Italian, that is, with the stress on the next to last syllable. In fact, the stress in Japanese can occur on almost any syllable. Connected with this is the fact that the vowels represented by <i, u> are not pronounced under one very special circumstance: when <i> or <u> comes *between two voiceless consonants*. The name Yamashita is sometimes pronounced as in Italian = [yah-mah-shee-tah], but it is actually [yah-mahsh-tah]. (Both [sh] and [t] are voiceless consonants, cf. Interlude 1, and the <i> between them is silent.) Do pronounce the second <i> in the city of Hiroshima = [hee-roh-shee-mah] since [sh] is voiceless, but [m] is voiced. (The more familiar English stress is [hee-roh-shee-mah].) The city of Nagasaki = [nah-gah-sah-kee]: both [s] and [k] are voiceless, but the [ah] between them is not subject to being skipped over.

CHINESE

The most striking feature of Chinese sound is the "tone" system. Every word has its own rising or falling voice, but this book does not attempt to represent these tones, nor does the announcing profession consider it appropriate to try to say them.

There are several different Latin-letter transcription systems for Chinese. One is called Wade-Giles, and the official modern one of the mainland government is called Pinyin. The Wade-Giles transcription of the city "Peking" has largely been replaced in the Western press by the Pinyin transcription "Beijing," that is, former ["pay-king"] is now [bay-jing]. It is far more complicated than is useful to discuss here, but the hints below will keep your announcing more or less on target.

Vowels

<ao> = [ow], <ai> = [y], <ei> = [ay]. The <e> letter is more [uh] than [eh]. Consequently, <eng> = [uhng] as in "Deng" = ["dung"].

The vowel letters <i, u> by themselves are [ee, oo], as in general European, but they also function as the consonants [y, w] when they are followed by another vowel letter, similarly to Italian or Spanish: <ua> = [wah], <ia> = [yah], <ueng> = [wuhng]. These are also the only two vowel letters than can follow the consonants <x, q>.

Consonants

Many Chinese consonants come in varieties called "aspirated" and "unaspirated." English has these varieties, too, but English speakers are generally unaware of them. Suffice it to say that <p> at the beginning of an English word is aspirated, that is, pronounced with a puff of air, as in "pot." Pinyin spells this <p>, and Wade-Giles spells it <p'>. Unaspirated <p> occurs in "spot." Pinyin spells this <b>, while Wade-Giles spells it <p>. The same holds true for Wade-Giles <t, t'>, <k, k'> vs. Pinyin <d, t>, <g, k>. There is no need to try these on the air. If you find apostrophes after *voiceless* consonants in the transcription of a Chinese name, it is a sign of Wade-Giles.

The most eye-arresting feature of Pinyin spelling for Westerners is the use of <xi, xu> = [shee, shoo] and <qi, qu> = [chee, choo]. When another vowel follows, read the <i, u> as a quick [y, w], as in the Chinese leader Deng Xiaoping = [duhng shyow-ping]. In addition, <sh> and <hs> = [sh], <ch> = [ch], <zh> = [j] (actually somewhere between [zh] and [j]).

<LETTER(S)>	[SOUND]	EXAMPLE	TRANSCRIPTION
<x> only before <i, u>; also <hs>, <sh>	sh	Deng Xiaoping Xiamen (city) Xinjiang	"dung" shyow ping shyah-mehn sheen-jyahng
<q> only before <i, u>;	ch	Qingdao (city) Qiu Jiu Da Qu	ching-dow chyoo-jyoo dah-choo

CODA

These reviews are an attempt to continue where such comparative charts as those in C. O. Mawson (1934, pp. xxi-xlii) and Deems Taylor (1940/1971), listed in Bibliography II, left off. The emphasis here, as throughout this book, is on system rather than alphabetical order of languages or letters.

Diacritic Review

This is a summary of each language's inventory of diacritics. This visual information will help you identify or eliminate a language—if the marks remain in the printing of the name. Marks on vowel letters are given first, then consonant letters.

MARK	NAME, DESCRIPTION	LANGUAGE(S)	LETTERS AFFECTED	PHONETIC REMARKS
x̄	Long mark (like macron)	Latvian	ā, ē, ī, ō, ū	[ah, eh, ee, oh, oo] (Long as in Interlude 3.)
x̃	Tilde (squiggle)	Estonian	õ	[oh, uh] (not nasal)
		Portuguese	ão	[õw] (nasal)
		Spanish	ñ	[nʸ]
x́	Acute (above, lower left to upper right)	Spanish	á, é, í, ó, ú	stress only
		Czech, Slovak	á, é, í-ý, ó, ú	long, not stress
		Slovak	r′ l′	long syllabic r, l
		Icelandic, Irish	á, é, í, ó, ú	long vowel
		Italian	é, ó	[ay, oh] (≠ [eh, aw])
		Polish	ó; ś ć ź ń	[oo]; [sh, zh, ch, nʸ]
		Serbo-Croatian	ć	[ch]
x̀	Grave (upper left- lower right)	Italian	à, è, ì, ò, ù	stress, also [eh, aw]
		French	è	[eh], rather than [ay]
x̂	Circumflex (above, pointing up)	French, Port.	â, ê, î, ô, û	[ah, eh, ee, oh, oo]
		Romanian	â, î	[ih]
		Welsh	ŷ, ŵ	long [ee, oo]
x̌	Haček (above, pointing down)	Czech	ě	[yeh]
			š č ž ň ť ď ř	[sh zh ch nʸ tʸ dʸ rzh]
		Slovak	š č ž ň ť ď	[sh zh ch nʸ tʸ dʸ]
		SC, Sv, Lt, Lv	š č ž dž	[sh zh ch j]
ẋ	Dotted	Lithuanian	ė	[ay]
		Polish	ż, dż	[zh, j]
		Turkish (un/dotted)	İ/i, I/ı	[ee], [ih] (upper, lower case)

x̊	Circled	Scandinavian	å	<å> = <aa> = [aw]
		Czech	ů	[oo] (same as <u, ú>)
ü (See below.)	Dieresis*	French, Dutch, (rarely English)	on second of two vowels	pronounce second vowel separately
	Umlaut	German,	ä, ö, ü	[eh, ay], [ö], [ü] [a] (Es, Fn.)
		Estonian	ä, ö	
		Finnish	ö, ü	
		Hung., Trk.	ö/ä	
		Swedish/Slovak		
	Special letters	Russian	ё, ї	[yoh], [ih]
		Ukrainian	ї	[yee]
		Albanian	ë	[uh]
		Dutch	ÿ	<ij> = [y]
ű	Long umlaut	Hungarian	ő, ű	treat as [ö], [ü]
x̆	Crescent (like English breve)	Rom., Blg.	ă	[uh]
		Turkish	ğ	silent before consonant
x̶	cross-through	Danish, Norw.	ø	[ö]
		Serbo-Croatian	Đ, đ	[j]
		Icelandic (upper)	Đ	[th] voiced
		Polish	Ł, ł	[w] (≠ [l])
x̨	Underhook (counterclockwise)	Lithuanian	ą ę į ǫ ų	same as plain
		Polish	ę ǫ	nasals [ẽhn], [õhn]
x̧	Cedilla/Comma (underhook, clockwise)	Latvian	b̦ ș d̦ l̦ *etc.*	"palatalized" cons.
		Romanian	ş ţ	[sh], [ts]
		Turkish	ş ç	[sh], [ch]
		French, Portuguese	ç	[s]
		Albanian		[ch]

* These two dots occur only on vowel letters and have different functions and correspondingly different names. In English, French, and Dutch they are called *dieresis* = [dy-ehr-ih-sihs] and mark the separation of two vowels. Read the second one as a separate sound and do not to take the two letters as a set. English occasionally spells "coöperate" = [koh-ah puh-rayt], ≠ [koo-puh-rayt], "reïnvest" = [ree-ihn-vehst], ≠ ["rain-vest"]. Dutch spells "België" = [behl-khee-uh] (the name for Belgium).

Some French names use dieresis to signal vowel sequences that are unusual for French, such as Saint-Saëns. In the Alsatian name Boëhlmann the dieresis prevents reading German <oe> = [ö]. Dutch <ij> can merge in print to form dotted <ÿ>.

In German, Swedish, Hungarian, Finnish, Estonian, the two dots are called *umlaut* and signal a difference in sound from the undotted letter: <u, ü> = [oo, ü], <o, ö> = [oh, ö], and in all of these languages but German, <a, ä> = [ah, a]. In German they are [ah, eh/ay].

Transcriptions of Russian may have <e> = [yeh] and <ë> = [yoh], though <e> usually serves for both. Either <y> or <ï> may give [ih]. Transcriptions of Ukrainian have <y> = [ih], <ï> = [yee], as in Kyïv. Albanian distinguishes <e> = [eh] from <ë> = [uh].

Letter-to-Sound Review

Some Consonant-Vowel Combinations

These are the usual readings of so-called "hard" and "soft" <c, g> in Interlude 2.

<table>
<tr><th><C></th><th>L
(Class.)</th><th>L (Church)
I, Rm.</th><th>E, F, Pt.</th><th colspan="2">S
Amer./Eur.</th><th>G</th><th>P*</th></tr>
<tr><td><ci></td><td>[kee]</td><td>[chee]</td><td colspan="2">[see]</td><td>[thee]</td><td>[tsee]</td><td>[chee]</td></tr>
<tr><td><ce></td><td>[keh]</td><td>[cheh]</td><td colspan="2">[seh]</td><td>[theh]</td><td colspan="2">[tseh]</td></tr>
<tr><td><ca></td><td colspan="6">[kah]</td><td>[tsah]</td></tr>
<tr><td><co></td><td colspan="6">[koh]</td><td>[tsoh]</td></tr>
<tr><td><cu></td><td colspan="6">[koo]</td><td>[tsoo]</td></tr>
</table>

<table>
<tr><th><G></th><th>L (Class.)</th><th>L (Church)
I, Rm., E</th><th>F, Pt.</th><th>S</th><th>N, Sw.</th><th>G, D</th></tr>
<tr><td><gi></td><td>[gee]</td><td>[jee]</td><td>[zhee]</td><td>[khee]</td><td>[yee]</td><td rowspan="3">G: all <g> = [g]
D: all <g> = [kh]</td></tr>
<tr><td><ge></td><td>[geh]</td><td>[jeh]</td><td>[zheh]</td><td>[kheh]</td><td>[yeh]</td></tr>
<tr><td><ga, go, gu></td><td colspan="5">[gah, goh, goo]</td></tr>
</table>

	E, F, Pt., D, R	S (Amer.)	S (Eur.)	G	I <z, zz>
<Z>	[z]	[s]	[th] = [θ]	[ts]	[dz]

Some Vowel Combinations

<table>
<tr><th><ie></th><th><ei></th><th><ai></th><th><au></th><th><oe></th></tr>
<tr><td>G, D, F [ee]</td><td colspan="2">G, D ["eye"]</td><td>G, D, Dn, N, S, I [ow]</td><td>G, F [ö]</td></tr>
<tr><td rowspan="2">P, R, S [yeh]</td><td rowspan="2">I [eh+ee]</td><td>S, I [ah+ee]</td><td>F [oh]</td><td rowspan="2">D [oo]</td></tr>
<tr><td>F, N, K [eh]</td><td>E [aw]</td></tr>
</table>

<eu>		<ou>		<oi>		<y>	
G	[oy]	F, Gk.	[oo]	E	[oy]	S, F, Cz., Lt.	[ee]
F, D	[ö]	D	[ow]	F	[wah]	P, U	[ih]
Pt.	[eh-oo]	Cz.	[oh-oo]	Gk.	[ee]	D	["eye"]

* Recall that in the haček languages (of which Polish is not one) all <c> = [ts].

Sound-to-Letter Review

This is the other side of the hard-soft coin. These are the major spellings for certain sound combinations, not all the possible spellings of the vowel sounds.

[k]	L (Class.)	L. (Church) I, Rm.	F, Pt., S	E
[kee]	<ci>	<chi>	<qui>	<kee, ki>
[keh]	<ce>	<che>	<que>	<ke>
[kah, koh, koo]	<ca, co, cu> (and French <cau, cou>)			

[kw]	L (Class.), I	E	Pt.	S
[kwee]	<qui>	<que>		<cui>
[kweh]	<que, qua>	<que, qua>		<cue>
[kwah]	<qua>	<qua, quo>	<qua>	<cua>
[kwoh]	<quo>	<quo>	<quo>	

[g]	L (Class.)	I, Rm.	F, Pt., S	E
[gee]	<gi>	<ghi>	<gui>	<gi, ge>
[geh]	<ge>	<ghe>	<gue>	<ge>
[gah, goh, goo]	<ga, go, gu>			

[s]	L (Class.)	L (Class.), I, Rm.	F, Pt., S (Am.)	E
[see]	<si>	<si>	<si, ci>	<see, cee>
[seh]	<se>	<se>	<se, ce>	<se, ce>
[sah]	<sa>		<sa, ça>	<sa, so>
[soh]	<so>		<so, ço>	<so>
			<sau, çau>	
[soo]	<su>		<su, çu>	<su, soo>
			<sou, çou>	

Recall that European Spanish has <ci, ce> = [thee, theh] and <za, zo, zu> = [thah, thoh, thoo].

The Palatal Challenge

The spelling of the palatal consonants (cf. Interlude 2) and of the dental affricate [ts] differ widely across European languages. Some languages share a spelling strategy. Open-sided boxes within a larger box indicate alternative spellings for a single language.

1	Voiceless fricative	Voiceless affricate	Voiced fricative	Voiced affricate
	[sh]	[ch]	[zh]	[j]
E	<sh, si, su>	<ch>	<-ge, -su->	<j, (-d)ge>
S				
C	<x, hs, sh>	<q, ch>	<zh>	<j>
Pt	<x>		<j, gi, ge>	
F	<ch>			
I	<sci, sce>	<ci, ce>		<gi, ge>
Rm	<ş>		<j>	
Trk.		<ç>		<c>
Alb.	<sh>		<zh>	<xh>
P	<ś, si, sz>	<ć, ci, cz>	<ź, zi, ż, rz>	<dź, dzi, dż>
H	<s>	<cs>	<zs>	<gy, dzs>
G	<sch>	<tsch>		
N-Sw.	<sj, kj, skj>			
D	<sj>	<tj, tsj>	<zj>	
Cz.-Sk.				
Lv.	<š>	<č>	<ž>	
SC		<ć>		<dž, đ>

2	Palatal Glide	Palatal Nasal	Palatal Liquid	Voiceless Dental Affricate
	[y] cons.	$[n^y]$	$[l^y]$	[ts]
E		<onion>	<million>	<-ts>
S	<ll>	<ñ>	<ll> (Eur.)	
Pt.	<y> , <i+vowel>	<nh>	<lh>	
F		<gn>		
I	<i+vowel>		<gli>	<z(z)> (= [ts, dz])
Rm				<ţ>
G	<j>			<z, -tz(-)>
D				
N-Sw.	<gi, ge, gj>			
P	<i+vowel>	<ń, ni>	<l>	
H	<ly>	<ny>		
Cz.-Sk.		<ň>	Sk. <l'>	<c>
Lv.		<ņ>	<ļ>	
SC		<nj>	<lj>	
Alb.				

FINALE

ANNOTATED BIBLIOGRAPHY

This three-part bibliography is not a complete reference list on music, just of those books where announcers can find musical and geographical names and terms. Commentary is provided on their usefulness for classical radio announcers, especially when used together with the present book. Bibliography I includes books with no phonetic help. (Some of them have enough information to make a reasonable guess at pronunciation possible.) Those in Bibliography II do have phonetics (some better, some worse), and Bibliography III ventures into phonetics for singers, books in related fields (art, cuisine) with phonetics, and general issues of producing and reading phonetic transcription. (There are many transcription systems in use for different purposes, and the better an announcer can determine any given author's system the more confidently s/he can use it to advantage.) Some radio stations may already have some of them, and they are usually found in the reference section of public and university libraries. Additional works can be found under such Library of Congress subject headings as Music—Terminology; Names, Personal or Names, Geographical with subheadings such as —Dictionaries, —Pronunciation; under the heading "X"-language with subheadings —Orthography, —Phonetics, —Textbooks; under more general headings such as Linguistics—Phonetics, Language and Languages, or Onomastics (the study of names).

Bibliography I. Names but No Phonetics

Information on music history and theory, terms and instruments, biographies, personal and geographical names, or foreign words in English. Some give country of origin or residence of a person, making them possibly useful for guessing at a pronunciation. Those that preserve diacritic marks are, of course, more useful than those that do not. Some books leave out diacritics either because they are too unwieldy to print or because authors assume that will confuse readers.The present book seeks to remedy that.

Arnold, Denis, ed., 1983. *New Oxford Companion to Music*. (Oxford University Press).

A greatly revised and expanded edition (two volumes) of Percy Sholes' *Oxford Companion to Music* (see Bibliography II). Unfortunately, Arnold does not continue Scholes' pronunciation guide, making this work far less useful than its predecessor, at least for announcing purposes.

Cummings, David, ed. 1986. *New Everyman Dictionary of Music.* (New York: Weidenfeld and Nicolson).

This is the 6th edition of a work first compiled by Eric Blom and revised in the 1970s by Sir Jack Westrup. It contains more names of performers than most dictionaries and the person's dates and country of origin. That ethnic hint, together with the present book, often suffices to suggest the pronunciation of the name. Titles of French, German, and Italian pieces are given in the original with translations in parentheses. Titles of Russian or Scandinavian pieces are given in English with the original title in parentheses. There is a useful 13-page appendix of names of characters in operas, though not a list of operas with the characters in them.

Cummings, David, ed. 1994-95. *International Who's Who in Music and Musicians Directory.* (Cambridge, England) 14th ed.

One-paragraph summaries of the lives and accomplishments of many people, living and not, Some ethnic information that might help in guessing a pronunciation, but the diacritic marks are spotty. (For diacritics, David Greene and Nicolas Slonimsky are better sources.)

Gilder, Eric, and June Port. 1978. *The Dictionary of Composers and Their Music: Arranged Chronologically and Alphabetically.* (London: Paddington Press).

Interesting listing to give a perspective on who wrote what when and who else was a toddler at the time. Compare with *Greene's Biographical Encyclopedia* in Bibliography II.

Greene, Frank. 1985. *Composers On Record.* (Metuchen, N.J. and London: The Scarecrow Press, Inc.)

Listing of 14,000 composers whose works have been recorded. Each name is tagged with a national origin and spelled with diacritics.

Grigg, Carolyn. 1978. *Music Translation Dictionary: An English-Czech-Danish-Dutch-French-German-Hungarian-Italian-Polish-Portuguese-Russian-Spanish-Swedish Vocabulary of Musical Terms.* (Westport, CT: Greenwood Press.) .

An impressive achievement and useful tool for researchers in music theory and history, however it contains only terms and no proper names. Compare W. Smith in Bibliography II.

Guinagh, Kevin. 1965. *Dictionary of Foreign Phrases and Abbreviations.* (New York: H.W. Wilson Co.).

Several thousand phrases from western European languages are given alphabetically with English translation and a language tag. They are then regrouped by language. It is listed here for practice in recognizing languages, though it gives no help in pronouncing them.

Hank, Patricia, and Flavia Hodges. 1988. *A Dictionary of Surnames.* and
__________. 1990. *A Dictionary of First Names.* (Oxford: Oxford University Press).

Informative entries on the history and meaning of thousands of names on the European continent. The possible usefulness of these two works for announcers is in identifying the nationality of a person and, therefore, possibly the pronunciation of the name. The First Names dictionary also has a supplement on names in the Arab world and on the Indian subcontinent.

Herbert, Jean, ed. 1967. *Glossary of Geographical Names in Six Languages.* (Amsterdam, London: Elsevier Publishing Co.).

Self-explanatory: place names but no phonetics. Nonetheless, useful for identifying places.

Jacobs, Arthur. 1990/1991. *The Penguin Dictionary of Musical Performers.* (New York: Viking Penguin Books).

Brief biographical and professional statistics on a limited selection of contemporary instrumentalists, vocalists, and conductors. There are no phonetics, but some of the biographical data allows one to make a guess at the probable pronunciation. The 1991 paperback by Penguin is slightly updated from the 1990 hardback by Viking.

Kennedy, Michael. 1985/1994. *Oxford Dictionary of Music.* (London: Oxford University Press).

In the first edition (1985), Kennedy admitted to being very conservative in the matter of transcribing Russian names and has "(rather reluctantly) conformed to the growing usage of Rakhmaninov and Skryabin, but too many record-labels and books prefer Chaliapin to Shalyapin, Diaghilev to Dyaghilev, and Tchaikovsky to Chaykovsky for any change to be anything but unnecessarily confusing" (pp. vii). In the 1994 edition he has gone back to Rachmaninov. His historical references distinguish earlier and later place names, such as St. Petersburg-Petrograd-Leningrad and Christiana-Oslo. He lists titles as they are "familiarly known, with a leaning towards the original-language title."

Libby, Ted. 1994. *The NPR Guide to Building a Classical CD Collection.* (New York: Workman).

Well-written sketches on performance quality, interpretation, and musicality for the listener who wants to collect classical disks, but no help in pronouncing the names of the people or pieces. (This could make it a little difficult to ask for the disks in a record store.)

Randel, Don Michael, ed. 1986. *New Harvard Dictionary of Music*
_______. 1995. *The Harvard Biographical Dictionary of Music.* (Cambridge, MA: Harvard University Press).

The first volume covers terms from "acoustics" to "zydeco," while the second covers composers and performers. This well-respected reference set sometimes tags terms with a language designation such as [Fr.] and [It.] but gives no information on how to pronounce French or Italian. The two volumes together offer classical listeners a serious alternative to the older 20-volume *Grove Dictionary,* see below. (Thanks to Bill Boggs of Harvard University Press for an enlightening conversation on this work.)

Sadie, Stanley, ed. 1980. *The New Grove Dictionary of Music.* (New York: Macmillan).

This standard encyclopedia—all 20 large volumes of it—for people in the music field offers no advice on pronounciation. The original *Grove* dates from the late 1800s, and this is the sixth edition.

___________. 1988. *The Norton/Grove Concise Encyclopedia of Music.* (New York: W.W. Norton Co.).

There is a lot of information in this single hefty volume, but none of it has to do with what words and names *sound* like.

Slonimsky, Nicholas, ed. 1992. *Baker's Biographical Dictionary of Musicians.* 8th ed. (New York: Schirmer).

One volume of biographical information but very spotty phonetic help. Names are, however, spelled with correct diacritic marks. In the preface Slonimsky, who is Russian, mentions some of the difficulties of transcribing Russian names into Latin letters, but only a few of the articles mention the pronunciation of a person's name, if it relates to the person's career or family history. He does specify Balakirev and Ippolitov-Ivanov. Slonimsky's preface to the 6th edition of *Baker* (reprinted in the 8th) relates anecdotes about big people in the music field.

Bibliography II. Names *and* Phonetics

Musical, biographical, and geographical information that do include phonetic help. Some items have straightforward phonetic transcriptions of great use to announcers, while others are less accessible or more concerned with "native" sound than with "announcing" sound.

Ageyenko (= Ageenko), F.L., and M.R. Zarva, eds. 1984. *Slovar' udareniy dlya rabotnikov radio i televideniya.* (Moscow: "Russkiy Yazik" Publishers).

This book is in Russian for Russian announcers, literally *Dictionary of Accent for Radio and Television Workers*, something like the Russian equivalent of the *NBC Handbook* or Noory's *Dictionary of Pronunciation*, discussed below. It appears here mostly because *Books in Print* gives it the misleading English title *Pronunciation Dictionary for Radio and Television Workers*, and the present author's purpose is only to save people who do not know Russian the trouble of looking for it. It is simply a list of words and names with their stress marked, which is all a Russian needs to pronounce a word. This book is also of historical-political interest as an artifact of the former Soviet Union, where famous people could be written out of history if they misbehaved. For example, Alexander Solzhenitsyn, winner of the Nobel prize in literature in the early 1970s, and cellist-conductor, Mstislav Rostropovich, are both conspicuously absent. (See the footnote under Rostropovich in Movement 2.) Just for the record, Ageenko's newest edition (1993) is now entitled simply *Slovar' udareniy russkogo yazika* (Dictionary of Russian Stress) and is not listed by an English title in *Books in Print.* It includes not only many new words that entered Russian in the period of perestroika and the dissolution of the Soviet Union, but also both Rostropovich and Solzhenitsyn.

Ammer, Christine. 1972. *Harper's Dictionary of Music.* (New York: Harper and Row).

Relatively good phonetics. Good for musicians because it has musical terms, but only minimally useful for announcers because it has names of composers but hardly any conductors or performers.

Barach, Stephanie. 1962. *An Introduction to the Language of Music* (Washington, D.C.: Luce, Inc.).

Basic dictionary of musical terms with decent phonetic assistance, but no proper names, so it is not of much use to radio announcers.

BBC Pronunciation Guides, Tenth Edition. (No author given). 1984. (London: BBC Data Publications).

This production of the BBC pronunciation unit was intended as an in-house manual for the BBC staff, and it is not generally available to the rest of the English-announcing world. It is in four volumes: "A Guide of the Pronunciation of Some Composers' Names," with successive volumes devoted to instrumentalists, singers, and conductors. The phonetic spellings, devised by the BBC's pre-war Advisory Committee on Spoken English, are good and consistent—with a British accent, of course. Names are provided with a language or country tag, and some names have notes on variants or difficulties.

Bollard, John K., ed., and Frank R. Abate and Katherine M. Isaacs, assoc. eds. 1993. *Pronouncing Dictionary of Proper Names*. (Detroit: Omnigraphics).

The full title is actually *Pronouncing Dictionary of Proper Names. Pronunciations for more than 23,000 Proper Names, Selected for Currency, Frequency, or Difficulty of Pronunciation, Including Places Names; Given Names; Names of Famous Individuals; Cultural, Literary, and Historical Names; Mythological Names; Names of Peoples and Tribes; Company Names and Product Names; with Pronunciations Transcribed into the International Phonetic Alphabet and a Simplified Phonetic Respelling; and Including an Explanatory Introduction*. This item is listed misleadingly in *Books In Print* as a reprint of Mackey 1922, see below, but it is a brand new work. Since it is all proper names it is much more useful for announcing purposes than the *NBC Handbook*. The explanatory introduction is like a mini-course in linguistics, complete with vowel systems and fine-tuned consonant differences. Variant spellings and pronunciations for English speakers from different regions are also given equal time and respect. Transcription is given in both "user-friendly" phonetic spelling and in International Phonetic Alphabet. There is more concern with representing sounds, themselves, than with showing the correspondences between spellings and sounds in any given language. Full names are given, but phonetics are given only for the last name, and many first names are listed as separate entries. As for coverage of musical names, the Dutch conductor "Ton Koopman" does not appear, but the Dutch-born American economist "Tjalling Koopmans" does appear. The economist, apparently, makes no pretense of Dutch pronunciation of his name, and he is given as [koop-muhnz], while Ton, if he were given, would be [kohp-muhn]. With general "frequency" cited in the title as one of the main criteria for inclusion of a name, the absence of a musician like Ton Koopman is no surprise, as well as many of the other musical names announcers need. A surprising omission is Ginastera. If the name of such a well-known figure in the music world is missing, one can hardly hope to find up-and-coming performers such as Tzimon Barto or Semyon Bychkov. At any rate, despite minor inconveniences, this dictionary is the most comprehensive for a maximally broad audience.

Clarke, H.A. 1896. *Pronouncing Dictionary of Musical Terms*. (Philadelphia: Theodore Presser Co.).

Quite good for general musical knowledge and quite a few names of classical composers and then-contemporary performers. It has been reprinted recently, though apparently without being updated.

Coveney, John and T.A. McEwen. 1960(?). *Pronouncing the Classics: Composers, Compositions, Artists*. (White Plains: Record Source International).

This was a landmark in its day: the first—and as far as this author knows, the only—attempt to provide audio-self-help for music people. It consists of a booklet with 1000 names, numbered and phoneticized, as an accompaniment to a phonograph record, a kind of "See It and Say It" of classical music. Coveney did the preparation and reads off the numbers on the list, and McEwen follows by pronouncing them once each. It is arranged alphabetically by composer's name, with titles of compositions given under the composer. This makes it difficult to locate any given piece. The French, German, and Italian are generally fine, but names from farther east present some problems. "Smetana" follows a German pronunciation (probably from Austro-Hungarian days) as [shmeh-tah-nah] instead of [smeh-tah-nah], and "Bartók," as [bar-tohk], instead of [bar-tohk]. As with almost all such helpful aids, the phonetics of individual names are not transferable tools that help users make their own stabs at new names.

Elson, Louis C. 1933. *Elson's Music Dictionary.* (Bryn Mawr, PA: Theodore Presser Co.).

The full title is spread over the entire title page in three sections of increasingly small type: (1) *Elson's Music Dictionary* (2) *Containing the definition and pronunciation of such terms and signs as are used in modern music* (3) *Together with a list of foreign composers and artists, with pronunciation of their names, rules for pronouncing foreign words, and a short English-Italian vocabulary of musical words and expressions.* The three-page introduction of "Rules for the Pronunciation of German, Italian, and French" is not bad but too terse for the non-specialist, and for anything farther east than Vienna, the reader is left high and dry.

Elson, Louis C., ed. 1918. *Modern Music and Musicians.*
________________. 1918. *Modern Music and Musicians for Vocalists.* (New York: The University Society).

Both of these two multi-volume works include a three-page "Guide to the Pronunciation of Fourteen Languages" with letter-sound correspondences for not only the expected German, French, and Italian, but also for Spanish, Dutch, Norwegian, Danish, Swedish, Polish, Russian, "Bohemian" (now Czech), Hungarian, Finnish, and Welsh. Unfortunately, the phonetic explanations are too brief and the examples too few for radio announcers. Besides that, the less familiar languages such as Hungarian, Polish, and Norwegian seem just as mysterious as before. The Russian section also has many unclear statements and outright mistakes. Elsons' later *Music Dictionary* (1933) deals only with the "Big Three" languages: German, French, and Italian.

Greene, David. 1985. *Greene's Biographical Encyclopedia of Composers.* (New York: Columbia University Press).

This is primarily a musician's or musicologist's reference work, but it can serve announcers quite well for the pronunciation of composers' names and English glosses of titles. Like Gilder 1978 (Bibliography I), Greene lists the names not alphabetically but by chronology.

Greet, W. Cabell. 1944. *World Words: Recommended Pronunciations.* (New York: Columbia University Press).

This listing of mostly geographical proper names was intended for newscasters. It was apparently the most complete such book of its day. There are editorial prefaces on pronunciation norms and questions of anglicization. This CBS project has at least two major advantages over the current *NBC Handbook*. First, there are introductory sketches on sound vs. letter in an amazing array of world languages: whole sections on Albanian, Burman (now Burmese), Dutch and Flemish, Estonian, Finnish, French, German, Greek, Hungarian, Italian, Japanese, Latvian, Lithuanian, Portuguese, Rumanian, the Scandinavian and Slavic languages as whole groups and as individuals (including a note on the Latin spellings of Russian names via French and German), Spanish, Thai or Siamese, and Turkish, as well as paragraphs with specific notes or hints on Arabic, "Names Of India," Korean, Languages of the Pacific, and Persian or Iranian. Second, the names are identified by the language they are in. The phonetics are quite good and are given both with dictionary diacritics and without. It does not claim to include the personal names that announcers in other fields need. The half-century since its publication seems not to have seen an update, but Munro 1988 and Webster's Geographical Dictionary 1988 are good alternatives. Bollard 1993 gives more even coverage to more fields.

Ho, Allan, and Dmitry Feofanov. 1989. *Biographical Dictionary of Russian/Soviet Composers.* (New York and London: Greenwood Press).

Mercifully much phonetics. Highly specialized, but a good reference tool for sorting people out into their current country.

Mackey, Mary S. and Maryette Goodwin Mackey. 1922. *Dictionary of Ten Thousand Proper Names* . (New York: Dodd, Mead, and Co., Republished by Gale Research Co., Detroit. 1979).

The subtitle goes on to read ...*Giving Geographical and Biographical Names of Books, Works of Art, Characters in Fiction, Foreign Titles, Etc.* The listing actually includes about twelve thousand names, each with a phonetic spelling. Fairly few musicians are represented, however.

Matthews, W.S.B., and Emil Liebling. 1925. *Pronouncing and Defining Dictionary of Music.* (Philadelphia: Theodore Presser Co.).

More detailed than Clarke 1896. Handy to have around but with the same obvious time limitation as Clarke.

Mawson, C.O. Sylvester. 1934. *International Book of Names.* (New York: Thomas Crowell Publishers).

The elaborate subtitle is ...*A Dictionary of the More Difficult Proper Names in Literature, History, Philosophy, Religion, Art, Music, and Other Studies, Together with the Official Form and Pronunciation of the Names of Present-Day Celebrities and Places Throughout the World, with Post-War Geographical Changes Duly Incorporated.* This book really does cover the whole world, and the phonetic introduction is very thorough. In addition to a list of phonetic symbols used to transcribe names, Mawson is unusual in providing (pp. xxi-xlii) a catalogue of special letters, diacritics and the typical stress characteristics of a long list of languages.

Morehead, Philip D. and Anne Mac Neil. 1991. *New American Dictionary of Music.* (New York: Dutton).

Phonetics for most non-English terms and for names assumed to need them. The usefulness of this work for announcers rests on the last eleven pages: a convenient four-column comparative

Italian-French-German-English glossary of terms for tempo, dynamics, expression, instruments, and voices. Attention is paid to differences between American and British usage, as well, including the British terminology for "eighth, sixteenth, thirty-second, and sixty-fourth" notes, namely, "quaver, semiquaver, demisemiquaver, and hemidemisemiquaver."

Munro, David, ed. 1988. *Chambers World Gazetteer.* (Cambridge: Chambers).

Good phonetics for geographical place names, which announcers have to announce almost as often as people's names.

Noory, Samuel. 1979. *Dictionary of Pronunciation,* 3rd edition. (South Brunswick: A.S. Barnes and Co., Inc.).

This very useful book has a separate sub-dictionary for proper names. Pages 1-384 contain about 45,000 words, including many names. The second part, pp. 385-505, contains some 13,000 proper names of people and places, complete with spelling variants and alternate pronunciations, from all over the globe, all periods of history, and just about all subjects. An announcer can get a lot of mileage out of it. Besides that, it starts off with a brief sketch of the history of English and tries to give an idea of how English spelling got to be so much more cumbersome and inconsistent than other European languages. (He discusses, for example, the Great Vowel Shift from Middle to Modern English.) Then Noory gives his own phonetic spelling system in great detail but without drowning the reader in terminology. The whole thing, then, is quite accessible to the patient non-specialist. As for limitations, as in Bollard 1993, it is impossible to include all names in a single volume, and a specialized purpose like classical music announcing usually draws the short straw. There are some composers, conductors, and performers, but it is hard to see a pattern. You will certainly find Bach, though not Busoni; Schumann, but not Scimone; Janáček, but not Josquin; Cimarosa, but not Cliburn. Nonetheless, it is certainly worthwhile knowing where to find this book on the shelf.

Pascoe, Harry. 1939. *Key To The Pronunciation of Foreign Words (Spanish, Portuguese, French, Italian, German, Hungarian, Russian) For Announcers, News Commentators, Singers, Teachers, Students.* (New York: Academy Photo-Offset, Inc.)

A booklet of only 75 pages of 6" x 9" format. For each language there are a few pages of helpful hints and a one-page list of typical personal names. This seems to be a homemade, photocopied aid that was not really published for wide distribution. This is regrettable, since in its day it seems to have been the only item of its kind designed with announcers in mind. It is better conceived than the current *NBC Handbook,* since it gives principles for self-study and not just an alphabetical list, but it is not nearly so extensive as Mawson 1934 and Greet 1944. It is offered here more for historical interest, given that it never developed into anything and is not available commercially.

Scholes, Percy A. 1936. *The Radio Times Music Handbook.* (London: Oxford University Press).

This small book bears the subtitle *being a complete book of reference giving both meaning and pronunciation of the technical words found in programmes,* and it was published for the BBC. The author wished to provide "first aid for the puzzled listener" by phonetically spelling over twelve hundred terms relevant for key signatures, scales, intervals, chords, rhythm, instruments, and dance forms. In addition to the usual French, German and Italian, there are also several terms for dance forms in Polish, Czech, Spanish, and even Basque. There are no proper names, but consult the same author's pronunciation glossary in his 1938 *Oxford Companion to Music*.

_______________. 1938. *The Oxford Companion to Music*. (London: Oxford University Press). (10th ed. by John Owen Ward, 1970).

There are no phonetics in the body of the text, but all the names and terms are collected in a separate pronouncing glossary (pp. 1130-1185) with an essay (pp. 1186-1189) advocating "a reasonably exact impression" of native pronunciation over an exact phonetic rendering, in which spirit the present book is conceived. See Arnold's 1983 *New Oxford Companion*, above.

Smith, W. J. 1961. *A Dictionary of Musical Terms in Four Languages*. (London: Hutchinson).

The title page has the title in English, French, Italian, and German. The terms (no proper names) are all phoneticized (including the English ones) and grouped by topic: instruments (including electronic), keys and harmony, conducting directions (orchestral and choral), different kinds of bands (brass, jazz, military). This small book makes a good complement to part of Grigg 1978 in Bibliography I.

Taylor, Deems, and Russell Kerr (originally compiled by Rupert Hughes). 1940/1971. *The Biographical Dictionary of Musicians*. (Garden City, N.Y.: Blue Ribbon Books).

This book has good, traditional phonetics with a separate pronunciation list of given names, titles and epithets. The most unusual feature of this dictionary is a comparative chart of spelling and sound correspondences in sixteen languages. (The 1940 edition places it at the end. The 1971 reprint moves it to the beginning.) This was a wonderful innovation but a difficult one for the non-specialist to follow, since the alphabetical order of the letters and the languages obscuresthe regularities of sound. Deems Taylor is also the author of *The Well-Tempered Listener* (Simon and Schuster, 1945), a popular book on music appreciation which has no connection to the present book.

Thompson, Oscar, ed. 1964. *International Cyclopedia of Music and Musicians*. 8th Ed. (New York: Dodd, Mead, and Co.).

This 2,500-page tome devotes the last twenty pages to a phonetic listing of mostly *last* names of the important people in music up to the late 1950s. The phonetic spelling is awkward, and one could quibble with the accuracy of some of them. Thompson, himself, died in 1945 having worked on the first few editions. Subsequent editions since the 8th are not listed here (the 11th appeared in 1985) because the phonetic appendix, minimal though it was, is left out altogether.

Webster's New Biographical Dictionary
Webster's New Geographical Dictionary. 1988. (Springfield, MA: G.&C. Merriam Co.).

Same good, consistent phonetics as in Webster's dictionaries of English. Announcers need them not only for music people but also for the names of places where concerts and festivals take place and where music composers and performers live and die. It takes practice to get used to reading the symbols, though. (See also Munro 1988 and Greet 1944, above.)

Westrup, J., and F.L. Harrison. 1960/1976. *The New College Encyclopedia of Music.* (New York: W.W. Norton and Co.).

There are phonetic spellings for several thousand titles, but the transcription is not very convenient. For example, "Bach" is given as [buckh], and "Saint-Saëns" is [s͡an s͡unce]. The 1976 version, revised by Conrad Wilson, gives a compact introductory list of some 1,800 names of people and compositions, as well as musical terms. Explanations and definitions are in the main text. Wilson, in his preface, expresses a strong preference for modern spellings of, for example, Rakhmaninov over Rachmaninov or Rachmaninoff, of Petrushka over Petrouchka, of Chaikovsky over Tchaikovsky. Such a practice, he believes, would make music parallel to other fields, such as literature, where the old spelling of Tchekhov has long been replaced by Chekhov. (Note that Kennedy 1985/1994 expresses the opposite opinion on transcription.)

Bibliography III. General References on Phonetics, Singing Diction, Transcription, etc.

These items are of direct relevance for singers, newscasters, and people interested in language for its own sake. Nonetheless, classical announcers can also benefit from them as sources for practice in reading different phonetic transcriptions and developing a common vocabulary for sounds, symbols sense of descriptions of sound

Adler, Kurt. 1967. *Phonetics and Diction in Singing: Italian, French, Spanish, German.* (Minneapolis: University of Minnesota Press).

Good as an introduction to relationships among sounds, even some linguistic comments on the use these languages make of their letters. Of course, this is much more than is needed in the announcing booth, and it leaves Eastern Europe and Asia untouched. There are several books on individual languages for singers, but only Piatak 1991, on Russian, is discussed below.

Allen, Charles G. 1975. *A Manual of European Languages for Librarians.* (London: Bowker). (Reprinted with minor corrections 1977).

Excellent source for basic information that helps identify texts in all 36 languages spoken—better to say, written—in Europe. There are short sketches of grammar, some basic vocabulary relevant to identifying publishers and editions, and notes on spelling variants, special letters and diacritics, and alphabetization conventions. The sections entitled "Spelling and Phonetics" for each language are more about spelling and not much about phonetics.

Edelstein, Debra, ed. 1993. *Pronouncing Dictionary of Artists' Names.* 3rd rev. ed. Art Institute of Chicago. A Bullfinch Press Book (Little, Brown and Co.).

Over 4,000 names of artists in alphabetical order with country of origin, medium (painting, etc.), and dates. The names are phoneticized according to Webster's dictionary symbols.

Ehrlich, Eugene and Raymond Hand, Jr., eds. 1991. *NBC Handbook of Pronunciation* 4th ed. (New York: Harper Collins).

Interesting foreward by Edwin Newman. 21, 000 common words and names in one continuous alphabetical listing with no grouping into fields—like "music names," "world leaders," "geographical places." The non-technical phonetic transcription is very much like the one used in the present book, but there is no indication of what language a word or name is in and no attempt to help an announcer attempt a word that is not in the *Handbook*. (Note that Noory 1979 keeps proper names separate from common nouns.) There are very few music names beyond the mega-stars like Mozart and Beethoven--and even those have only last names. One may refer to such figures this way in casual conversation, but classical radio announcers usually do them the courtesy of including their given names, as well.

Elster, Charles Harrington. 1988. *There Is No 'Zoo' In 'Zoology' and Other Beastly Mispronunciations (An Opinionated Guide For the Well-Spoken)*. (New York: Collier Books).

Opinionated is putting it mildly! This is a mildly entertaining look at common mispronunciations of English words, dressing familiar words in unfamiliar phonetic garb. It is of no immediate use to broadcasters because it specifically avoids proper names and foreign words but is listed here as a possible training ground for reading popularized phonetic spelling. Elster accepts only those pronunciations sanctioned by the standard dictionaries. He is interested in correcting individual mistakes and not in presenting general principles to help readers approach other material.

Gilyarevsky (Giliarevskii), R. S. and V.S. Grivnin. (tr. from Russian by Lev Navrozov). 1970. *Languages Identification Guide*. (Moscow: Nauka).

Sample paragraphs and brief descriptions (in English) of virtually all the written languages in the world. Several appendices. Good for visual reference on writing systems.

Herman, Lewis, and Marguerite Shalett Herman. 1943. *Foreign Dialects: A Manual for Actors, Directors, and Writers*. (New York: Theatre Arts Books).

The full copyright title is *Manual of Foreign Dialects for Radio, Stage, and Screen*, and it has a preface by Garson Kanin. The phonetic spellings in this invaluable manual are meant to lead English speakers into producing authentic accents of several regionally or socially marked varieties of English and of many of the world's major languages. Some instructions on intonation and mannerisms are given in terms of musical notes to indicate rising and falling voice contours. This is certainly of interest to announcers as training in speech awareness and the ways that letters can represent sound.

Katzner, Kenneth. 1995. *The Languages of the World, New Edition*. (London: Routledge).

Similar in format and scope to Gilyarevsky 1970 but with more focus on language families. This new edition also has up-to-date information on location, number of speakers, and in some cases, political status of these languages.

McConkey, Wilfred J. 1992. *Klee as in Clay*. 3rd ed.
__________________. 1989. *Haute as in Oat: A Pronunciation Guide to European Wines and Cuisines*. (Lanham, MD: Madison Books).

These books give the other side of Elster's coin: only foreign names, particularly those "commonly mispronounced" in several areas of life. *Klee* deals with architecture, literature, dance, and music, while *Haute* covers food and wine. The phonetic spelling takes the "whole

English word" approach to phonetic approximation, but not all names submit so readily to such representation. Announcers will find the selection of music names in *Klee* quite small.

Piatak, Jean, and Regina Avrashov. 1991. *Russian Songs and Arias.* (Phonetic readings, word-by-word translations, and a concise guide to Russian diction). (Dallas: Pst.... Inc.).

Useful for learning the Russian alphabet in a musical context. (See also C. Allen for the other Cyrillic-letter Slavic languages.) Surprisingly, the book is of greater use to announcers than it is to singers because Piatak's phonetic information is more accurate for modern *spoken* Russian than for good Russian singing diction. She reproduces 19th-century song texts, which are essentially modern Russian, in their "old" spelling—by which she means pre-1917 revolution (not Old Russian, which means the Russian spoken until about the fourteenth century). This is odd since modern Russians publish such texts in modern spelling. (After the revolution a minor reform streamlined Russian spelling by replacing a few letters deemed superfluous with letters that had the same sound.)

Pullam, Geoffrey and William Ladusaw. 1986. *Phonetic Symbol Guide.* (University of Chicago Press).

This reference book showcases every IPA symbol with its name(s), linguistic descriptions of the sound(s) it represents, and some discussion of the languages that have it.

von Ostermann, Georg. 1952. *Manual of Foreign Languages, For the Use of Librarians, Bibliographers, Research Workers, Editors, Translators, and Printers.* (New York: Central Book Co.)

Consider this the iceberg of which Charles Allen's *Manual of European Languages* is just the tip. Van Ostermann has short descriptions of hundreds of languages including—most importantly for announcing—their spelling and grammatical characteristics with several comparative appendices on diacritics, special and adjusted letters, and typical combinations. This is good both for visual identification and attempts at pronunciation, not to mention a wealth of facts for the language-hungry. (In short, it makes the Coda of the present book look like a church picnic. Of course, von Ostermann goes far beyond the needs of classical announcers.)

Wall, Joan. 1989. *International Phonetic Alphabet For Singers.* (A Manual For English and Foreign Language Diction.) (Dallas: Pst.... Inc.).

A full-scale course for reading IPA tailored to the needs of singers. Announcers could find it very valuable for learning how sounds are produced in the mouth and how they relate to traditional spellings.

Wall, Joan, Robert Caldwell, et al. 1990. *Diction For Singers: A Concise Reference for English, Italian, Latin, German, French, and Spanish Pronunciation.* (Dallas: Pst.... Inc.).

Much more detailed than the present book can possibly be, with eye-challenging comparisons of how the same sounds can be spelled differently in different languages and hints on how to form unfamiliar sounds and blend them with a musical line. Of course, all those hints are given in the International Phonetic Alphabet (See Wall's manual of IPA just above).

INDEXES

Phonetic Terms, Names of Symbols and Diacritic Marks, Phonetic Commentary on Particular Names

Languages Discussed and Mentioned

Special Letters, Combinations, and IPA Symbols

Vowels